Palgrave Macmillan Studies in Banking and Financial Institutions

The Palgrave Macmillan Studies in Banking and Financial Institutions series is international in orientation and includes studies of banking systems in particular countries or regions as well as contemporary themes such as Islamic Banking, Financial Exclusion, Mergers and Acquisitions, Risk Management, and IT in Banking. The books focus on research and practice and include up to date and innovative studies that cover issues which impact banking systems globally.

Timothy King · Jonathan Williams
Editors

Corporate Governance in the Banking and Financial Sector

Innovations and Adaptations in a Changing Landscape

palgrave
macmillan

Editors
Timothy King
School of Accounting and Finance
University of Vaasa
Vaasa, Finland

Jonathan Williams
Surrey Business School
University of Surrey
Guildford, UK

ISSN 2523-336X ISSN 2523-3378 (electronic)
Palgrave Macmillan Studies in Banking and Financial Institutions
ISBN 978-3-031-83352-6 ISBN 978-3-031-83353-3 (eBook)
https://doi.org/10.1007/978-3-031-83353-3

Cover illustration: ASKA getty images

This Palgrave Macmillan imprint is published by the registered company Springer Nature Switzerland AG
The registered company address is: Gewerbestrasse 11, 6330 Cham, Switzerland

Contents

Notes on Contributors

Shaker Ahmed is a Lecturer in Finance at the University of Surrey, UK. He received his Ph.D. in Finance from the University of Vaasa, Finland, and has held visiting scholar positions at the Skema Business School in France and the Hanken School of Economics in Finland and taught at Umeå University, Sweden, as a guest lecturer. His research focuses on the influence of executive characteristics, corporate strategic decisions, and political risk on firm-level and financial market outcomes. He has published in the *British Journal of Management*, *European Financial Management*, *Journal of Economics and Business*, and *Finance Research Letters*, among others. His work has featured in international media outlets, including the *Financial Times*, *Wall Street Journal*, *Daily Mail*, and *Harvard Business Manager*. For his doctoral research, he received €127,000 in research grants from three foundations in Finland: OP Group Research Foundation, Jenny and Antti Wihuri Foundation, and the Saving Banks Research Foundation.

Selena Aureli is an Associate Professor at Bologna University, Italy, and previously Assistant Professor of Business Administration and Accounting Studies at Urbino University, Italy. Selena teaches Financial Reporting, Managerial Accounting, Sustainability and Social Reporting. She has published contributions to books, essays, and journal articles. Her research interests are non-financial reporting, sustainability, governance, and performance measurement. Selena participates in conferences and has presented her work at Universities in Italy and abroad. She has been a visiting professor at the Institute of Technology Tallaght (Dublin, Ireland), the Higher School of Economics (Moscow, Russia), Tampere University (Tampere, Finland), and Universitè Catholique de Lille (France).

Laura Baselga-Pascual is an Associate Professor in Accounting and Finance at Deusto Business School (San Sebastián, Spain). Her research explores board characteristics, ethics, risk determinants in financial institutions, and corporate tax avoidance. She has contributed chapters to several books and published in scientific journals, such as the *Journal of Business Ethics*, the *North American Journal of Economics and Finance*, *Emerging Markets Review*, the *Spanish Journal of Finance and Accounting*, and *Finance Research Letters,* among others. Laura has presented her work at international conferences and is an active member of two research groups: *Innovación, Competitividad, Emprendimiento y Sostenibilidad* at Universidad de Deusto and the *Banking and Entrepreneurial Finance Research Group (BANEF)* at Universidad Pablo de Olavide.

Alessio Bongiovanni is a Lecturer in Banking and Finance in the Accounting and Finance Department at the University of Leeds. Before joining Leeds, he was a Lecturer and a Post-Doctoral Research Fellow in Financial Markets and Institutions at the University of Turin. His current research interests include bank stability and governance, and sustainable finance. He has held visiting positions at the Bank of Lithuania, the University of Orléans, and Bangor University.

Paola Brighi is a Professor of Economics of Financial Intermediation at the University of Milan. She obtained her M.A. from the University of Louvain-la-Neuve, Belgium, and Ph.D. from the University Politecnica delle Marche, Italy. Previously, she was a Visiting Scholar at the University of Wisconsin, USA, and the University of Essex, UK. She teaches Economics of Financial Intermediation at undergraduate level and Empirical Legal Studies at graduate level and has lectured on the Ph.D. programme in Management and the European Master in Consumer Affairs (EMCA) at the University of Bologna. She has published on ESG, banking structure, relationship lending, bank geographic diversification, efficiency, cooperative banks, and SME finance. She participates in national conferences and workshops (ADEIMF, AIDEA, and the Bank of Italy) as well as international (Financial Management Association-FMA, European Financial Management Association-EFMA,

International Finance and Banking Society-IFABS, and the Wolpertinger Annual Conference). She is a member of ADEIMF (National Association of Financial Intermediary Economists), AIFIRM (Italian Association of Financial Industry Risk Managers), and NED-Community (Non-Executive Directors Community).

María Cantero-Saiz is an Associate Professor in Finance at the University of Cantabria (Spain) and Researcher at Santander Financial Institute (SANFI) who teaches on undergraduate and postgraduate programmes. After taking her BS in Business Management (2010) and MBA in 2011, she completed her Ph.D. in finance at the University of Cantabria (2015). Her research interests focus on banking, monetary policy, sovereign risk, corporate finance, sustainable finance, and climate risks. She has published in scientific journals, such as the *Journal of International Money and Finance*; *International Review of Economics and Finance*; *Finance Research Letters*; *Journal of Macroeconomics*; *Journal of Regulatory Economics*; *Journal of Asian Economics*; *Journal of Money, Credit and Banking*; *BRQ Business Research Quarterly*; or *Research in International Business and Finance*. She has also collaborated in several books, presented papers at national and international conferences, and received awards for her research, such as "Doctoral Theses Santander Financial Institute Award (2016)", the Prize for the Best Presentation of the Finance Section at the "International Conference on Applied Economics and Business" (Amsterdam, 2017), and Best Paper Award at the "9th International Conference on Corporate Social Responsibility (CSR), Sustainability, Ethics and Governance" (Santander, 2023). She has participated in national and international research projects and was a visiting researcher at Norwich Business School (University of East Anglia) (2013–2014), Berlin School of Economics and Law (2017), and Università degli Studi di Palermo (2022–2023, 2024–2025). Since 2015, she leads the University of Cantabria Classroom Debate to promote communicative skills among students.

Lauri Hiltunen is a recent Masters degree graduate from the University of Vaasa. He has an active research interest in understanding corporate transactions, including the factors that influence outcomes. He currently works in Finland for a company as an analyst specialising in financial modelling and M&A.

Tatiana King is an Associate Professor of Accounting (tenure-track) and the head of the Auditing and Control in Accounting research group at the University of Vaasa, Finland. Her research focuses on sustainability and the disclosure of ESG-related information. She has published in journals, such as *Accounting, Auditing & Accountability Journal*, *Journal of Business Research*, *International Business Review*, *Journal of Accounting, Auditing and Taxation*. Tatiana presents her papers at international accounting and management conferences.

Timothy King is a Professor of Finance and Director of the Centre for Finance and Financial Accounting at the School of Accounting & Finance, University of Vaasa. His research is in the areas of banking, FinTech, corporate governance, corporate finance as well as ESG. He has published in journals, such as the *Journal of Corporate Finance* and *British Journal of Management*. He holds an Undergraduate degree in Business Studies and Economics, Masters degree in Banking and Finance, and a Doctorate in Banking and Finance—all from Bangor University. He currently serves as Editor of the *Multinational Finance Journal* as well as an Associate Editor of several other journals including the *Business Research Quarterly*. He is the co-editor of the book *Disruptive Technology in Banking and Finance: An International Perspective on FinTech*, part of the Palgrave Studies in Financial Services Technology series.

Juha Mäki is a postdoctoral researcher at the School of Accounting and Finance at the University of Vaasa, Finland. His main research interests are in the areas of accounting and auditing with a specific focus on the real estate industry. More recently he is looking at such issues with respect to the banking sector. His publications are in journals including the *Journal of Accounting Literature*, the *Journal of European Real Estate Research*, the *International Journal of Accounting*, and *Accounting in Europe*.

Muddassar Malik is a researcher in the fields of risk governance, banking regulation, and financial performance, with a focus on OECD banks. His Ph.D. in Economics and Finance examined the impact of risk governance on banking performance. He has published in journals, such as the *Journal of Financial Regulation and Compliance*, and *Risk Governance and Control: Financial Markets & Institutions*. His research delves into the role of risk governance, financial performance, and regulatory frameworks in shaping bank risk and financial outcomes. He has presented his findings at international forums contributing to critical discussions on risk management and corporate governance. His research activity includes collaborations and visiting scholar positions at institutions, such as Queensland University of Technology, George Washington University, University of Bologna, Maastricht University, Universidad Carlos III de Madrid, and Copenhagen Business School. His work is supported by competitive grants reflecting his dedication to advancing knowledge and fostering impactful contributions to the academic and banking communities.

Elizabeth Morton is a Lecturer of Taxation in the School of Accounting, Information Systems and Supply Chain Management at RMIT University (Australia) as well as a Research Fellow at the RMIT Blockchain Innovation Hub. Her research traverses both accounting and taxation systems, with particular concern directed towards blockchain and related technologies, information disclosure, and tax compliance. Her research is published in journals, such as *Accounting Forum*, *Accounting History*, *the Australian Tax Forum*, *the Financial Services Review*, and *The Tax Specialist*.

Salvatore Polizzi is Assistant Professor in Banking & Finance at the Department of Economics, Business and Statistics, University of Palermo, Italy. His research interests include banking, risk management, bank narrative reporting, disclosure and internal audit. During his academic career, he has worked for the European Central Bank and Banca d'Italia and held visiting researcher positions at Bangor University (UK) and Autonoma University of Madrid (Spain). He is member of the European Association of University Teachers in Banking and Finance (Wolpertinger), the Italian Association of University Teachers in Banking and Finance (ADEIMF) and Italian Academy of Management (AIDEA). He has published in the *Journal of International Money and Finance*, *Review of Quantitative Finance and Accounting*, *European Financial Management*, *European Journal of Finance*, and *Journal of Financial Services Research* amongst others. He has also published two books on disclosure and securitisation in the banking industry. He is an Associate Editor or Editorial Board Member of several international journals, including *Management Decision*, the *Review of Pacific-Basin Financial Markets and Policies*, and the *Journal of Banking Regulation*.

Enzo Scannella is Professor of Banking and Finance at the Department of Economics, Business, and Statistics, University of Palermo (Italy) where he teaches Corporate Banking, Economics and Management of Financial Institutions, and Risk Management. His main research interests include banking, financial regulation, risk management, and financial innovation. He has held visiting positions at Harvard Business School (Boston, USA), Universidad Autónoma de Madrid (Madrid, Spain), and Carleton University (Ottawa, Canada) among others. He has published in national and international journals and has contributed to several books. He is a member of various scientific associations, university research groups, editorial boards, and scientific committees for conferences. He is a member of the European Association of University Teachers in Banking and Finance (Wolpertinger), the Italian Academy of Management (AIDEA), and Italian Association of University Teachers in Banking and Finance (ADEIMF). He is Editor-in-Chief of the *International Journal of Financial Innovation in Banking*.

Ville Valkama is a recent Masters degree graduate from the University of Vaasa. He has been working under the supervision of Timothy King and holds an interest in understanding the dynamics of retail investing.

Paola Vezzani is Professor of Banking and Finance at the Department of Communication and Economics of the University of Modena and Reggio Emilia, Italy, where she was previously the Dean of the Faculty and the Head of the Department. She graduated from the University of Modena and obtained a Ph.D. in Capital Markets and Financial Management from the University of Bergamo. She was a visiting Ph.D. student at the Graduate School of Business Administration in the Finance Department of New York University. She is a member of AIDEA (Italian Academy of Business Administration and Management), ADEIMF (Italian Association of University Teachers of Financial Intermediaries, Markets and Finance), and the European Association of University Teachers in Banking and Finance (Wolpertinger). She is a member of the Scientific Committee of Banking and Financial Diploma of the Italian Banking Association (ABI). Her research topics include the diversification strategies of banking groups, organisational and business models, bank performance analysis, intellectual capital, customer complaints, non-financial reporting, banks' remuneration policies, corporate governance, and the Nobel Prize in Economic Sciences.

Jonathan Williams is Professor of Banking and Finance in the Discipline of Finance and Accounting, Surrey Business School, University of Surrey. He is the Series Editor of the Palgrave Macmillan Studies on Banking and Financial Institutions and co-editor of *Digital Transformation and the Economics of Banking: Economic, Institutional, and Social Dimensions* (2024) and *Disruptive Technology in Banking and Finance: An International Perspective on FinTech* (2021). He is the Chair of the European Association of University Teachers of Banking and Finance (Wolpertinger). His early research examined the efficiency and productivity of banks and policy-related issues, such as competition and privatisation. More recently, he has published on banking union and negative interest rate policy. Currently, he is researching executive compensation and corporate governance in banking as well as fintech and macroprudential policy.

List of Figures

List of Tables

CHAPTER 1

Introduction

Timothy King and Jonathan Williams

The governance of corporations captivates the interest of governments, policymakers, business leaders, academics, and stakeholders in corporations, such as shareholders and debtholders as well as the executive teams who run our businesses. However, it has been acknowledged for a long time that the separation of firm ownership from its control has the potential to create principal-agent problems which, in turn, can undermine good corporate governance and lead to adverse outcomes for corporations, their stakeholders, and the wider society.

The typical corporation is owned by its shareholders who appoint a board of directors to run the firm on behalf of its owners. Boards hire a professional manager or Chief Executive Officer (CEO) to run the firm. Hence, a vital function of the board is to monitor the performance of the CEO. Boards are composed of executive directors who run the firm

T. King (✉)
University of Vaasa, Vaasa, Finland
e-mail: timothy.king@uwasa.fi

J. Williams
University of Surrey, Guildford, UK
e-mail: jon.williams@surrey.ac.uk

T. King and J. Williams (eds.), *Corporate Governance in the Banking and Financial Sector*, Palgrave Macmillan Studies in Banking and Financial Institutions, https://doi.org/10.1007/978-3-031-83353-3_1

and non-executive directors (NEDs) who are independent of the firm's daily operations. NEDs provide advice and guidance according to their specialisms and experience and they monitor executive directors on behalf of shareholders. It is common for corporations to operate various sub-committees which support the main board. Examples include the audit committee, nomination committee, and remuneration committee.

Whilst the corporate structure outlined above *should* create good governance, it is not insulated from poor governance practices which, in turn, require laws, regulations, and/or codes of practice to ensure that corporations comply with best practice corporate governance. Several potential anomalies may be attributed to powerful CEOs who extract rents and expropriate shareholders. Practically, a powerful CEO can interfere in the monitoring function by nominating preferred candidates to become NEDs. Matters may be compounded if CEO appointees sit on the firm's remuneration committee, which decides the compensation to be paid to the CEO and all other executives. It has been common at some corporations for the CEO to be the chair of the board of directors, which is a practice known as duality that is perceived to be another signal of CEO power.

Over time, corporate governance best practice has been evolving and expanding in scope with recommendations made on a variety of issues. Examples include significantly increasing the proportion of independent directors on boards and advising the separation of CEO and chair roles. Other developments reflect wider societal movements. For instance, some countries have introduced laws and/or quotas to increase the participation of women on boards. A body of academic research qualifies the benefits of greater female participation which include, for example, moderating the risk appetite of (certain types of) males whilst increasing male attendance at board meetings. The emergence and increasing importance of corporate social responsibility (CSR) and ESG (environment, social and *governance*) emphasise the role that good governance is expected to play in helping society tackle major challenges, such as responsible behaviour and climate risks. Good corporate governance prioritises obtaining the best outcomes through diversity, equity and inclusion (DEI) in the workplace and on boards.

The Global Financial Crisis (GFC) of 2007–09 shed an unfavourable light on corporate governance practices in the banking sector. Specific attention and ire were directed at the compensation arrangements of executives and the incentives they created which had fuelled the excessive risk-taking and short-term focus that characterised the pre-GFC environment. Also, under the microscope was how powerful some bank CEOs were, the underrepresentation of women and minority groups on bank boards, and a perceived lack of conscience or social responsibility by bankers for the economic turmoil caused by the GFC.

Much has changed following the GFC. The regulatory response enshrined in Basel 3 set out how important the three pillars approach is by requiring an enhanced supervisory review and greater market discipline via increased disclosure of information in addition to stricter capital and new liquidity requirements. The Financial Stability Board (FSB) recommendations on remuneration have passed into law at least in the European Community (EC). Codes of corporate governance have been modified and enhanced across the world. For many reasons suggested above, there is greater scrutiny of the governance of corporations including banks. This book will underscore the importance of corporate governance in banks via a combination of vigorous theoretical discourse and robust empirical evidence. The next section will highlight the organisation of this book by summarising the contributions of each of its chapters.

1.1 Organisation of the Chapters in This Book

Chapters 2 to 4 provide an analysis of how markets have assessed changes to corporate governance arrangements. The chapters employ event study methods to gauge stock market reactions to the announcement of specific events to determine whether news of the events creates value for shareholders.

In Chapter 2, Ahmed, King, and Mäki examine the reaction of stock markets to news of the appointments of new CEOs. The authors obtain their evidence from non-financial firms operating in the Nordic countries. Specifically, they compare reactions to the appointments of inside CEOs (internal candidates) and outside CEOs (external candidates). Their analysis finds that more than half of new CEOs at large firms were outside candidates. Furthermore, their analysis of cumulative abnormal returns (CARs) around announcement dates shows unequivocally that markets respond positively to outside CEO appointments only. Changing CEO, irrespective of inside or outside candidature, fails to generate improvements in firms' operating performance in the subsequent three-year period. However, firms which appoint an outside do realise an increase in sales growth and capital expenditure post appointments.

In Chapter 3, Ahmed, Baselga-Pascual, and King evaluate the impact of diversification on the long-term performance and risk profile of banks operating in 11 Eurozone countries. Motivation for the analysis draws on the prospect following the GFC that regulators might formally implement the functional separation of commercial banking and investment banking to protect the former from the riskier activities of the latter. The authors examine the effects of asset and revenue diversification on bank franchise values at listed banks. Their results show that revenue diversification increases bank risk but does not affect franchise values whereas a greater concentration on lending adversely affects franchise values but does not increase risk.

In Chapter 4, Hiltunen and King examine the role that ESG metrics play in mergers and acquisitions (M&A). Obtaining their evidence from a sample of M&A transactions involving listed firms in the United States, the authors estimate CARs for acquiring and target firms and examine the impact of firms' ESG criterion finding that the abnormal returns to acquiring firms vary according to their ESG scores. Specifically, CARs are less negative for acquiring firms which have higher ESG scores and when target firms have higher ESG scores. Markets react most negatively to deals in which a low ESG scoring firm acquires a high ESG scoring target. The univariate analysis unambiguously demonstrates the significance of ESG credentials in driving value creation.

Chapters 5 to 7 focus explicitly on the banking sector to provide a snapshot of the corporate governance landscape pertaining to banks. The chapters are presented in chronological order in terms of the timings of the governance events each discusses.

In Chapter 5, Aureli, Brighi, and Malik consider the impact of banks having a Risk Committee on their financial stability and appetite for risk as captured by the total capital ratio. The authors construct a sample of European and US public banks for a four-year period beginning immediately prior to the GFC. Their analysis shows that the presence of a risk committee is positively associated with the total capital ratio. It implies that risk committees enhance the risk management capabilities of banks. That the effect is stronger during the GFC emphasises the critical role that good corporate governance structures, in this case the formation of risk committees, can play during episodes of financial stress.

In Chapter 6, Vezzani provides a comprehensive analysis of the role and duties of specialist remuneration committees (RemCo) and of various supra-national and national regulations and corporate governance codes affecting RemCo. The increasing importance of a strong and independent RemCo with a focus on executive compensation arrangements supports contention that incentives implicit in compensation contracts were a causal factor of the GFC and signals intention to prevent a reoccurrence of this anomaly. An analysis of board committee structures and director characteristics at Global Systemically Important Banks (G-SIBs) provides fresh insights into the features of RemCo at the G-SIBs.

In Chapter 7, Bongiovanni and Williams consider the effect of the COVID-19 pandemic on deposit market outcomes affecting bank holding companies operating in the US. Whilst evidence elsewhere shows that exogenous shocks lead to changes in deposit flows and deposit interest rates, it is uncertain whether deposit market dynamics were influenced by banks ESG scores following the shock arising from the pandemic. The authors contend that a bank's ESG credentials proxy for trust and show that depositors use the information embedded in ESG scores to discipline or reward banks. Specifically, depositors reward high ESG scoring banks with faster growth of noninterest-bearing deposits and acceptance of lower deposit interest rates following the shock.

Chapters 8 to 11 examine emerging areas of interest pertaining to corporate governance and as such these chapters constitute the final section of this book. Given the focus on emerging areas, the topics of the chapters are diverse and wide ranging.

In Chapter 8, King and Valkama use unique brokerage data to examine the stock trading of investors using the Robintrack dataset from Robinhood. Specifically, the authors explore the relationship between stock price volatility and individual investor ownership which yields valuable insight into the impact of the behaviour of individual investors. The analysis shows that individual investors are associated with more volatile stocks which suggests that higher volatility stocks attract individual investors and/or the observed higher volatility might result from an increase in interest in those stock by individual investors.

In Chapter 9, King and Williams examine the concept of shareholder voice which has become an important feature of corporate governance with shareholder proposals serving as a mechanism for outside owners to try to induce favourable performance outcomes and/or desirable changes in firms by conveying the expectations of shareholders to firm management. The authors compile a dataset of shareholder proposals which if accepted would increase the relative power and direct access of shareholders in large, publicly listed US corporations. Using CARs and a regression discontinuity approach, the analysis reveals that it matters how close a vote is to the pass/fail threshold. The results offer little support for the notion that shareholders desire increased access and power except in firms where the existing governance quality is particularly low and managers highly entrenched. Arguably, shareholders consider existing shareholder access and power sufficient, and vote against proposals that would increase their power possibly reflecting a perception that executives are better positioned to make firm-level decisions. It implies also that whilst shareholders might desire some degree of improved power, they are concerned that additional shareholder power will concentrate on certain powerful and influential shareholders. In such circumstances, an increase in shareholder power could work to reduce the overall welfare of shareholders.

In Chapter 10, King (Tatiana) and Morton reflect on the emergence and rapid growth of new financial technologies. The authors propose a novel framework that complements the extant literature by contextualising blockchains' impact on financial reporting functions. The framework is based on two theories, namely, the diffusion of innovation theory and norm lifecycle theory, and it reflects the differing stages of the norm adoption lifecycle. The authors highlight the difficulty of blockchains being effective without the development of proper norm legitimacy (since norms are not yet established). They clarify that, at the infrastructure level, the diffusion of blockchain technology for financial reporting is bound by two key limitations: first, a limitation of scope and second, a limitation of discretion. These limitations may or may not prevent the adoption of blockchain technology; the technology's further diffusion with central government support can facilitate decentralised blockchain infrastructure within the broader digital ecosystem. The authors posit that blockchains can be obsolete, sustaining, or disruptive for the accounting profession, depending on when and where in the lifecycle they are adopted.

In Chapter 11, Cantero-Saiz, Polizzi, and Scannella bring this book to an almost close by reviewing and carrying out a forward-looking analysis of research that focuses on the relationship between ESG and banks' asset quality and discussing how this relationship might be shaped by the financial performance of banks in the future.

Finally, Chapter 12 provides a short conclusion to the book.

CHAPTER 2

Stock Market Reaction to External CEO Appointments: Evidence from the Nordic Countries

Shaker Ahmed, Timothy King, and Juha Mäki

2.1 Introduction

The Chief Executive Officer (CEO), as the principal decision-maker in a firm, has the most direct and significant impact on its policies and outcomes. A turnover in this key position implies possible upcoming

We wish to thank Gonul Colak, Denis Davydov, Mikko Lepämäki, Seppo Pynnönen, Jorge Soria Ruiz-Ogarrio, Timo Rothovius, Sami Vähämaa, and the participants at the Graduate School of Finance (GSF) Summer Workshop in Finance, 2019 for their helpful comments and suggestions.

S. Ahmed
University of Surrey, Surrey, UK
e-mail: shaker.ahmed@surrey.ac.uk

T. King (✉) · J. Mäki
University of Vaasa, Vaasa, Finland
e-mail: timothy.king@uwasa.fi

T. King and J. Williams (eds.), *Corporate Governance in the Banking and Financial Sector*, Palgrave Macmillan Studies in Banking and Financial Institutions, https://doi.org/10.1007/978-3-031-83353-3_2

changes in the firm's strategic direction (Hambrick & Quigley, 2014; Parrino, 1997). A CEO chosen from within the ranks of current executives indicates continuation of the firm's current strategic orientation, while the appointment of an external executive signifies the firm's willingness to shift toward a new course of action (Datta & Rajagopalan, 1998; Herrmann & Datta, 2002; Kesner & Sebora, 1994; Schepker et al., 2017). Observing such a visible signal based on CEO origin, investors are expected to reassess the firm's prospects with the stock price reacting to revised assessments. We investigate if the short-term market reaction to executive appointment announcements varies based on CEO origin in Nordic countries.

The difference between internal and external CEOs centers around their perceived competence and expected impact on firm outcomes. Internal CEOs have specialized firm-specific knowledge and skills. However, their long history of working in the firm makes them more committed to the organizational status quo and less likely to initiate substantial strategic changes. If the market views that the strategic direction the internal appointees adopt is not expected to change firm outcomes, we can find no market reaction following such appointments (Friedman & Singh, 1989).

In contrast, external CEOs bring relatively novel knowledge and skills to the firm and possess a lesser degree of emotional commitment to the organizational status quo (Zhang & Rajagopalan, 2010). As a result, outside CEOs with fresh perspectives and diverse experience are likely to initiate more strategic changes and consequently affect firm outcomes. The expectation about future performance change can lead to a significant market reaction around the appointment announcement days of external CEOs. A positive market reaction would indicate investors view the external appointment favorably, whereas a negative response implies investors consider the adverse effects of the new hiring to outweigh its positive impacts.

Prior literature shows top management turnover announcements are associated with significantly positive abnormal stock returns (Bonnier & Bruner, 1989; Weisbach, 1988). Huson et al. (2004) find these positive

J. Mäki
e-mail: juha.maki@uwasa.fi

abnormal returns are related to subsequent improvements in firms' operating performance. Furthermore, the degree of improvement is positively related to external rather than internal hiring. Thus, we can expect the CEO appointment announcement, especially the external CEO hiring, to have a positive market reaction as the firm performance is expected to improve after the event.

We start our empirical analysis by testing if CEO appointment is associated with higher abnormal return in the Nordic markets. Then, we focus on the firm's performance around the event year. A common finding in the literature is that CEO appointment is normally preceded by poor firm performance even though the bad performance is caused by factors beyond incumbent executives' control (Eisfeldt & Kuhnen, 2013; Fiordelisi & Ricci, 2014; Jenter & Kanaan, 2015; Peters & Wagner, 2014). In addition, firms with a high demand for changing their direction, especially after a period of poor performance, are likely to appoint an outside CEO for their fresh perspectives and willingness to initiate strategic changes (Parrino, 1997). Thus, firms appointing outside CEOs are likely to have worse performance prior to the appointment than firms promoting internal executives.

Finally, we investigate if the market reaction aligns with the post-turnover firm operating performance. To better understand how the firm's performance changes following the turnover, we study the firm's assets and operating efficiency changes. A poorly performing firm can improve its operating performance by restructuring its assets by reducing capital intensity, eliminating underperforming businesses, or writing down certain assets (Huson et al., 2004). Alternatively, higher performance can derive from increased revenue or operating returns. By analyzing the changes in assets and operating efficiencies around the CEO turnover years, we can find if there is any difference in strategic orientation between internal and external CEOs.

Our chapter contributes to the CEO succession literature by investigating the market reaction to CEO appointments in the Nordic markets. Earlier studies report that between 15 and 19% of CEOs from large publicly traded US firms have an outside origin (see, e.g., Huson et al., 2001; Parrino, 1997). The proportion of external CEOs has increased to over 24% over the period 2011–2017 for S&P 500 firms (Schloetzer et al., 2018). Conventionally, the rate of outside CEOs is even higher for Nordic firms. Rose (2019) reports more than half of the newly appointed executives are external CEOs.

Oxelheim et al. (2013) argue that because of smaller domestic product and financial markets, large Nordic firms depend heavily on foreign products and capital markets. Consequently, these firms inherit a heightened demand for outside orientation, flexibility, and adaption (Menon & Pfeffer, 2003). Given the characteristics of external CEOs offer the best match for these characteristics, the large Nordic firms offer an expedient setting to test the effect of internal vs. external CEO appointments. It is also interesting to study whether the natural expectation of having outside CEOs leads to a significantly negative market reaction in the events of internal appointments. Overall, our paper contributes to the small body of literature looking into the effect of corporate policies in the Nordic countries (see, e.g., Berglund & Mäkinen, 2019; Enqvist et al., 2014; Lending & Vähämaa, 2017).

Another important contribution is that we focus only on large and most-traded stocks from the thinly traded Nordic markets. Chung and Luo (2013) argue that investors' reactions to succession announcements in thinly traded markets may be muddier than in mature markets in the presence of information asymmetry. To mitigate this problem, we choose to study the large Nordic firms as they offer the most visibility in these markets. This setup, thus, increases the relevance of our results regarding the impact of CEO succession on shareholder wealth. Besides, because of the rich information availability of these stocks, special situation investors can attempt to design trading strategies by observing how the stock market reacts to information about new CEO appointments.

Using CEO appointment announcements of large non-financial firms from the four Nordic countries, we observe the large firms' unusually higher percentage of external CEOs. Over 56% of the newly appointed Nordic top executives are outsiders compared to less than a quarter in the US. We also find that external CEO announcements lead to a significantly positive market reaction and have no significant effect on the internal promotion of executives. Further, we find that the positive market reaction sustains for several days leading up to the announcement day. Interestingly, we do not find any persistent improvement in operating profit following CEO turnover. However, external CEO appointments lead to higher efficiency gain, but that does not result in higher operating returns, perhaps due to higher expenditure on capital assets.

We proceed as follows. Section 2.2 describes the data and event-study methodology. Section 2.3 shows results for abnormal returns around CEO announcements and robustness tests. Section 2.4 focuses on the change in operating outcomes around the event years. Finally, Sect. 2.5 provides concluding remarks.

2.2 Data and Methodology

Data and Summary Statistics

We start our data collection by compiling the list of constituent non-financial firms of OMX Copenhagen 20, OMX Helsinki 25, Oslo SE OBX, and OMX Stockholm 30 indices for Denmark, Finland, Norway, and Sweden.[1] These four indices contain the 20, 25, 25, and 30 largest and most-traded firms from the Nordic countries. We use these firms to mitigate the illiquidity problem that affects the returns of thinly traded stocks.

We collect the announcement dates of CEO appointments from stock market press releases and company websites for the period 2006 to 2017 and check the biographies of new appointees from company websites and Bloomberg to determine whether the newly appointed CEO was recruited from within the firm or externally. Following Huson et al. (2001), we define a newly appointed CEO as an external executive if they have less than one year of working experience in the firm as an executive or board of members preceding the announcement of their appointment.

Our final sample includes 99 CEO appointment announcements[2] from 61 Nordic firms[3] with 55 outside CEO appointments. Table 2.1 shows about 56% of the appointed CEOs in our sample are outsiders. Notably (2011) and 2015 had the highest proportion of external CEO appointments, while the lowest percentage of 29% came from 2017.

For our sample firms and four indices, we collect the daily stock prices from Thomson Reuters DataStream over the period 2006–2017.

[1] The list of constituent firms was compiled in May 2018.

[2] The total number of CEO announcements for Denmark, Finland, Norway, and Sweden are 17, 26, 25, and 31. The proportion of outside CEOs for these four countries are approximately 59%, 65%, 52% and 48%, respectively.

[3] Of these 61 firms, 11, 18, 14, and 18 firms are from Denmark, Finland, Norway, and Sweden. Names of the sample firms are presented in Appendix Table 2.9.

Table 2.1 Number of CEO appointment announcements by years

	All appointments		*External appointments*		*Internal appointments*	
Year	*Obs. (a)*	*% of total appointments*	*Obs. (b)*	*% of appointments (b/a)*	*Obs. (c)*	*% of appointments (c/a)*
2006	1	1	1	100	0	0
2007	3	3	2	67	1	33
2008	14	14	9	64	5	36
2009	12	12	5	42	7	58
2010	10	10	5	50	5	50
2011	6	6	5	83	1	17
2012	3	3	1	33	2	67
2013	8	8	4	50	4	50
2014	12	12	6	50	6	50
2015	13	13	10	77	3	23
2016	10	10	5	50	5	50
2017	7	7	2	29	5	71
Total	99	100	55	56	44	44

Note The table presents the number of CEO appointment announcements by year

Following Huson et al. (2004), we use *Operating Return on Assets (OROA)* to proxy firm performance that we define as *operating earnings before interest expenses and income taxes (EBIT)-to-total assets*. We collect the two financial variables from Thomson Reuters's WorldScope database. As we study the growth in the firm's performance from three years before the CEO succession to three years after the event, our sample period for financial variables ranges from 2002 to 2020.

Table 2.2 tabulates summary statistics for our two main variables. The daily stock return is, on average, four basis points that corresponds to about 10% annualized percentage return (APR) and annualized standard deviation or realized volatility is about 39%. The average firm *OROA* is 10.28%, with a standard deviation of 12.65%. The maximum and minimum values of 74.64% and −48.32%, beyond three standard deviations of the mean indicate our sample includes some extreme outliers.

Apart from *total assets* and *EBIT*, we collect data on four more firm-level variables from WorldScope for the years 2002 to 2020 in local currencies to conduct our additional tests. These four variables are: (i) *Capital expenditure (CAPEX)* is the amount used to acquire fixed assets

Table 2.2 Summary statistics

	Mean	*Median*	*Std. dev*	*Minimum*	*Maximum*	*Observations*
Entire sample: 2006–2017						
Return	0.0004	0.0000	0.0244	−1.0600	0.4308	187,085
Firm-level variable: 2002–2020						
OROA	0.1009	0.0887	0.1299	−0.6813	0.7464	1080

Note The table presents the stock return and operating return for our sample firms. *OROA* is the proxy for the firm performance and is defined as the operating earnings before interest expenses and income taxes divided by total assets. The sample period for *OROA* is from 2002–2020

other than those associated with acquisitions; (ii) *Property, Plant and Equipment (PPE)* is the gross tangible assets used to produce goods or distribute services; (iii) *Employees* represents the number of both full and part-time employees of the firm excluding seasonal and emergency workers; and (iv) *Sales* is the gross operating revenue earned by the firm and operating return is the earnings of a firm before interest expense and income taxes.

Since the variables we use are ratios, we use local currency-denominated variables to avoid incorporating currency-related gains or losses in the results. However, we present summary statistics for all financial variables denominated in USD in Appendix 2.10.

Event-Study Methodology

Our measure of market-model-adjusted daily abnormal return around the CEO appointment announcement days is

$$AR_{i,t} = R_{i,t} - (\alpha_i + \beta_i R_{m,t}) \tag{2.1}$$

where, $AR_{i,t}$ is the daily abnormal return for the event i at day t, $R_{m,t}$ is the proxy for the market return, $R_{i,t}$ is the daily stock return for the event i at day t. The parameters of the market model α_i and β_i are estimated through OLS regression using a 180-day estimation window from 205 to 26 days preceding to the event day. From the estimated $AR_{i,t}$ we calculate cumulative abnormal return (CAR_i) by summing the daily abnormal of event i over the period $[\tau 1, \tau 2]$.

$$CAR_i = \sum_{t=\tau 1}^{\tau 2} AR_{i,t} \tag{2.2}$$

Further, we standardize the CAR_i using the estimation window standard deviation of residuals corrected for sampling error following Campbell et al. (1997, p. 159).

$$SCAR_i = \frac{CAR_i}{\sigma_i} \tag{2.3}$$

To test the null hypothesis of no event effect, we employ the standardized cross-sectional test of Boehmer et al. (1991) (henceforth the BMP test). Under this BMP test, a t-test is performed on the cross-sectional SCARs.

Event-study methodology usually assumes cross-sectional independence of the abnormal returns leading to underestimation of standard errors and severe over-rejection of null hypotheses (Kolari & Pynnönen, 2010). To address this problem, we use the Kolari and Pynnönen (2010) cross-sectional correlation adjustment for the BMP test statistics using forecasted abnormal returns over the period [–25, 25].

2.3 Empirical Analysis

We start our empirical analysis by showing the daily abnormal return from five days prior to the announcement day to five days following it. From Fig. 2.1, we find the cross-sectional average abnormal return is positive from three days before the event to the event day for all CEO appointments. After the event day, the abnormal return remains mostly negative. Abnormal returns rise sharply on the day before the announcement for both internal and external appointees. On other days, the abnormal returns pattern differs for inside and outside CEOs.

Daily abnormal returns show an instantly recognizable pattern for external CEO appointments. All the days leading up to the event have positive abnormal returns. From three days before the event, the abnormal return increases each day progressively. The mean daily abnormal return reaches its peak on the event day to about 0.94%, which is substantially higher than the daily return of 0.04% for our sample firms, as reported in Table 2.1.

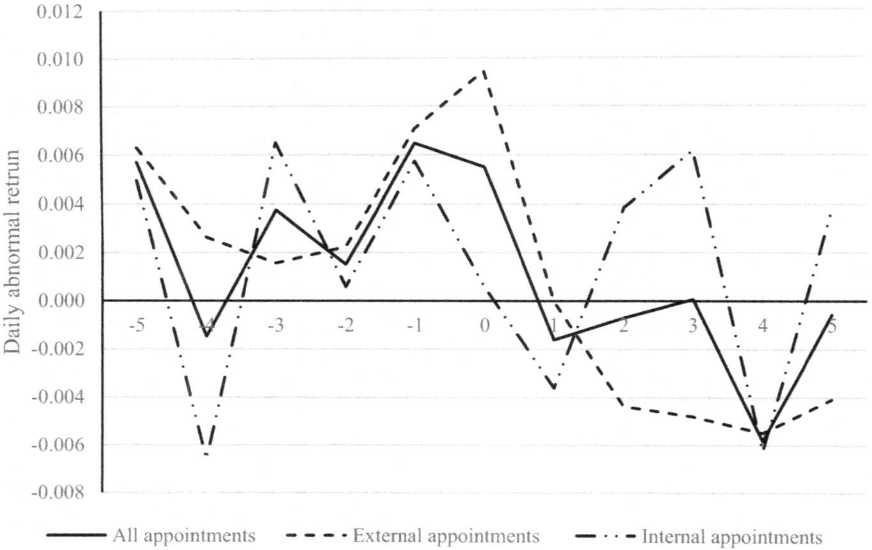

Fig. 2.1 Daily abnormal return around the CEO appointment announcements (*Note* This figure shows the cross-sectional average of daily Abnormal Return (AR) around the CEO appointment announcements. External CEOs are defined as having less than one year of working experience in the firm as an executive or a board member. The market-model-adjusted daily AR is calculated for each event using a 180-day estimation window from 205 to 26 days preceding the event day)

Following the event, the stock price declined severely and becomes negative from the second day. Further, we find the abnormal return rebounds on the fourth day and continues to grow the next day. Overall, we pick up an upward trend on the [−3, 0] window and an uninterrupted downward trend over the [1, 4] window. Because of the concentration of positive cumulative returns during the pre-event window, it is unlikely to find any significant positive cumulative return beyond the second days after the event.

For internal appointments, we do not find any instantly noticeable pattern in daily abnormal returns. There is a positive reaction on the event day. However, the average abnormal return of about 0.06% is relatively meager compared to the event day abnormal return for external CEO appointments. For the rest of the days, abnormal return appears to fluctuate randomly. Overall, Fig. 2.1 indicates that the stock market reaction to new CEO appointments is likely limited to the appointment of outside CEOs.

Cumulative Abnormal Returns

We present the significance of cumulative abnormal returns for various event windows around the event day. Consistent with our expectation from Fig. 2.1, Table 2.3 shows that stock markets react significantly only to the appointments of external CEOs. For internal appointments, the cumulative abnormal returns are positive but statistically insignificant for all event windows. Moreover, *CAR*s for all appointment announcements mimic the pattern of *CAR*s for external appointments with lower economic and statistical significance.

The event day abnormal return for external appointments is 0.94%, which is significant at 5% level. The *CAR* increases to 1.65% for the window [−1, 1] but starts to decline as the event window becomes wider around the event day. The declining cumulative abnormal return indicates that the post-event negative returns reduce the gain from the pre-event period. Interestingly, we find the significant cumulative return for the window [−5, 2] of about 2.5% is significant at 1% level. This finding is also in line with our intuition that the positive CAR concentrates mainly on the pre-event period.

The lack of significant market reaction when CEOs are promoted within the firm, suggests that the market expects internal CEOs to continue to maintain the current strategic orientation of the firm and,

Table 2.3 Cumulative abnormal return around CEO appointment announcements

Panel A: All CEO appointments				
Period	*CAR*	*BMP*	*ADJ. BMP*	*Obs*
[0, 0]	0.0055	1.722*	1.782*	99
[−1, 1]	0.0104	1.789*	1.852*	99
[−2, 2]	0.0112	1.584	1.639	99
[−3, 3]	0.0150	1.501	1.553	99
[−3, 2]	0.0149	1.934*	2.002**	99
[−5, 2]	0.0192	2.227**	2.305**	99
Panel B: External CEO appointments				
[0, 0]	0.0094	2.032**	1.938*	55
[−1, 1]	0.0165	2.326**	2.218**	55
[−2, 2]	0.0144	1.835*	1.749*	55
[−3, 3]	0.0111	1.325	1.264	55
[−3, 2]	0.0159	1.965*	1.873*	55
[−5, 2]	0.0249	2.792***	2.662**	55
Panel C: Internal CEO appointments				
[0, 0]	0.0006	−0.030	−0.031	44
[−1, 1]	0.0027	−0.103	−0.108	44
[−2, 2]	0.0072	0.247	0.258	44
[−3, 3]	0.0198	0.835	0.871	44
[−3, 2]	0.0137	0.786	0.821	44
[−5, 2]	0.0120	0.523	0.546	44

Note This table presents Cumulative Abnormal Returns (CAR) around CEO appointment announcement days, where external CEOs are defined as having less than one year of working experience in the firm as an executive or a board member. CARs are the cross-sectional average of the market-model-adjusted cumulative daily abnormal return calculated for each event using Eqs. (2.1) and (2.2). The coefficients of the market model are estimated using a 180-day estimation window from 205 to 26 days preceding the event day. BMP reports the t-statistics from the standardized cross-sectional test of Boehmer et al. (1991), and Adj-BMP presents the BMP t-statistics adjusted for cross-sectional correlation following Kolari and Pynnönen (2010)

*** $p < 0.01$, ** $p < 0.05$, * $p < 0.10$

thus, less likely to have any change in firm performance (Friedman & Singh, 1989). On the other hand, external CEOs are viewed as initiating changes that are likely to improve firm performance. In general, our result is consistent with that of Borokhovich et al. (1996), who identify shareholder benefit from external CEO appointments.

The insights from our study are novel for the Nordic markets. Specifically, our results substantially differ from Rose (2019), who finds significantly negative CAR for internal CEO appointments and positive but insignificant for external CEO hiring using a sample of Nordic firms. In contrast, we find a significant positive reaction to external CEO appointments, but shareholders do not penalize the internal CEO appointment by discounting the share price for the large Nordic firms. Thus, our results suggest that larger Nordic firms behave differently from smaller firms. Furthermore, Chung and Luo (2013) argue that the lack of information availability around the corporate event can lead to a muddier market response. Therefore, the difference in results can also be caused by the availability of better information for large firms compared to their smaller counterparts.

Robustness Check

The section reports three robustness tests based on our preliminary results in Table 2.3. The first test involves using an alternative definition of external CEO. In our primary analysis, we define a newly appointed CEO with less than one year of working experience as an executive or board member as an outsider. Given independence from the organizational status quo is the central attribute of external CEOs, we use this restrictive classification to limit the oncoming CEOs' exposure to the firm.

Having known the firm, a long-serving board member is likely to have more attachment to the firm's policies than an executive hired from outside but less involved in the firm's status quo than an existing executive actively managing the day-to-day operation. In the alternative definitions, we relax the requirement about external CEOs' experience as board members and redefine such appointees as outsiders. This new approach leads to previously identified three insider CEOs being re-classified as external CEOs.

The results for the new classification of external CEO are presented in Table 2.4. The change of definition does not change our baseline results in Table 2.3. We find significant market reaction only for the external CEO appointments. Panel B in Table 2.4 shows that the event day reaction to external hiring is about 0.73%. Compared to Table 2.3, the magnitude of CARs for the external CEO sub-sample reduced for all event windows. This result suggests investors do not view the board members as independent outsiders because of their involvement with the firm. Thus, their inclusion in the external CEO category resulted in a less accurate definition of outsiders and a more diluted market reaction.

In our second robustness test, we only include firms primarily listed in the Nordic market. Because of higher investors' attention, local firms can have a heightened market reaction than cross-listed firms. Therefore, we drop four events from our initial sample to construct a subset of firms

Table 2.4 CAR around CEO appointments for alternative external CEO definition

Panel A: All CEO appointments				
Period	*CAR*	*BMP*	*ADJ. BMP*	*Obs*
[0, 0]	0.0055	1.722*	1.782*	99
[-1, 1]	0.0104	1.789*	1.852*	99
[-2, 2]	0.0112	1.584	1.639	99
[-3, 3]	0.0150	1.501	1.553	99
[-3, 2]	0.0149	1.934*	2.002**	99
[-5, 2]	0.0192	2.227**	2.305**	99
Panel B: External CEO appointments				
[0, 0]	0.0073	1.696*	1.683*	58
[-1, 1]	0.0144	2.032**	2.017**	58
[-2, 2]	0.0120	1.522	1.511	58
[-3, 3]	0.0085	0.924	0.918	58
[-3, 2]	0.0136	1.633	1.621	58
[-5, 2]	0.0232	2.566**	2.547**	58
Panel C: Internal CEO appointments				
[0, 0]	0.0029	0.484	0.495	41
[-1, 1]	0.0047	0.215	0.219	41
[-2, 2]	0.0100	0.603	0.616	41
[-3, 3]	0.0241	1.179	1.204	41
[-3, 2]	0.0168	1.082	1.105	41
[-5, 2]	0.0135	0.664	0.678	41

Note This table presents the Cumulative Abnormal Returns (CAR) around the CEO appointment announcement days, where external CEOs are defined as having less than one year of working experience in the firm as an executive. CARs are the cross-sectional average of the market-model-adjusted cumulative daily abnormal return calculated for each event using Eqs. (2.1) and (2.2). The coefficients of the market model are estimated using a 180-day estimation window from 205 to 26 days preceding the event day. BMP reports the t-statistics from the standardized cross-sectional test of Boehmer et al. (1991), and Adj-BMP presents the BMP t-statistics adjusted for cross-sectional correlation following Kolari and Pynnönen (2010)

*** $p < 0.01$, ** $p < 0.05$, * $p < 0.10$

primarily listed in the Nordic countries. Out of these four events, three are categorized as external appointments. From Table 2.5, we find similar results as in Table 2.3. However, Panel B demonstrates that the market reaction to outside CEO appointments is higher when we exclude the cross-listed firms. Our finding supports the view that local investors pay more attention to local firms.

For the third robustness test, we use USD-denominated stock returns to take into account the return of international investors. An appreciating (depreciating) local currency can increase (reduce) the total return of international investors. Considering the movement in currencies is beyond the direct control of individual firms, we use local currency-denominated stock returns in our primary analysis to measure investors' reaction to CEO announcements. Moreover, due to the stable economic condition of the Nordic countries, it is unlikely that short-term stock returns from these markets would vary substantially due to currency conversion.

The results with the USD-denominated stock returns are presented in Table 2.6. The levels of statistical significance remain virtually the same as in Table 2.3. The marginal differences in the magnitude of CARs arising from currency conversion do not affect the economic significance of the external CEO appointment in any meaningful way. Thus, there are no significant differences between local or USD-denominated abnormal stock returns.

2.4 Firm Performance

The positive stock market reaction we documented in the previous section at the appointment of new CEOs, especially at external CEOs' hiring, suggests the market expects the firm performance to improve following the CEO succession. Also, prior studies find that poor firm performance is the main reason for CEO turnover. In this section, we study the change in the firm's operating performance around the CEO appointment. Specifically, holding the financial year at which the announcement is made as the event year, we test the growth in firms' operating performance in three preceding and succeeding years.

Table 2.5 CAR for Local firms

Panel A: All CEO appointments				
Period	*CAR*	*BMP*	*ADJ. BMP*	*Obs*
[0 0.0]	0.0060	1.745*	1.810*	95
[-1 0.1]	0.0109	1.815*	1.883*	95
[-2 0.2]	0.0120	1.592	1.652	95
[-3 0.3]	0.0153	1.412	1.464	95
[-3 0.2]	0.0159	1.927*	1.999**	95
[-5 0.2]	0.0199	2.189**	2.270**	95
Panel B: External CEO appointments				
[0 0.0]	0.0107	2.148**	2.079**	52
[-1 0.1]	0.0179	2.427**	2.350**	52
[-2 0.2]	0.0164	1.991*	1.928*	52
[-3 0.3]	0.0118	1.335	1.293	52
[-3 0.2]	0.0180	2.093**	2.026**	52
[-5 0.2]	0.0267	2.859***	2.768***	52
Panel C: Internal CEO appointments				
[0 0.0]	0.0003	–0.167	–0.176	43
[-1 0.1]	0.0025	–0.177	–0.187	43
[-2 0.2]	0.0066	0.073	0.077	43
[-3 0.3]	0.0195	0.709	0.747	43
[-3 0.2]	0.0133	0.661	0.696	43
[-5 0.2]	0.0117	0.427	0.449	43

Note This table presents the Cumulative Abnormal Returns (CAR) around the CEO appointment announcement days for firms with headquarters in the four Nordic countries. External CEOs are defined as having less than one year of working experience in the firm as an executive or a board member. CARs are the cross-sectional average of the market-model-adjusted cumulative daily abnormal return calculated for each event using Eqs. (2.1) and (2.2). The coefficients of the market model are estimated using a 180-day estimation window from 205 to 26 days preceding the event day. BMP reports the t-statistics from the standardized cross-sectional test of Boehmer et al. (1991), and Adj-BMP presents the BMP t-statistics adjusted for cross-sectional correlation following Kolari and Pynnönen (2010)

*** $p < 0.01$, ** $p < 0.05$, * $p < 0.10$

Table 2.6 CAR using USD-denominated returns

Panel A: All CEO appointments

Period	*CAR*	*BMP*	*ADJ. BMP*	*Obs*
[0, 0]	0.0056	1.702*	1.776*	99
[-1, 1]	0.0105	1.797*	1.875*	99
[-2, 2]	0.0106	1.451	1.514	99
[-3, 3]	0.0149	1.428	1.490	99
[-3, 2]	0.0144	1.792*	1.869*	99
[-5, 2]	0.0191	2.192**	2.287**	99
Panel B: External CEO appointments				
[0, 0]	0.0094	2.011**	1.932*	55
[-1, 1]	0.0167	2.377**	2.284**	55
[-2, 2]	0.0143	1.852*	1.780*	55
[-3, 3]	0.0112	1.328	1.276	55
[-3, 2]	0.0158	1.976*	1.899*	55
[-5, 2]	0.0257	2.922***	2.808***	55
Panel C: Internal CEO appointments				
[0, 0]	0.0007	–0.029	–0.031	44
[-1, 1]	0.0028	–0.135	–0.142	44
[-2, 2]	0.0060	0.032	0.033	44
[-3, 3]	0.0195	0.741	0.777	44
[-3, 2]	0.0125	0.588	0.617	44
[-5, 2]	0.0109	0.382	0.401	44

Note This table presents the Cumulative Abnormal Returns (CAR) around the CEO appointment announcement days using USD-denominated stock returns. External CEOs are defined as having less than one year of working experience in the firm as an executive or a board member. CARs are the cross-sectional average of the market-model-adjusted cumulative daily abnormal return calculated for each event using Eqs. (2.1) and (2.2). The coefficients of the market model are estimated using a 180-day estimation window from 205 to 26 days preceding the event day. BMP reports the t-statistics from the standardized cross-sectional test of Boehmer et al. (1991), and Adj-BMP presents the BMP t-statistics adjusted for cross-sectional correlation following Kolari and Pynnönen (2010)
*** $p < 0.01$, ** $p < 0.05$, * $p < 0.10$

Change in Operating Return Around Turnover

Figure 2.2 presents the cross-sectional mean and median of yearly growth in OROA around the event years. The median *OROA* declines before the event year for all appointments, with the highest single year drop for firms promoting executives internally than firms hiring external CEOs. Following the internal CEO appointment, *OROA* growth becomes positive in the next year. In contrast, firms appointing an external CEO experience a sharp decline in operating performance in the event year that worsens in the succeeding year. Firm performance improves dramatically in the second year before starting to decline again in the next year. For mean *OROA*, we observe similar patterns, but the rate of change is even higher. Overall, both figures show poor firm performance before the event year but no systematic performance improvement after that.

After looking into the year-to-year growth in *OROA*, we now examine if the percentage change in OROA over different event windows is statistically significant. We use the *t*-test and Wilcoxon signed-rank test for the mean and median values. Table 2.8 shows the median firm experiences lower growth over the [−2, 0] and [−3, 0] pre-event windows. Further, firms appointing external CEOs suffer more drops in *OROA* than firms promoting internal CEOs. This results in line with the expectation that firms with a higher degree of loss need more radical change and consequently appoint outsiders.

The appointment of an external CEO, however, does not improve firm performance instantly. There is significant negative growth in the first year following the appointment. Moreover, the decline in performance is higher for the median firm than the average firm, indicating that the average growth is subject to severe outlier problems.

Contrary to our assumption that external CEO appointments should lead to higher performance in subsequent years, we find some evidence that firms with internal CEOs record positive growth in the first year following the new CEO appointment. The median firm's *OROA* improves by 13.4%, and the result is significant at the 1% level. Interestingly, we do not find any evidence that firm performance improves following internal and external executives when a longer window is considered.

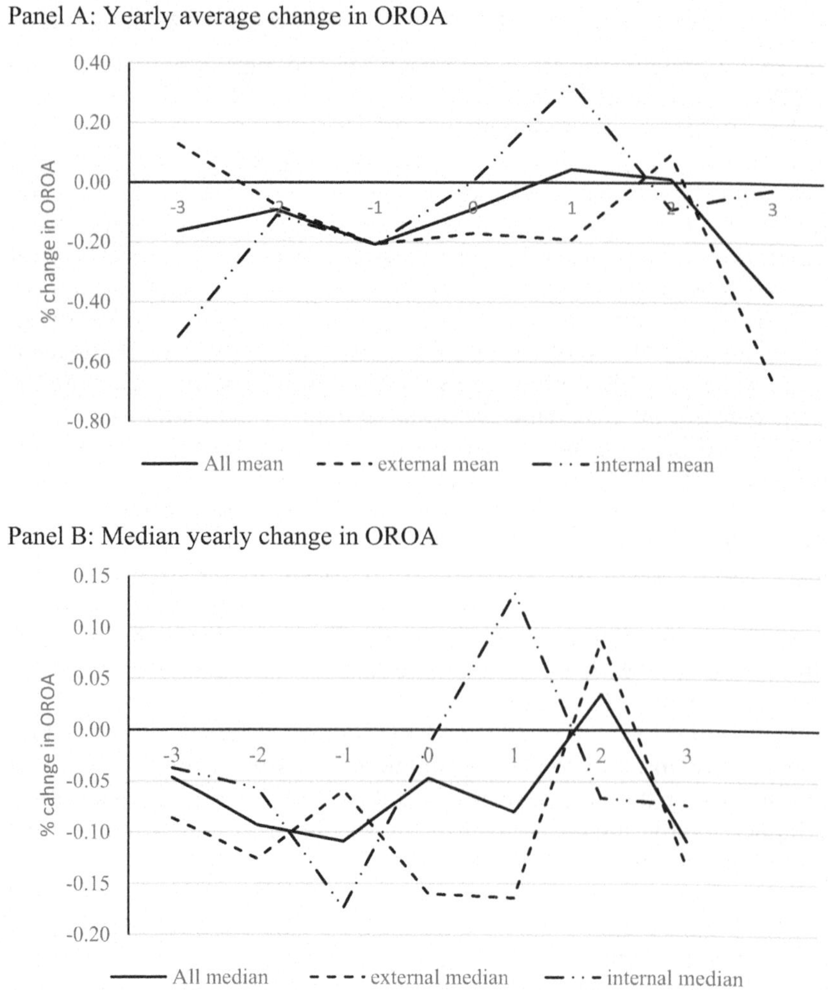

Fig. 2.2 Yearly change in Operating Return on Assets (OROA) (*Note* This figure shows the yearly mean and median percentage changes in OROA from three years before the CEO appointment announcements to three years after the event. External CEOs are defined as having less than one year of working experience in the firm as an executive or a board member)

Other Operating Changes Around Turnover

To better understand how firm performance changes around the CEO succession, following Huson et al. (2004), we study the change in six variables: *total assets*, *CAPEX*, *PPE*, *employees*, *sales per employee*, and *operating profit per employee*. To avoid the outliner problem, in this section, we only provide the median values of the growth in these variables over different event windows and their associated significance based on the Wilcoxon signed-rank test.

Panel A of Table 2.8 shows the change in *total assets* leading to and moving from the event year. We find firms' asset growth decreases before CEO succession. The median firm grows only 1% in the event year compared to 10% over the three years before the succession. However, the trend rebounds after the event year. After the announcement, the median firm experiences a growth of 3.7% in the first year, which progressively increases each following year, leading to a 12.3% growth in the third year.

There is a striking difference in the trend of asset growth for firms appointing internal and external CEOs. Firms appointing internal CEOs do not have any significant asset growth in the pre-announcement years, whereas firms appointing external CEOs have higher asset growth. Following the appointment, the asset growth in both internal and external CEO firms increases sharply. In three years, internal CEOs increase the firm size by 11.4%, whereas firms with external CEOs have marginally higher asset growth of 12.3%.

Like the asset growth, the results show that CEO origin is also associated with changes in *CAPEX* and *PPE*. After the succession, the median firm experiences faster growth in capital expenditure under the external CEO, reaching 17.1% in the second year. Under internal CEOs, capital expenditure reduces in the first year following the turnover but reaches the peak in the second year and continues to grow at a slower rate in the third year. At the end of the third year, the external CEO increases *CAPEX* by 7.5% compared to internal CEOs.

For *PPE*, the growth declines as the event year approaches and again starts to increase afterwards. Internal CEOs increase the *PPE* more than external CEOs. There is a 17.2% increase in *PPE* for firms with inside CEOs in three years compared to 12.4% for firms having external CEOs. The newly appointed internal CEOs are more inclined to increase the *PPE,* while external CEOs increase the *CAPEX*.

Panel D shows that firms appointing external CEOs experience significant growth in the number of employees leading to the event year. However, following the appointment, there is no significant increase in *employees* for both internal and external successions. From Panel E, we observe a modest growth in *sales per employee* in all prior years to the announcement for both outside and inside CEO appointments. However, firms appointing inside CEOs have higher revenue growth than those hiring outside. Following the appointment, only outside CEO firms have significant growth in *sales per employee*. While there is only 2.7% revenue growth three years before the event, following CEO turnover, *sales per employee* reaches 12.7%. Thus, we observe a substantial change in firm performance following external CEO appointments.

Interestingly, the growth in sales does not help external CEOs' firms realize a higher operating profit in any significant way. Instead, similar to our finding in Table 2.7, we observe that the operating profit per employee reduces significantly in the year after the turnover and that there is no improvement in the subsequent years. Internal CEO firms only show weak evidence of improved operating profit in the first year following the event and no significant changes afterwards.

The results in Table 2.8 indicate firms hiring external CEOs have higher asset growth and new employees but worse efficiency in the pre-succession years than firms appointing internal CEOs. The efficiency improves following the external appointment, but the asset growth continues to grow at a higher rate. A likely explanation is that the diluted operating income from increasing asset base offsets the gains from increased efficiency.

2.5 Conclusions

Nordic firms exhibit a tendency to hire outside CEOs. Over half of CEO appointments in our sample are external appointees; in comparison, less than a quarter of large US firms' CEOs are outsiders. This overdependence on external CEOs leads to the question of how these appointments benefit shareholders. We address this question by studying the short-term abnormal return of large Nordic firms around CEO appointment announcements.

Table 2.7 Change in Operating Return on Assets (OROA)

	All appointments			*External Appointments*			*Internal Appointments*		
Period	*Mean*	*Median*	*Obs*	*Mean*	*Median*	*Obs*	*Mean*	*Median*	*Obs*
[−3, 0]	−0.193	−0.272***	93	−0.253	−0.286**	52	−0.118	−0.267*	41
	(−0.67)	(−2.9)		(−0.86)	(−2.22)		(−0.22)	(−1.87)	
[−2, 0]	−0.361**	−0.223***	92	−0.430**	−0.224**	51	−0.275	−0.179**	41
	(−2.46)	(−3.28)		(−2.07)	(−2.18)		(−1.34)	(−2.53)	
[−1, 0]	−0.084	−0.041	91	−0.163	−0.130	49	0.008	−0.015	42
	(−0.53)	(−1.25)		(−0.78)	(−1.32)		(0.03)	(−0.41)	
[0, 1]	0.236	−0.070	91	−0.021	−0.164***	50	0.548*	0.134*	41
	(1.23)	(−0.72)		(−0.08)	(−2.59)		(1.95)	(1.78)	
[0, 2]	−0.082	−0.108	92	−0.160	−0.021	50	0.010	−0.149	42
	(−0.64)	(−1.4)		(−0.96)	(−1.21)		(0.05)	(−0.69)	
[0, 3]	0.007	−0.053	94	0.169	−0.031	52	−0.193	−0.094	42
	(0.05)	(−1.12)		(0.69)	(−0.59)		(−1.44)	(−1.14)	

Note This table reports the cross-sectional mean and median percentage change in OROA around the CEO appointment announcement year. External CEOs are defined as having less than one year of working experience in the firm as an executive or a board member. For mean values, t-statistics are reported in the parenthesis. For median values, we report the z-statistics from the Wilcoxon signed-rank test in parenthesis

*** $p < 0.01$, ** $p < 0.05$, * $p < 0.10$

Table 2.8 Change in firm policies around the CEO appointments

	All appointments		External appointments		Internal appointments	
Period	*Median*	*Obs*	*Median*	*Obs*	*Median*	*Obs*
Panel A: Change in total assets						
[−3, 0]	0.101***	93	0.072***	52	0.158	41
	(3.71)		(3.36)		(1.59)	
[−2, 0]	0.07***	93	0.079***	52	0.065	41
	(3.01)		(3.00)		(1.08)	
[−1, 0]	0.011*	93	0.009	53	0.024	40
	(1.77)		(1.18)		(1.37)	
[0, 1]	0.037***	94	0.026**	52	0.047*	42
	(2.8)		(2.08)		(1.89)	
[0, 2]	0.070***	94	0.07***	52	0.063**	42
	(3.61)		(2.63)		(2.46)	
[0, 3]	0.123***	93	0.123***	51	0.114***	42
	(4.62)		(3.36)		(3.12)	
Panel B: Change in capital expenditure						
[−3, 0]	−0.033	94	−0.004**	52	−0.062	42
	(1.54)		(2.17)		(−0.24)	
[−2, 0]	−0.059	93	−0.045	52	−0.079	41
	(0.09)		(0.95)		(−1.00)	
[−1, 0]	0.005	92	0.041	52	−0.051	40
	(0.02)		(0.92)		(−0.94)	
[0, 1]	0.019	94	0.035	52	−0.004	42
	(1.53)		(1.27)		(0.89)	
[0, 2]	0.168***	94	0.171***	52	0.118*	42
	(3.44)		(2.99)		(1.92)	
[0, 3]	0.146***	94	0.185***	52	0.110*	42
	(3.72)		(3.26)		(1.89)	
Panel C: Change in gross property, plant, and equipment						
[−3, 0]	0.201***	91	0.221***	50	0.191**	41

Panel A: Change in total assets

	All appointments		*External appointments*		*Internal appointments*	
Period	*Median*	*Obs*	*Median*	*Obs*	*Median*	*Obs*
	(5.42)		(5.50)		(2.17)	
[−2, 0]	0.095***	91	0.110***	51	0.089*	40
	(4.67)		(4.47)		(1.95)	
[−1, 0]	0.047***	92	0.051***	52	0.035**	40
	(4.05)		(3.45)		(2.18)	
[0, 1]	0.028***	94	0.043***	52	0.017*	42
	(3.25)		(2.62)		(1.96)	
[0, 2]	0.081***	94	0.075***	52	0.090***	42
	(4.06)		(2.84)		(2.89)	
[0, 3]	0.141***	94	0.124***	52	0.172***	42
	(5.15)		(3.71)		(3.53)	
Panel D: Change in number of employees						
[−3, 0]	0.043**	92	0.055***	51	−0.002	41
	(2.22)		(3.05)		(0.01)	
[−2, 0]	0.029**	89	0.040***	50	0.010	39
	(2.01)		(2.69)		(−0.01)	
[−1, 0]	0.010	90	0.009	50	0.011	40
	(1.49)		(1.31)		(0.73)	
[0, 1]	0.006	91	0.008	51	0.004	40
	(0.83)		(1.06)		(−0.06)	
[0, 2]	0.021	92	0.031	52	0.019	40
	(1.37)		(1.03)		(0.99)	
[0, 3]	0.023*	93	0.041	51	0.013	42
	(1.67)		(1.64)		(0.77)	
Panel E: Change in sales per employee						
[−3, 0]	0.062***	92	0.027**	51	0.073**	41
	(3.34)		(2.19)		(2.46)	
[−2, 0]	0.038***	90	0.025*	50	0.045**	40
	(3.12)		(1.94)		(2.57)	
[−1, 0]	0.013***	93	0.026**	52	0.010*	41

(continued)

Table 2.8 (continued)

Panel A: Change in total assets

	All appointments		*External appointments*		*Internal appointments*	
Period	*Median*	*Obs*	*Median*	*Obs*	*Median*	*Obs*
	(2.63)		(1.97)		(1.68)	
[0, 1]	0.014*	92	0.016	51	0.005	41
	(1.65)		(0.91)		(1.41)	
[0, 2]	0.069**	94	0.073*	52	0.044	42
	(2.21)		(1.78)		(1.29)	
[0, 3]	0.100***	91	0.127***	50	0.063	41
	(3.4)		(2.85)		(1.61)	
Panel F: Change in operating profit per employee						
[−3, 0]	−0.229**	92	−0.278**	51	−0.150	41
	(−2.18)		(−2.32)		(−0.63)	
[−2, 0]	−0.164*	87	−0.229*	48	−0.086	39
	(−1.93)		(−1.76)		(−0.82)	
[−1, 0]	−0.025	92	−0.168	50	0.045	42
	(−0.47)		(−1.05)		(0.54)	
[0, 1]	−0.035	93	−0.183**	51	0.150*	42
	(−0.66)		(−2.57)		(1.89)	
[0, 2]	−0.036	93	0.000	51	−0.039	42
	(−0.35)		(−0.42)		(−0.09)	
[0, 3]	0.009	92	−0.027	50	0.070	42
	(−0.3)		(−0.32)		(−0.13)	

Note This table reports the cross-sectional mean and median percentage change in OROA around the CEO appointment announcement year. External CEOs are defined as having less than one year of working experience in the firm as an executive or a board member. For median values, we report the z-statistics from the Wilcoxon signed-rank test in parenthesis

*** $p < 0.01$, ** $p < 0.05$, * $p < 0.10$

Our results show that the significant positive abnormal return in the appointment of new CEOs is driven by outside CEO appointment events. Moreover, the positive returns mainly concentrate during the pre-event period. The result is consistent with the organizational-adaptation view suggesting that the benefit of an outsider CEO's knowledge, network, and willingness to initiate operating changes outweighs any associated costs, such as lack of firm-specific knowledge (Georgakakis & Ruigrok, 2017; Zhang & Rajagopalan, 2010).

To better understand why the market favorably reacts to the external CEO appointment, we further study the circumstances around which new CEOs are appointed and the outcomes that follow. We find firms perform poorly years before the turnover. Moreover, firms appointing external CEOs experience worse operating returns and higher asset growth than firms promoting internal executives. We don't find any persistent improvement in the operating returns in the following three years after the turnover occurs. However, *sales per employee* increase after the external CEO takes over, suggesting some efficiency gain. Nevertheless, the simultaneous increase in capital expenditure that these firms undertake may have an adverse effect on their operating profit.

Our analysis provides two interesting sets of findings for the Nordic market. First, the positive stock market reaction is not directly associated with the improvement of firm operating performance. Instead, it reflects on the anticipated efficiency gain. Therefore, it would be interesting to study if this efficiency gain improves the firm performance in the long run. Second, the concentration of positive abnormal return leading up to the event day indicates that CEO turnovers are highly anticipated events. Therefore, further studies need to scrutinize how informed traders, such as institutional investors and firm executives, react to the CEO appointment announcement compared to individual investors.

Appendix

See Tables 2.9, 2.10.

Table 2.9 List of sample firms

Company Name	*Country*	*Company Name*	*Country*
Amer Sports	Finland	Skanska	Sweden
Cargotec	Finland	SKF	Sweden
Huhtamaki	Finland	SSAB	Sweden
Kesko	Finland	Swedish Match	Sweden
Kone	Finland	Volvo	Sweden
Konecranes	Finland	Carlsberg	Denmark
Metsa Board	Finland	Chr. Hansen	Denmark
Metso	Finland	Coloplast	Denmark
Neste	Finland	Genmab	Denmark
Nokia	Finland	GN Store Nord	Denmark
Nokian Renkaat	Finland	H. Lundbeck	Denmark
Orion	Finland	Novo Nordisk	Denmark
Outokumpu	Finland	Novozymes	Denmark
Outotec	Finland	Pandora	Denmark
Stora Enso	Finland	Vestas Windsystems	Denmark
Tieto	Finland	William Demant Holding	Denmark
Wartsila	Finland	Aker BP	Norway
YIT	Finland	DNO	Norway
ABB	Sweden	Grieg Seafood	Norway
Alfa Laval	Sweden	Leroy Seafood	Norway
AstraZeneca	Sweden	Marine Harvest/Mowi	Norway
Atlas Copco	Sweden	Norsk Hydro	Norway
Boliden	Sweden	Orkla	Norway
Electrolux	Sweden	Petroleum Geo-Services	Norway
Ericsson	Sweden	Salmar	Norway
Fingerprint Cards	Sweden	Schibsted	Norway
Getinge	Sweden	Statoil/Equinor	Norway
Hennes & Mauritz	Sweden	Subsea 7 SA	Norway
Sandvik	Sweden	TGS-Nopec	Norway
SCA	Sweden	Yara International	Norway
Securitas	Sweden		

Table 2.10 USD-denominated summary statistics

Variables	*Mean*	*Median*	*Std. dev*	*Minimum*	*Maximum*	*Obs*
Total assets	10 167 054	4 400 447	17 140 989	7 253	164 550 267	1082
Gross PPE	6 776 291	1 961 856	20 549 210	216	220 245 504	1075
Capital expenditure	515 979	163 121	1 580 886	12	20 723 023	1079
Employees	27 378	12 041	41 999	11	302 055	1070
Sales	9 012 731	3 865 943	13 586 983	366	127 975 617	1081
Operating profit	1 091 713	351 977	3 020 852	−4 297 766	39 545 172	1080

Note Variables other than employees are in thousand USD

References

Berglund, T., & Mäkinen, M. (2019). Do banks learn from financial crisis? The experience of Nordic banks. *Research in International Business and Finance, 47*, 428–440.

Boehmer, E., Masumeci, J., & Poulsen, A. B. (1991). Event-study methodology under conditions of event-induced variance. *Journal of Financial Economics, 30*(2), 253–272.

Bonnier, K. A., & Bruner, R. F. (1989). An analysis of stock price reaction to management change in distressed firms. *Journal of Accounting and Economics, 11*(1), 95–106.

Borokhovich, K. A., Parrino, R., & Trapani, T. (1996). Outside directors and CEO selection. *Journal of Financial and Quantitative Analysis, 31*(3), 337–355.

Campbell, J. Y., Lo, A. W. C., & MacKinlay, A. C. (1997). *The econometrics of financial markets*. Princeton University Press.

Chung, C. N., & Luo, X. R. (2013). Leadership succession and firm performance in an emerging economy: Successor origin, relational embeddedness, and legitimacy. *Strategic Management Journal, 34*(3), 338–357.

Datta, D. K., & Rajagopalan, N. (1998). Industry structure and CEO characteristics: An empirical study of succession events. *Strategic Management Journal, 19*(9), 833–852.

Eisfeldt, A. L., & Kuhnen, C. M. (2013). CEO turnover in a competitive assignment framework. *Journal of Financial Economics, 109*(2), 351–372.

Enqvist, J., Graham, M., & Nikkinen, J. (2014). The impact of working capital management on firm profitability in different business cycles: Evidence from Finland. *Research in International Business and Finance, 32*, 36–49.

Fiordelisi, F., & Ricci, O. (2014). Corporate culture and CEO turnover. *Journal of Corporate Finance, 28*, 66–82.

Friedman, S. D., & Singh, H. (1989). CEO succession and stockholder reaction: The influence of organizational context and event content. *Academy of Management Journal, 32*(4), 718–744.

Georgakakis, D., & Ruigrok, W. (2017). CEO succession origin and firm performance: A multilevel study. *Journal of Management Studies, 54*(1), 58–87.

Hambrick, D. C., & Quigley, T. J. (2014). Toward more accurate contextualization of the CEO effect on firm performance. *Strategic Management Journal, 35*(4), 473–491.

Herrmann, P., & Datta, D. K. (2002). CEO successor characteristics and the choice of foreign market entry mode: An empirical study. *Journal of International Business Studies, 33*(3), 551–569.

Huson, M. R., Malatesta, P. H., & Parrino, R. (2004). Managerial succession and firm performance. *Journal of Financial Economics, 74*(2), 237–275.

Huson, M. R., Parrino, R., & Starks, L. T. (2001). Internal monitoring mechanisms and CEO turnover: A long-term perspective. *The Journal of Finance, 56*(6), 2265–2297.

Jenter, D., & Kanaan, F. (2015). CEO turnover and relative performance evaluation. *The Journal of Finance, 70*(5), 2155–2184.

Kesner, I. F., & Sebora, T. C. (1994). Executive succession: Past, present & future. *Journal of Management, 20*(2), 327–372.

Kolari, J. W., & Pynnönen, S. (2010). Event study testing with cross-sectional correlation of abnormal returns. *The Review of Financial Studies, 23*(11), 3996–4025.

Lending, C. C., & Vähämaa, E. (2017). European board structure and director expertise: The impact of quotas. *Research in International Business and Finance, 39*, 486–501.

Menon, T., & Pfeffer, J. (2003). Valuing internal vs. external knowledge: Explaining the preference for outsiders. *Management Science, 49*(4), 497–513.

Oxelheim, L., Gregorič, A., Randøy, T., & Thomsen, S. (2013). On the internationalization of corporate boards: The case of Nordic firms. *Journal of International Business Studies, 44*(3), 173–194.

Parrino, R. (1997). CEO turnover and outside succession a cross-sectional analysis. *Journal of Financial Economics, 46*(2), 165–197.

Peters, F. S., & Wagner, A. F. (2014). The executive turnover risk premium. *The Journal of Finance, 69*(4), 1529–1563.

Rose, C. (2019). Stock market reactions to CEO succession announcements: inside versus outside recruitment? *Journal of Management and Governance*, 1–33.

Schepker, D. J., Kim, Y., Patel, P. C., Thatcher, S. M., & Campion, M. C. (2017). CEO succession, strategic change, and post-succession performance: A meta-analysis. *The Leadership Quarterly, 28*(6), 701–720.

Schloetzer, J. D., Tonello, M., & Larkin, G. (2018). *CEO Succession Practices: 2018 Edition*. The conference board, Inc.

Weisbach, M. S. (1988). Outside directors and CEO turnover. *Journal of Financial Economics, 20*, 431–460.

Zhang, Y., & Rajagopalan, N. (2010). Once an outsider, always an outsider? CEO origin, strategic change, and firm performance. *Strategic Management Journal, 31*(3), 334–346.

CHAPTER 3

How Do Stock Markets Value Bank Diversification? Evidence from the Eurozone

Shaker Ahmed, Laura Baselga-Pascual, and Timothy King

3.1 Introduction

Since the Global Financial Crisis (GFC) of 2008, regulators and supervisors around the world have focused on reforming the banking industry. A pressing issue concerned the future role of large, universal banks and whether to separate non-banking activities from traditional banking activities thereby creating more specialized banks in the process. In

Shaker Ahmed gratefully acknowledges the research grant by the OP Group Research Foundation, the Finnish Savings Banks Research Foundation, and the Jenny and Antti Wihuri Foundation.

S. Ahmed
University of Surrey, Surrey, UK
e-mail: shaker.ahmed@surrey.ac.uk

L. Baselga-Pascual
University of Deusto, Donostia, Spain

T. King (✉)
University of Vaasa, Vaasa, Finland
e-mail: timothy.king@uwasa.fi

T. King and J. Williams (eds.), *Corporate Governance in the Banking and Financial Sector*, Palgrave Macmillan Studies in Banking and Financial Institutions, https://doi.org/10.1007/978-3-031-83353-3_3

2012, the Liikanen Report recommended separating proprietary trading and market-making activities from other banking activities in the European Union (EU) banking sector. Earlier, both the Volcker Rule in the United States and the Vickers Commission report in the United Kingdom proposed similar restrictions on non-banking financial services. However, such recommendations contradicted the spirit and intent of earlier deregulatory acts[1] that had facilitated functional diversification in the banking industry. To provide an economic assessment of the debate, we investigate whether functional diversification affects bank franchise value or riskiness.

Prior literature on bank diversification suggests that banks offering non-banking products can reduce earnings volatility by diversifying into activities that are imperfectly correlated with traditional banking revenue streams without decreasing their expected returns (DeYoung & Roland, 2001; Heggestad, 1975; Johnson & Meinster, 1974; Litan, 1985; Wall & Eisenbeis, 1984). Banks especially so-called "global financial supermarkets" and "global banks" diversify their asset portfolios and access to alternative sources of income, such as underwriting, securities trading, brokerage, and investment banking, as well as other untraditional banking activities (Meslier et al., 2014; Wilmarth, 2011).

Diversification is beneficial if the potential benefits are larger than the associated costs. Through diversification, banks can improve their revenue generating capacity and reduce costs by sharing inputs, such as labor, technology, and information across multiple functional units. Further, banks can use acquired information from underwriting securities and insurance to improve loan organization and credit risk management. The benefits derived from economies of scope and economics of information can have a positive impact on banks' market value. However, organizational complexity, agency problems, and informational asymmetries can lead to unprofitable diversification activities and overweigh any diversification benefits. In this case, diversification adversely affects bank market value. Theoretically, it is unclear how functional diversification affects Tobin's Q. Empirically, Laeven and Levine (2007) report a diversification discount in financial conglomerates across 43 countries. Their

[1] In 1989, the Second Banking Coordination Directive laid the groundwork for functional diversification of European banks. In 1999 in the U.S., the Gramm–Leach–Bliley Act. (GLBA), also known as the Financial Services Modernization Act repealed the Glass–Steagall Act (GSA) of 1933 that had prohibited commercial banks from participating in investment banking business.

results support the view that diversification leads to agency problems and mitigates the effects of benefits.

From the risk dimension, standard portfolio theory predicts that the combined cash flows from non-correlated revenue sources should be less risky than each component. Stiroh and Rumble (2006) find non-interest activities are much more volatile while not more profitable than interest-generating activities. Similar findings lead Stiroh (2006) to conclude that some banks may have over-extended in diversifying activities. Therefore, the benefit from diversification largely depends on the type and riskiness of non-banking activities that diversified banks undertake (Kwan & Laderman, 1999).

We focus on the Eurozone banking sector where economic and monetary integration provides a unique opportunity to capture the effect of bank diversification. Compared to US banks, European banks have engaged in a broader range of activities for a more extended period (Baele et al., 2007). Further, Europe has suffered a prolonged financial crisis beyond the GFC. Thus, Europe provides an expedient ground for testing how bank diversification affects bank performance and riskiness.

We use an unbalanced panel of 769 bank-year observations that includes 66 individual banks from 11 countries from 2002 to 2017 to test whether a bank's non-interest income ratio and loans-to-asset ratio affect its franchise value and riskiness. To measure riskiness, we use total volatility, idiosyncratic risk, and systematic risk. The lengthy sample period will allow us to capture the long-term effects of diversification on bank performance and risk as well as the effect of different market conditions, such as the GFC and European sovereign debt crisis.

We find that revenue diversification does not affect bank franchise values whereas asset diversification reduces it. This is new evidence. It contrasts findings in Baele et al. (2007) that higher non-interest income ratios increase franchise values. We also find that revenue diversification raises bank risk mostly through increasing idiosyncratic risk. For asset diversification, we do not find any relationship with bank risks.

The remainder of the chapter is as follows. Section 3.2 describes the data and variables. Section 3.3 reports empirical analysis and results. Section 3.4 offers concluding remarks.

3.2 Data and Variables

Data

We collect bank stock prices traded in Euro from Thomson Reuters DataStream for 12 Eurozone countries: Austria, Belgium, Finland, France, Germany, Greece, Ireland, Italy, Luxembourg, Netherlands, Portugal, and Spain. These countries had adopted the Euro as their currency by 2001 and are subject to a similar monetary policy. We collect MSCI country indices for these countries and the one-month Euribor interest rate from DataStream. We obtain bank-specific annual accounting data from Worldscope.

From our initial sample, we eliminated banks with missing stock return data and secondary listing data. Since stocks that are traded infrequently may yield uninformative returns, we disregard stock market data for a particular bank if more than 15% of the bank's daily stock returns are zero for all sample years.[2] We also exclude bank-year observations with missing data on accounting variables. Our final sample includes 769 bank-year observations that contain 66 individual banks from 11 countries over 2002 to 2017.[3] In 2017, our sample banks represent close to 98% of the market value of listed banks in the 11 countries. Panel A of Table 3.2 presents the number of bank-year observations for each country in each year while panel B reports the number of individual banks for each country (Table 3.1).

Dependent Variables

Franchise value reflects a bank's long-run earnings potential and comparative advantages. To capture the market's expectation of the future profitability of a bank, we use Tobin's Q to proxy the franchise value, which we measure by the ratio of market-to-book value of equity. To assess the market-based riskiness of banks, we use total volatility

[2] To control for banks with infrequent trading in Europe, Baele et al. (2007) adopt a similar approach of disregarding a bank-year data for a bank when more than 15% of the bank's daily stock returns are zero in that year.

[3] Seven banks in our sample are considered global systemically important banks (G-SIBs) by the Financial Stability Board (FSB) in 2017. These banks are Dexia (Belgium), BNP Paribas (France), Groupe Crédit Agricole (France), Societé Générale (France), Deutsche Bank (Germany), Unicredit Group (Italy), Santander (Spain).

Table 3.1 Year and countrywise number of observations

Panel A: Year and countrywise number of observations											
Year	*AT*	*BE*	*DE*	*ES*	*FI*	*FR*	*GR*	*IE*	*IT*	*NL*	*PT*	*Total*
2002	1	3	2	3	0	8	6	2	13	1	1	40
2003	1	3	2	3	0	9	6	2	13	1	1	41
2004	1	3	3	4	0	11	6	2	14	1	2	47
2005	1	3	3	4	0	12	7	2	14	1	2	49
2006	2	3	3	4	0	12	7	2	14	1	2	50
2007	2	3	2	4	0	12	8	2	14	1	2	50
2008	2	3	3	4	0	14	8	2	14	1	2	53
2009	2	3	3	5	0	14	8	2	14	1	2	54
2010	2	3	2	5	1	14	8	2	14	1	2	54
2011	2	3	3	4	1	14	6	2	13	1	2	51
2012	2	3	3	6	1	14	6	2	14	1	2	54
2013	2	2	2	4	0	12	4	2	10	0	2	40
2014	2	2	5	7	1	14	4	2	9	1	1	48
2015	2	2	3	6	0	11	3	3	12	2	2	46
2016	2	2	5	4	0	13	2	3	13	2	2	48
2017	2	0	5	6	0	14	2	2	10	1	2	44
Total	28	41	49	73	4	198	91	34	205	17	29	769
Panel B: Countrywise number of banks												
Obs	2	3	7	8	1	14	8	3	16	2	2	66

Note Panel A presents the number bank-year observation for Austria (AT), Belgium (BE), Germany (DE), Spain (ES), France (FR), Greece (GR), Ireland (IE), Italy (IT), Netherlands (NL), Portugal (PT). Panel B presents the number of individual banks from each country

(VOL), idiosyncratic risk (IVOL), and systematic risk (Beta). Stock return volatility captures the overall riskiness of banks and reflects market perceptions about the risks inherent in banks business strategies, management, assets, liabilities, off-balance-sheet positions, and the variability of cash flows (Ahmed et al., 2018). We calculate total volatility as the logarithm of the annualized standard deviation of daily stock returns over a calendar year.

We decompose total volatility into firm-specific and systematic risk components. Whereas Beta indicates firm-level riskiness related to systematic market developments and uncertainty, IVOL measures bank-specific risk unrelated to market conditions and movements. Well-diversified investors are mainly concerned about systematic risk that cannot be mitigated through portfolio diversification. However, regulators, bank managers, large stakeholders, and bank customers care about idiosyncratic

Table 3.2 Descriptive statistics

Variables	*Mean*	*Median*	*Min*	*Max*	*Std. Dev*	*No. of obs*
Dependent variables:						
Tobin's Q	0.066	0.051	0.000	0.579	0.054	769
VOL[a] (%)	36.755	30.062	5.500	321.334	25.554	769
IVOL[a] (%)	33.373	26.955	5.499	321.294	24.301	769
BETA	0.536	0.479	−0.194	1.879	0.410	769
Main variables of interest						
NII	0.473	0.467	0.012	0.961	0.160	769
LTA	0.671	0.702	0.090	0.920	0.174	769
Control variables						
Size (in millions)	237,327	55,003	484	2,193,953	424,074	769
ETA (%)	6.900	6.287	−5.096	17.641	3.555	769
ROA (%)	0.687	0.770	−12.420	4.990	1.204	769
CIR (%)	66.911	66.901	−560.976	401.833	41.639	769
LLP (%)	18.169	8.584	−75.610	628.164	44.711	769
LG (%)	6.430	4.032	−83.743	202.666	19.436	769

This table presents the correlation matrix among all the variables used in the empirical analysis. ***Tobin's Q*** is calculated as the ratio of the market value of a bank and its book value of assets, ***Volatility (VOL)*** is the logarithm of the annualized standard deviation of daily stock returns over a calendar year, ***Idiosyncratic risk (IVOL)*** is calculated as the standard deviation of the residuals from Eq. (3.1) estimated using daily stock returns over a calendar year, ***Systematic risk (beta)*** is the coefficient of market return obtained from the same model regression. ***Non-interest income share (NII)*** calculated as the Non-interest income divided by the sum of the absolute values of net interest income and non-interest income. ***Loans to total assets (LTA)*** is calculated as the ratio of net loans to total assets. The control variables are defined as follows: (i) ***Size*** is the natural logarithm of total assets, (ii) ***Capital ratio (ETA)*** is calculated as the ratio of equity capital to total assets, (iii) ***Profitability*** is proxied by the return on assets calculated as net income divided by total assets, (iv) ***Cost to income ratio (CIR)*** is calculated as non-interest expenses divided by the sum of net interest income and non-interest income, (v) ***Loan loss provision (LLP)*** is the ratio of Loan loss provision to sum of Net interest income and Non-interest income, (vi) ***Loan growth (LG)*** is the annual growth rate of net loans.

[a] *VOLA* and *IVOLA* are annualized using 252 trading days in a year.

risk and total volatility to understand the risk profile of banks (Baele et al., 2007).

$$R_{i,t} = \alpha + \beta_i R_{m,i,t} + \varepsilon_{i,t} \tag{3.1}$$

To obtain the measures for IVOL and Beta in a given year, we estimate Eq. 3.1 using the daily stock returns over that calendar year. In Eq. 3.1,

$R_{i,t}$ is the excess stock return, $R_{m,i,t}$ is the excess stock return of MSCI country index and $\varepsilon_{i,t}$ is the residual. IVOL is calculated as the standard deviation of the residuals. The coefficient of market return β_i in Eq. 3.1 is our measure of Beta. Via IVOL and Beta, we can understand through which channel bank functional diversification affects bank riskiness.

Bank Diversification

We use the ratio of non-interest income-to-total operating income (NII) to proxy revenue diversity. Total operating income is the sum of the absolute values[4] of net interest income and non-interest income. Non-interest income includes revenue earned from investments gains/losses, trust, and fiduciary income, commissions and fees, foreign exchange income, and income from trading accounts. An increase in NII indicates a diversified income structure.

Following Baele et al., (2007), we use the ratio of net loans to total assets (LTA) to measure a bank's asset diversity. An increase in LTA implies a bank is more concentrated in traditional banking activities or lacks diversification. However, asset diversification is not proxy for revenue diversification since assets other than loans can also generate interest revenue.

Control Variables

In common with empirical banking literature, we specify several control variables to account for potentially confounding effects on bank performance and risk-taking. Specifically, we account for bank size, capital ratio, performance, efficiency, credit risk, and growth in our regressions. We define the control variables as follows: (i) *Size* is the natural logarithm of total assets, (ii) *Capital ratio (ETA)* is the ratio of equity capital to total assets, (iii) *Profitability* is return on assets calculated as net income to total assets, (iv) *Cost to income ratio (CIR)* equals the ratio of non-interest

[4] If revenues are positive, our measure of revenue diversification takes values between zero and one. However, negative income shares from any of the revenue streams would lead to income shares of other revenue streams greater than one. Consequently, the revenue diversification measure can take values lower than zero and greater than one, which in turn can produce outliers and adversely affect the reliability of the diversification index. Following Elsas et al. (2010), we control for negative income by using the sum of absolute values of income streams to calculate total operating income.

expenses-to-the sum of net interest income and non-interest income, (v) *Loan loss provision* (LLP) is the ratio of loan loss provisions-to-the sum of net interest income and non-interest income (vi) *Loan growth* (LG) is the annual growth rate of net loans.

3.3 Results

Descriptive Statistics and Correlation

Table 3.2 presents selected descriptive statistics of our variables. The average non-interest income ratio (NII) is 0.473 with a standard deviation of 0.160; the loans to total assets (LTA) has mean value of 0.671 and standard deviation of 0.174. The total volatility (idiosyncratic volatility) of our sample banks is about 36.76% (33.37%) per year. The beta of the average bank is about 0.536.

The average bank has total assets of about 237 billion Euro, a 6.9% capital ratio, and profitability (ROA) of 0.69%. The average bank uses 66.91% of total operating income to finance banking operations leaving a profit margin of 33.09% from which around 18.17% is used as provisions for loan loss. Furthermore, the average bank has a yearly loan growth of 6.4%. The descriptive statistics hint at the presence of outliers in the sample. Therefore, and to address the problem, we winsorize variables at 1% and 99% levels, respectively. The following tests are applied to winsorized variables.

Table 3.3 presents bivariate correlations among variables. Table 3.3 shows Tobin's Q is strongly negatively correlated with all three risk measures, and the three risk measures are strongly positively associated with each other. Furthermore, Tobin's Q is strongly positively associated with LTA and negatively associated with NII. LTA is strongly negatively associated with all risk measures indicating that concentration on assets in traditional baking activities reduces bank risks. On the contrary, correlation with NII and risk measures indicate that revenue from non-traditional banking sources reduces idiosyncratic risk but increases systematic risk.

Table 3.3 Correlation matrix

	Variables	*1*	*2*	*3*	*4*	*5*	*6*	*7*	*8*	*9*	*10*	*11*	*12*
1	TOBIN'S Q	1											
2	VOL	−0.213***	1										
3	IVOL	−0.189***	0.987***	1									
4	BETA	−0.262***	0.608***	0.506***	1								
5	NII	−0.113***	−0.176***	−0.208***	0.082**	1							
6	LTA	0.073**	−0.107***	−0.043	−0.376***	−0.371***	1						
7	Size	−0.259***	0.085**	−0.005	0.452***	0.346***	−0.631	1					
8	ETA	0.154***	−0.269***	−0.222***	−0.350***	−0.119***	0.431	−0.383***	1				
9	ROA	0.380***	−0.451***	−0.473***	−0.237***	0.154***	0.045	−0.030	0.191***	1			
10	CIR	−0.138***	0.238***	0.207***	0.311***	0.304***	−0.290***	0.250***	−0.252***	−0.35***	1		
11	LLP	−0.162***	0.603***	0.634***	0.321***	−0.335***	0.094***	−0.088**	−0.094***	−0.64***	0.204***	1	
12	LG	0.230***	−0.296***	−0.292***	−0.227***	−0.016	0.022	−0.005	−0.045	0.315***	−0.164***	−0.250***	1

Note This table presents the correlation matrix among all the variables used in the empirical analysis. *Tobin's Q* is calculated as the ratio of the market value of a bank and its book value of assets, *Volatility (VOL)* is the logarithm of the annualized standard deviation of daily stock returns over a calendar year, *Idiosyncratic risk (IVOL)* is calculated as the standard deviation of the residuals from Eq. (3.1) estimated using daily stock returns over a calendar year, *Systematic risk (beta)* is the coefficient of market return obtained from the same model regression. *Non-interest income share (NII)* calculated as the Non-interest income divided by the sum of the absolute values of net interest income and non-interest income. *Loans to total assets (LTA)* is calculated as the ratio of net loans to total assets. The control variables are defined as follows: (i) *Size* is the natural logarithm of total assets, (ii) *Capital ratio (ETA)* is calculated as the ratio of equity capital to total assets, (iii) *Profitability* is proxied by the return on assets calculated as net income divided by total assets, (iv) *Cost to income ratio (CIR)* is calculated as non-interest expenses divided by the sum of net interest income and non-interest income, (v) *Loan loss provision (LLP)* is the ratio of Loan loss provision to sum of Net interest income and Non-interest income, (vi) *Loan growth (LG)* is the annual growth rate of net loans. All the variables are winsorized at 1% and 99% level

*** $p < 0.01$, ** $p < 0.05$, * $p < 0.10$

Univariate Results

We perform univariate tests to examine whether banks with high and low non-interest income ratios and loans-to-asset ratios have different characteristics. We define the bottom 25% banks in NII (LTA) distribution as low NII (LTA) banks. Correspondingly, we define banks in the top 25% of NII (LTA) distribution as high NII (LTA) banks. We conduct two-tailed *t*-tests to test the null hypothesis that there is no difference between high and low NII (LTA) banks. In Table 3.4, panel A shows comparisons between high and low NII banks while panel B compares high and low LTA banks. We cluster standard errors at the bank level.

The average banks in the high NII and low NII groups have scores of 0.679 and 0.279, respectively. The univariate results suggest that banks in the higher NII group have higher systematic risk (*beta*) but lower idiosyncratic risk (*ivola*), total volatility and franchise value. The average LTA score for the high LTA group is 0.854 and for the low NII group is 0.428. Statistically, we cannot uncover a significant difference in Tobin's Q between the groups of low and high LTA banks. However, banks with higher LTA scores are less risky than banks with low LTA scores. In general, the results indicate that whereas asset diversification is not associated with bank franchise value it is associated with higher riskiness.

The univariate results show that banks with higher degrees of revenue diversification are bigger in size, hold less capital, and generate higher profits. Moreover, these banks are less efficient and preserve lower loan loss provisions. We do not find that high and low diversified banks differ by loan growth in a statistically significant way. On the contrary, those banks lack asset diversification, that is, they have higher LTA scores, are smaller in size, hold more capital, and achieve higher efficiency. However, there is no statistically significant difference between low and high LTA banks with respect to profitability, loan loss provisions, and loan growth.

Table 3.4 Univariate tests

Panel A: Banks with high NII vs. Banks with low NII						
Variables	*High mean*	*obs*	*Low mean*	*obs*	*t-test*	*t-value*
Dependent variables:						
TOBIN'S Q	0.061	192	0.079	192	−0.019*	−1.766
VOL	3.455	192	3.620	192	−0.165*	−1.922
IVOL	3.322	192	3.541	192	−0.220**	−2.487
BETA	0.660	192	0.547	192	0.113*	1.673
Bank Diversification:						
RD	0.679	192	0.279	192	0.400***	20.841
AD	0.536	192	0.698	192	−0.162***	−3.879
Control variables:						
Size	11.845	192	10.553	192	1.292***	2.600
ETA	5.215	192	6.477	192	−1.262**	−1.976
ROA	0.778	192	0.469	192	0.309**	2.201
CIR	76.687	192	64.505	192	12.182***	3.355
LLP	7.074	192	28.702	192	−21.628***	−4.586
LG	5.846	192	7.210	192	−1.364	−0.754
Panel B: Banks with high LTA vs. Banks with low LTA						
Dependent variables:						
TOBIN'S Q	0.063	192	0.056	192	0.007	0.668
VOL	3.200	192	3.525	192	−0.325***	−3.225
IVOL	3.162	192	3.375	192	−0.213**	−2.150
BETA	0.246	192	0.717	192	−0.471***	−7.332
Bank Diversification:						

(continued)

Table 3.4 (continued)

Panel A: Banks with high NII vs. Banks with low NII						
Variables	*High mean*	*obs*	*Low mean*	*obs*	*t-test*	*t-value*
RD	0.448	192	0.567	192	−0.118***	−3.065
AD	0.854	192	0.428	192	0.427***	15.914
Control variables:						
Size	9.425	192	12.416	192	−2.991***	−6.373
ETA	9.900	192	5.008	192	4.892***	5.989
ROA	0.740	192	0.644	192	0.095	0.517
CIR	63.641	192	74.466	192	−10.825***	−2.692
LLP	13.096	192	10.631	192	2.466	0.531
LG	6.218	192	4.696	192	1.522	0.939

Note The table reports the results of *t*-tests for the null hypothesis that there is no difference in the means between subgroups high *NII(LTA)* and low *NII (LTA)*. Both high (low) NII and LTA subgroups include bottom (top) 25% banks in NII and LTA distribution, respectively. ***Tobin's Q*** is calculated as the ratio of the market value of a bank and its book value of assets, ***Volatility (VOL)*** is the logarithm of the annualized standard deviation of daily stock returns over a calendar year, ***Idiosyncratic risk (IVOL)*** is calculated as the standard deviation of the residuals from Eq. (3.1) estimated using daily stock returns over a calendar year, ***Systematic risk (beta)*** is the coefficient of market return obtained from the same model regression. ***Non-interest income share (NII)*** calculated as the Non-interest income divided by the sum of the absolute values of net interest income and non-interest income. ***Loans to total assets (LTA)*** is calculated as the ratio of net loans to total assets. The control variables are defined as follows: (i) ***Size*** is the natural logarithm of total assets, (ii) ***Capital ratio (ETA)*** is calculated as the ratio of equity capital to total assets, (iii) ***Profitability*** is proxied by the return on assets calculated as net income divided by total assets, (iv) ***Cost to income ratio (CIR)*** is calculated as non-interest expenses divided by the sum of net interest income and non-interest income, (v) ***Loan loss provision (LLP)*** is the ratio of Loan loss provision to sum of Net interest income and Non-interest income (vi) ***Loan growth (LG)*** is the annual growth rate of net loans. All the variables are winsorized at 1% and 99% level. The *t*-statistics (in parentheses) are based on robust standard errors which are adjusted for heteroskedasticity and are clustered by firm

*** $p < 0.01$, ** $p < 0.05$, * $p < 0.10$

Regression Results

We estimate different versions of Eq. (3.2) to test the null hypothesis that bank diversification affects bank franchise values and riskiness.

$$y_{i,t+1} = \alpha + \beta_1 x_{i,t} + \beta_2 size_{i,t} + \beta_3 ETA_{i,t} + \beta_4 ROA_{i,t}$$
$$+\beta_5 CIR_{i,t} + \beta_6 LLP_{i,t} + \beta_7 LG_{i,t} + \sum_{t=2003}^{2017} \delta_t year_t + \sum_{j=1}^{10} \delta_j Country_j + \varepsilon_{i,t} \tag{3.2}$$

where $y_{i,t+1}$ represents one year ahead dependent variables either Tobin's Q or the bank riskiness measures: total volatility, idiosyncratic volatility, systematic risk. Our main variables of interest are denoted as $x_{i,t}$ namely, NII and LTA.

Table 3.5 presents regression results for revenue diversification. All models1–2 include year and country fixed effects. Model indicates that revenue diversification does not affect bank franchise values. Interestingly, the direction of effect is positive in model 1 and negative in model 2 after controlling for LLP and LG. The stro positive relationship between the credit risk measure (i.e., LLP) and Tobin's Q may have mediated the relationship between NII and Tobin's Q. The two models explain around 40% and 43% of the variation in Tobin's Q, respectively.

Models 3–8 consistently show that revenue diversification positively affects bank riskiness at the 1% percent level. The increase in total risk mostly comes from the rise of idiosyncratic risk. According to model 4, a one standard deviation increase in NII (i.e., 0.16) increases total volatility by 1.09%. Models 6 and 8 suggest the same increase in NII contributes to a rise in idiosyncratic risk of 1.08% and systematic risk by about 0.05. Models 3–6 explain between 63 and 66% of the variation in total risk and idiosyncratic risk. Models 7–8 illustrate about 71% variation in systematic risk. In general, Table 3.5 revenue diversification increases bank risk without having any effect on franchise value. Our result is consistent with the view that income from non-interest activities is riskier than traditional banking activities while they are not more profitable than conventional income sources.

Table 3.6 reports the regression results for loan concentration. Models 1–2 suggest a negative relationship between LTA and franchise value. From model 2, a one standard deviation increase in LTA is associated

Table 3.5 Revenue diversification and stock market reaction

	Tobin's Q		*VOL*		*IVOL*		*Beta*	
Variables	*Model 1*	*Model 2*	*Model 3*	*Model 4*	*Model 5*	*Model 6*	*Model 7*	*Model 8*
Constant	0.115**	0.112**	3.247***	3.306***	3.511***	3.577***	−0.792***	−0.784***
	(2.23)	(2.37)	(12.39)	(12.73)	(13.81)	(14.07)	(−4.76)	(−4.71)
Main variables of interest:								
NII	0.004	−0.002	0.546***	0.531***	0.516***	0.504***	0.306***	0.288***
	(0.24)	(−0.12)	(3.08)	(2.96)	(2.87)	(2.81)	(2.92)	(2.72)
Control variables:								
Size	−0.005	−0.006*	0.010	0.009	−0.020	−0.020	0.107***	0.104***
	(−1.45)	(−1.96)	(0.62)	(0.55)	(−1.28)	(−1.23)	(11.81)	(11.67)
ETA	0.002	0.000	−0.034***	−0.035***	−0.034***	−0.035***	−0.007	−0.010
	(0.87)	(0.23)	(−3.35)	(−3.45)	(−3.43)	(−3.45)	(−1.07)	(−1.63)
ROA	−0.000	0.000	0.002	0.002	0.001	0.001	0.004***	0.005***
	(−0.27)	(0.54)	(1.12)	(0.97)	(0.63)	(0.44)	(4.00)	(4.00)
CIR	−0.000	0.000	0.005***	0.005***	0.005***	0.005***	0.001***	0.002***
	(−0.35)	(1.18)	(5.58)	(4.84)	(5.95)	(5.10)	(2.68)	(3.16)
LLP		0.015***		0.008		−0.000		0.035*
		(3.62)		(0.28)		(−0.02)		(1.87)
LG		−0.000		−0.004**		−0.004***		−0.001
		(−0.20)		(−2.48)		(−2.62)		(−1.42)
Year fixed effect	Yes	Yes	Yes	Yes	Yes	Yes	Yes	Yes
Country fixed effect	Yes	Yes	Yes	Yes	Yes	Yes	Yes	Yes

	Tobin's Q		*VOL*		*IVOL*		*Beta*	
Variables	*Model 1*	*Model 2*	*Model 3*	*Model 4*	*Model 5*	*Model 6*	*Model 7*	*Model 8*
Obs	703	703	703	703	703	703	703	703
R^2	0.40	0.43	0.65	0.66	0.63	0.63	0.71	0.71
F-stat	16.85***	18.39***	46.52***	44.59***	41.43***	39.96***	59.91***	56.88***

Note The dependent variables are defined as follows: *Tobin's Q* is calculated as the ratio of the market value of a bank and its book value of assets, ***Volatility (VOL)*** is the logarithm of the annualized standard deviation of daily stock returns over a calendar year, ***Idiosyncratic risk (IVOL)*** is calculated as the standard deviation of the residuals from Eq. (3.1) estimated using daily stock returns over a calendar year, ***Systematic risk (beta)*** is the coefficient of market return obtained from the same model regression. ***Non-interest income share (NII)*** calculated as the Non-interest income divided by the sum of the absolute values of net interest income and non-interest income. ***Loans to total assets (LTA)*** is calculated as the ratio of net loans to total assets. The control variables are defined as follows: (i) *Size* is the natural logarithm of total assets, (ii) ***Capital ratio (ETA)*** is calculated as the ratio of equity capital to total assets, (iii) ***Profitability*** is proxied by the return on assets calculated as net income divided by total assets, (iv) ***Cost to income ratio (CIR)*** is calculated as non-interest expenses divided by the sum of net interest income and non-interest income, (v) ***Loan loss provision (LLP)*** is the ratio of Loan loss provision to sum of Net interest income and Non-interest income, (vi) ***Loan growth (LG)*** is the annual growth rate of net loans. All the variables are winsorized at 1% and 99% level. The *t*-statistics (in parentheses) are based on robust standard errors which are adjusted for heteroskedasticity and are clustered by firm

*** $p < 0.01$, ** $p < 0.05$, * $p < 0.10$

with a fall of 0.009 in Tobin's Q. Model 1 shows the relationship is significant at the 10% level. After controlling for loan loss provisions and loan growth in Model 2, the relationship becomes significant at 5% level. The explanatory power of these models is 41% and 45% respectively.

LTA also negatively affects bank riskiness, but they are not statistically significant for any of three risk measures. The explanatory power of the models 3–8 in Table 3.6 is similar to those in Table 3.5. For total volatility and idiosyncratic risk, the models explain between 62 and 65% variation in them. For systematic risk, the explanatory power is around 71%. In general, Table 3.6 suggests that the stock market perceive the concentration on traditional banking activities as a sign of decline in future earning potential even though the univariate tests suggest that banks in Higher LTA group are more efficient and have higher growth than more diversified banks.

Additional Tests

We conduct a number of additional robustness tests. To control possible multicollinearity problems among regressors, we estimate Eq. 3.2 with only two control variables: size and ROA. Table 3.2 indicates the pairwise correlation between these two variables are statistically insignificant while the rest of the control variables are correlated with each other. The results are similar to Tables 3.5 and 3.6. In addition, we find that LTA affects total volatility and systematic risk at 10% and 1% statistical significance level respectively.

To test the effect of outliers, we estimate Eq. 3.2 with unwinsorized variables. As in Table 3.5, we find NII positively affects all three risk measures, and the results are significant at 1% level. LTA negatively affects franchise value and all three bank risk measures.

Considering around 80% of our observation comes from Italy, France, Greece, Spain, and Germany, we re-estimate Eq. 3.2 using a truncated sample consisting of bank-year observations only from these five countries. The results are qualitatively similar to those with unwinsorized variables and thus raise the possibility of extreme observations in this sub-sample. In fact, Greece was severely affected during the sovereign debt crisis, and it is possible that Greece banks somewhat drive our results. Therefore, we drop observations from Greece and estimate Eq. 3.2 with the remaining four countries. The resultant sub-sample represents around

Table 3.6 Bank assset diversification and stock market reaction

	Tobin's Q		*VOL*		*IVOL*		*Beta*	
Variables	*Model 1*	*Model 2*	*Model 3*	*Model 4*	*Model 5*	*Model 6*	*Model 7*	*Model 8*
Constant	0.176***	0.181***	3.621***	3.668***	3.800***	3.847***	−0.522**	−0.497**
	(3.06)	(3.47)	(9.76)	(10.29)	(10.52)	(11.07)	(−2.21)	(−2.04)
Main variables of interest:								
LTA	−0.047*	−0.054**	−0.220	−0.213	−0.158	−0.146	−0.170	−0.185
	(−1.72)	(−2.15)	(−1.28)	(−1.23)	(−0.98)	(−0.89)	(−1.35)	(−1.46)
Control variables:								
Size	−0.007**	−0.009***	0.006	0.004	−0.021	−0.021	0.103***	0.098***
	(−2.22)	(−2.91)	(0.38)	(0.25)	(-1.34)	(−1.29)	(11.34)	(10.36)
ETA	0.002	0.001	−0.037***	−0.040***	−0.038***	−0.039***	−0.008	−0.012*
	(1.03)	(0.46)	(−3.52)	(−3.74)	(−3.54)	(−3.67)	(−1.34)	(−1.90)
ROA	−0.000	−0.000	0.003	0.003	0.002	0.002	0.005***	0.005***
	(−0.64)	(−0.00)	(1.60)	(1.51)	(1.22)	(1.07)	(3.91)	(3.92)
CIR	−0.000	0.000	0.004***	0.004***	0.005***	0.004***	0.001**	0.002***
	(−0.16)	(1.48)	(4.56)	(4.01)	(4.96)	(4.23)	(1.98)	(2.88)
LLP		0.015***		0.018		0.008		0.042**
		(3.97)		(0.61)		(0.28)		(2.25)
LG		−0.000		−0.004**		−0.004**		−0.001
		(−0.03)		(−2.39)		(−2.53)		(−1.38)
Year fixed effect	Yes	Yes	Yes	Yes	Yes	Yes	Yes	Yes
Country fixed effect	Yes	Yes	Yes	Yes	Yes	Yes	Yes	Yes

(continued)

Table 3.6 (continued)

	Tobin's Q		*VOL*		*IVOL*		*Beta*	
Variables	*Model 1*	*Model 2*	*Model 3*	*Model 4*	*Model 5*	*Model 6*	*Model 7*	*Model 8*
Obs	703	703	703	703	703	703	703	703
R^2	0.41	0.45	0.64	0.65	0.62	0.62	0.70	0.71
F-stat	17.86***	19.82***	44.79***	43.01***	39.85***	38.47***	58.81***	56.17***

Note The dependent variables are defined as follows: *Tobin's Q* is calculated as the ratio of the market value of a bank and its book value of assets, ***Volatility (VOL)*** is the logarithm of the annualized standard deviation of daily stock returns over a calendar year, ***Idiosyncratic risk (IVOL)*** is calculated as the standard deviation of the residuals from Eq. (3.1) estimated using daily stock returns over a calendar year, ***Systematic risk (beta)*** is the coefficient of market return obtained from the same model regression. ***Non-interest income share (NII)*** calculated as the Non-interest income divided by the sum of the absolute values of net interest income and non-interest income. ***Loans to total assets (LTA)*** is calculated as the ratio of net loans to total assets. The control variables are defined as follows: (i) *Size* is the natural logarithm of total assets, (ii) ***Capital ratio (ETA)*** is calculated as the ratio of equity capital to total assets, (iii) ***Profitability*** is proxied by the return on assets calculated as net income divided by total assets, (iv) ***Cost to income ratio (CIR)*** is calculated as non-interest expenses divided by the sum of net interest income and non-interest income, (v) ***Loan loss provision (LLP)*** is the ratio of Loan loss provision to sum of Net interest income and Non-interest income, (vi) ***Loan growth (LG)*** is the annual growth rate of net loans. All the variables are winsorized at 1% and 99% level. The *t*-statistics (in parentheses) are based on robust standard errors which are adjusted for heteroskedasticity and are clustered by firm

*** $p < 0.01$, ** $p < 0.05$, * $p < 0.10$

68% of row observations. The results show NII positively affects all three risk measures at 5% level and LTA affects franchise values and beta.

To capture the effect of the global financial crisis, we reproduce Eq. 3.2 without the data of 2008 and 2009 and find similar results in Tables 3.5 and 3.6. All these tests indicate that results presented in Tables 3.5 and 3.6 are robust to different model specification and alternative sampling methods. However, the relationship between Beta and LTA is present in all four exercises, which indicates that the relationship is subject to extreme market conditions.

3.4 Conclusions

We have investigated how functional diversification affects bank stock valuations and riskiness. We find revenue diversification does not affect bank franchise values whereas increases in loans reduce franchise values. We also find revenue diversification increases bank risk mostly by increasing idiosyncratic risk. Even though our results show LTA does not affect bank riskiness, additional tests show when we take extreme market conditions into account, LTA can exert a negative effect on systematic risk.

The construction of NII and LTA may shed light on the difference in results in Tables 3.5 and 3.6. For example, LTA does not include all interest-bearing assets, such as bond holdings. However, revenue diversification includes all revenue streams other than interest income, which includes earnings from loans as well as bond holdings. So, the results indicate that earnings from sources other than interest income considered to be riskier than the traditional banking activities and banks need to hold a diversified asset portfolio to increase the franchise value. Therefore, in future research, it is important to focus on the level of asset and revenue mixture to find the optimal diversification that can positively impact banks' market value and risk profiles. For regulators, our results suggest that constraining banks from earning revenues from non-banking activities can reduce bank risk, which in turn could reduce bank franchise values. Therefore, regulators must consider the benefits of asset diversification to ensure the robust growth of the banking industry.

Appendix A: Description of variables

Classification	*Variable*	*Notation*	*Data Source*
Measure of stock market reaction:			
Tobins'q	The market value of a company divided by the book value of assets	Tobin's Q	WorldScope
Volatility	Yearly realized stock return volatility calculated from the logarithmic daily stock return over a year	VOLA	DataStream
Idiosyncratic risk	Idiosyncratic volatility measured as the residual from the market model using daily stock returns over a given year	IVOLA	DataStream
Systematic risk	Market beta from the market model using daily stock returns for a year	Beta	DataStream
Bank functional diversification:			
Non-interest income	Non-interest income divided by the sum of the absolute values of net interest income and non-interest income	NII	WorldScope
Asset structure	Net loans divided by the total assets	LTA	WorldScope
Bank-specific variables:			
Size	Total Assets	Size	WorldScope
Capital ratio	Equity divided by the total assets	ETA	WorldScope
Profitability	Return on Assets (%)	ROA	WorldScope
Cost to income ratio	It is calculated as non-interest expenses divided by the sum of net interest income and non-interest income	CIR	WorldScope
Credit risk	Loan loss provision divided by the sum of net interest income and non-interest income)	LLP	WorldScope
Loan growth	Loan growth calculated as the first difference of the logarithm loan series	LG	WorldScope

Appendix B: List of Banks

No	*Bank names*	*Country*
1	Erste Group Bank	Austria
2	Raiffeisen Bank Intl	Austria
3	KBC Group	Belgium
4	Banque Nale.de Belgique	Belgium
5	Dexia	Belgium
6	Deutsche Bank	Germany
7	Commerzbank	Germany
8	DT.Pfandbriefbank	Germany
9	Merkur Bank	Germany
10	Procredit Holding	Germany
11	Quirin Privatbk	Germany
12	Umweltbank	Germany
13	Banco Santander	Spain
14	BBV Argentaria	Spain
15	Caixabank	Spain
16	Bankia	Spain
17	Banco de Sabadell	Spain
18	Bankinter R	Spain
19	Liberbank	Spain
20	CAJA de Ahorros del Mediterraneo	Spain
21	Aktia A	Finland
22	BNP Paribas	France
23	Credit Agricole	France
24	Societe Generale	France
25	Natixis	France
26	Credit Agr.Ile de France	France
27	Cr.Agricole Morbihan	France
28	Crcam Atlantique Vendee	France
29	Crcam Ille	France
30	Crcam Langued CCI	France
31	Crcam Nord de France CCI	France
32	Credit Agr.Toulouse	France
33	Credit Agr.Touraine	France

(continued)

(continued)

No	*Bank names*	*Country*
34	Credit Agricole Brie Picardie	France
35	Credit Foncier de Monaco	France
36	National Bk.of Greece	Greece
37	Alpha Bank	Greece
38	Bank of Piraeus	Greece
39	Eurobank Ergasias	Greece
40	Bank of Greece	Greece
41	Attica Bank	Greece
42	T Bank Susp	Greece
43	TT Hellenic Postbank Susp	Greece
No	Bank names	Country
44	AIB Group	Ireland
45	Bank of Ireland Group	Ireland
46	Permanent Tsb GHG	Ireland
47	Intesa Sanpaolo	Italy
48	Unicredit	Italy
49	Mediobanca Bc.Fin	Italy
50	Banco BPM	Italy
51	Unione di Banche Italian	Italy
52	Banca Monte dei Paschi	Italy
53	Finecobank Spa	Italy
54	Banca Ppo.di Sondrio	Italy
55	BPER Banca	Italy
56	Credito Emiliano	Italy
57	Banca Carige	Italy
58	Banco di Sardegna RSP	Italy
59	Banca Finnat Euramerica	Italy
60	Banca Profilo	Italy
61	BCA.Piccolo Cdt.Valtell	Italy
62	BNC.di Desio E Delb	Italy
63	ING Groep	Netherlands
64	V Lanschot Kempen Dutch Cert	Netherlands
65	Banco Comr.Portugues R	Portugal
66	Banco BPI	Portugal

References

Abedifar, P., Molyneux, P., & Tarazi, A. (2018). Non-interest income and bank lending. *Journal of Banking & Finance, 87*, 411–4268.

Acharya, V. V., Hasan, I., & Saunders, A. (2006). Should banks be diversified? Evidence from individual bank loan portfolios. *The Journal of Business, 79*(3), 1355–1412.

Altunbas, Y., Manganelli, S., & Marques-Ibanez, D. (2011). *Bank risk during the financial crisis: Do business models matter?* (Working Paper 1394). European Central Bank.

Baele, L., De Jonghe, O., & Vennet, V. R. (2007). Does the stock market value bank diversification? *Journal of Banking & Finance, 31*(7), 1999–2023.

Baselga-Pascual, L., del Orden-Olasagasti, O., & Trujillo-Ponce, A. (2018). Toward a more resilient financial system: Should banks be diversified? *Sustainability, 10*(6), 1–16.

Baselga-Pascual, L., Trujillo-Ponce, A., & Cardone-Riportella, C. (2015). Factors influencing bank risk in Europe: Evidence from the financial crisis. *The North American Journal of Economics and Finance, 34*, 138–166.

Berger, P. G., & Ofek, E. (1995). Diversification's effect on firm value. *Journal of Financial Economics, 37*(1), 39–65.

Brighi, P., & Venturelli, V. (2014). How do income diversification, firm size and capital ratio affect performance? Evidence for bank holding companies. *Applied Financial Economics, 24*(21), 1375–1392.

Choi, J. J., Elyasiani, E., & Kopecky, K. J. (1992). The sensitivity of bank stock returns to market, interest and exchange rate risks. *Journal of Banking & Finance, 16*(5), 983–1004.

Demsetz, R. S., & Strahan, P. E. (1997). Diversification, size, and risk at bank holding companies. *Journal of Money, Credit, and Banking*, 300–313.

DeYoung, R., & Roland, K. P. (2001). Product mix and earnings volatility at commercial banks: Evidence from a degree of total leverage model. *Journal of Financial Intermediation, 10*, 54–84.

Docking, D. S., Hirschey, M., & Jones, E. (1997). Information and contagion effects of bank loan-loss reserve announcements. *Journal of Financial Economics, 43*(2), 219–239.

Elsas, R., Hackethal, A., & Holzhäuser, M. (2010). The anatomy of bank diversification. *Journal of Banking & Finance, 34*(6), 1274–1287.

Heggestad, A. (1975). Riskiness of investments in nonbank activities by bank holding companies. *Journal of Economics and Business, 27*, 219–223.

Johnson, R. D., & Meinster, D. R. (1974). Bank holding companies: Diversification opportunities in nonbank activities. *Eastern Economic Journal, 1*, 316–323.

Köhler, M. (2015). Which banks are more risky? The impact of business models on bank stability. *Journal of Financial Stability, 16*, 195–212.

Kwan, S. H., & Laderman, E. S. (1999). On the portfolio effects of financial convergence–A review of the literature. *Economic Review-Federal Reserve Bank of San Francisco, 2*, 18.

Laeven, L., & Levine, R. (2007). Is there a diversification discount in financial conglomerates? *Journal of Financial Economics, 85*(2), 331–367.

Lee, C. C., Hsieh, M. F., & Yang, S. J. (2014). The relationship between revenue diversification and bank performance: Do financial structures and financial reforms matter? *Japan and the World Economy, 29*, 18–35.

Litan, R. E. (1985). Evaluating and controlling the risks of financial product deregulation. *Yale Journal on Regulation, 3*, 1–52.

Meslier, C., Tacneng, R., & Tarazi, A. (2014). Is bank income diversification beneficial? Evidence from an emerging economy. *Journal of International Financial Markets, Institutions and Money, 31*, 97–126.

Stiroh, K. J. (2004). Diversification in banking: Is noninterest income the answer? *Journal of Money, Credit, and Banking, 36*(5), 853–882.

Stiroh, K. J. (2006). New evidence on the determinants of bank risk. *Journal of Financial Services Research, 30*(3), 237–263.

Stiroh, K. J., & Rumble, A. (2006). The dark side of diversification: The case of US financial holding companies. *Journal of Banking & Finance, 30*(8), 2131–2161.

Uhde, A., & Heimeshoff, U. (2009). Consolidation in banking and financial stability in Europe: Empirical evidence. *Journal of Banking & Finance, 33*(7), 1299–1311.

Van Lelyveld, I., & Knot, K. (2009). Do financial conglomerates create or destroy value? Evidence for the EU. *Journal of Banking & Finance, 33*(12), 2312–2321.

Villalonga, B. (2004). Diversification discount or premium? New evidence from the business information tracking series. *The Journal of Finance, 59*(2), 479–506.

Wall, L. D., & Eisenbeis, R. A. (1984). Risk considerations in deregulating bank activities. *Federal Reserve Bank of Atlanta Economic Review, 69*, 6–19.

Wilmarth, A. E. (2011). The Dodd-Frank act: A flawed and inadequate response to the too-big-to-fail problem. *Oregon Law Review, 89*, 951–1058.

CHAPTER 4

Creating Value in M&A: Does ESG Performance Matter for Acquirer Returns?

Lauri Hiltunen and Timothy King

4.1 Introduction

Mergers and acquisitions (M&A) represent critical strategic initiatives for firms aiming to achieve inorganic growth, leverage synergies, and expand market presence. They serve as catalysts for strategic renewal and competitive repositioning, offering avenues for accessing new markets, optimizing resources, and driving value creation. Despite their potential benefits, M&A transactions entail complexities and challenges such as cultural integration, regulatory scrutiny, and stakeholder resistance, necessitating careful planning to maximize their success and realize sustainable value. The advantages of M&A activities are frequently attributed to the synergistic effects that arise from the operational efficiencies of the

L. Hiltunen · T. King (✉)
School of Accounting and Finance, University of Vaasa, Vaasa, Finland
e-mail: timothy.king@uwasa.fi

L. Hiltunen
e-mail: c115535@student.uwasa.fi

T. King and J. Williams (eds.), *Corporate Governance in the Banking and Financial Sector*, Palgrave Macmillan Studies in Banking and Financial Institutions, https://doi.org/10.1007/978-3-031-83353-3_4

combined entity (Renneboog & Vansteenkiste, 2019). However, M&As are generally found to be value destroying for acquirers (Renneboog & Vansteenkiste, 2019).

Regardless of the potential issues with value creation through M&A, PwC (2023) reports a global increase in M&A activities. As depicted in Fig. 4.1, following the subsidence of COVID-19 pandemic-related hesitations, the subsequent year has witnessed a surge in new deals, predominately in mega-deals valued at over US$ 1 billion. The current year has seen increases in inflation and cost of financing, which influenced the eagerness for M&A transactions. The role of market timing and merger waves influencing deal flow is high and tends to coincide with economic, political, and regulatory revisions (Martynova & Renneboog, 2008). The relevance of market timing is further emphasized by Nguyen et al. (2012), who find that market timing considerations impact 73% of M&A deals and the underlying valuations.

Against this background, this chapter returns to the debate as to what factors influence acquirer returns in M&A transactions by considering whether the environmental, social and governance (ESG) performance of both acquirer and target entities influence the returns to acquirers following M&A announcements. We do for a sample of 429 domestic and cross-border M&A transactions by US listed firms between 2010 and 2023. Our investigation speaks to a need to consider the financial implications of incorporating sustainability and responsible business practices into M&A considerations.

By way of preview, we present mixed findings. First, employing a classic event study approach, we uncover initial evidence that acquirer announcement returns, while still negative on average, differ significantly for acquirers based on their ESG performance and when there are differences between acquirer and target ESG indicators. We find that acquirer returns are less negative when acquirers have higher ESG scores and when targets have high-ESG scores. Further analyzing deals according to acquirer and target ESG scores, we show that returns are least negative when the deal involves both a high-ESG acquirer and target but most negative when low-ESG acquirers acquire a high-ESG target. However, the significance of ESG as a factor influencing acquirer announcement returns disappears in a multivariate setting. Taken together, the mixed findings may reflect several factors, including ambiguity over the effects of ESG, changes in the importance of ESG over time, and, to some extent, the relatively small sample size.

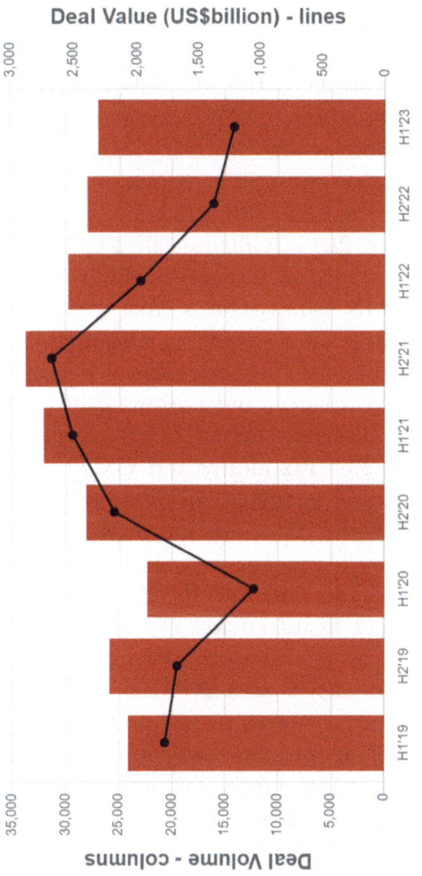

Fig. 4.1 Global M&A volumes (PwC, 2023)

4.2 Environmental, Social, and Governance (ESG) Considerations

The intersection of M&A with environmental, social, and governance (ESG) considerations represents a pivotal frontier in contemporary corporate strategy and sustainable development discourse. Over the past twenty years, the concepts of accountability and sustainability have evolved within the realm of investments with initiatives like the United Nations' Principles of Responsible Investing (PRI), EU Taxonomy, and the Central Securities Depository Regulation (CSDR) are gaining broad acceptance among corporations and investors (Eurosif, 2023). Further, in 2018, sustainability or corporate responsibility reports were published by 86% of companies included in the S&P 500 index, a significant increase from the under 20% reported in 2011 (Gillan et al., 2021). As firms increasingly recognize the importance of integrating ESG principles into their operational frameworks, M&A transactions emerge as potent vehicles for driving transformative change and advancing sustainability agendas. ESG encompasses three non-financial categories about a company's environmental impact, social performance, and corporate governance practices. Various agreements and directives mandate companies to divulge this information, such as the EU Taxonomy and CSDR. Following disclosure, numerous private rating agencies can derive ESG scores and other non-financial metrics from the reported information (Christensen et al., 2022).

By embedding ESG criteria into the due diligence process, acquirers can, in theory, assess target firms' environmental impact, social responsibility practices, as well as governance structures, thereby mitigating risks and uncovering potential synergies (KPMG, 2022). Moreover, M&A activities offer opportunities for firms to realign their strategic priorities, enhance stakeholder engagement, and foster long-term value creation in alignment with ESG objectives. Firms can improve their sustainability credentials through strategic acquisitions and even create industry-wide shifts toward more responsible business practices. However, the relative limited prior literature on the relevance of ESG for M&A performance presents mixed results. In what follows we provide a detailed review of the key extant literature.

Bose et al. (2021) explore the connection between a company's carbon risk and its decisions to acquire other companies, as well as the market's response to such announcements. Further, the study also examines whether CSR can alleviate or amplify the effects of carbon risk. Carbon emissions served as a proxy for measuring carbon risk. The results reveal that companies with high carbon risk tend to transfer their risks to foreign targets. The authors identify that acquiring companies with high carbon emissions are more likely to choose targets in less regulated, poorer countries with weaker shareholder protection and environmental controls. This trend is particularly noticeable when the acquiring company's home country has robust shareholder protection laws. Furthermore, their results imply focusing on CSR in this context can exacerbate the negative impact of carbon risk, leading to unfavorable market reactions, especially when the target country has strong governance or environmental protection and is affluent.

Zheng et al. (2023) consider a related research question to the present chapter but in the context of M&As in China. They analyze the overall level of ESG and its changes prior to M&As. The results suggest that acquiring firms with robust ESG practices tend to exhibit better post-M&A performance compared to those with weaker ESG frameworks, supporting the instrumental stakeholder theory. This theory suggests that a high-ESG rating fosters trust and stakeholder support, facilitating smoother integration processes and ultimately contributing to improved performance outcomes. More granularly, they find that firms with low initial ESG levels experience performance improvements post-M&A upon enhancing their ESG performance. However, those with high initial ESG levels face performance declines if their ESG levels deteriorate before the transaction.

Departing from M&As, Crifo et al. (2015) examine the impact of disclosing ESG practices on private equity financing. The authors utilize an unconventional method to the existing literature, by researching professional private equity investors in simulated firm auctions and analyzing the effect of disclosing positive and negative ESG practices. Their findings suggest that investors consider non-financial ESG information as valuable insight when making investment decisions. Furthermore, investors tend to react negatively toward unfavorable ESG practices, leading to reduced bidding and lower firm valuation. These findings highlight the significance of implementing ESG practices as companies without responsible processes in place may face difficulties in accessing private equity financing and higher capital costs, ultimately harming the shareholders by reducing firm value.

Several studies focus more broadly on corporate social responsibly (CSR). Deng et al. (2013) investigate the relationship between CSR and merger outcomes. The authors find that high CSR acquirers experience higher announcement returns, improved long-term operating performance, and increased stock returns compared to low CSR acquirers. Additionally, Deng et al. (2013) argue that mergers conducted by high CSR acquirers are more likely to be completed and the completion is done in a shorter period, indicating a positive relationship between CSR and overall merger outcomes. A related study by Arouri et al. (2019) argue that high acquirer CSR should be associated with lower M&A uncertainty. More specifically, they conjecture that through fostering trust and collaboration with stakeholders higher CSR ultimately facilitates smoother M&A processes with reduced uncertainty and disruption. Using data on 726 international M&A deals from 2004–2016, they find a negative correlation between acquirer CSR and completion uncertainty, measured using arbitrage spreads. High-CSR acquirers face narrower arbitrage spreads, indicating stronger market confidence in deal completion. Furthermore, individual CSR dimensions contribute separately to decreased uncertainty, highlighting the multifaceted impact of responsible business practices. These findings imply a competitive edge in the M&A market as a risk mitigation strategy and potentially enhance deal success rates.

4.3 Data and Methodology

Data

The data used in this study is collected from the London Stock Exchange Group (LSEG) database. The study focuses on listed US acquirers and limits data to the two largest stock exchanges in the US: the New York Stock Exchange (NYSE) and NASDAQ. The initial unfiltered dataset consists of 42,076 M&A transactions between 2010 and 2023, with a total of 6772 unique acquirers. Standard M&A filters, and a need for ESG data for both acquirers and targets reduce this initial sample substantially to the final sample of 429 M&A transactions and 348 unique acquirers. The final sample includes all M&As that meet the following criteria: The acquirer is publicly listed on NASDAQ or NYSE, the deal value is disclosed and exceeds US $1 million, the acquirer and target are in the LSEG ESG database and through the transaction, a change of control takes place. The change of control means that the final sample includes only transactions, where the acquirer purchases majority interest or a merger takes place.

Berg et al. (2022) and Christensen et al. (2022) state that there is variance in ESG ratings across providers, thus the study implements ESG rating from one leading source: the LSEG (formerly: Thomson Reuters and Refinitiv) ESG combined Score (TRESGCS) based on reported information for each of the three ESG pillars along with an overlay for ESG controversies. The ESG controversies category measures a company's exposure to ESG controversies, as well as negative events highlighted in global media. Figure 4.2 illustrates the ESG score considerations further. These scores range from 0 to 100 and the third and fourth quartiles are considered good and excellent relative ESG performance, respectively. Thus, the thesis considers a rating of fifty to be the dividing score for the split between high and low-ESG-rated firms.

Methodology

This study has two empirical approaches for answering the hypotheses and utilizes accounting indicators and stock returns. The first method is to estimate the average returns acquirers' experience in the event window around an M&A announcement, as per common practice in the M&A literature (Renneboog & Vansteenkiste, 2019; Wang et al., 2021) and then examine differences in CARs based on acquirer and target ESG performance. The second approach is to utilize a multiple linear regression model, where the CARs from the event study are further analyzed with a set of key control variables, similar to Wang et al. (2021) and Zheng et al. (2023).

Event Study

Following established practice in the literature (e.g., Renneboog & Vansteenkiste, 2019; Wang et al., 2021), we employ a classic event study methodology to estimate acquirer cumulative abnormal returns (CARs) around M&A announcements. We estimate abnormal returns from the market model using daily stock returns in the two hundred trading days and ending 11 days before the M&A announcement (Wang et al.,

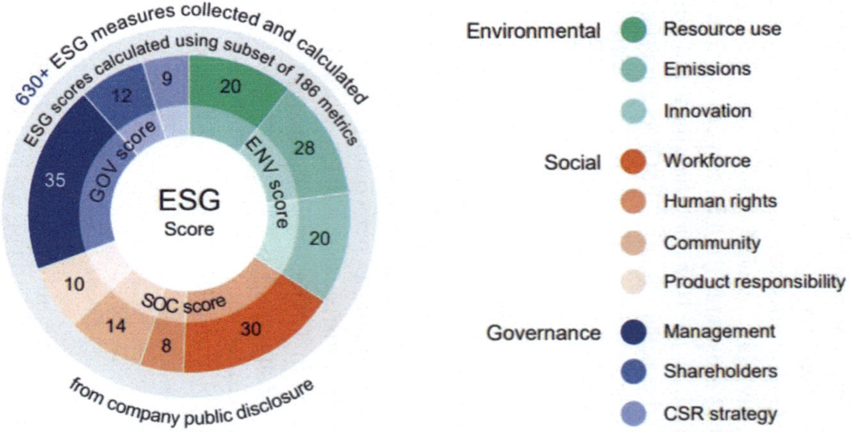

Fig. 4.2 ESG score methodology (LSEG, 2024)

2021). The market model, introduced by Brown and Warner (1985), is as follows:

$$AR_{i,t} = R_{i,t} - \hat{\alpha} - \hat{\beta} R_{m,t} \tag{4.1}$$

where, $\hat{\alpha} and \hat{\beta}$ = Ordinary Least Squares values from the estimation period. S&P 500 returns are used as a proxy for the market return. Daily abnormal stock returns are accumulated to obtain the CAR from day t_1 before the M&A announcement date to day t_2 after the M&A announcement date. This study utilizes multiple event windows to comprehensively analyze the market reaction to the announcement. The study further utilizes the findings of Brown and Warner (1985) to test the statistical significance of the CARs. Where the derived t-values consider the cross-sectional dependence in security-specific excess returns.

Multiple Linear Regression Model

The study follows approaches derived from the existing literature, such as Wang et al. (2021) and Zheng et al. (2023). The multivariate regression specification is as follows:

$$Acquirerperformance_{i,t} = \beta_0 + \beta_k \Sigma ESG_{i,t-1} + \beta_k \Sigma Acquirercontrols_{i,t-1} + \beta_k Dealcontrol_{i,t-1} + \int_{i,t} \tag{4.2}$$

where, i = acquirer index; t = time; *Acquirer performance* = CAR, ROA (return on assets), or ROE (return on equity); *ESG rating* represents the acquirer and target ESG ratings or an ESG upgrade dummy; *Acquirer controls* are size, leverage, and market to book value; *Deal control* is the deal value. Details of all these variables are discussed in the next section.

4.4 Study Variables

Dependent Variables

The dependent variables used in the study include multiple variations, since as Renneboog and Vansteenkiste (2019) note, the use of accounting data alone to measure post-merger performance suffers from inherent noisiness. M&A often come with special depreciation or amortization, write-downs, and restatements following divestitures of some acquired assets, or subsequent M&A deals, making it difficult to isolate the effect of a merger event.

First, CARs, as previously mentioned, are computed using the market model, and CAR (*−1,1*) is the daily abnormal stock returns in percentages, cumulated from one day before the M&A announcement date to one day after the M&A announcement date. CARs (*−2,2*) and (*−5,5*) are calculated similarly to CAR (*−1,1*), with the event window extended to two and five days before and after the transaction date, respectively. We also utilize a binary version of the CARs, where the dummy variable takes a value of 1 if the acquirer CAR is above the mean and zero if otherwise. Second, we also employ return ROA and ROE as alternative measures of performance, similar to Zheng et al. (2023). ROA is measured as operating income before depreciation scaled by the book value of total assets, while ROE is measured as operating income before depreciation scaled by the book value of equity.

Other Variables

The main independent variables include ESG characteristics. ESG ratings used are Thomson Reuters ESG Combined Score (TRESGCS) at the end of the fiscal year before the acquisition announcement to capture the ESG performance before the transaction. Further, the ESG rating is not available for the targets' post-transaction. The other variable used in the study is ESG upgrade, a binary variable that takes the value of 1 if the acquirer has an ESG rating upgrade in the year prior to the M&A announcement year, and zero otherwise.

Control variables include firm- and industry-specific characteristics derived from the literature (Wang et al., 2021; Zheng et al., 2023). These include acquirer size (SIZE), calculated as the natural logarithm of the acquirer's book value of assets at the end of the fiscal year before the acquisition announcement, acquirer leverage (LEV), calculated as the ratio of total debt to total assets at the end of the fiscal year before the acquisition announcement, MTBV, which is the market value of equity divided by the book value of equity. Additionally, the study includes a transaction-specific control variable, the deal size (DSIZE), calculated as the natural logarithm of the deal value, excluding net debt. These variables have been widely employed to examine the relationship between post-M&A performance and ESG in the limited existing literature (Zheng et al., 2023).

Table 4.1 Descriptive statistics

Variable	*Number*	*Mean*	*Median*	*Maximum*	*Minimum*	*Std. Dev*
CAR (−1,1)	429	−2.176	−1.592	28.344	−39.124	7.338
CAR (−2,2)	429	−2.165	−1.601	27.505	−40.783	7.940
CAR (−5,5)	429	−2.174	−1.418	35.386	−40.082	8.918
ROA	429	5.052	4.690	48.640	−91.310	10.724
ROE	429	14.072	10.920	92.050	−85.000	20.793
Acquirer ESG	429	48.536	48.750	92.930	0.000	22.751
Target ESG	429	27.686	26.070	86.550	0.000	19.281
Deal size	429	7.827	7.782	11.341	2.531	1.563
LEV	429	0.292	0.282	0.0991	0.000	0.202
MTBV	429	6.420	2.450	49.477	−76.450	28.160
SIZE	429	16.429	16.396	20.874	11.746	1.593
ESGUP	429	0.529	1.000	1.000	0.00	0.500

4.5 Results and Discussion

Descriptive Statistics

Table 4.1 shows the descriptive statistics of the full data sample. CARs are presented in percentages and further analyzed in the subsequent chapter. The acquirer ESG ratings are mostly balanced in the range of 0 to 100 and the average acquirer has a rating of 49. Contrarily, targets exhibit, on average, poor relative ESG performance and an insufficient degree of transparency in reporting material based on the score range provided by LSEG. The lower ratings are somewhat expected, given that achieving a high-ESG rating typically requires substantial investments, which might not be a priority in small and medium-sized enterprises (SME).

Event Study Results

The event study results are presented in Table 4.2, where the values presented represent mean CAR across the sample. The negative CAR results are consistent with prior literature that typically find negative CAR for acquirers on average (Renneboog & Vansteenkiste, 2019). The full sample, in the first row of Table 4.2, does not consider the ESG status and shows statistically significant negative returns across all event windows. Further, the economic significance holds considerable importance across

Table 4.2 Event study results

Variable	*Obs*	*CAR (−1,1)*	*CAR (−2,2)*	*CAR (−5,5)*
Full sample	429	−2.165***	−2.176***	−2.174***
		(17.707)	(−13.648)	(−9.239)
High ESG acquirer	188	−1.368***	−1.586***	−1.492***
		(−9.226)	(−6.166)	(−4.532)
Low ESG acquirer	241	−2.787***	−2.636***	−2.706***
		(−13.596)	(−11.133)	(−7.289)
High ESG target	61	−1.749***	−1.660***	−1.790***
		(−5.821)	(−4.750)	(−3.278)
Low ESG target	368	−2.234***	−2.261***	−2.238***
		(−16.156)	(−12.364)	(−8.348)

Superscripts *, **, and *** denote significance at the 10%, 5%, and 1% levels, respectively. T-statistics are in parentheses.

the samples in Table 4.2. The results imply that market reaction is, on average, fully accumulated in the first days around the announcement.

The results presented in Table 4.2 show that, on average, high-ESG acquirers realize less negative CAR compared to low-ESG acquiring peers. More specifically, the CARs are statistically significant, and the mean returns are higher by 1.05 percentage points in the five-day window yet are still negative at −1.59%. The last two rows of Table 4.2 show similar results with the target split, as the five-day window returns of acquirers targeting low-ESG firms are 0.6 percentage points lower than those acquiring high-ESG targets. This tentatively suggests it may be in the interest of acquirers to seek out high-ESG performing targets.

Do the Results Hold in a Multivariate Setting?

An important question is whether differences in acquirer returns attributable to differences in acquirer and target ESG performance hold in a multivariate setting. This is not necessarily the case, with the afore discussed literature presenting inconclusive results regarding the relevance of ESG as a factor in M&A, and related, transactions.

Table 4.3 presents the baseline results, where the main independent variables include both acquirer and target ESG ratings. The dependent variables in the first three columns are CAR −*1,1*; −*2,2*; and −*5,5*, respectively. The final two columns, left to right, show results for ROA and ROE. The table reveals that the ESG performance of acquirers' or targets does not appear to be a statistically significant factor influencing returns to acquirers when we control for key variables including size, leverage and the size of deals. While there is no confirmative evidence of an influence of ESG on CAR we do find some evidence that higher acquirer ESG performance is associated with greater ROE in M&As.

In terms of control variables, interestingly deals involving larger acquirers are associated with positive and statistically significant CAR and

Table 4.3 Baseline multivariate regression results

Variable	*CAR (−1,1)*	*CAR (−2,2)*	*CAR (−5,5)*	*ROA*	*ROE*
Acquirer ESG	0.010	0.17	0.005	0.039	0.120**
	(0.557)	(0.890)	(0.236)	(1.531)	(2.433)
Target ESG	0.003	0.004	−0.006	0.003	0.004
	(0.170)	(0.200)	(−0.236)	(0.092)	(0.072)
SIZE	0.674**	0.745***	0.668**	0.478	1.848**
	(2.530)	(2.590)	(2.504)	(1.269)	(2.509)
LEV	−1.670***	1.268***	1.724***	7.479***	14.979***
	(0.949)	(0.667)	(0.802)	(3.807)	(3.077)
MTBV	0.003	0.005	0.003	0.027	−0.028
	(0.275)	(0.396)	(0.177)	(1.542)	(0.810)
Deal Size	−0.346	−0.397	0.248	0.914	−0.689
	(−1.262)	(−1.338)	(−0.742)	(2.357)	(−0.907)
Observations	429	429	429	429	429
R-squared	0.022	0.025	0.014	0.085	0.083
Adj R-squared	0.008	0.011	0.000	0.072	0.070
F-statistics	1.568	1.793	0.966	6.571	6.348
S.D. dependent var	7.338	7.940	8.918	10.724	20.793
Akaike info criterion	6.832	6.987	7.231	7.524	8.867
Schwarz criterion	6.898	7.053	7.297	7.590	8.933
Hanan-Quinn criter	6.858	7.013	7.257	7.550	8.893
Durbin-Watson stat	2.085	2.100	2.072	2.168	2.097

Superscripts *, **, and *** denote significance at the 10%, 5%, and 1% levels, respectively. T-statistics are in parentheses.

ROE, which could reflect a greater scope for deal synergies and potential for target integration in larger acquirers. Given that our sample contains only firms with ESG data, the positive effect of acquirer size on deal performance could reflect some systematic differences between acquiring firms with ESG data and those without, given that prior research has often found acquirer size negatively related to M&A deal performance (e.g., Golubov et al., 2015). Although beyond the scope of the current chapter, we consider that this would be an interesting avenue for future research to explore further. Finally, consistent with prior studies (e.g., Golubov et al., 2015) we find some evidence of a positive effect of acquirer leverage on acquirer M&A performance, albeit the effect is only statistically significant at conventional levels for the models with ROE and ROA as the dependent variables.

To test whether these results are sensitive to how the ESG factor is included, in Table 4.4 we repeat the analysis from Table 4.3 but replace the raw composite ESG scores with dummy variables for acquirer and target ESG performance, whereby a value of 1 indicates above sample mean ESG scores and a 0 otherwise. Results for the positive effect of acquirer ESG score on ROE hold and in fact become stronger in magnitude. Coefficients for other control variables remain unchanged., which suggests ESG performance may matter for ROE in M&As, although we make no claims toward causality given, we do not address potential endogeneity concerns including omitted variables and selection effects.

Do ESG Upgrades Matter for Initial Post-M&A Financial Performance?

To this point we have examined whether acquirer and target ESG scores impact CAR to acquirers as well as their financial performance post-M&A. In this subsection, we consider another related question: whether upgrades to acquirer ESG scores around M&As influence their post-M&A financial performance. Zheng et al. (2023) hypothesize that acquirers with a low-ESG score that improve it should realize a more positive change in financial performance post-M&A, consistent with the law of diminishing marginal utility (DMU) that posits that value benefits may accrue to increases in the perception of the firm by stakeholders.

To test this conjecture, in Table 4.5, we present regression estimates of ESG ratings on the one-year post-M&A performance. We divide the full sample into two subsamples by the median of ESG acquirer ratings.

Table 4.4 Multivariate regression results: ESG acquirer and target dummy

Variable	*Obs*	*CAR (−1,1)*	*CAR (−2,2)*	*CAR (−5,5)*	*ROA*	*ROE*
Acquirer ESG		0.391	0.721	0.618	1.811	4.583**
		(0.475)	(0.811)	(0.615)	(1.560)	(2.012)
Target ESG		0.568	0.356	0.290	1.116	2.390
		(0.519)	(0.301)	(0.217)	(0.722)	(0.788)
SIZE		0.683**	0.753***	0.624*	0.471	1.938**
		(2.551)	(2.602)	(1.910)	(1.247)	(2.614)
LEV		1.681	1.291	1.728	7.530***	15.163***
		(0.956)	(0.679)	(0.805)	(3.031)	(3.112)
MTBV		0.004	0.006	0.003	0.028	0.031
		(0.297)	(0.412)	(0.179)	(1.582)	(0.884)
Deal Size		−0.377	−0.406	−0.320	0.828**	−0.808
		(−1.355)	(1.348)	(−0.941)	(2.106)	(−1.048)
Observations		429	429	429	429	429
R-squared		0.022	0.025	0.014	0.087	0.066
Adj R-squared		0.008	0.011	0.000	0.074	0.053
F-statistics		1.603	1.788	1.025	6.727	4.990
S.D. dependent var		7.338	7.940	8.918	10.724	20.793
Akaike info criterion		6.898	7.053	7.230	7.522	8.869
Schwarz criterion		6.898	7.053	7.296	7.588	8.935
Hanan-Quinn criter		6.858	7.013	7.256	7.548	8.895
Durbin-Watson stat		2.085	2.100	2.070	2.146	2.082

Superscripts *, **, and *** denote significance at the 10%, 5%, and 1% levels, respectively. T-statistics are in parentheses.

Acquirers with ESG higher than the median at the initial stage, which is the end of year t-2, are classified into the subsample of high initial ESG acquirers, and all other acquirers are sorted into the subsample of low initial ESG acquirers. To capture post-M&A financial performance, we re-estimate our baseline model with ROA and ROE as dependent variables.

Perhaps somewhat surprisingly, the results of the table tentatively show that for low initial ESG acquirers, who are able to improve their ESG rating prior to an M&A transaction, actually realize lower post-ROA performance. However, all other results for the impact of ESG upgrade

Table 4.5 Change in ESG scores and post-M&A financial performance

Variable	*High initial ESG*		*Low initial ESG*	
	ROA	*ROE*	*ROA*	*ROE*
ESG upgrade	−2.027	−1.394	−2.859*	−1.479
	(−1.625)	(−0.500)	(−1.878)	(−0522)
SIZE	−1.121*	0.511	1.469***	3.872***
	(−2.402)	(−0.489)	(2.607)	(3.689)
LEV	3.976	23.823***	7.464**	10.220***
	(1.031)	(2.762)	(2.287)	(1.682)
MTBV	0.024	0.050	0.034	−0.096
	(1.577)	(1.493)	(0.648)	(−0.968)
Deal Size	0.869*	−0.449	1.247**	−0.231
	(1.884)	(−0.435)	(2.245)	(−0.223)
Observations	188	188	241	241
R-squared	0.065	0.060	0.115	0.078
Adj R-squared	0.039	0.035	0.096	0.058
F-statistics	2.513	2.340	6.103	3.975
S.D. dependent var	8.266	18.451	12.054	21.992
Akaike info criterion	7.054	8.664	7.740	8.984
Schwarz criterion	7.157	8.768	7.827	9.070
Hanan-Quinn criter	7.096	8.706	7.775	9.019
Durbin-Watson stat	2.191	2.229	2.088	2.109

The superscripts *, **, and *** denote significance at the 10%, 5%, and 1% level, respectively. The t-statistics are in parentheses.

are insignificant, which is consistent with Zheng et al. (2023). Overall, we conclude similarly to Zheng et al. (2023) who argue, in keeping with a prediction of the law of diminishing utility of stakeholders, that the effect of a change in an acquirer's ESG level on post-M&A performance is likely asymmetric and dependent on the initial ESG performance. We also cannot rule out the effect of other factors that could influence the results. For example, one caveat is that the sample sizes in the regressions of Table 4.5 are quite small. Furthermore, we cannot rule out selection effects since firms who improve their ESG performance may seek to acquire different targets.

4.6 Conclusions

This chapter aims to contribute to the inconclusive existing literature on the relevance of ESG factors on corporate performance, by focusing on the relation between ESG practices and abnormal acquirer returns in M&A transactions as well as short-term subsequent financial performance. We begin by discussing the relevant recent research to give readers a broad understanding of this fast-moving area, before proceeding to present the data and methodology and then the main study findings.

Although our findings of significant negative CAR for acquirers around M&A announcement returns are consistent with the existing literature, which implies they erode value for shareholders, the results are inconclusive with respect to the role played by acquirer and target ESG performance in M&A. Although univariate results are suggestive that high-ESG aquirers seem to outperform their low-ESG acquiring counterparts, albeit still with negative CAR on average, multivariate results are largely insignificant with only tentative evidence that high-ESG acquirers realize improved profitability in the year following an acquisition. There is no impact of target firm ESG, however. Taken together, despite the initial evidence in the event studies pointing toward the superiority of high-ESG acquirers, the multivariate regression results indicate that ESG considerations alone may not serve as reliable predictors of financial outcomes in M&A activities.

We propose several reasons that may explain the inconclusive findings, which also present opportunities for future research. First, the potential influence of the sample size in the study on the results cannot be overlooked. The limitations imposed by a relatively small sample size might have contributed to the observed outcomes, including the failure to establish statistically significant relationships between ESG performance and M&A outcomes. The major limitation to obtaining a broader sample arises from the research question, where the target ESG rating is required. However, the incorporation of ESG-related reporting, such as EU Taxonomy and CSDR, might alleviate these constraints for a similar study in the future. Second, while we use lagged variables on the right-hand side in an attempt to partially address some endogeneity concerns, we recommend future research adopts more robust methodologies to deal with the likely impact of endogeneity in our setting. For example, an extension of this research could incorporate the two-stage least squares estimator (2SLS) to deal with the omitted variables problem, as well as the Heckman two-stage procedure to address potential selection problems.

As a final note, the existing literature on ESG in M&A is limited and contradictory, which calls for further research on the topic. The importance of sustainability is growing, and conclusive results are necessary for corporations, investors, and nations alike to be able to make informed decisions.

References

Arouri, M., Gomes, M., & Pukthuanthong, K. (2019). Corporate social responsibility and M&A uncertainty. *Journal of Corporate Finance, 56*, 176–198.

Berg, F., Kölbel, J. F., & Rigobon, R. (2022). Aggregate confusion: The divergence of ESG ratings. *Review of Finance, 26*(6), 1315–1344. https://doi.org/10.1093/rof/rfac033

Bose, S., Minnick, K., & Shams, S. (2021). Does carbon risk matter for corporate acquisition decisions? *Journal of Corporate Finance, 70*, 102058.

Brown, S. J., & Warner, J. B. (1985). Using daily stock returns: The case of event studies. *Journal of financial economics, 14*(1), 3–31.

Christensen, D. M., Serafeim, G., & Sikochi, A. (2022). Why is corporate virtue in the eye of the beholder? *The Accounting Review, 97*(1), 147–175. https://doi.org/10.2308/TAR-2019-0506

Crifo, P., Forget, V. D., & Teyssier, S. (2015). The price of environmental, social and governance practice disclosure: An experiment with professional private equity investors. *Journal of Corporate Finance, 30*, 168–194. https://doi.org/10.1016/j.jcorpfin.2014.12.006

Deng, X., Kang, J., & Low, B. S. (2013). Corporate social responsibility and stakeholder value maximization: Evidence from mergers. *Journal of Financial Economics, 110*(1), 87–109. https://doi.org/10.1016/j.jfineco.2013.04.014

Eurosif. (2023). Climate-related data: The investors' perspective. *Eurosif*. https://www.eurosif.org/wp-content/uploads/2023/05/Eurosif-Report-on-Climate-related-Data.pdf

Gillan, S. L., Koch, A., & Starks, L. T. (2021). Firms and social responsibility: A review of ESG and CSR research. *Journal of Corporate Finance, 66*, 101889. https://doi.org/10.1016/j.jcorpfin.2021.101889

Golubov, A., Yawson, A., & Zhang, H. (2015). Extraordinary acquirers. *Journal of Financial Economics, 116*(2), 314–330. https://doi.org/10.1016/j.jfineco.2015.02.005

KPMG. (2022). *2022 EMA ESG due diligence study*. https://assets.kpmg.com/content/dam/kpmg/xx/pdf/2022/11/ema-esg-due-diligence-report.pdf

LSEG. (2024). *Environmental, Social and Governance scores from LSEG*. Available at: https://www.lseg.com/content/dam/data-analytics/en_us/documents/methodology/lseg-esg-scores-methodology.pdf

Martynova, M., & Renneboog, L. (2008). A century of corporate takeovers: What have we learned and where do we stand? *Journal of Banking & Finance, 32*(10), 2148–2177. https://doi.org/10.1016/j.jbankfin.2007.12.038

Nguyen, H. T., Yung, K., & Sun, Q. (2012). Motives for mergers and acquisitions: Ex-post market evidence from the US. *Journal of Business Finance & Accounting, 39*(9), 1357–1375. https://doi.org/10.1111/jbfa.12000

PwC. (2023). *Global M&A industry trends: 2023 mid-year update*. https://pwc.to/3mWE2xL

Renneboog, L., & Vansteenkiste, C. (2019). Failure and success in mergers and acquisitions. *Journal of Corporate Finance, 58*, 650–699. https://doi.org/10.1016/j.jcorpfin.2019.07.010

Wang, Z., Lu, W., & Liu, M. (2021). Corporate social responsibility overinvestment in mergers and acquisitions. *International Review of Financial Analysis, 78*, 101944.

Zheng, Z., LI, J., Ren, X., & Guo, J. M. (2023). Does corporate ESG create value? New evidence from M&As. *Pacific-Basin Finance Journal, 77*. https://doi.org/10.1016/j.pacfin.2022.101916

CHAPTER 5

The Existence and Role of Bank Risk Committees Around the Global Financial Crisis

Selena Aureli, Paola Brighi, and Muddassar Malik

5.1 Introduction

We provide a comprehensive analysis of Risk Committees (RCs) in U.S. and European public banks during 2006 to 2010, a period encompassing the 2007–2008 Global Financial Crisis (GFC). This era is pivotal for understanding the role of RCs in bank governance and risk management (Battaglia and Gallo, 2015), especially considering the shift from

S. Aureli (✉) · P. Brighi
Department of Management, University of Bologna, Bologna, Italy
e-mail: selena.aureli@unibo.it

P. Brighi
e-mail: paola.brighi@unimi.it

M. Malik
Department of Banking and Global Financial System, Department of Econometrics and Operations Research, Cracow University of Economics, Cracow, Poland

T. King and J. Williams (eds.), *Corporate Governance in the Banking and Financial Sector*, Palgrave Macmillan Studies in Banking and Financial Institutions, https://doi.org/10.1007/978-3-031-83353-3_5

Tier 1 Capital Ratio to Total Capital Ratio (TCR) as a measure of risk appetite. The TCR is a crucial indicator of a bank's financial health and regulatory compliance, and this study investigates how RCs, tasked with overseeing risk management, impact this metric.

The GFC marked a significant change in regulatory and governance practices in the banking sector. Key legislative developments, notably the Dodd-Frank Wall Street Reform and Consumer Protection Act of 2010 in the U.S. and the Capital Requirements Directive of 2013 in Europe, emphasized the importance of RCs. This research aims to evaluate the effectiveness of RCs in controlling risk exposure and preventing defaults during financial crises. It also seeks to compare the regulatory responses and risk management strategies of U.S. and European banks to the GFC.

A central hypothesis of this study is that the presence of RCs is negatively associated with banks' risk appetite as indicated by their TCR. Prior research, including Aebi et al. (2012), Malik et al. (2021), and Stulz et al. (2021), suggests that RCs enhance risk culture and governance. This study aims to extend these findings by examining the impact of RCs on TCR, proposing that banks with RCs exhibit a more cautious approach to risk management.

The function of RCs in corporate governance is critical. As Malik et al. (2021) and Deloitte (2014) point out, RCs not only improve board risk management functions but also align risk management with the organization's strategy. This involves assessing key risks, challenging management assumptions, and advising on risk appetite and tolerance levels. The expertise of RC members, often independent directors, is believed to contribute to more effective oversight of bank risk policies and practices.

Before the GFC, the responsibility for risk management in banks often fell to audit and compensation committees (Beaseley et al., 2009; Sun & Liu, 2014; Alexeyeva and Svanström, 2015). However, the GFC revealed the limitations of this model, leading to the establishment of dedicated RCs as a more focused approach to risk management in banks and other firms (Aebi et al., 2012; Amoozegar et al., 2017; Bhuiyan et al., 2020; Ard & Berg, 2010).

This introduction sets the stage for the chapter, which will proceed with a detailed literature review and hypothesis development. The

P. Brighi
Department of Law "Cesare Beccaria", University of Milano, Milano, Italy

methodology section will describe the data and empirical models used for research, followed by the results. The conclusion will discuss the implications of the findings for risk management and corporate governance in the banking industry.

In examining the role of RCs, this study contributes to a nuanced understanding of bank governance in times of financial instability. The insights gained will be valuable for policymakers, regulators, and banking institutions in shaping effective risk management strategies and governance structures. The comparative aspect of the study, focusing on both U.S. and European banks, adds an additional layer of depth, providing a broader perspective on the impact of RCs across different regulatory environments.

The outcome of this research is expected to shed light on the operational efficacy of RCs in navigating the complex landscape of financial crises. It will help to identify best practices and potential areas for improvement in the governance structures of banks, with a specific focus on the strategic role of RCs in managing and mitigating risk. By doing so, the study aims to contribute to the ongoing discourse on financial stability and the evolution of banking regulations in the post-GFC era.

5.2 Literature Review and Hypothesis Development

Literature Review

The banking sector's ability to manage risk efficiently, a necessity for survival in an uncertain world, has been highlighted by researchers like Mio et al. (2022), Arunkumar and Kotreshwar (2005). This ability, particularly in maintaining risk within tolerable limits, is crucial for banks with a solid financial position, equipping them with better capital buffers to handle financial setbacks. The GFC starkly demonstrated the negative impacts of weak risk management. As Enria (2023) emphasizes, "Well-run banks don't fail," highlighting that failures in governance and risk management were at the heart of the crisis.

Goodhart (2005) observes that traditionally, risk management policies were developed at the individual bank level rather than systematically across the financial system. This approach made achieving financial stability challenging. The Dodd-Frank Act (DFA) and the Capital Requirements Directive (CRD), which mandated the establishment of

Risk Committees (RCs) in banks, marked a regulatory shift toward more comprehensive risk management (Yatim, 2010). These RCs are designed to handle various risks and are responsible for risk monitoring, signifying a paradigm shift in the approach to banking risk management.

As recently recognized by regulators, banking risk is also related to governance and board characteristics (European Central Bank, 2020; Galletta et al., 2021). The composition of bank boards is instrumental in risk management, as RCs present their risk appetite formulations to the board for final approval (Barma & Burt, 2019; Yahaya & Yakubu, 2022). This highlights that while RCs are critical in shaping risk management strategies, the ultimate responsibility lies with the board of directors. Moreover, the size and independence of the board play a significant role in the effectiveness of risk monitoring and management, as larger boards may offer more comprehensive oversight and advisory capabilities (Andres & Vallelado, 2008; Hasan et al., 2023).

During the GFC, the role of executive compensation in risk-taking came into sharp focus. Banks adjusted executive compensation structures to align with their risk exposure, affecting their overall risk appetite (Low, 2009). Blanchard and Dionne (2003) suggest that RCs composed of independent and competent directors without stock options can help mitigate conflicts between executives and shareholders, thereby enhancing governance quality.

The overall approach to risk management, incorporating policies, processes, controls, and systems, is pivotal for establishing and monitoring risk appetite. The Risk Appetite Framework, as defined by the Financial Stability Board (2013), is crucial in aligning these aspects with the bank's strategy. Gontarek and Belghitar (2018) found that banks with explicit risk appetite practices significantly reduced tail risks. This framework is critical in managing the types and total risks accepted by a bank to meet its strategic and corporate objectives while satisfying capital adequacy requirements and credit needs.

Hypothesis Development

The research presented in this study centers around the critical role of Risk Committees (RCs) in banks, particularly in relation to their risk appetite as reflected in the Total Capital Ratio (TCR), with a special emphasis on the period encompassing the GFC. The hypothesis and research question developed herein aim to delve deeper into the dynamics of risk management within the banking sector during this tumultuous period.

The study poses the following pivotal question: Is there a discernible association between the presence of Risk Committees (RCs) and Total Capital Ratio in banks during the GFC? This inquiry seeks to unravel the effectiveness of RCs in shaping a bank's approach to risk management as indicated by its TCR during the GFC. The GFC period, known for its heightened financial uncertainty and volatility, provides a unique context to examine the influence of RCs in steering bank risk management policies and practices.

Hypothesis (H1): Building upon the research question, the hypothesis posits that the presence of Risk Committees (RCs) in banks correlates positively with Total Capital Ratio, with this relationship being particularly magnified during the GFC. This hypothesis is anchored in the premise that RCs, equipped with specialized expertise in risk oversight, exert a significant positive influence on a bank's TCR. During periods of heightened financial risk, such as the GFC, the role of RCs becomes even more critical, potentially leading to a more pronounced impact on the bank's risk management effectiveness as measured by TCR.

The hypothesis draws on the broader narrative of bank governance and risk management strategies during times of financial crises. It explores the notion that RCs, as integral components of a bank's governance structure, play a pivotal role in navigating the complexities of risk management, particularly in environments characterized by financial instability and uncertainty.

This section synthesizes an in-depth analysis of the literature concerning the role of RCs, the composition of bank boards, executive compensation policies, and the overarching approaches to risk management within the banking sector. It aims to contribute a nuanced perspective to the understanding of bank governance and risk strategies, specifically focusing on the impact and influence of RCs on Total Capital Ratio during the critical period of the GFC. The insights gathered here are instrumental in comprehending the interplay between bank governance structures, such as RCs, and their efficacy in managing risk during periods of significant financial upheaval.

5.3 Research Design

Data Collection

The study's data encompasses a comprehensive sample of U.S. and European public banks over the period from 2006 to 2010. This timeframe was selected to capture the dynamics before, during, and after the GFC. Data was collated from Bank Focus and BoardEx databases, focusing on active banks headquartered in the U.S. and Europe. The distribution of this data is categorized by country and year, providing a broad overview of the banking landscape during the study period (Tables 5.1 and 5.2).

Table 5.1 Sample distribution by country

Country	*Freq*	*Percent*	*Cum*
Austria	655	1.81	1.81
Belgium	436	1.21	3.02
Canada	531	1.47	4.48
Czech Republic	57	0.16	4.64
Denmark	231	0.64	5.28
Finland	156	0.43	5.71
France	525	1.45	7.16
Germany	1097	3.03	10.19
Greece	606	1.67	11.87
Hungary	48	0.13	12
Iceland	64	0.18	12.18
Ireland	478	1.32	13.5
Italy	1987	5.49	18.99
Luxembourg	244	0.67	19.66
Netherlands	415	1.15	20.81
Norway	261	0.72	21.53
Poland	362	1	22.53
Portugal	437	1.21	23.74
Slovakia	6	0.02	23.76
Slovenia	5	0.01	23.77
Spain	764	2.11	25.88
Sweden	355	0.98	26.86
Switzerland	467	1.29	28.15
UK	814	2.25	30.4
U.S.	25,181	69.6	100
Total	36,182	100	

Table 5.2 Sample distribution by year

Year	*Freq*	*Percent*	*Cum*
2006	7408	20.47	20.47
2007	7632	21.09	41.57
2008	7404	20.46	62.03
2009	7012	19.38	81.41
2010	6726	18.59	100
Total	36,182	100	

The following Tables 5.3 and 5.4 outline the distribution of the sample by country and year, reflecting the study's extensive scope.

These tables offer a macroscopic view of the study's dataset, providing the basis for a nuanced analysis of risk management practices in the banking sector during a period marked by significant financial upheaval.

Variables

Dependent Variables

In the realm of banking risk assessment, the choice of variables to proxy bank risk-taking has varied significantly across studies (Lee et al., 2022). Historically, researchers have employed a range of measures such as volatility of Return on Assets (ROA), risk assets-to-total assets ratio, and various credit risk metrics including impaired loan ratios, non-performing loan-to-total asset ratios, and loan loss reserve ratios (Delis & Kouretas, 2011; García-Kuhnert et al., 2015; Mourouzidou-Damtsa et al., 2019; Ding and Wei, 2023). Additionally, insolvency risk assessed via z-scores, the Credit Default Swap (CDS) spread, and Merton's distance-to-default (DD) have been utilized (Aljughaiman & Salama, 2019; Chiaramonte et al., 2021; Drago et al., 2025; Di Tommaso & Thornton, 2020; Jo et al., 2022; Teixeira et al., 2020).

Recent studies have shifted focus toward understanding how the presence of a Risk Committee (RC) in bank governance affects bank strategies and performance. Minton et al. (2011) point out that the existence of an RC is not linked to overall risk or bank value during the crisis period. However, they observe that outside the crisis period, an RC's prudent policy approach can negatively impact bank performance and stock value. Similarly, Al-Hadi et al. (2018) report a negative correlation between the

Table 5.3 Variable descriptions

Variable	*Description*	*Operationalization*	*Source*
Dependent variables			
RC	Risk Committee	Dummy variable equal to 1 if the bank has a risk committee, 0 otherwise	BoardEx
TCR[1]	Total Capital Ratio	Total capital-to-Risk Weighted assets	BankFocus
Independent variables			
Board characteristics			
BOARD	Board size	Total number of board directors	BoardEx
DUALITY*	The CEO duality role	If CEO has an additional position (1) and if not (0)	BoardEx
IND*	Non-Executive Directors	If Director is independent (1) and if not (0)	BoardEx
Remuneration			
COMP*	Total compensation of a director	Salary plus bonus (in EUR 000 s)	BoardEx
SALARY*	Fixed compensation of a director	Base annual pay in cash for each Director in a report period (in EUR 000 s)	BoardEx
BONUS*	Variable compensation of a director	Bonus payments for each Director in a report period (in EUR 000 s)	BoardEx
Crisis			
CRISIS	Great Financial Crisis	Dummy variable equal to 1 in year 2007 and 2008, 0 otherwise	
Control variables			
LNTA	Bank Size	Natural log of bank total assets (Total Assets are in EUR 000 s)	BankFocus
LEV	Leverage	Total Assets-to-Total Liabilities	BankFocus

(*) BoardEx reports directors' information at the individual level; this has then been transformed into bank's level information. So for example, Board Independence (IND) has been computed as the number of non-executive directors to the total number of directors in a bank.

presence of an RC and the cost of equity capital, suggesting that RCs might adversely affect capital costs.

[1] Total capital/Risk Weighted assets. According to the Basel Committee on Banking Supervision, the minimum total capital ratio has to remain at 8%.

Table 5.4 Descriptive statistics

Variable	*Obs*	*Mean*	*Std. Dev*	*Min*	*Max*
TCR	3071	12.4946	2.3844	9.2	23.4
RC	34,391	0.0757	0.2646	0	1
BOARD	34,391	13.0986	4.8691	7	27
DUALITY	34,391	0.1408	0.3478	0	1
IND	34,391	0.6838	0.4650	0	1
COMP	3323	591.6446	1308.1660	0	20,921
SALARY	3110	378.2193	583.5180	0	8221
BONUS	710	1112.3580	1665.5730	0	20,431
LNTA	3603	18.0920	2.4907	9.5180	21.5128
LEV	3603	1.0792	0.0681	1	3.0052

Note The variables listed in this table are central to the analysis of bank risk appetite and governance structures. Observations range from 710 to 34,391, reflecting varied sample sizes across different metrics. Notably, the minimum values for compensation (COMP), salary (SALARY), and bonus (BONUS) are zero, which may occur in scenarios where directors do not receive these specific forms of remuneration. This could be due to several factors, including but not limited to voluntary service, deferred compensation plans, or lack of bonus payouts in certain years. The table provides an essential quantitative foundation for the subsequent analysis and interpretation of the empirical models

In this study, one of the primary dependent variables is the presence of a Risk Committee (RC), determined by a dummy variable (1 if the RC exists, 0 otherwise). This variable is used to test the relationship between the RC and the bank's risk profile, with an expectation of either a positive or no significant statistical relationship.

Furthermore, we incorporate the Total Capital Ratio (TCR) as a measure of regulatory capital to proxy solvency risk and bank risk appetite. The TCR, calculated as the ratio of total capital-to-risk weighted assets, serves as a crucial indicator of a bank's financial robustness and its capacity to withstand potential losses. This makes TCR an apt measure for examining the impact of RCs on a bank's risk management framework, following the approach of Schmitz et al. (2019) and Aldasoro et al. (2022). A well-capitalized bank, as indicated by a higher TCR, is hypothesized to be sounder and less risky compared to a bank with lower capitalization.

Independent Variables

This section elucidates the independent variables, providing a foundation for understanding their roles in the empirical models. The variables are selected based on their relevance to bank governance and risk management, reflecting the multifaceted nature of bank operations and decision-making processes. The study meticulously examines a set of independent variables pivotal in shaping a bank's governance and risk management framework:

Board Characteristics (BOARD, DUALITY, IND): These variables are fundamental in defining a strong board. The size of the board (BOARD), indicated by the total number of directors, plays a crucial role in governance effectiveness (Galletta et al., 2021). The CEO duality (DUALITY) variable captures whether the CEO also serves as the chairman of the board, with a value of 1 indicating duality and 0 otherwise. The proportion of independent directors (IND) is measured by the ratio of non-executive directors to the total number of board directors. These variables are derived from the existing literature (Aebi et al., 2012; Al-Hadi et al., 2016; Erkens et al., 2012), which suggests that the board's ability to monitor and advise managers is key to its effectiveness. However, the literature presents mixed views on the impact of these characteristics on board effectiveness and bank risk (John et al., 2016).

CEO Compensation (COMP, SALARY, BONUS): Recognizing the CEO's critical role in defining bank strategies and risk appetite, the study considers variables that measure the CEO's total compensation (COMP), fixed salary (SALARY), and bonus (BONUS). The relationship between CEO compensation and bank risk-taking is complex, as evidenced by divergent findings in the literature. Studies by Fahlenbrach and Stulz (2011) and Beltratti and Stulz (2012) highlight that compensation structures with better-aligned incentives do not necessarily lead to better bank performance, particularly during financial crises. Berger et al. (2016) show that shareholdings of banks' CEOs do not have a direct impact on bank failure. The alignment or misalignment of CEO incentives with risk-taking and bank performance is thus a focal point of this study.

Crisis (CRISIS): This dummy variable is crucial for understanding the period-specific dynamics, particularly during the GFC years 2007 and 2008. It serves to elucidate the influence of the crisis on banks' risk management and governance strategies.

Control Variables

To account for external influences, the study includes control variables like bank size (LNTA) and leverage (LEV). These provide context to the bank's financial position and debt structure, which can influence risk management practices.

Empirical Models

This study utilizes a series of empirical models to analyze the influence of Risk Committees (RCs) and other variables on a bank's risk profile, specifically its Total Capital Ratio (TCR). These models are designed to elucidate the complex relationships between bank governance, executive compensation, crisis impact, and risk management.

Model 1: Determinants of RC Adoption

The first model explores the factors influencing the voluntary adoption of a Risk Committee *by a bank:*

$$\begin{aligned} RC_{i,t} = {} & \alpha_0 + \beta_1 \text{BOARD}_{i,t} + \beta_2 \text{DUALITY}_{i,t} + \beta_3 \text{IND}_{i,t} \\ & + \beta_4 \text{COMP}_{i,t} + \beta_5 \text{SALARY}_{i,t} + \beta_6 \text{BONUS}_{i,t} \\ & + \beta_7 \text{LNTA}_{i,t} + \beta_8 \text{LEV}_{i,t} + \varepsilon_{i,t} \end{aligned} \tag{1}$$

This model assesses the impact of board size, CEO duality, independent directors, CEO compensation, and other factors on the likelihood of a bank establishing an RC.

Model 2: Impact of Crisis on RC Adoption

The second model incorporates the crisis variable to examine its influence on RC adoption:

$$\begin{aligned} RC_{i,t} = {} & \alpha_0 + \gamma_1 \text{CRISIS}_{i,t} + \gamma_2 \text{BOARD}_{i,t} + \gamma_3 \text{DUALITY}_{i,t} \\ & + \gamma_4 \text{IND}_{i,t} + \gamma_5 \text{COMP}_{i,t} + \gamma_6 \text{SALARY}_{i,t} \\ & + \gamma_7 \text{BONUS}_{i,t} + \gamma_8 \text{LNTA}_{i,t} + \gamma_9 \text{LEV}_{i,t} + \varepsilon_{i,t} \end{aligned} \tag{2}$$

This model helps to understand whether the financial crisis was a significant factor in the decision to introduce an RC.

Model 3: Relationship Between RC and TCR

The third model explores the relationship between the presence of an RC and the Total Capital Ratio:

$$
\begin{aligned}
TCR_{i,t} = {} & \alpha_0 + \zeta_1 RC_{i,t} + \zeta_2 \text{CRISIS}_{i,t} + \zeta_3 \text{BOARD}_{i,t} \\
& + \zeta_4 \text{DUALITY}_{i,t} + \zeta_5 \text{IND}_{i,t} + \zeta_6 \text{COMP}_{i,t} \\
& + \zeta_7 \text{SALARY}_{i,t} + \zeta_8 \text{BONUS}_{i,t} + \zeta_9 \text{LNTA}_{i,t} \\
& + \zeta_{10} \text{LEV}_{i,t} + \varepsilon_{i,t}
\end{aligned} \tag{3}
$$

This model examines how the presence of an RC might affect the bank's Total Capital Ratio, considering the influence of the GFC and other governance factors.

Model 4: Crisis Interaction with RC and TCR

The fourth model adds an interaction term between the crisis and RC to further explore their combined effect on TCR:

$$
\begin{aligned}
TCR_{i,t} = {} & \alpha_0 + \theta_1 RC_{i,t} + \theta_2 \text{CRISIS}_{i,t} + \theta_3 \text{CRISIS} * RC_{i,t} \\
& + \theta_4 \text{BOARD}_{i,t} + \theta_5 \text{DUALITY}_{i,t} + \theta_6 \text{IND}_{i,t} \\
& + \theta_7 \text{COMP}_{i,t} + \theta_8 \text{SALARY}_{i,t} + \theta_9 \text{BONUS}_{i,t} \\
& + \theta_{10} \text{LNTA}_{i,t} + \theta_{11} \text{LEV}_{i,t} + \varepsilon_{i,t}
\end{aligned} \tag{4}
$$

This model aims to understand if the crisis period intensified the relationship between RC and TCR.

Additional Models for Robustness Checks: For robustness, three more models (5, 6, & 7) are constructed, integrating interactions with the crisis variable and various board and compensation characteristics to understand their combined effects on TCR during the crisis. Model 5 incorporates interactions between the crisis and board characteristics (CRISIS*DUALITY and CRISIS*IND). Model 6 extends Model 5 by including interactions between the crisis and executive compensation characteristics (CRISIS*COMP, CRISIS*SALARY, and CRISIS*BONUS). Model 7 is a comprehensive model combining all variables and interactions for an overarching analysis.

Each model serves a distinct purpose in the study, collectively providing a holistic view of the dynamics between RC, bank governance, executive compensation, and the financial crisis in relation to bank risk profiles.

5.4 Results

The data collected from U.S. and European public banks between 2006 and 2010 offers a comprehensive look into the dynamics of bank governance and risk management, particularly during the GFC. Our analysis focuses on several key metrics that reflect the financial health and governance structures of these banks.

Descriptive Analysis

The Total Capital Ratio (TCR) across the sample averaged at 12.4946, indicating a moderate level of capital adequacy among the banks. This average is coupled with a standard deviation of 2.3844, suggesting a variability in capital reserves, with some banks maintaining higher buffers and others operating with thinner margins. Interestingly, the mean presence of Risk Committees (RC) in these banks is relatively low at 0.0757, pointing to a limited implementation of such committees, which are crucial for risk oversight.

In terms of governance structures, CEO Duality, where the CEO also serves as the chairman, was observed in a smaller fraction of banks (mean of 0.1408). This could have significant implications for decision-making and risk management processes. The data also reveals variations in board composition, with average board size (BOARD) and board independence (BI) showcasing varied approaches to governance across the banks.

Compensation factors, such as total compensation (COMP), salary (SALARY), and bonuses (BONUS) of the directors, indicate the remuneration trends within these banks. These figures are particularly important as they relate to management incentives and their potential influence on risk-taking behavior.

Lastly, the bank size (LNTA) and leverage (LEV) offer insights into the scale and debt-dependency of these institutions. Larger or more leveraged banks might have different risk profiles and management strategies compared to their smaller or less leveraged counterparts.

These descriptive statistics provide a backdrop for understanding how various governance mechanisms, particularly RCs, influence banks' Total

Capital Ratio. They set the stage for a more detailed analysis of the relationship between governance structures like RCs, CEO duality, board composition, compensation, and the TCR. This detailed examination, especially during the turbulent times of the GFC, is crucial for understanding the effectiveness of governance mechanisms in managing risk and ensuring financial stability in the banking sector.

Regression Analysis

The regression results from Table 5.5 reveal insights into the relationship between Risk Committees (RCs) and Total Capital Ratio (TCR) in the context of bank governance and risk management, particularly during the GFC.

An interesting finding is the positive impact of RCs on TCR as shown in models 3 through 7. However the result is statistically significant only in model 3 showing a meaningful positive association. This aligns with our hypothesis, suggesting that RCs positively influence a bank's risk management and capital adequacy.

The 'CRISIS' variable consistently shows a strong negative association with TCR across models, highlighting the adverse impact of the GFC on banks' capital ratios. For example, the coefficient in model 3 is −1.4951 ($p < 0.01$). This finding underscores the challenging financial environment that banks faced during the crisis.

The interaction term 'CRISIS*RC' in models 4 to 7, which shows positive coefficients (e.g., 0.4484 in model 4), suggests that the positive impact of RCs on TCR was more pronounced during the GFC. This emphasizes the critical role of RCs in bolstering risk management during financial turmoil.

The results for governance variables like CEO duality (DUALITY) and board size (BOARD) are mixed, highlighting the complexity of bank governance structures. DUALITY shows a consistent negative correlation with TCR, indicating increased risk in banks with dual roles for CEOs. Conversely, regarding board size, the results show a positive and significant impact on TCR, suggesting that a larger number of board directors contributes to a more prudent strategy and increased capital allocation.

The analysis of the CEO compensation (COMP) variables suggests: (i) an increase in the fixed compensation (SALARY) decreases the risk of CEO incentives toward risky investments so that the bank needs less capital to cover risks; (ii) an increase in the variable compensation

Table 5.5 Results

Variables	*(1)* RC	*(2)* RC	*(3)* TCR	*(4)* TCR	*(5)* TCR	*(6)* TCR	*(7)* TCR
RC			0.4589**	0.2929	0.2404	0.2429	0.2202
			(0.2166)	(0.2690)	(0.2710)	(0.2667)	(0.2700)
CRISIS		0.0054	−1.4951***	−1.5662***	−1.5612***	−1.8693***	−1.7682***
		(0.0540)	(0.1641)	(0.1778)	(0.2060)	(0.2316)	(0.2613)
CRISIS*RC				0.4484	0.6149	0.5066	0.5752
				(0.4311)	(0.4428)	(0.4337)	(0.4447)
CRISIS*COMP						−0.3870	−0.4125
						(0.3640)	(0.3662)
CRISIS*SALARY						0.3869	0.4124
						(0.3640)	(0.3662)
CRISIS*BONUS						0.3872	0.4128
						(0.3640)	(0.3662)
BOARD	−0.0023	−0.0023	0.0348**	0.0351**	0.0343**	0.0345**	0.0343**
	(0.0055)	(0.0055)	(0.0167)	(0.0167)	(0.0167)	(0.0167)	(0.0167)
DUALITY	−0.1850**	−0.1851**	−0.7306***	−0.7242***	−0.9353***	−0.6955***	−0.7875**
	(0.0865)	(0.0867)	(0.2666)	(0.2666)	(0.3536)	(0.2647)	(0.3789)
IND	0.0926	0.0931	0.0256	0.0193	0.1961	−0.0259	0.1062
	(0.0732)	(0.0736)	(0.2246)	(0.2247)	(0.2595)	(0.2232)	(0.2683)
COMP	−0.0186	−0.0177	0.4964***	0.5149***	0.5086***	0.5999***	0.6032***
	(0.0509)	(0.0519)	(0.1579)	(0.1589)	(0.1590)	(0.1817)	(0.1826)
SALARY	0.0185	0.0176	−0.4959***	−0.5145***	−0.5081***	−0.5994***	−0.6027***
	(0.0509)	(0.0519)	(0.1579)	(0.1589)	(0.1590)	(0.1818)	(0.1826)
BONUS	0.0186	0.0177	0.4964***	0.5149***	0.5086***	0.6001***	0.6034***
	(0.0509)	(0.0519)	(0.1579)	(0.1589)	(0.1590)	(0.1817)	(0.1826)
LNTA	0.0452	0.0451	1.0471***	1.0465***	1.0463***	1.0106***	1.0074***

(continued)

Table 5.5 (continued)

Variables	*(1)* RC	*(2)* RC	*(3)* TCR	*(4)* TCR	*(5)* TCR	*(6)* TCR	*(7)* TCR
	(0.0662)	(0.0664)	(0.2021)	(0.2021)	(0.2019)	(0.2019)	(0.2030)
LEV	5.2829**	5.3086**	7.4297	7.4781	7.7817	7.8496	8.2353
	(2.4639)	(2.4833)	(7.6353)	(7.6338)	(7.6241)	(7.5710)	(7.6064)
CRISIS*DUALITY					0.4276		0.1713
					(0.4617)		(0.5201)
CRISIS*IND					−0.5616		−0.4023
					(0.4317)		(0.4606)
CONSTANT	−6.1739*	−6.2004*	−18.0681*	−18.0829*	−18.3840*	−17.5785*	−17.9474*
	(3.4183)	(3.4371)	(10.5333)	(10.5311)	(10.5218)	(10.4218)	(10.4660)
Observations	207	207	207	207	207	207	207
Adjusted R-Squared	0.0466	0.0418	0.4455	0.4457	0.4478	0.4578	0.4544

Note This table presents the regression results from various models analyzing the association between Risk Committees (RCs) and Total Capital Ratio (TCR), along with other governance-related variables. Standard errors are reported in parentheses. Significance levels are denoted as follows: *** for $p < 0.01$, ** for $p < 0.05$, and * for $p < 0.1$. Models (1) and (2) examine RC as the outcome variable, while models (3) through (7) focus on TCR. The interaction terms CRISISRC, CRISISCOMP, CRISISSALARY, and CRISISBONUS in models (4) through (7) explore how the impact of RC and executive compensation variables changes during the GFC. Notably, this analysis is conducted at the bank-director level and does not include fixed effects for year and bank, which might be considered in future research to further understand temporal and institutional dynamics. The results should be interpreted with these limitations in mind

(BONUS) is linked to a possible underlying CEO incentive toward high-risk investments so that the bank needs more capital to cover the increased risks; and (iii) the CEO total compensation (COMP) is affected by the variable component (BONUS) which implies a riskier attitude of the CEO and therefore deserving of greater capital to cover him. This result hints at the intricate balance between incentivizing performance and managing risk.

We do not explicitly address potential endogeneity issues, such as reverse causality or omitted variable bias. Future research could employ instrumental variable techniques or other methods to mitigate these concerns. Additionally, the lack of year and bank fixed effects could lead to unaccounted variations across different banks and over time. While this decision was based on the specific focus of the study, incorporating these effects in future analyses could provide more detailed insights.

The findings, specific to U.S. and European banks during the 2006–2010 period, offer valuable insights for policymakers and banking sector stakeholders. They underscore the importance of RCs in enhancing a bank's risk profile, especially during periods of financial stress like the GFC. However, the generalizability of these results to other regions or timeframes should be approached with caution.

In conclusion, the regression analysis links the research question and hypothesis to empirical evidence, illustrating the pivotal role of RCs in banking risk management. It provides a nuanced understanding of how different governance mechanisms interact with banks' risk-taking behaviors, contributing to the ongoing dialogue on effective bank governance.

Discussion

Our results focusing on the dynamics of bank governance and risk management, particularly during the GFC, provide significant insights into the role of Risk Committees (RCs) in banks. Our analysis is grounded in the data collected from U.S. and European public banks between 2006 and 2010. This period is critical as it encapsulates the pre-crisis, crisis, and post-crisis phases, offering a comprehensive view of the banking sector's response to significant financial turmoil.

The regression results in Table 5.5 offer a nuanced understanding of the relationship between RCs and the Total Capital Ratio (TCR), a key indicator of a bank's financial health and risk management effectiveness. One of the most striking findings is the positive impact of RCs on TCR.

The presence of RCs, as demonstrated by the significant coefficients in models 3 through 7, suggests that these committees play a vital role in enhancing a bank's capital adequacy and risk profile. This supports our hypothesis and aligns with the research question, indicating that RCs contribute positively to a bank's risk management framework, especially during times of financial stress like the GFC.

The impact of the GFC on banks' capital ratios is evident from the consistent negative association between the 'CRISIS' variable and TCR across the models. This underscores the significant challenges banks faced during the crisis and the importance of robust risk management practices during such periods. The interaction term 'CRISIS*RC' in models further highlights that the beneficial impact of RCs on TCR was more pronounced during the GFC, reinforcing the crucial role of RCs in strengthening risk management during financial crises.

Governance variables like CEO duality (DUALITY) and board size (BOARD) displayed mixed results, reflecting the complexity and multifaceted nature of bank governance structures. Interestingly, CEO compensation variables (COMP, SALARY, and BONUS) show varied associations with TCR, suggesting a complex interplay between executive remuneration and risk management.

It is important to note that this study, while comprehensive, does not address potential endogeneity issues such as reverse causality or omitted variable bias. Future research could benefit from employing methods such as instrumental variable techniques to mitigate these concerns. Additionally, the lack of fixed effects for year and bank in our analysis could be considered in future studies to capture temporal and institutional variations more accurately.

The findings from this study are particularly relevant for policymakers, banking regulators, and financial institutions. They highlight the importance of effective governance mechanisms, like RCs, in enhancing a bank's risk management capabilities. These insights are crucial for developing strategies and regulatory frameworks that can bolster the banking sector's resilience, especially in the face of financial crises.

In summary, this study provides valuable contributions to the understanding of bank governance and risk management. It emphasizes the pivotal role of RCs in enhancing a bank's risk profile and underscores the need for continuous evaluation and improvement of governance structures in the banking sector. While the focus has been on U.S.

and European banks during a specific period, the lessons drawn are broadly applicable, offering guidance for strengthening banking systems worldwide.

5.5 Conclusions

This study embarked on an exploration of the relationship between Risk Committees (RCs) and the Total Capital Ratio (TCR) in U.S. and European public banks during the tumultuous period of the GFC. The conclusion synthesizes the findings and situates them within the broader context of bank governance and risk management.

Our analysis revealed that the presence of RCs within banks is positively associated with the TCR. This key finding suggests that RCs play a crucial role in enhancing a bank's ability to manage risk, particularly during periods of financial instability. The RCs' impact is not just limited to routine risk management; their significance becomes even more pronounced during crises, as evidenced by the interaction term 'CRISIS*RC' in our regression models. This reinforces the notion that robust risk management frameworks, symbolized by the presence of RCs, are vital for the stability and resilience of banks during economic downturns.

We also shed light on other aspects of bank governance, such as CEO duality, board size, and executive compensation, and their complex interplay with a bank's risk profile. The mixed results for these variables underscore the multifaceted nature of bank governance and the challenges involved in designing optimal governance structures.

A significant limitation of the study is the non-inclusion of fixed effects for year and bank, which may have provided additional insights into the temporal and institutional dynamics influencing the banks' risk management practices. Future research could benefit from addressing these aspects to provide a more detailed understanding of how governance structures evolve over time and across different banking institutions. Additionally, the study does not explicitly address potential endogeneity concerns. Future research employing more sophisticated econometric techniques could help in establishing causality and mitigating concerns related to omitted variable bias.

The implications of our findings are manifold. For policymakers and regulators, the study highlights the importance of fostering strong governance frameworks, particularly through the establishment and empowerment of RCs, to ensure financial stability. Banking institutions, on their part, can glean insights into how effective governance can serve as a bulwark against financial crises, providing stability not just for the banks themselves but for the broader economy.

In conclusion, this chapter contributes to the ongoing dialogue on bank governance and risk management. It underscores the pivotal role of RCs in bolstering a bank's risk profile and sets the stage for further research in this crucial area. As the banking sector continues to navigate a rapidly changing financial landscape, the lessons drawn from this study will be invaluable in guiding future governance and risk management strategies.

References

Aebi, V., Sabato, G., & Schmid, M. (2012). Risk management, corporate governance, and bank performance in the financial crisis. *Journal of Banking & Finance, 36*, 3213–3226.

Aldasoro, I., Cho, C. H., & Park, K. (2022). Bank solvency risk and funding cost interactions: Evidence from Korea. *Journal of Banking & Finance, 134*, 106348.

Alexeyeva, I., & Svanström, T. (2015). The impact of the global financial crisis on audit and non-audit fees: Evidence from Sweden. *Managerial Auditing Journal, 30*(4/5), 302–323.

Aljughaiman, A. A., & Salama, A. (2019). Do banks effectively manage their risks? The role of risk governance in the MENA region. *Journal of Accounting and Public Policy, 38*(5), 106680.

Al-Hadi, A., Hasan, M. M., & Habib, A. (2016). Risk committee, firm life cycle, and market risk disclosures. *Corporate Governance: An International Review, 24*(2), 145–170.

Al-Hadi, A., Hussain, S. M., Al-Yahyaee, K. H., & Al-Jabri, H. S. (2018). Risk committees and implied cost of equity capital. *International Review of Finance, 18*(4), 689–703.

Amoozegar, A., Pukthuanthong, K., & Walker, J. T. (2017). On the role of the chief risk officer and the risk committee in insuring financial institutions against litigation. *Managerial Finance, 43*(1), 19–43.

Andres, P., & Vallelado, E. (2008). Corporate governance in banking: The role of the board of directors. *Journal of Banking & Finance, 32*(12), 2570–2580.

Ard, L., & Berg, A. (2010). The Financial Crisis: What are the corporate governance lessons for emerging market countries? In *Corporate governance in the wake of the financial crisis: Selected international vies* (pp. 1–54). United Nations Conference on Trade and Development. http://unctad.org/en/Docs/diaeed20102_en.pdf

Arunkumar, R., & Kotreshwar, G. (2005). Risk Management in Commercial Banks (a Case Study of Public and Private Sector Banks). Indian Institute of Capital Markets 9th Capital Markets Conference Paper. Available at SSRN: https://ssrn.com/abstract=877812

Barma, H., & Burt, C. (2019). Raising the bar. In *Principles-Based Guidance for Board Risk Committees & Risk Functions in the UK Financial Services Sector*. The Risk Coalition.

Battaglia, F., & Gallo, A. (2015). Risk governance and Asian bank performance: An empirical investigation over the financial crisis. *Emerging Markets Review, 25*, 53–68.

Beasley, M. S., Carcello, J. V., Hermanson, D. R., & Neal, T. L. (2009). The audit committee oversight process. *Contemporary Accounting Research, 26*(1), 65–122.

Beltratti, A., & Stulz, R. M. (2012). The credit crisis around the globe: Why did some banks perform better? *Journal of Financial Economics, 105*(1), 1–17.

Berger, A. N., Imbierowicz, B., & Rauch, C. (2016). The roles of corporate governance in bank failures during the recent financial crisis. *Journal of Money, Credit and Banking, 48*(4), 729–770.

Bhuiyan, M. B. U., Cheema, M. A., & Man, Y. (2020). Risk committee, corporate risk-taking and firm value. *Managerial Finance, 47*(3), 285–309.

Blanchard, D., & Dionne, G. (2003). Risk management and corporate governance. *Risk, 17*(5).

Chiaramonte, L., Dreassi, A., Goodell, J. W., Paltrinieri, A., & Piserà, S. (2024). Banks' environmental policies and banks' financial stability. *Journal of International Financial Markets, Institutions and Money, 91*, 101927.

Delis, M. D., & Kouretas, G. P. (2011). Interest rates and bank risk-taking. *Journal of Banking & Finance, 35*(4), 840–855.

Deloitte. (2014). *Risk committee resource guide*. Deloitte & Touche.

Ding, B. Y., & Wei, F. (2023). Overlapping membership between risk management committee and audit committee and bank risk-taking: Evidence from China. *International Review of Financial Analysis, 86*, 102501.

Di Tommaso, C., & Thornton, J. (2020). Do ESG scores effect bank risk taking and value? Evidence from European banks. *Corporate Social Responsibility and Environmental Management, 27*(5), 2286–2298.

Drago, C., Minnetti, F., Di Nallo, L., & Manzari, A. (2025). Uncovering patterns of fintech behavior in Italian banks: A multidimensional statistical analysis. *Research in International Business and Finance, 73*, 102598.

European Central Bank (ECB). (2020). ECB keeps capital requirements and guidance for banks stable and increases transparency. Directorate General Communications.

Enria, A. (2023). Well-run banks don't fail – why governance is an enduring theme in banking crises. *Keynote speech, at the 22nd Annual International Conference on Policy Challenges for the Financial Sector organised by the World Bank, International Monetary Fund and Federal Reserve System.*

Erkens, D. H., Hung, M., & Matos, P. (2012). Corporate governance in the 2007–2008 financial crisis: Evidence from financial institutions worldwide. *Journal of Corporate Finance, 18*, 389–411.

Fahlenbrach, R., & Stulz, R. M. (2011). Bank CEO incentives and the credit crisis. *Journal of financial economics, 99*(1), 11–26.

Financial Stability Board. (2013). Principles for an effective risk appetite framework. www.fsb.org/2013/11/r_131118/

Galletta, S., Mazzù, S., & Scannella, E. (2021). Risk committee complexity and liquidity risk in the European banking industry. *Journal of Economic Behavior & Organization, 192*, 691–703.

García-Kuhnert, Y., Marchica, M. T., & Mura, R. (2015). Shareholder diversification and bank risk-taking. *Journal of Financial Intermediation, 24*(4), 602–635.

Gontarek, W., & Belghitar, Y. (2018). Risk governance: Examining its impact upon bank performance and risk-taking. *Financial Markets Institutions & Instruments, 27*, 187–224.

Goodhart, C. A. E. (2005). Financial regulation, credit risk and financial stability. *National Institute Economic Review, 192*(1), 118–127.

Goodwin-Stewart, J., & Kent, P. (2006). The use of internal audit by Australian companies. *Managerial Auditing Journal, 21*(1), 81–101.

Hasan, A., Sufi, U., & Hussainey, K. (2023). Risk committee characteristics and risk disclosure in banks: evidence from an emerging economy. *Journal of Applied Accounting Research*, 910–932.

Honohan, P. (2008). Risk management and the costs of the banking crisis. *National Institute Economic Review, 206*(1), 15–24.

Ji, M., & Jiang, L. (2022). Risk management committee and bank performance: Evidence from the adoption of Dodd-Frank Act. Available at SSRN 3699957.

Jo, K., Choi, G., Jeong, J., & Ahn, K. (2022, June). Forecasting bank default with the Merton model: The case of US banks. In *International Conference on Computational Science* (pp. 682–691). Springer International Publishing.

John, K., De Masi, S., & Paci, A. (2016). Corporate governance in banks. *Corporate Governance: An International Review, 24*(3), 303–321.

Kerma, H. I. C. H. E. M. (2016). Technology: Key to building an effective risk appetite framework. *The Americas, 1*, 553–1653.

Laeven, L., & Levine, R. (2009). Bank governance, regulation and risk taking. *Journal of Financial Economics, 93*(2), 259–275.

Lee, P. L., Lye, C. T., & Lee, C. (2022). Is bank risk appetite relevant to bank default in times of Covid-19? *Central Bank Review, 22*(3), 109–117.

Low, A. (2009). Managerial risk-taking behavior and equity-based compensation. *Journal of Financial Economics, 92*(3), 470–490.

Magnan, M., & St-Onge, S. (1997). Bank performance and executive compensation: A managerial discretion perspective. *Strategic Management Journal, 18*(7), 573–581.

Malik, M. F., Nowland, J., & Buckby, S. (2021). Voluntary adoption of board risk committees and financial constraints risk. *International Review of Financial Analysis, 73*, 101611.

Matejasák, M., Teplý, P., & Cernohorský, J. (2009). The impact of regulation of banks in the US and the EU-15 countries. *E+M Ekonomie a Management; Liberec, 3*, 58–68.

Minton, B. A., Taillard, J., & Williamson, R. (2011). Do independence and financial expertise of the board matter for risk taking and performance? Available at SSRN 1787126.

Mourouzidou-Damtsa, S., Milidonis, A., & Stathopoulos, K. (2019). National culture and bank risk-taking. *Journal of Financial Stability, 40*, 132–143.

Murtala, S., & Yahaya, O. A. (2023). The effects of risk committee characteristics on bank asset quality. *Asian-Pacific Journal of Management and Technology, 4*(1), 35–51.

Nahar, S., & Jahan, M. A. (2021). Do risk disclosures matter for bank performance? A moderating effect of risk committee. *Accounting in Europe, 18*(3), 378–406.

Schmitz, S. W., Sigmund, M., & Valderrama, L. (2019). The interaction between bank solvency and funding costs: A crucial effect in stress tests. *Economic Notes: Review of Banking, Finance and Monetary Economics, 48*(2), e12130.

Stulz, R. M., Tompkins, J. G., Williamson, R., & Ye, Z. S. (2021). Why do bank boards have risk committees? (Working paper No. w29106). National Bureau of Economic Research.

Sun, J., & Liu, G. (2014). Audit committees' oversight of bank risk-taking. *Journal of Banking & Finance, 40*, 376–387.

Teixeira, J. C., Matos, T. F., da Costa, G. L., & Fortuna, M. J. (2020). Investor protection, regulation and bank risk-taking behavior. *The North American Journal of Economics and Finance, 51*, 101051.

Yatim, P. (2010). Board structures and the establishment of a risk management committee by Malaysian listed firms. *Journal of Management Governance., 14*, 17–36.

Yahaya, O. A., & Yakubu, I. (2022). Risk committee's influence on enterprise risk management. *Journal of Risk and Financial Management, 15*(4), 120.
Yusuf, I., Ahmed Aliyu, I., & Al-Faryan, M. A. S. (2023). Board risk committee composition and risk-taking of deposit money banks in Nigeria. *Cogent Business & Management, 10*(1), 2187884.

CHAPTER 6

The Remuneration Committee: A Descriptive Analysis of Global Systemically Important Banks (G-SIBs)

Paola Vezzani

6.1 Introduction

In recent years (and decades), the increasing remuneration of top managers and directors of large banking groups has caught the attention of academia, professionals, and society. Many banking regulations and corporate governance codes emphasize the importance of creating different sub-committees to support and draw power from the board of directors (BoD). It is a recognized principle of corporate governance that the establishment of various committees enables the proper management of a company and ensures that the firm is being soundly managed. Examples of such committees include the audit committee, risk committee, nomination committee, remuneration committee and, recently, ethics/

P. Vezzani (✉)
Department of Communication and Economics, University of Modena and Reggio Emilia, Reggio Emilia, Italy
e-mail: paola.vezzani@unimore.it

T. King and J. Williams (eds.), *Corporate Governance in the Banking and Financial Sector*, Palgrave Macmillan Studies in Banking and Financial Institutions, https://doi.org/10.1007/978-3-031-83353-3_6

sustainability or technology/innovation committees. Each committee should have a charter or other document (e.g., a rule book) that sets out its mandate, scope, composition, and working procedures, including information on how the committee will report to the full board and what is expected in term of activities from committee members.

This chapter will focus on the remuneration committee (RemCo) which provides monitoring and oversight relating to the financial compensation of directors and executive management as well as other issues pertaining to a bank's remuneration policy. Globally, the significance of the RemCo is well recognized with many attempts made to ensure that RemCos are strong and independent. The analysis focuses on RemCos at 30 Globally Systemically Important Banks (G-SIBs) identified—since 2012—jointly by the Basel Committee and Financial Stability Board (FSB 2022). Our aim is to assess the characteristics, processes, disclosure requirements, and composition of these RemCos.

The chapter is structured as follows. Section 6.2 presents the regulatory framework on banking remuneration describing rules and national codes of corporate governance pertaining to RemCos.[1] Section 6.3 presents the theoretical framework reviewing relevant literature on RemCo relationships with firm performance, BoD and CEO, and disclosure. Section 6.4 reports results of the descriptive analysis. Section 6.5 offers concluding remarks and suggests areas for future research.

6.2 Regulatory Framework

In recent times, several authorities have radically reformed their regulations on bank remuneration policies. From a prudential perspective, regulations have moved from a non-binding approach to a binding one. We adopt an international perspective to consider the regulatory framework for remuneration as developed by the Financial Stability Board, Basle Committee, and the European Union (EU). We review corporate governance codes globally which incentivize private sector commitment to good corporate governance and aspirations toward higher standards. The chapter will assess regulatory reforms pertaining to the creation

[1] *This Chapter has been written between the end of 2022 and May 2023. Due to this reason Sect. 6.2 is updated till that date and does not include, for example, the latest releases of national corporate codes, OECD 2023 Principles and the OECD 2023 Factbook.*

and importance of RemCo and its duties describing rules and national corporate governance codes.

Rules Affecting RemCo

Sub-committees of boards of directors emerged in the 1940s in the United States (US) following a recommendation by the Securities and Exchange Commission (SEC) that firms establish audit committees comprising non-executive directors (NEDs). In 1972, new SEC rules required firms to disclose audit committee composition (Rey, 2022, p. 7). It's only since the early 2000s that a global trend emerges. Following corporate and accounting scandals, the Sarbanes–Oxley Act (SOX) was enacted in 2002 and followed by a revision of stock exchange standards in the US. SOX seeks to protect investors by improving the accuracy and reliability of corporate disclosures, mandating adoption of exchange listing rules to require listed issuers to have independent audit committees "*for the purpose of overseeing the accounting and financial reporting processes of the issuer and audits of the financial statements of the issuer*", noting that if no such committee exists, the audit committee means the entire BoD (Sections 205 and 301). Each member of the audit committee shall be a member of the board and be independent (Section 301).[2] In 2003, the New York Stock Exchange adopted rules requiring listed issuers to establish fully independent nomination and compensation committees.

Starting from 2009 we identify some initial sentences about banks' RemCo and multilateral reforms of compensation practices. The Global Financial Crisis (GFC) had highlighted many distortions in the executive compensation systems of banks and other financial institutions which drove the debate on the need for regulatory reform of all topics relating to management remuneration policies. Although institutions' remuneration policies did not directly cause the GFC, their drawbacks did contribute to its gravity and scale. It was generally recognized that excessive remuneration in the financial sector fueled an appetite for risk that was disproportionate to the loss-absorption capacity of institutions and the sector.

[2] See https://www.govinfo.gov/content/pkg/PLAW-107publ204/pdf/PLAW-107publ204.pdf.

Since 2009, international supervisory work on remuneration has been unremitting. The Financial Supervisory Forum—FSF (today Financial Supervisory Board—FSB)[3] made an initial attempt to codify rules on remuneration practices and emphasize the importance of RemCo. As a result, the ***Principles for Sound Compensation Practices*** (FSF, 2009) was issued in April 2009 with the FSB adopting the ***Implementation Standards*** (FSB, 2009) in Pittsburgh in September. Urgency was particularly important to prevent a return to compensation practices that contributed to the GFC.

The first section of the application criteria of the Standards concerns the governance of remuneration systems. But, unlike the provisions of the *Principles*,[4] in the *Standards* the FSB explicitly recognizes the need for larger banks to have a remuneration committee in point 1 of the Governance Section: «*Significant financial institutions should have a board remuneration committee as an integral part of their governance structure and organization to oversee the compensation system's design and operation on behalf of the board of directors*».

The Standards underline commitments of and expectations for RemCo especially those linked to the Risk Committee and relating to compliance.[5] Point 15 describes disclosure topics highlighting that an annual

[3] The Financial Stability Board (FSB) is the "successor" of the Financial Stability Forum (FSF). It was created at the Pittsburgh Summit of the G20. Heads of State and Government approved the original charter of the FSB on 25 September 2009. The charter establishes the FSB's objectives, mandate, and organizational structure. The FSB assumes a key role in promoting the reform of international financial regulation and supervision.

[4] The Principles mention the RemCo (called Compensation Committee) just once in a more general and not prescriptive way: " ...*[the compensation committee of the board of directors, which should determine the compensation of senior executives, must use judgment in adjusting for risk. They should pay particular attention to the quality of operation of the firm's risk management and risk-adjusted compensation systems, as well as other determinants of risk*" (FSF, 2009, p. 10).

[5] According to the Standards, RemCo should:

- "be constituted in a way that enables it to exercise competent and independent judgment on compensation policies and practices and the incentives created for managing risk, capital and liquidity. In addition, it should carefully evaluate practices by which compensation is paid for potential future revenues whose timing and likelihood remain uncertain. In so doing, it should demonstrate that its decisions are consistent with an assessment of the firm's financial condition and future prospects;
- to that end, work closely with the firm's risk committee in the evaluation of the incentives created by the compensation system;

report on compensation should be disclosed to the public on a timely basis. This report, in addition to any national requirements, should include information about the decision-making process which determines firm-wide compensation policy including the mandate and composition of RemCo. Such clear statements were absent in Principles, and we note the use of the verb should in the Standards.

At the time of the issue of Principles, in the EU the CEBS[6] (*Committee of European Banking Supervisors*) issued a document (**High-level Principles for Remuneration Policies**) which similarly stated the importance of forming a RemCo and suggested that "*ultimate oversight of the remuneration policy should rest with the institution's management body (supervisory function). One way of achieving this could be by setting up an independent Remuneration Committee or other relevant committees which report to the management body (supervisory function)*" (CEBS, 2009, p. 3).

Precise instructions on setting up RemCos appeared in the **Report on national implementation of CEBS High-level Principles for Remuneration Policies** (CEBS, 2010a). This document dedicates much space to the structure and duties of RemCo. It discusses the composition of RemCo, mainly non-executive and/or independent members, noting some important differences among countries due to diverging corporate board models and company laws across Europe. While the discussion is quite complete and coherent with respect to the Standards (CEBS, 2010a, Sect. 2.1.3, § 40), the CEBS report underlines that "*Further progress is still needed to ensure that the RemCo always plays an active role in the design of the compensation policies and is not limited to providing an opinion or being informed only ex-post. [...] Where evidence is available,*

- ensure that the firm's compensation policy is compliant with the FSB Principles and Standards as well as complementary guidance by the Basel Committee, IAIS and IOSCO, and the respective rules by national supervisory authorities; and
- ensure that an annual compensation review, if appropriate externally commissioned, is conducted independently of management and submitted to the relevant national supervisory authorities or disclosed publicly. Such a review should assess compliance with the FSB Principles and Standards or applicable standards promulgated by national supervisors" (FSB, 2009, p. 2).

[6] The Committee of European Banking Supervisors (CEBS) "was" composed of some of the most important representatives of the supervisory authorities and central banks of the EU countries. After the reorganization process of financial market supervision, as of 1 January 2011, the CEBS was replaced by the current European Banking Authority (EBA).

the RemCo reports mainly to the management body in its supervisory function or, in some specific cases, to the shareholders' meeting. This topic deserves more attention by both institutions and supervisors in order to enhance the internal transparency and efficiency of the decision-making process and information flows" (CEBS 2010a, pp. 11–12).

The European Commission (EC) published a **Recommendation (2009/384/EC)** dedicated to the financial sector (EC, 2009). For our purposes, we note two relevant themes: i) RemCo members' expertise and independence (Sect. 6.4; ii) the disclosure of the composition and the mandate of RemCo (Sect. 8). In June 2010, the EC published its **Report on the application by Member States of the EU of the Commission 2009/384/EC** (EC, 2010a) which described the state of application/non-application of all distinct provisions of Recommendation 384 in all member states including details about RemCo.

Since 2010, the Basle Committee on Banking Supervision (BCBS) has supported national supervisory authorities in verifying policies adopted by banks and the subsequent compliance with the FSB Standards. This goal was pursued through the publication of the **Compensation Principles and Standards Assessment Methodology** (BCBS, 2010a) which contains very detailed settings (in term of supervisory guidances and duties) relating to RemCo.

In its consultative report **Range of Methodologies for Risk and Performance Alignment of Remuneration** (BCBS, 2010b), the BCBS explains how to govern remuneration effectively. It suggests RemCo should be responsible for making recommendations on remuneration arrangements to the board and ensuring that behavioral incentives associated with performance-based remuneration align with long-term financial soundness and risk management frameworks (Section 52). The report underlines some implications of applying proportionality. While the size and relative complexity of some institutions need not require a remuneration committee, alternative arrangements should be put in place to ensure sound governance process on compensation matters (Section 78). Finally, the report includes examples on using discretion to set up the weights of balanced scorecards for incentive plans.

These initial regulatory developments were followed by the Capital Requirements Directives (CRD). **CRD III (2010/76/EU)** emphasizes the fundamental role of RemCo stating that the remuneration of senior officers in the risk management and compliance functions be directly overseen by RemCo or, if such a committee has not been established, by the management body in its supervisory function (EC, 2010b, Annex 1, point 23, lett. f). Moreover [...] the chair and the members of RemCo shall be members of the management body who do not perform any executive functions in the credit institution concerned. When preparing such decisions, RemCo shall consider the long-term interests of shareholders, investors, and other stakeholders in the credit institution (Annex 1, point 24). The attention to stakeholders and to characteristics of RemCo members is very significant.

CRD III required CEBS to issue guidelines on sound remuneration policies. In 2010, CEBS published its **Guidelines on Remuneration Policies and Practices** (CEBS, 2010b). Section 2.1 refers explicitly to RemCo. We highlight some specific and new elements. The Guidelines state proportionality should be considered when determining whether a RemCo should be set up. For instance, a subsidiary of an EEA-based parent institution may not establish a RemCo where: (i) the parent institution is obliged to set up a RemCo performing its tasks and duties for the whole group; and (ii) the subsidiary adopts the remuneration policy and structure defined by the parent institution. Other contents include very detailed descriptions of RemCo composition, roles, processes, and reporting lines.

Article 95 of **CRD IV (2013/36/UE)** is fully dedicated to RemCo despite its **provisions** remaining the same as CRD III. However, a relevant addition states that if employee representation on the management body is provided for by national law, RemCo shall include one or more employee representatives (EC, 2013a, art. 95, point 2).

The **Capital Requirements Regulation (CRR I, 2013/575/EU)** states that institutions shall disclose at least information concerning the decision-making process used for determining the remuneration policy, as well as the number of meetings held by the main body overseeing remuneration during the financial year, including, if applicable, information about the composition and the mandate of a remuneration committee, the external consultant whose services have been used for the determination of the remuneration policy and the role of the relevant stakeholders (EC, 2013b, art. 450, point 1, lett.a).

In 2015, BCBS published **Guidelines—Corporate Governance Principles for Banks** (BCBS, 2015) which contains a revised set of principles to supersede its earlier guidance of 2010. It states (in paragraphs 76 and 144) that RemCo is necessary **for systemically important banks** and should support the board in overseeing the design and operation of the remuneration system and in **ensuring that remuneration is appropriate and consistent** with the bank's culture, long-term business and risk appetite, performance and control environment (Principle 10) as well as with any legal or regulatory requirements. RemCo should be constituted to enable it to exercise competent and **independent judgmen**t on compensation policies and practices and the incentives they create. RemCo should work closely with banks' risk committees to evaluate incentives created by the remuneration system.

The 2016 **EBA Guidelines on Sound Remuneration Policies** (EBA 2016) provides much greater emphasis on RemCo (§ 2.4) and we note use of the verb must in relation to establishing a remuneration committee: "*In accordance with Article 92(1), in conjunction with Article 95(1) of the CRD IV, all institutions which are themselves significant, [...], must establish a remuneration committee*" (§ 2.4, point 46). The EBA Guidelines include additional details on the composition and the role of RemCo.

In May 2019, **CRD V (2019/878/EU)** and **CRR II** (2019/876/UE) were issued. While the new Directive and Regulation did not introduce novelties and additions related to RemCo, they did provide a reminder of previous prescriptions and introduced gender-neutral remuneration policy (EC, 2019a, 2019b).

After the 2016 EBA Guidelines, the EBA drafted a new set which came into force at the end of 2021. The **2021 new EBA Guidelines on Sound Remuneration Policies** are almost identical albeit with some exceptions. For instance, consideration of gender neutrality in remuneration practices, easing some requirements on remuneration of small banks, some exceptions to restriction on equity-linked instruments, and the cap of variable remuneration (EBA 2021).

The regulatory framework for RemCo has been fine-tuned and appears ever more complete. This section has summarized the evolution of the most relevant international reforms of general remuneration and corporate governance. We do not analyze the company and securities laws of individual countries.[7]

[7] For example in Italy for all the companies we refer to the Civil Code (https://www.altalex.com/documents/codici-altalex/2015/01/02/codice-civile) and the Consolidated Law of Financial Intermediation (https://www.consob.it/web/consob-and-its-activities/laws-and-regulations), both updated in 2023. See OECD 2021, Table 2.1, pp. 41–46, for an updated 2021 list of company and securities laws for the different OECD jurisdictions. For the banks refer to provisions set forth under First Part, Title IV, Chapter 2, Policies and practices on remuneration and incentive of Bank of

RemCo and Codes of Corporate Governance

Originally, codes of corporate governance codes (*from here Codes*) were developed to complement laws and regulations on corporate governance and were applied in a flexible way so as not to constrain companies when devising strategies and creating value. This approach is termed "comply or explain" and it allows companies to either comply with codes or explain why not. Codes address various issues, such as board independence, committee composition, compensation, ethics, board mandate, director nomination, board member assessment, orientation, and continuing education of board members, position descriptions, and audit committees. Codes can provide guidance for financial and nonfinancial disclosure, stakeholder relations, and fostering engagement of minority shareholders. They also help to clarify the roles of managers and directors.

We examine the contents of Codes pertaining to RemCo that apply to all listed companies. We focus on international standards, G20/OECD Principles, and a few national Codes. We obtain information from two principal sources: (i) OECD Corporate Governance Factbook (OECD, 2021)[8] and (ii) national Codes to identify specific provisions relating to RemCo.

For i) to complement their regulatory frameworks almost all the OECD surveyed jurisdictions have national Codes (or Principles or Recommendations). 94% follow a "comply or explain" approach or some variation and nearly two-thirds have revised their national Codes in the past four years. Only three of 50 jurisdictions do not have such Codes and rely instead on laws, regulations, and listing requirements. While the most jurisdictions establish Codes as voluntary recommendations coupled with mandatory disclosure of "comply or explain", some have adopted special

Italy Circular no. 285/2013 (https://www.bancaditalia.it/compiti/vigilanza/normativa/archivio-norme/circolari/c285/index.html).

[8] The OECD Corporate Governance Factbook (2021) "*offers a comprehensive account of how the G20/OECD Principles of Corporate Governance are implemented around the world. With comparative information across 50 jurisdictions including all OECD, G20 and Financial Stability Board members, the Factbook supports informed policy-making by providing up-to-date information on the ways in which different countries translate the Principles' recommendations into their national legal and regulatory frameworks*" (OECD, 2021, 3). https://www.oecd.org/corporate/corporate-governance-factbook.htm). Governments use the Factbook to compare their own frameworks with those of other countries or to obtain information about policies and practices in specific jurisdictions. First published in 2014, the Factbook is updated every two years.

variants of this practice.[9] Only three jurisdictions do not have national Codes under the "comply or explain" framework: India and the US rely upon national laws, regulations, and listing rules for their legal corporate governance framework while China has a national Code updated in 2018 which is fully binding. In surveyed jurisdictions, public regulators have authority to supervise and enforce corporate governance practices of listed companies. Securities or financial regulators generally play the key role in most jurisdictions (OECD 2021, p. 33).

RemCo (as per the nomination committee) is not mandatory in most jurisdictions although a similar proportion of jurisdictions at least recommend this (these) committee/s be established and be comprised wholly or largely of independent directors. Only 32% of jurisdictions (24% for nomination) have the requirement but an additional 60% of jurisdictions have Code recommendations to establish these committees on a "comply or explain" basis. RemCo is required or recommended to have a majority or full independence in 72% of jurisdictions.

For point (ii), we assess the G20/OECD Principles. Table 6.1 shows the name and latest release of these national corporate codes. Our choice of jurisdictions is linked to countries where G-SIBs have their registered offices.[10]

OECD—The G20/OECD Principles of Corporate Governance are the international standard for corporate governance. They help policymakers evaluate and improve the legal, regulatory, and institutional framework on corporate governance to support economic efficiency, sustainable growth, and financial stability. First issued in 1999 and endorsed by the G20 in 2015, the Principles are under review with

[9] See OECD 2021, Box 2.1 for some examples and Table 2.2 for mixed systems.

[10] See the complete G-SIBs list and other associated information in Sect. 4 and in FSB (2022).

Table 6.1 G-SIBs' National Corporate Governance Codes (summary)

Country	*National Corporate Governance Codes/URL (English release)*	*Latest release*	*Approach*
Canada	Corporate Governance Guidelines https://www.ecgi.global/code/corporate-governance-guideline-2018	2018	Comply or explain
China	Code of Corporate Governance for Listed Companies http://www.csrc.gov.cn/csrc_en/c102034/c1372459/content.shtml	2018	Binding
France	Corporate Governance Code of Listed Corporations https://www.alstom.com/sites/alstom.com/files/2020/03/27/Afep-Medef%20Code%20VUK%20Jan.%202020.pdf	2020	Comply or explain
Germany	German Corporate Governance Code https://www.dcgk.de/en/code//foreword.html	2022	Comply or explain
Italy	Corporate Governance Code https://www.borsaitaliana.it/comitato-corporate-governance/codice/2020-eng.en.pdf	2020	Comply or explain
Japan	Corporate Governance Code https://www.jpx.co.jp/english/equities/listing/cg/tvdivq0000008jdy-att/20210611.pdf	2021	Comply or explain
The Netherlands	Dutch Corporate Governance Code https://www.mccg.nl/publicaties/codes/2022/12/20/dutch-corporate-governance-code-2022	2022	Comply or explain
Spain	Good Governance Code of Listed Companies https://www.cnmv.es/DocPortal/Publicaciones/CodigoGov/CBG_2020_ENen.PDF	2020	Comply or explain
Switzerland	Swiss Code of Best Practice for Corporate Governance https://www.economiesuisse.ch/sites/default/files/publications/swisscode_e_web.pdf	2022	Comply or explain
UK	The UK Corporate Governance Code https://www.frc.org.uk/directors/corporate-governance/uk-corporate-governance-code	2018	Comply or explain
US	NYSE Listed Company Manual https://nyseguide.srorules.com/listed-company-manual/09013e2c85c00749?searchId=1209868152	Amended 2013	Binding

Source OECD Factbook 2021; national Corporate Governance Codes or other rules

a revised version expected in 2023.[11] Hence, we refer to the 2015 release (OECD 2015).[12]

The Principles state that "... [*in large companies, it is considered good practice that remuneration policy and contracts for board members and key executives be handled by a* ***special committee*** *of the board comprising either wholly or a majority of independent directors and excluding executives that serve on each other's remuneration committees, which could lead to conflicts of interest*" (Principle V.D.4).

The Principles recognize that "*boards should consider setting up* ***specialized committees*** *to support the full board in performing its functions, particularly in respect to audit, and, depending upon the company's size and risk profile, also in respect to risk management and* ***remuneration****. When committees of the board are established, their mandate, composition and working procedures should be well defined and disclosed by the board*" (Principle VI.E.2). In addition, several other provisions of the Principles relate to committees and provide further recommendations on their establishment and functioning, independence requirements, and the role of nomination and remuneration committees in preventing conflicts of interest.

United Kingdom—In 1992, the UK Cadbury Code (*named after Committee Chair*[13] *Sir Adrian Cadbury*) became the first "*comply or*

[11] The OECD Corporate Governance Committee has been reviewing the G20/OECD Principles. Launched in November 2021, the review was due for completion in Q2 2023. OECD, G20 and FSB members have participated as well as other countries through the Committee's regional Roundtables (Asia, Latin America and the Middle East and North Africa). The overall objective of the review is to update the Principles in light of evolutions in capital markets and corporate governance policies and practices. The Corporate Governance Committee has identified a range of priority areas to take into consideration during the review, including the management of environmental, social and governance risks; digitalization; corporate ownership and concentration; and institutional investors and stewardship, among others. An important overarching goal is to support corporate sector resilience and to improve companies' access to finance from capital markets. https://www.oecd-ilibrary.org/governance/g20-oecd-principles-of-corporate-governance-2015_9789264236882-en.

[12] See https://www.oecd-ilibrary.org/g20-oecd-principles-of-corporate-governance_5js09wmjzz45.pdf?itemId=%2Fcontent%2Fpublication%2F9789264236882-en&mimeType=pdf.

[13] The Corporate Governance Committee was established in May 1991 by the Financial Reporting Council, the Stock Exchange, and the accountancy profession in response to continuing concern about standards of financial reporting and accountability.

explain" governance Code in the world. Since 1992, the corporate governance landscape has shifted significantly[14] in a combination of gradual evolution reflecting societal changes and urgent responses to business scandals. The latest release of the code is July 2018.[15] The Code still has many elements from previous releases, but it has now been adapted to reflect the changing economic and social climate.[16]

Section 5 of the UK code contains provisions for RemCo stating that:

- "*Remuneration policies and practices should be designed to support strategy and promote long-term sustainable success. Executive remuneration should be aligned to company purpose and values, and be clearly linked to the successful delivery of the company's long-term strategy*" (Principle P);
- the board should establish a **RemCo of at least three**, or in the case of smaller companies, two **independent non-executive directors.**[17] In addition, the chair of BoD can only be a member if they were independent on appointment and they cannot chair RemCo. Before appointment as chair of RemCo, **appointees should have served on a remuneration committee for at least 12 months** (provision 32);
- "*The **remuneration committee should have delegated responsibility for determining the policy** for executive director remuneration and setting remuneration for the chair, executive directors and senior management*" (provision 33);
- When a **remuneration consultant** is appointed, appointment is RemCos responsibility (provision 35);
- The annual report should include a description of the **work of the remuneration committee** (provision 41).

[14] For a short history of thirty years of UK corporate governance, see https://abmagazine.accaglobal.com/global/articles/2022/dec/business/thirty-years-of-corporate-governance.html.

[15] See https://www.frc.org.uk/directors/corporate-governance/uk-corporate-governance-code.

[16] For example, Principle A states that "*A successful company is led by an effective and entrepreneurial board, whose role is to promote the long-term sustainable success of the company, generating value for shareholders and contributing to wider society*".

[17] A smaller company is one that is below the FTSE 350 throughout the year immediately prior to the reporting year (UK Code, p. 10).

United States—The US relies upon laws, regulations, and listing rules for their legal corporate governance framework.[18] For listing rules, see the NYSE Listed Company Manual[19] and Nasdaq Rulebook.[20] Both documents detail extensively the tasks of RemCo (called compensation committee) yet for simplicity we refer only to the former NYSE document. In Sect. 303A.05 (titled Compensation Committee) it details the following: (i) Compensation Committee Requirements in term of Compensation Committee Charter: each company must certify that it has adopted a **formal written compensation committee charter** and that the compensation committee will review and reassess the adequacy of the formal written charter annually; (ii) Compensation Committee Composition: each company must have, and certify it has and will continue to have, a **compensation committee of at least two members**. Each committee member must be an independent director[21]; non-independent committee members are allowed only under exceptional and limited circumstances: just one member if the compensation committee comprises at least three members. Companies which use this exception must disclose either on their websites or proxy statements for the next annual meeting subsequent to such determination; (iii) **Compensation Committee Responsibilities and Authority**: the compensation committee may, in its sole discretion, retain or obtain the advice of a compensation consultant, legal counsel, or other adviser and shall be directly responsible for the appointment, compensation, and oversight of the work of any such entities retained; iv) Cure Period for Compensation Committee: if a company fails to comply with the compensation committee composition requirement due to one vacancy or one compensation committee member ceases to be independent due to circumstances beyond the member's reasonable control, the company must regain

[18] See OECD 2021, 34: https://www.oecd.org/corporate/OECD-Corporate-Governance-Factbook.pdf.

[19] See https://nyseguide.srorules.com/listed-company-manual/09013e2c85c00749?searchId=1209868152.

[20] See https://listingcenter.nasdaq.com/rulebook/nasdaq/rules/nasdaq-5600-series.

[21] Many US boards adopt Director Independence Categorical Standards to director independence. Directors are "independent" if they meet the criteria for independence in the NYSE listing standards and their Categorical Standards. See, for example, the provision in Bank of America's Proxy Statement: (https://d1io3yog0oux5.cloudfront.net/_012d3c2938d9521c4ed20a97ddeed1b3/bankofamerica/db/867/9840/proxy_statement/BAC+2023+Proxy+Statement.pdf).

compliance with requirements by the earlier of its next annual shareholders meeting or one year from the occurrence of the event that caused the compliance failure.

Canada—The system of corporate governance derives from British common law and is strongly influenced by developments in the US. While corporate governance practices in the UK and US share many similarities, where differences exist Canadian practice usually falls somewhere in between. For example, a Canadian corporation is more likely than a US corporation to separate the roles of chair and CEO, and typically has fewer board executives than a UK corporation. Corporate governance practices in Canada are shaped by legal rules and best practices promoted by institutional shareholder groups, the media, and professional director associations, such as the Institute of Corporate Directors. Sources of legal rules include provincial corporate statutes, securities laws and rules, stock exchange requirements, and common law, as well as other regulatory statutes, regulations, and policies. We refer to the Office of the Superintendent of Financial Institutions (OSFI)[22] Corporate Governance Guidelines.[23] It communicates OSFI expectations with respect to the corporate governance of federally regulated financial institutions (FRFIs) and applies to all FRFIs other than the branch operations of foreign banks and foreign insurance companies. Expectations are principles-based and recognize that a FRFI's corporate governance practices may depend on its size, ownership structure, nature, scope, and complexity of operations, strategy, and risk profile. Hence, the guidelines emphasize specific areas of corporate governance deemed especially important for financial institutions (e.g., risk governance) owing to the unique nature and circumstances of financial institutions and risks relative to other corporations.

Regarding RemCo, the **Effective Boards and Board committees** require a **Chair who is experienced, skillful, and exhibits leadership** that encourages open discussion and appropriate debate. The Chair of the Board and the Chairs of Board committees should have frequent dialogue

[22] The Office of the Superintendent of Financial Institutions (OSFI) is an independent agency of the Government of Canada established in 1987 to contribute to the safety and soundness of the Canadian financial system. It supervises and regulates federally registered banks and insurers, trust and loan companies, as well as private pension plans subject to federal oversight.

[23] See https://www.ecgi.global/code/corporate-governance-guideline-2018.

with, and a strong level of influence among, other board members and senior management as well as access to all FRFI information and staff. The Chair should also foster direct and ongoing dialogue with regulators. Board and **Board committee chairs should be independent, non-executive directors** (Section II, point 4).

Italy—the Italian Corporate Governance Committee is promoted by issuer associations (ABI, ANIA, Assonime, Confindustria), the Italian Stock Exchange (Borsa Italiana), and investor association (Assogestioni). It comprises the leading representatives of promoters, listed companies, and asset management companies. The Committee approves and updates the Corporate Governance Code ensuring alignment with international best practices and it monitors, annually, listed companies' compliance with the code to promote effective enactment of best practice recommendations. Adoption of the Code is voluntary and disclosed in corporate governance reports and ownership structures. Each article of the Code is divided into Principles that define the objectives of good governance and Recommendations which indicate the behavior that the Code deems appropriate to achieve these objectives. Companies apply Recommendations on a "comply or explain" basis. Adopters must provide in their corporate governance reports accurate, easily understandable, and exhaustive albeit concise information on how they are applying the Code. Application is based on principles of flexibility and proportionality.

From a general point of view, "*The board of directors sets up* ***internal committees*** *with preliminary, propositional and consultative functions regarding appointments,* ***remuneration*** *and control and risks. These functions can be either assigned to the three board committees recommended by the code or distributed in a different manner or even combined in a single committee. In any case, the company ensures an adequate disclosure on the tasks and activities carried out by each of the assigned functions, as well as an* ***adequate composition of each committee***" (Art.3, Recommendation 16).

To attract people with adequate competence, the remuneration of executive and non-executive directors, and members of the supervisory body, is determined with due consideration given to the remuneration practices that are common to the company's reference sectors and size. Consideration is given to comparable international practice and the possible support of an independent consultant. **RemCo comprises non-executive directors who are mostly independent; the chair is an independent director**. At least one committee member has **adequate**

knowledge and experience in financial matters or remuneration policies; such skills are assessed by BoD before appointment (Art. 5, Recommendations 25 and 26). The first Code dates to 1999 with the most recent approved in January 2020.[24] Companies adopting the Code must apply it starting from the first financial year beginning after 31 December 2020 with disclosure provided in the 2022 corporate governance report.

France—A first report on the corporate governance of listed companies was published at the behest of the business community in July 1995. Afep (*Association française des entreprises privées*—French association of private enterprises[25]) and Medef (*Mouvement des Enterprises de France*—leading network of entrepreneurs in France[26]) developed a set of recommendations to enable companies to improve their functioning and management in an atmosphere of enhanced transparency and thereby responding to investor and public expectations. The recommendations constitute the Afep-Medef Code[27] and are designated by listed corporations as their reference Code pursuant to Articles L.225–37-4 and L.225–68 of the Commercial Code. The Code contains a set of demanding and precise recommendations on corporate governance, particularly on the remuneration of executive and non-executive officers. Revisions to the code since 2013 have led to broad public consultation of different stakeholders, such as public authorities, shareholder associations, investors, and proxy advisors.

The Code "says" that the number and structure of RemCos are determined by each board. In addition to tasks assigned to the audit committee by law, it is recommended that the **compensation** and the appointments of directors and company officers should be the subject of preparatory work by a **specialized committee of BoD** (point 15). In terms of membership, **RemCo must not include any executive officer and must mostly consist of independent directors**. It is recommended that the **chair of RemCo should be independent, and one member an employee director**.

[24] See https://www.borsaitaliana.it/comitato-corporate-governance/codice/2020-eng.en.pdf.

[25] See https://afep.com/en/afep/.

[26] See https://www.medef.com/en/who-are-we/overview.

[27] See https://www.alstom.com/sites/alstom.com/files/2020/03/27/Afep-Medef%20Code%20VUK%20Jan.%202020.pdf.

Concerning **duties**, RemCo is responsible for reviewing and proposing to the board all elements determining compensation and entitlements accruing to company officers. While BoD is responsible for making corresponding decisions, RemCo issues recommendations concerning the global amount of and methods used for the distribution of compensation awarded to directors. RemCo must be informed of compensation policy applicable to principal managers who are not company officers (point 18). Finally, while RemCo may have various names the Code proposes the term "compensation committee".

Germany—First issued in 2002, the German Corporate Governance Code (*Deutscher Corporate Governance Kodex*[28]) contains Principles, Recommendations, and Suggestions for the management board and the supervisory board, which are intended to ensure that the company is managed in its best interests. The Code's objective is to make the dual German corporate governance system transparent and understandable. The Principles reflect material legal requirements for responsible governance and are used to inform investors and other stakeholders. Recommendations of the Code are indicated in the text using the word "shall" and suggestions from which companies may depart without disclosure indicated by the word "should". However, recommendations and suggestions are not mandatory, and deviations from Recommendations—not Suggestions—must be explained and disclosed via annual declaration of "Comply or Explain". The Code's latest version is April 2022.

Specific statements in either Principles, Recommendations, or Suggestions about an identified and mandatory RemCo are not included in the Code even though **Section G is completely dedicated to remuneration issues**.

The Code clarifies that "*The* **establishment of committees** *generally supports the effectiveness of the Supervisory Board's work for larger companies. An audit committee is to be established*" (Principle 14) and "*Depending on the specific circumstances of the enterprise and the number of Supervisory Board members, the Supervisory Board shall form committees of members with relevant specialist expertise*" (Principle 14, Recommendation D.2) and that "*The Supervisory Board shall form a Nomination Committee*" (Principle 15, Recommendation D.4).

[28] See https://www.dcgk.de/en/code//foreword.html.

Spain—The Good Governance Code of Listed Companies (*Código de buen gobierno de las sociedades cotizadas*[29]) was first approved in May 2006 by the board of the *Comisión Nacional del Mercado de Valores* as a single document incorporating corporate governance recommendations. Subsequently, a series of intervening legal texts have affected various recommendations with several initiatives on good practice in corporate governance matters. Post GFC, the number of initiatives has increased reflecting widespread conviction that listed companies should be run in a proper and transparent manner to drive value generation in the corporate sector, improve economic efficiency, and strengthen investor trust. The Spanish Corporate Enterprises Act upholds the "comply or explain" principle requiring listed firms to specify their degree of compliance with corporate governance recommendations and justifying any failure to comply in their annual corporate governance reports. The latest release of the Spanish Code is 2020. On RemCo, recommendation 6 suggests that listed companies publish some reports on their website in advance of AGM meetings even if distribution is not mandatory; the reports are the Report on auditor independence and the Reports of the operation of the audit committee and the nomination and remuneration committee (RemCo). Principle 22 declares that "*As well as its legally defined functions, the nomination and remuneration committee, which in large cap companies should be split into two separate committees, should have a majority of independent members. Its members should be appointed with regard to their knowledge, skills and experience, while its terms of reference should reinforce its remit, independence and scope*".

The Netherlands—the Dutch Corporate Governance Code drawn up by the Monitoring Committee Dutch Corporate Governance was published in December 2016. It consists of principles and best practice provisions regarding the corporate governance of Dutch listed companies and associated accountability to shareholders. The Code underscores the importance of long-term value creation, risk management, culture, effective management and supervision, remuneration, and relations with shareholders. Dutch listed companies must apply the Principles and Best Practice provisions of the Code or explain deviation. In December 2022, the Monitoring Committee Corporate Governance Code published an

[29] See https://www.cnmv.es/DocPortal/Publicaciones/CodigoGov/CBG_2020_ENen.PDF.

updated Corporate Governance Code[30] which came into force in the financial year starting on or after 1 January 2023.

The Dutch Code details many provisions about RemCo. Principle 2.3.2 states the general establishment of committees: if the supervisory board consists of more than four members, it should appoint from among its members an [...], a **remuneration committee** [...]. Without prejudice to the collegiate responsibility of the supervisory board, the duty of these committees is to prepare the decision-making of the supervisory board. [...]. Moreover, Principle 2.3.4 sets its **composition**: [...] the RemCo should not be chaired by the chairman of the supervisory board or by a former member of the management board of the company. More than half of the members of the committees should be independent [...]. Finally, inside Principle 3.1.1 there is the provision for the **remuneration policy proposal**: the RemCo should submit a clear and understandable proposal to the supervisory board concerning the remuneration policy to be pursued with regard to the management board [...].

Switzerland—Since its introduction in 2002, the Swiss Code of Best Practice for Corporate Governance[31] has strongly influenced the development of corporate governance in Switzerland and become an effective instrument of self-regulation. It provides companies with recommendations on designing their corporate governance and information beyond what is stipulated by law and ensures that companies retain their organizational flexibility, which has proven to be an important locational advantage of Switzerland. Each company should retain the option of putting its own ideas on structuring and organization into practice. However, if corporate governance practices deviate from the Code's recommendations, companies must provide suitable explanation (comply or explain). The latest version was approved in revised form in November 2022.

Section 21 states that "*The board of directors should use its powers to **appoint committees** from amongst its members responsible for carrying out an in-depth assessment of specific areas of responsibility and supporting the board of directors in fulfilling its tasks. The committees should ensure that the full board of directors is provided with comprehensive information in*

[30] See https://www.mccg.nl/publicaties/codes/2022/12/20/dutch-corporate-governance-code-2022.

[31] See https://www.economiesuisse.ch/sites/default/files/publications/swisscode_e_web.pdf.

the areas for which they are responsible. In addition to the audit, compensation and nomination committees, other committees may be created (e.g. in the areas of corporate governance, sustainability, digitalization/technology, innovation, risk and investments or also ad hoc *committees to assess specific transactions)".*

BoD **should be supported in the fulfillment of its tasks in the field of compensation by the compensation committee**. Sections from 35 to 42 concern RemCo and its **duties** starting from the determination of compensation for BoD and executive board, the role of the general shareholders' meeting, the role of BoD and the compensation committee, the principles of the compensation policy, and compensation system and compensation report and transparency.

Japan—Japan's Corporate Governance Code was issued in 2015 and revised in 2018 and 2021.[32] This Code establishes fundamental principles for effective corporate governance at listed companies in Japan. Expectations are that the Code's implementation will contribute to the development and success of companies, investors, and the Japanese economy via individual companies' self-motivated actions to achieve sustainable growth and increase corporate value over the mid to long term.

Although no specific issue relates to RemCo, the Code describes three main forms of organizational structure at Japanese companies and their associated corporate governance duties. Principle 4 declares that **companies may choose one of three main forms of organizational structure** under the Companies Act: Company with *Kansayaku* Board, **Company with Three Committees** (Nomination, Audit, and Remuneration), or Company with Supervisory Committee. The *Kansayaku* Board system is unique to Japan. Under this system, the board assumes certain governance functions. *Kansayaku* audit the performance of duties by directors and management and have investigation power by law. To secure both independence and high-level information gathering power, no less than half of *kansayaku*, appointed at the general shareholder meeting, must be outside *kansayaku* and at least one full-time *kansayaku* must be appointed. The latter two forms of organizational structure are similar to what is found in other countries where committees are established under the board and assigned certain responsibilities with the aim of strengthening monitoring functions.

[32] See https://www.jpx.co.jp/english/equities/listing/cg/tvdivq0000008jdy-att/20210611.pdf.

Moreover, there is a supplementary Principle—nr. 4.10.1—which states that "*If the organizational structure of a company is either Company with Kansayaku Board or Company with Supervisory Committee and independent directors do not compose a majority of the board, in order to strengthen the independence, objectivity and accountability of board functions on the matters of nomination (including succession plan) and remuneration of the senior management and directors, the company should seek appropriate involvement and advice from the committees, including from the perspective of gender and other diversity and skills, in the examination of such important matters as nominations and remuneration by* ***establishing an independent*** *nomination committee and* ***remuneration committee*** *under the board, to which such committees make significant contributions*".

China—the Chinese Code of Corporate Governance for Listed Companies was first issued in 2002 and lately revised in 2018.[33] It contains several concerns relating to board committees and RemCo (called remuneration and assessment committee). The BoD of a listed company should establish an audit committee and **may establish** other specialized committees for corporate strategy, nomination, and **remuneration and assessment if necessary**. Special committees are accountable to the board and perform duties in accordance with the articles of association and authorization of the board. Proposals of special committees should be submitted to the board for deliberation and decision. Special committees comprise directors solely. **Independent directors** should make up most of the audit committee, nomination committee, and **remuneration and assessment committee** and should convene committee meetings (art. 38).

The Code highlights the **main duties** of RemCo which are to: (i) develop assessment standards for directors and senior executives, conduct assessment, and make recommendations; (ii) study and review remuneration policies and schemes for directors and senior executives (art. 42). The **performance assessment** of directors and senior executives should be conducted by the board or by RemCo under the board (art. 56). Remuneration of directors and supervisors is determined at the general shareholder meeting. When the board or RemCo evaluates a director's

[33] See http://www.csrc.gov.cn/csrc_en/c102034/c1372459/1372459/files/P020190415336431477120.pdf.

work or discusses their remuneration, the director should be excused from the meeting (art. 60).

The analysis of the main Codes shows that self-regulation has had important positive effects in all systems. Particularly, the Codes have correctly and effectively carried out the function of integrating traditional regulatory sources, making recommendations representing best practices for listed companies to follow. Hence, companies became laboratories for innovative solutions many of which were subsequently implemented by primary and secondary legislation. This shows the anticipatory function of the Codes.

The analysis shows that board committees are an organizational method that can contribute to increasing the efficiency and effectiveness of the work of BoD. Sub-boards perform advisory and propositional functions with reference to matters in which the risk of conflicts of interest is particularly relevant or where the need for more specific skills is felt. The fact that these committees are composed entirely or largely of independent directors offers greater guarantee that decisions in delicate matters, such as appointments, remuneration, and internal control and risk management, are taken in company's best interests.

6.3 Theoretical Framework

RemCo is a board sub-committee whose duties concern the rewards, salary, bonus, and share options as well as company cars, private health insurance, and pension contributions of corporate executives. This section proposes some questions as the basis for a brief review of relevant literature.

i) Is the existence and relevance of RemCo supported by a specific managerial theory?
ii) How extensive is the research on RemCo activities and which relationships have been analyzed?

A Theoretical Perspective on RemCo

Agency theory is commonly used to explore relationships between corporate governance features like board characteristics and company performance. The creation of RemCo is consistent with an agency perspective[34] that underlines the separation of management and control functions.

Traditionally, remuneration is used to align the interests of shareholders and executives through pay-for-performance compensation arrangements. The GFC prompted a debate on banks' governance structures. A controversial issue was the size of compensation awards to executives and the incentives implicit in compensation contracts that prioritized short-term goals over long-term firm performance, which consequently led to new remuneration guidelines and regulation. RemCo was established to create incentives for agents which aligned the interests of principals and increased the accountability of agents for their actions (Abugu, 2012). Ruigrok et al. (2006) note that the quality of the board's activities is increased by the delegation of functions to specific committees. Consistent with agency theory, RemCo is one of the most important committees for enhancing the work of management, mitigating agency problems, and ensuring better alignment to stakeholders' interests. In turn, this can improve corporate disclosure.

Holmstrom (1979)[35] states that the principal is always better off with more information about agent behavior than less. Also, principals and agents can work together when both have the same attitude to risk toward projects and the same goals and interests in the firm (Eisenhardt, 1989). Thus, common interests in projects can solve conflicting interests between principal and agent.

[34] The existence of board committees and RemCo is not only linked to agency theory but to other theories, for example, managerial power theory (Bebchuk & Fried, 2003).

[35] Bengt Holmstrom won the Nobel Prize in 2016 (together with Oliver Hart) with the following motivation: "*for their contributions to contract theory*".

Earlier Literature

Theoretical and empirical research on board committees, particularly RemCo, is scarce compared to literature on boards of directors and executive compensation.[36] Hence, this section avoids literature in the broader executive remuneration and corporate governance streams and focuses on studies directly relevant to our preferred topic. Most studies about RemCo consider the following:

i) Relationship between the presence/absence of RemCo and company performance;
ii) The presence (in terms of majority) of independent/non-executive members on RemCo (a sub-detail regarding its composition) and relationships with CEO remuneration and compensation packages;
iii) The existence of RemCo and better (or worse) CSR-ESG disclosure.

It is widely recognized that committees have a valuable impact in terms of board monitoring, executive behavior, accounting and nomination practices, and investor and stakeholder perceptions. Adams et al. (2021) show that committees play an important role in firms' functioning and corporate governance with their growing over time due to increased legal requirements and recommendations, shareholder and stakeholder pressure on boards, and the more complex business environment (Rey, 2022, p. 6). In addition to tighter regulatory frameworks, the proliferation of board committees has been driven by other factors, such as stakeholder and institutional pressure, class action lawsuits, increased competence and expertise of independent directors, the evolution of CEO role and behavior, and diversity requirements (Kolev et al., 2019). Other evidence finds that committee structures are relevant to firms. Klein (1998) evaluates the link between board composition and firm performance for firms S&P 500 listed firms by assessing the composition of boards' committee structures. Results show that inside directors' membership of finance and investment committees adds value. The market explicitly acknowledges this by rewarding firms whose boards significantly increase percentages of insiders on either committee. However, board committees present

[36] See Kovačević (2009) for a review which critically analyzes and synthesizes literature relevant to executive remuneration committee processes.

costs and disadvantages that should be considered when evaluating board efficiency and productivity (OECD, 2021). Committees can also impair communication, create silos within the board, and create problems of inside information due to some members having more information than others that they might strategically withhold or manipulate even if "*it is not clear how [committees] affect aggregate group information production and decision-making*" (Adams et al., 2021, p. 1120).

Directors appointed to powerful committees may enjoy improved status and greater power on boards (Chen & Wu, 2016; Gilson & Gordon, 2019; Kolev et al., 2019). The proliferation of committees creates additional expenses. Faleye et al. (2011) find that independent director majorities on committees are costly to firms as workload and responsibilities increase together with the occurrence and length of committee meetings. Furthermore, directors sitting on multiple boards participate in more committees in each company (Lee, 2020). Multitasking independent directors can improve board performance they can create diversion. Hiring external experts and advisors to support many committees is costly. Reeb and Upadhyay (2010) suggest that while committees help large boards the effect may not generalize to small or insider-oriented boards.

Next, we review studies exclusively related to RemCo. The available evidence on the effectiveness of RemCo is mixed. Regarding point (i), Agyemang-Mintah (2016) investigates the association between the presence of RemCo and firm performance. Results show establishing RemCos exerted a positive impact on the profitability of UK financial institutions measured as ROA and market value. However, other research on RemCo together with other committees reports a negative impact. Klein (1998) samples 486 US firms from 1992 to 1993 and examines the association between the presence of audit, remuneration, and nomination committees and financial performance finding no significant relationships. Results are robust irrespective of changes to the composition of committees. Vafeas and Theodorous (1998) sample 250 UK-listed firms in 1994 to investigate the impact of audit, remuneration, and nomination committees on firm performance finding no evidence to suggest that the existence of board committees affects financial performance. Vafeas (1999) investigates 307 US-listed firms from 1990 to 1994 reporting a negative relationship between the establishment of board committees (audit, remuneration, and nomination) and the value of a firm. Fratini and Tettamanzi

(2015) analyze 182 Italian-listed companies. Firm performance is positively related to board size and audit committee's effort while negatively related to leverage albeit the relationship is economically unimportant. Audit committee and leverage lost their relevance in 2007 when the presence of RemCo positively impacted performance.

Concerning point (ii), Main and Johnston (1993) sample 220 large British-listed firms and examine the role of RemCo in UK boards. They find that the presence of RemCo is associated with higher executive pay which reduces shareholder value. Conyon and Peck (1998) study RemCo and the executive pay of 94 UK companies over 1991 to 1994. The proportion of non-executive directors sitting on RemCo is positively related to senior management pay and the sensitivity of pay-to-performance. Remuneration levels are greater in companies with RemCo. Belliveau et al. (1996) find that when the RemCo chair's status is higher than the CEOs, CEO is lower, and when the CEO's status is higher than the chair, the CEO's pay is higher. Daily et al. (1998) find no link between excessive pay received by CEOs and RemCos dominated by executive directors. Similarly, Newman and Mozes (1999) analyze 161 firms in the US in 1992 and confirm there is no relationship between CEO pay and executive director participation in RemCo. The findings imply that executive directors do not necessarily influence CEO pay during remuneration meetings. Indeed, Bertrand and Mullainathan (2001) find CEO compensation is less strong or weak when the firm is better managed.

Gregory-Smith (2012) tests the impact of RemCo independence on CEO pay. FTSE 350 companies between 1996 and 2008 are used to assess whether RemCo facilitates optimal contracting or CEOs capture the pay-setting process and inflate their own remuneration. The study finds no evidence of a relationship between CEO pay and director independence which challenges the notion of managerial power. Acero and Alcade (2023) investigate whether the proportion of proprietary directors (blockholders or their representatives) on RemCo influences vertical pay inequality at Spanish-listed companies and whether this relationship is conditioned by concentration of ownership. Their results indicate that the presence of "these" directors on RemCo serves to reduce vertical pay inequality even in the context of high ownership concentration.

Some studies examine jointly points (i) and (ii). Harymawan et al. (2020) determine that RemCo is essential in the remuneration of senior company officers which is associated with higher firm performance and, in consequence, higher CSR disclosure. Their study examines relationships between RemCo, executive and board of director remuneration, and firm performance in Indonesia using 847 observations of firms listed on the Indonesian Stock Exchange over 2014 to 2017. Results indicate that RemCo is positively related to executive remuneration and firm performance. Higher remuneration is only linked to higher performance in firms with an established RemCo. Regarding point (iii), CSR-ESG disclosure, Kanapathippillai et al. (2019) show that RemCo tends to voluntarily disclose attribution and higher levels of information thereby increasing the quality of this committee. Similarly, RemCo encourages disclosure of ESG information in Thai-listed companies (Suttipun, 2021) while Abeysekera (2012) shows that RemCo influences human capital disclosure on the Colombo Stock Exchange. In contrast, Alotaibi (2016) suggests that RemCo that is too big is less effective in its functions leading to reduced CSR disclosure.

Bel-Oms and Segarra-Moliner (2022) analyze whether the existence of RemCo increases disclosure of more CSR information. They test the moderating role played by the proportion of independent directors on boards of directors with the relationship between the constitution of RemCo and CSR disclosure. Using an international sample of 28,610 listed companies in 2018 their evidence shows that existence of RemCo is more likely to disclose CSR information while the existence of independent board members positively moderates the association between the existence of remuneration committees and CSR disclosure.

6.4 Descriptive Analysis

Sample and Data

We investigate the main characteristics of RemCos in G-SIBs in 2022, which is a small albeit international sample of very large banks, to derive an updated map of the role and duties of RemCos globally. A G-SIB is a bank whose systemic risk profile is deemed to be of such importance that its failure would trigger a wider financial crisis and threaten the global economy. The Basel Committee has developed a formula for determining which banks are G-SIBs deploying criteria including size, interconnectedness, and complexity. For this reason, regulators subject G-SIBs to stricter prudential regulation, such as higher capital requirements. All data and information in this analysis derive from public information from bank websites and official documents (financial statements, proxy statements, corporate governance and remuneration reports, term of references, and charters) for 2022.

Over time, the list of G-SIBs has seen revisions and alternating entries and exits even definitive ones especially for European G-SIBs due to the reduction of their indicators of systemic importance. In addition, various migrations between buckets have occurred. Table 6.2 shows the list of G-SIBs from 2011 to 2022 (FSB 2022). It lists the G-SIB, country of origin, and for each year its allocated risk bucket (an empty box means the bank was not included in the list that year). For example, Agricultural Bank of China entered the list three years later (2014) and was always placed in the least risky bucket (n.1) which implies an additional capital buffer of 1% of CET1 (see Note in Table 6.2 for buckets). Whereas 36 banking groups have been on the list at some point, in 2022 the list contains 30 G-SIBs of which 13 are European banks, 8 American, 7 Asian, and 2 Canadian. Our analysis excludes the following ex-G-SIBs reflecting their absence from the 2022 list: BBVA, Commerzbank, Dexia, Lloyds Banking Group, Nordea, and Royal Bank of Scotland. On average, the cluster of US G-SIBs has a higher level of systemic importance. Noting this is based on a simple "average value" (not shown), at the end of 2012 the average bucket value of the 8 US G-SIBs equaled 2.25 *c.f.* 1.81 for European banks and 1.25 for Asian banks. In 2022, the systemic importance of US G-SIBs remains essentially the same with an average bucket value of 2. The average bucket value for Asian banks increased to 1.43 whereas it has decreased for European banks to 1.38.

Board of Directors and Board Committees: An Overview

This section provides an overview of corporate boards and sub-committees at G-SIBs in 2022. Table 6.3 presents hand-collected information on board composition in term of size, gender diversity, director independence (NED), age, tenure, and number of meetings held during the year.[37]

[37] We do not analyze the regulatory framework (rules or codes) for individual countries and refer the reader to OECD (2021). Our comments concern the hand-collected data for 2022.

Table 6.2 G-SIBs and allocated risk buckets

#	*G-SIB*	*Country*	*2011*	*2012*	*2013*	*2014*	*2015*	*2016*	*2017*	*2018*	*2019*	*2020*	*2021*	*2022*
1	Agricultural Bank of China	China				1	1	1	1	1	1	1	1	1
2	Bank of America	US		2	2	2	2	3	3	2	2	2	2	3
3	Bank of China	China		1	1	1	1	1	2	2	2	2	2	2
4	Bank of New York Mellon	US		2	1	1	1	1	1	1	1	1	1	1
5	Barclays	UK		3	3	3	3	2	2	2	2	2	2	2
6	BBVA	Spain		1	1	1								
7	BNP Paribas	France		3	3	3	3	3	2	2	2	2	3	2
8	China Construction Bank	China					1	1	2	1	1	2	2	1
9	Citigroup	US		4	3	3	3	4	3	3	3	3	3	3
10	Commerzbank	Germany												
11	Credit Suisse	Switzerland		2	2	2	2	2	1	1	1	1	1	1
12	Deutsche Bank	Germany		4	3	3	3	3	3	3	2	2	2	2
13	Dexia	Belgium												
14	Goldman Sachs	US		2	2	2	2	2	2	2	2	1	2	2
15	Group Crédit Agricole	France		1	2	1	1	1	1	1	1	1	1	1
16	Groupe BPCE	France		1	1	1	1	1		1	1	1	1	1
17	HSBC	UK		4	4	4	4	3	3	3	3	3	3	3
18	Industrial & Commercial Bank of China	China			1	1	1	2	2	2	2	2	2	2
19	ING Bank	The Netherlands		1	1	1	1	1	1	1	1	1	1	1
20	JP Morgan Chase	US		4	4	4	4	4	4	4	4	3	4	4

#	*G-SIB*	*Country*	*2011*	*2012*	*2013*	*2014*	*2015*	*2016*	*2017*	*2018*	*2019*	*2020*	*2021*	*2022*
21	Lloyds Banking Group	UK												
22	Mitsubishi UFJ FG	Japan		2	2	2	2	2	2	2	2	2	2	2
23	Mizuho FG	Japan		1	1	1	1	1	1	1	1	1	1	1
24	Morgan Stanley	US		2	2	2	2	1	1	1	1	1	1	1
25	Nordea	Norway		1	1	1	1	1	1					
26	Royal Bank of Canada	Canada							1	1	1	1	1	1
27	Royal Bank of Scotland	UK		2	2	2	1	1	1					
28	Santander	Spain		1	1	1	1	1	1	1	1	1	1	1
29	Société Générale	France		1	1	1	1	1	1	1	1	1	1	1
30	Standard Chartered	UK		1	1	1	1	1	1	1	1	1	1	1
31	State Street	US		1	1	1	1	1	1	1	1	1	1	1
32	Sumitomo Mitsui FG	Japan		1	1	1	1	1	1	1	1	1	1	1
33	Toronto Dominion	Canada									1	1	1	1
34	UBS	Switzerland		2	2	1	1	1	1	1	1	1	1	1
35	Unicredit Group	Italy		1	1	1	1	1	1	1	1	1	1	1
36	Wells Fargo	US		1	1	1	1	2	2	2	2	1	1	1
	TOTAL		29	28	29	30	30	30	30	29	30	30	30	30

Note The allocation of G-SIBs to risk buckets began in 2012. The following are the required levels of additional capital buffers: Bucket 5 (3.5%) Bucket 4 (2.5%) Bucket 3 (2.0%) Bucket 2 (1.5%) Bucket 1 (1.0%). *Source* https://www.bis.org/bcbs/gsib/index.htm

Table 6.3 Boards of directors: Salient characteristics

Statistics	*Directors (#)*	*of which: women (#)*	*Women, %*	*NED, %*	*Avg Age BoD (yrs)*	*Avg Age women BoD (yrs)*	*Avg Age CEO (yrs)*	*Avg Age Chair (yrs)*	*Avg BoD tenure (yrs)*	*BoD meetings (#)*
Total Mean	13.9	4.8	34.4	73.4	61.7	59.8	58.8	63.9	5.0	14.7
Coefficient of variation [(SD/Mean)*100]	18.2	40.7	37.1	32.6	5.1	6.3	8.3	8.6	40.2	40.2
Minimum	9	1	8.3	26.3	55.7	49.7	46	51	2.4	8
Maximum	21	9	58.3	100.0	67.8	67.8	67	75	8.9	31
Geography Means										
Asia (G-SIBs: 7)	14.1	2.3	15.9	44.4	61.6	58.4	58.9	59.3	3.3	12.9
US-Canada (G-SIBs: 10)	12.8	5.1	39.9	90.7	63.7	62.1	60.6	64.8	6.6	14.2
Europe (G-SIBs: 13)	14.7	5.9	40.5	75.6	60.2	58.7	57.3	65.8	4.7	16.2

Table 6.4 Boards: Size, gender diversity, and independence

Directors (#)	*G-SIBs (#)*	*Women, %*	*G-SIBs (#)*	*NEDs, %*	*G-SIBs (#)*
< 10	1	0–24.99	6	< 39.99	4
11–13	13	25–49.99	2	40–74.99	8
14–16	13	25–49.99	18 (of which 8 at least 40%)	> 75	18 (of which 4 at 100%)
> 17	3	> 50	4		

The average **size** of the board is 13.9 members[38]; only one bank has less than 10 directors while for 13 banks the board size ranges between 11 and 13 members. A further 13 banks have a board with between 14 and 16 members. The mode is 14. Three G-SIBs have larger boards (Table 6.4). Board size shows moderate variability measured by the coefficient of variation. US and Canadian banks, on average, have smaller board size compared to European and Asian banks.

The G20/OECD Principles recognize the importance of diversity of thought in board discussions and suggest that "*countries may wish to consider measures such as voluntary targets, disclosure requirements, boardroom quotas and private initiatives that enhance gender diversity on boards and in senior management*" (Principle VI.E.4). The ability of boards to ensure strategic guidance of the company depends in part on its composition which should include directors with the right mix of background and competencies.[39]

In recent years, a growing number of jurisdictions have adopted measures to promote female participation on boards often via disclosure requirements and regulatory measures, such as mandated quotas and/or voluntary targets. To foster **gender diversity** on boards, many jurisdictions have adopted mandatory quotas for listed companies requiring a

[38] In some G-SIBs, data relates to the Supervisory Board which typically comprises NEDs while the management board (not examined) comprises executives only.

[39] Directors' CVs include many details regarding skills and experiences. Each G-SIB maps and discloses such competencies having regard to topics like (the following is not a fixed list) financial and international markets, strategic planning, sustainability (ESG), banking business, legal and regulatory, corporate governance, compliance, risk and control, accounting and audit, and digital and technological areas. We do not analyze these skills.

certain percentage of board seats to be filled by women,[40] while others apply more flexible mechanisms, such as voluntary goals while a few have introduced a combination of both (OECD 2021, pp. 165–166).

In our sample of G-SIBs, on average, over one-third of directors are women. The variability across banks is quite high with very big differences between Asian banks where women hold only 16% of board seats[41] and the US and Europe where female presence is around one-third and over with a further twelve cases where the percentage exceeds 40% (Table 6.4). However, only three G-SIBs have a female CEO or chair: Jane N. Fraser is CEO at Citigroup, Jacynthe Coté is Chair of the Board at Royal Bank of Canada, and Ana Botin is the Executive Chair at Santander. We analyze gender diversity because each G-SIB discloses in a different way (or does not disclose) other types of diversity (nationality, ethnicity, etc.).

Tables 6.3 and 6.4 provide information on director **independence** (such directors are termed Non-Executive Director, NED). Despite differences in board structure, almost all countries have introduced a requirement or recommendation regarding the minimum number or ratio of independent directors. Recommendation that boards be composed of at least 50% independent directors is the most prevalent voluntary standard. Within G-SIBs, the overall percentage of NED exceeds 70% with differences across geographical areas: in US and Canadian banks the proportion of NEDs exceeds 90% because it is common for the board, with the sole exception of CEO, to comprise NEDs.[42] In 18 G-SIBs, the

[40] For example, Italy adopted a gradual approach to the imposition of quotas starting with a 2011 law taking effect in 2012. The law applying to companies listed on the Italian Stock Exchange initially required a minimum of 20% of board seats for each gender with the first board appointment following August 2012, and a minimum of 33% for the second term expiring with the third term of board appointments. A 2019 law increased the minimum threshold from 33 to 40% starting from 2020 and extended its application to six successive terms of board appointments.

[41] In their annual reports, Asian G-SIBs state that the composition of their BoDs complies with national requirements for listing rules and codes on gender diversity, and bank policies on diversity.

[42] At the French bank, Groupe BPCE, the BoD comprises members from the Banque Populaire Banks (7), the Caisses d'Epargne (7), independent members (3), and employee representatives (2). The majority representation of Crédit Agricole's Regional Banks on the BoD of Crédit Agricole constitutes an atypical representation reflecting the group's cooperative structure: 7 out of 11 are Chairs and 3 CEOs; excluding the three directors representing employees, 33% of board directors are independent in accordance with the recommendation of the AFEP/MEDEFCode. We consider inside NEDs' percentage,

percentage of NEDs % is over 75%; among this cohort there are 4 cases where the value is 100%, namely, Credit Suisse, UBS, Deutsche Bank, and ING Bank, that is cases where we analyze the Supervisory Board (not the Management Board) and the CEO does not have a board seat. On other BoDs, the CEO has a seat.

We next consider the average **age** of board members, which is 61.7 years for all G-SIBs. On average, US and Canadian directors are slightly older (63.7 years)[43] and European directors younger (60.2 years). Female directors are younger still (59.8 years). Like their male counterparts, the average woman director at US and Canadian is older (62.1 years) than her European peer (58.7 years). The average CEO is 58.8 and Chair 63.5 years. In all but two of 8 US G-SIBs the CEO is also the chair. Duality, however, depends on corporate governance models with some countries prohibiting this practice with other models prohibiting the CEO from a board seat.

We analyze the average **tenure** of BoDs. Some G-SIBs have a tenure policy that outlines term limits to balance the benefits of experience with the need for new perspectives and achieving ongoing board renewal. We recognize that national approaches to defining independence for NEDs vary considerably particularly regarding maximum tenure and independence from significant shareholders. Many jurisdictions establish a maximum tenure for board members to be considered as independent. On average, tenure at 30 G-SIBs is 5 years with notable geographical differences. At US banks, there are 3 cases where tenure exceeds 8 years whereas average tenure is lower in Europe (4.7 years) and Asia (3.3 years).

Our final piece of information relates to the annual "activity" of the board. Hence, we analyze the **number of meetings** held during the year. On average, this figure is 14.7 meetings including regular scheduled

independent members, and employees' representatives. Differences in these metrics exist between Chinese and Japanese G-SIBs with the latter recording a higher percentage of NEDs.

[43] In their Corporate Governance Guidelines, some US banks state that an individual who would be age 72 (or 75 in some cases) at the time of election shall not be nominated for initial election to the Board, that the Board may approve the nomination for reelection of a director who would be age 72 (or 75) at the time of election (see for example https://investor.bankofamerica.com/2022-proxy-statement, p.9). In two French G-SIBs, these two limits are lower.

meetings and special (ad hoc) ones[44]; medium variability exists among G-SIBs with European banks holding an average of 16.2 meetings compared to 12.9 at Asian banks and 14.2 at US and Canadian banks. We do not collect data on directors' attendance since this figure is compliant with internal rules, or if a director did not attend the bank explained the reason (normally health-related issues, bereavements, etc.). Moreover, we do not examine data on the total number of BoD proposals and resolutions for two reasons: first, this information is not easily available; second, we could incur the risk of comparing different counting methods and different levels of board mandates.

Board Committees, which meet separately from BoD, comprise subsets of board members and tend to have specific, narrowly defined functions. These qualities make sub-committees desirable for large banking groups since these companies tend to have heterogeneous boards that meet, on average, 15 times a year. The board has ultimate responsibility for the bank's business strategy and financial soundness, key personnel decisions, internal organization and governance structure and practices, and risk management and compliance obligations. The board may delegate some functions though not its responsibilities to board committees where appropriate. The role of sub-committees has been increasing due to the growing complexity of the business environment and evolving nature of risks. Hence, their functions have expanded from a strictly monitoring role to providing more encompassing and forward-looking advice to the board. Indeed, boards may need additional support to deal with their broadening and challenging responsibilities, emerging complex risks, and more technical and specific issues. Although boards may rely more on committees, they retain responsibility for decision-making. The average number of board committees at G-SIBs is 5.3. The average bank has at least four committees and some boards eight or nine. 63% of banks have five or six committees. Geographical differences are insignificant (Table 6.5).

Table 6.6 shows the specific committees reporting to their boards, their denomination, joint situations with other committees, and average size. Four types of board-level sub-committees, namely, risk, audit, nomination, and remuneration are most common and/or required by law/

[44] Normally, special meetings are called on a shorter notice than regular scheduled meetings which are planned a year or a semester in advance.

Table 6.5 Numbers of board sub-committees

Board Coms (#)	*G-SIBs (#)*	*G-SIBs, %*	*G-SIB*
4	7	23.3	Bank of America, BNP Paribas, Mitsubishi UFJ FG, Mizuho FG, Royal Bank of Canada, Société Générale, Toronto Dominion
5	14	46.7	Barclays, China Construction Bank, Citigroup, Goldman Sachs, Groupe BPCE, HSBC, ING Bank, JP Morgan Chase, Morgan Stanley, Standard Chartered, State Street, Sumitomo Mitsui FG, UBS, Unicredit Group
6	5	16.7	Bank of China, Bank of New York Mellon, Groupe Crédit Agricole, Wells Fargo, Santander
7	2	6.7	Agricultural Bank of China, Credit Suisse
8	1	3.3	Industrial and Commercial Bank of China Ltd
9	1	3.3	Deutsche Bank
5.3 (avg)	**30**	**100.0**	

listing rules or recommended by codes in most jurisdictions in the financial services sector. Nomination and remuneration committees are not mandatory in some jurisdictions.

Over time, other committees that also serve on a continuous basis have emerged to support and advise the board on issues, such as sustainability, ethics, corporate social responsibility, environment, technology, and innovation. Besides the most common committees, practices vary and are influenced by the company's size, structure, sectors, or level of development. Normally, outside directors serve as chair and members of the banks' legally mandated and voluntarily established committees.

From our analysis, we observe the following points:

First, all 30 G-SIBs have established a *Risk Committee* with an average size of 6 members. In high-risk or regulated industries (e.g., banking, insurance), the separation of audit and risk committees may be valuable as audit is traditionally more focused on financial risks and responsible for the accuracy of financial positions, while risk is conceived to be forward-looking and go beyond financial matters to address all types of risks. The global pandemic, the acceleration of climate change, social pressures, and technological developments have drawn increased attention to the large range of risks facing companies and the need for adequate risk mitigation strategies.

Table 6.6 Board sub-committees; by type, size, and membership

Type of Board Committee (#)	*G-SIBs (#)*	*Committee Name* (# of G-SIBs adopting that name)	*Avg size (#) §*	*Min (#) §*	*Max (#) §*
Risk Committee	30 (standalone)	Risk/Risks Committee (21)^ Risk Management Committee (3) Risk Management and Consumers' Interests Protection Committee (1) Enterprise Risk Committee (1) Risk Policy Committee (1) Internal Control, Risk Management and Compliance Committee (1) Risk Supervision, Regulation and Compliance Committee (1) Internal Controls & Risks Committee (1) Risk Management Committee of Institutions in the US Regions* US Risk Committee (2)*	6	3	9

Type of Board Committee (#)	*G-SIBs (#)*	*Committee Name* (# of G-SIBs adopting that name)	*Avg size (#) §*	*Min (#) §*	*Max (#) §*
Audit Committee	28 (standalone) 2 (joint)	Audit Committee (24) Audit and Compliance Committee (1) Group Audit Committee (1) Audit and Internal Control Committee (1) Examining and Audit Committee (1) *Together with Risk (2)*	5	3	10
Nomination Committee	27 (standalone) 3 (joint)	Corporate Governance & Nomination Committee (15)^ Nomination/Nominating Committee (6) Corporate Governance, ESG and Sustainability Committee (4)^ Appointments Committee (2) *Together with RemCo (3)*	5	3	11
RemCo	**30 (standalone)**	**See focus on the next Section**			

(continued)

Table 6.6 (continued)

Type of Board Committee (#)	*G-SIBs (#)*	*Committee Name* (# of G-SIBs adopting that name)	*Avg size (#) §*	*Min (#) §*	*Max (#) §*
ESG Committee	17 (standalone) 7 (joint)	Sustainability/ESG Committee (5)^ Public Responsibility/ies Committee (2) Responsible Banking, Sustainability and Culture Committee (1) Strategic Planning and Sustainable Development Committee (1) Strategic and Corporate Social Responsibility Committee (1) Strategy and Sustainability Committee (1) Cooperative and CSR Committee (1) Corporate Culture and Consumer Protection Committee (1) Corporate Social Responsibility and Consumer Protection Committee (1) Culture and Sustainability Committee (1) Corporate Culture and Responsibilities Committee (1) Corporate Responsibility Committee (1) *Together with Nomination Committee (4)* *Together with Risk Committee (1)* *Together with Related Party Committee (1)* *Together with RemCo (1)*	5	2	8

Type of Board Committee (#)	*G-SIBs (#)*	*Committee Name* (# of G-SIBs adopting that name)	*Avg size (#) §*	*Min (#) §*	*Max (#) §*
Technology Committee	7 (standalone)	Technology Committee (2) Operations and Technology Committee (2)^ Technology, Data and Innovation Committee (2)^ Digital Transformation and Technology Committee (1)	6	4	8
Related Party Committee	5 (standalone)	Related Party Transactions Management Committee (2)^ Connected Transactions Control Committee (1) Related Party Transaction, Social Responsibility and Consumer Protection Committee (1) Related-Parties Committee (1)	3	3	4

(continued)

Table 6.6 (continued)

Type of Board Committee (#)	*G-SIBs (#)*	*Committee Name* (# of G-SIBs adopting that name)	*Avg size (#) §*	*Min (#) §*	*Max (#) §*
Strategic / Finance Committee	7 (standalone) 1 (joint)	Strategic Development Committee (2) Finance Committee (2) Financial Statements Committee (1) Strategy Committee (1) County Area Banking Business/Inclusive Finance Development Committee (1) *Together with ESG Committee (1)*	7	3	11
Others	n.s	Chairman's Committee (2) Conduct and Financial Crime Control Committee (1) Regulatory Oversight Committee (1) Joint Risk and Audit Committee (1) Mediation Committee (1)	n.s	n.s	n.s

Note ^In this count we include very similar denominations; § the average size (rounded), minimum, and maximum, in term of committees' members, refer to standalone committees and not joint committees; * c*ommittees* belong to G-SIBs where a Risk Committee already exists

Second, the *Audit Committee*, which plays a key role in corporate governance by overseeing companies' financial reporting and disclosure, exists in 28 G-SIBs.[45] The average size is 5 members. Setting up audit, together with remuneration and nomination committees, is considered as way to address conflicts of interest: "*The board should consider establishing specific committees to consider questions where there is a potential for conflict of interest*" (Principle VI.E.1). Another function relates to accounting policies: "*it should also be regarded as good practice for this committee, or equivalent body, to review and report to the board the most critical accounting policies which are the basis for financial reports*" (VI.D.7); moreover, Principles V.C and V.D suggest that it is good practice that external auditors are recommended by an independent audit committee or an equivalent body, and that external auditors are appointed either by that committee/body or at the shareholders' meeting.[46]

Third, another important issue is the role of committees in monitoring and approving related party transactions. Several recommendations of the G20/OECD Principles deal with this topic. Chapter VI notes that an important board function is "*to guard against abusive related party transactions*", a function often assigned to the internal auditor who should maintain direct access to the board (Principle VI.D.6). Only 5 G-SIBs run a specific and dedicated *Related Party Committee*. The size is small (3 members). In other groups this function, where necessary, is exercised by other committees. The *Nomination Committee* usually identifies and recommends board members and executive candidates. It deals with the identification of individuals qualified to become board members in terms of skills and diversity, guiding the BoD in its annual review, reviewing succession plans, independence, and tenure of BoD. This committee is mandatory in only 24% of jurisdictions surveyed by the OECD. However, 60% of jurisdictions have code recommendations to establish them on a "comply or explain" basis and 64% require or recommend having a majority of independent members (Rey, 2022, p. 15). While there are

[45] For example, Italy's 2020 Code of Corporate Governance takes an alternative approach—in companies adopting the traditional governance system—by combining risk management and internal control within a single control and risk committee. This committee supports the board's assessments and decisions relating to the internal control and risk management system and the approval of periodical financial and non-financial reports. This is the case of the Italian G-SIB Unicredit Group.

[46] Rey (2022, pp. 10–15) details the work of the Audit committee.

large variations in the composition of nomination committees (between 3 and 11 members), their functions are relatively similar. All G-SIBs have a nomination committee, but 3 Asian banks combine it with RemCo.

Fourth, it is interesting to examine ESG-related disclosures and climate-related disclosures. Banks are increasingly considering assigning an oversight role to dedicated committees. 17 G-SIBs have a standalone *ESG Committee* with a great variety of denominations and average size of 5 members. Moreover, another committee type has emerged which we refer to as the *Technology Committee.* 7 G-SIBs have established this specific committee. It deals with the challenging role of digital financial transformation and innovation and advises the board on managing digital security risks. It also recommends technology-related procedures to meet the bank's financial and regulatory obligations with respect to privacy, data retention, and data protection. It is also necessary to mention other committees at the G-SIBs, for example, the *Strategic* or *Finance* Committees and others, such as the *Conduct and Financial Crime Control* Committee and *Regulatory Oversight* Committee.[47]

Remuneration Committee

RemCos are formally constituted committees of company boards of directors. While BoD is ultimately responsible for oversight of executive remuneration, RemCo is an appropriate and efficient mechanism to assist the BoD in ensuring effective and responsible remuneration practices. All the G-SIBs have created a RemCo, some since 2000. First, we examine the names of these RemCos in 2022. The 30 G-SIBs use 13 names some of which are similar that we can create five almost homogeneous groups. Table 6.7 shows that most banks (60%) use the term "*Compensation*" and "*Remuneration*" Committee. About 20% prefer a name including the term "*Human Resources*" or "*Human Capital*" (common in Canada and some US banks) while three Asian banks use a joint "*Nomination and Remuneration*" committee which addresses both governance and remuneration issues. Moreover, three US G-SIBs use different names for this committee including words, such as "*Management Development*", "*Succession*", and "*Culture*". Soana and Crisci (2017) carry out similar

[47] Rey (2022, pp. 19–27) discusses the various practices to establishing different sub-committees to support certain tasks and address specific issues.

analysis of Nomination Committees in 2016. Our analysis of RemCo shows similar variability in the choice of names.

We analyze the structure of G-SIBs RemCos for 2022 according to size, gender, independence, average age, and number of meetings (Table 6.8). In terms of **size**, the average RemCo has 5 members with a minimum of 3 and maximum of 8. In 73% of G-SIBs, RemCo comprises 4, 5, or 6 members. European RemCos are slightly smaller size (4 to 6 members) compared to Asian (5 to 3), and US and Canadian banks (5 to 2). Generally, it is unadvisable for RemCo to comprise only one or two members yet regarding efficiency there is little advantage to having a large committee. Mostly, RemCos have 4 or 5 members. This reflects

Table 6.7 RemCo; by names

Denomination of the Committee	*Name of adopting G-SIB*	*# of G-SIBs*	*%*
Compensation Committee/ Compensation Control Committee	Credit Suisse, Goldman Sachs, Groupe Crédit Agricole, Industrial and Commercial Bank of China Ltd, Mitsubishi UFJ FG, Mizuho FG, Société Générale, Sumitomo Mitsui FG, UBS/Deutsche Bank	10	33.3
Remuneration Committee/ Group Remuneration Committee	Barclays, BNP Paribas, Groupe BPCE, ING Bank, Santander, Standard Chartered, UniCredit Group / HSBC	8	26.7
Human Resources Committee/ Human Resources and Compensation Committee/ Compensation and Human Capital Committee	Royal Bank of Canada, State Street, Toronto Dominion, Wells Fargo/Bank of New York Mellon/Bank of America	6	20.0
Nomination and Remuneration Committee/Personnel and Remuneration Committee	Agricultural Bank of China, China Construction Bank/Bank of China	3	10.0
Compensation and Management Development Committee/ Compensation, Management Development and Succession/ Compensation, Performance Management and Culture Committee	JP Morgan Chase/Morgan Stanley/Citigroup	3	10.0
Total		30	100

Note The / separates the bank/s with different name/s as reported in the 1st column

Table 6.8 RemCo membership

	RemCo (#)	*Women, %*	*NEDs, %*	*Avg Age*	*Meetings (#)*
Total Mean	5.0	31.5	87.6	62.6	7.6
*CV [(St.Dev/ Mean)*100]*	*26.2*	*57.5*	*21.8*	*7.5*	*31.6*
Minimum	3	0.0	25.0	52.7	4
Maximum	8	66.7	100.0	74.0	14
Geographical Means					
Asia (G-SIBs: 7)	5.3	18.2	72.4	64.8	6.9
US-Canada (G-SIBs: 10)	5.2	30.5	97.5	64.1	8.0
Europe (G-SIBs: 13)	4.6	41.9	88.2	60.3	7.7

concerns that RemCo requires members possessing appropriate knowledge, expertise, and professional experience of remuneration policies and practices, such as mechanisms for aligning the remuneration structure to institutions' risk and capital profiles.

If we analyze the **gender** of RemCo members, we find that the average incidence of women on RemCo is 31.5%. Notable differences exist across geographical areas: for European G-SIBs (41.9%) female participation exceeds the average; US and Canadian banks (30.5%) roughly equal average; and for 6 out of 7 Asian G-SIBs female membership of RemCo is very low (18.2%). Table 6.9 shows that 23.3% of G-SIBs have a RemCo where women make up at least 50% or more of the membership. This is a positive message together with another statistic: 12 RemCo Chairs out of 30 are women.[48] For most G-SIBs, the percentage of women on RemCo ranges between 25% and 49.99%. Only three banks have a smaller percentage of women (below 15%) while for two banks the percentage is 0%. Notwithstanding, our results are encouraging given evidence elsewhere that about 96% of G-SIB RemCos comprised mainly men, and that males were most represented on audit and nomination committees, and BoD (Soana & Crisci, 2017).[49]

[48] The situation is evolving. In 2023, two G-SIGs (UniCredit Group and HSBC) changed their RemCo chair with a man.

[49] Soana and Crisci (2017) examine the same number (30) of G-SIBs. However, our sample differs from theirs in the following ways. The 2016 list of G-SIBs included Nordea and the Royal Bank of Scotland who no longer are on the list. Since 2017 and 2019,

Table 6.9 RemCo composition: gender

Women, %	*G-SIBs, #*	*G-SIBs, %*	*Cumulative %*	*G-SIBs (in **bold** if the Chair is a woman)*
0–14.99	3	10.0	10.0	Agricultural Bank of China. Mizuho FG (0%). Morgan Stanley (0%)
15–24.99	7	23.3	33.3	Bank of China. China Construction Bank. Deutsche Bank. Industrial and Commercial Bank of China Ltd. Royal Bank of Canada. Santander. Sumitomo Mitsui FG
25–49.99	13	43.3	76.7	**Bank of America. Bank of New York Mellon**. BNP Paribas. Citigroup. **Goldman Sachs. Groupe BPCE**. **Mitsubishi UFJ FG.** Société Générale. Standard Chartered. **State Street. Toronto Dominion. Unicredit Group**. Wells Fargo
> 50	7	23.3	100.0	Barclays. Credit Suisse. **Group Crédit Agricole**. **HSBC**. **ING Bank**. JP Morgan Chase. UBS

An area of concern for committees is **independence**. Depending on the country, membership comprises independent directors or mostly independents. Arguments exist whether committees should be entirely independent to avoid bias or have some non-independent members to ensure adequate functioning. One issue resulting from an overly independent committee concerns determining directors' remuneration and ensuring a correlation between compensation and performance by understanding the functioning of the corporation. The complexities of current remuneration packages demand a degree of expert knowledge and specialized information. If pay is to be linked to performance, it seems wise to give attention to this detail and that the dominant perspective on such matters comes from those who represent the shareholders, i.e., NEDs.

two Canadian banks have entered (Royal Bank of Canada and Toronto Dominion). Soana and Crisci (2017) analyze 29 G-SIBs since Nordea was excluded because its nomination committee is external to BoD as required by the Norwegian corporate governance code.

Many rules and codes recommend the creation of RemCo and exclude from its membership executive directors and CEOs in favor of mainly independent directors. These rules suggest that banks should establish a RemCo or similar body, which comprises a sufficient proportion of NEDs. The independence of RemCo can be strengthened by not appointing executive directors unless necessary. Our evidence shows that about 63% of G-SIB RemCos comprise entirely independent directors. Furthermore, 87.6% of RemCo members are independent with percentages highest at US and Canadian Banks (97.5%) followed by European G-SIBs (88.2%). RemCo has higher levels of independence (87.6%) than the board (73.4%).

Table 6.8 shows the average **age** of RemCo members is 62.7 years which is a little higher than the average board (61.7 years). At the minimum RemCo, average age is 52.7 years (the Italian case updated in 2023[50]) and the maximum is 74 years (the Japanese banking group Mizuho FG). Even with this very limited difference in average age compared to the BoD, it is likely that RemCo members have higher seniority since, by law, they must have, at least as regards the chair, high competences and skills.

There is a paucity of literature and empirical analysis on the operations of RemCo. Annual reports and other documents disclose information and the **frequency of meetings** and who attends. Our analysis finds a high degree of variation in the number of RemCo meetings held at G-SIBs. On average, RemCo effectively meets 7.6 times per year with a minimum of 4 and maximum of 14 times. While some charters specify minimum requirements for the number of annual RemCo meetings, say three or four, Adams et al. (2021) note that a committee that never meets exists in name only.

6.5 Conclusions and Recommendations for Future Research

BoD is primarily responsible for monitoring managerial performance and providing strategic guidance to management. In doing so, BoD typically sets up specialized committees to carry out specific tasks to support

[50] At the beginning of 2023, UniCredit changed the Chair of its RemCo following the resignation of the previous one.

and improve its work. Even if BoD is ultimately responsible for the oversight of executive remuneration, RemCo is an appropriate and efficient mechanism to assist BoD in ensuring effective and responsible remuneration practices. Typically, RemCo's purpose is to advise BoD on remuneration policy to attract talent while achieving the long-term interests and values of the company. RemCo usually recommends the level of remuneration of board directors and senior management, determines their terms of engagement, oversees stock options packages and overall compensation, and reviews and operates performance-related pay plans for executives. Overall, its monitoring role consists of ensuring transparency and compliance, exercised through appropriate disclosures.

Despite the important role of RemCo in the governance of executive remuneration, research into its operation, especially in Europe, is limited. Existing studies are insufficient to make broad generalizations regarding the overall efficacy of RemCo recommendations. Research as to whether remuneration committees are associated with more effective remuneration practice is limited and largely yielded mixed results. Further research is required to enable a detailed understanding of the determinants, quality, operation, and efficacy of this important committee. Consequently, testing whether remuneration committees are effective at aligning the interests of shareholders and executives remains an open and important research goal.

Our analysis of G-SIBs shows wide variation in the structures of RemCo with differences reflecting the size of banks, size of their board, geography, and internal rules. While the chapter has limitations, several potential further research opportunities exist. First, the sample size is small, the banks are the largest and most interconnected, which makes generalization difficult. Second, the analysis is specific to banking. Future research could enhance the existing literature on RemCo by examining larger samples of banks and other industrial and service companies. Research could consider whether corporate behavior and the efficacy of remuneration committees has changed following the introduction of mandated rules. An extension of this analysis would be to determine whether the data pertaining to G-SIBs are persistent over time. Finally, it would be useful to describe in greater depth the duties and responsibilities of RemCOs at G-SIBs.

References

Abeysekera, I. (2012). Role of remuneration committee in narrative human capital disclosure. *Accounting & Finance, 52*, 1–23. https://doi.org/10.1111/j.1467-629X.2011.00441.x

Abugu, J. E. O. (2012). Monitoring directors' remuneration, fat cat packages and perks of office. *Journal of Financial Crime, 19*(1), 6–19. https://doi.org/10.1108/13590791211190696/full/html

Acero, I., & Alcalde, N. (2023). The composition of the remuneration committee and the vertical pay gap: the role of proprietary directors in Spain. *Baltic Journal of Management, 18*(3), 386–401. https://doi.org/10.1108/BJM-09-2022-0354/full/pdf?casa_token=RRbKu_gvufAAAAAA:8Kv0vQx_9PfBp-oS5i-8N0RXLmXwBo2n6KVq_k-0Y7yOHcjTvWAMACd-Xnanoq7KpvuBbQpX0w_JvZmkf6JLfTFoIlTaxrTL6_QIX4WfkLPJn9DsWW4

Adams, R. B., Ragunathan V., & Tumarkin R. (2021). Death by committee? An analysis of corporate board (sub-) committees. *Journal of Financial Economics, 141*(3), 1119–1146. https://www.sciencedirect.com/science/article/abs/pii/S0304405X21002257

Agyemang-Mintah, P. (2016). Remuneration Committee governance and firm performance in UK financial firms. *Investment Management and Financial Innovations, 13*(1), 176–190. https://www.utupub.fi/bitstream/handle/10024/170589/remuneration%20committee%20.pdf?sequence=1&isAllowed=y

Alotaibi, K. (2016). Determinants and Consequences of CSR Disclosure Quantity and Quality: Evidence from Saudi Arabia, Ph.D. Thesis, Faculty of Business, Plymouth University, Plymouth, UK. https://pearl.plymouth.ac.uk/bitstream/handle/10026.1/5332/2016Alotaibi10416096PhDd..pdf?sequence=1&isAllowed=y

Basle Committee on Banking Supervision (BCBS). (2010a). *Compensation principles and standards assessment methodology.* https://www.bis.org/publ/bcbs166.pdf

Basle Committee on Banking Supervision (BCBS). (2010b). *Range of methodologies for risk and performance alignment of remuneration.* https://www.bis.org/publ/bcbs178.pdf

Basle Committee on Banking Supervision (BCBS). (2015). *Guidelines - Corporate governance principles for banks.* https://www.bis.org/bcbs/publ/d328.pdf

Bebchuk, L. A., & Fried, J. M. (2003). Executive compensation as an agency problem. *Journal of Economic Perspectives, 17*(3), 71–92. http://www.law.harvard.edu/faculty/bebchuk/pdfs/2003.Bebchuk-Fried.Executive.Compensation.pdf

Belliveau, M. A., O'Reilly, C. A. I., & Wade, J. B. (1996). Social capital at the top: Effects of social similarity and status on CEO compensation. *Academy of Management Journal, 39*(6), 1568–1593. https://www.jstor.org/stable/257069

Bel-Oms, I., & Segarra-Moliner, J. R. (2022). How do remuneration committees affect corporate social responsibility disclosure? Empirical evidence from an international perspective. *Sustainability, 14*(2), 860. https://www.mdpi.com/2071-1050/14/2/860#B20-sustainability-14-00860

Bertrand M., & Mullainathan, S. (2001). Are CEOs rewarded for luck? The ones without principals are. *Quarterly Journal of Economics, 116*, 901–932. https://inequality.stanford.edu/sites/default/files/media/_media/pdf/Reference%20Media/Bertrand%20and%20Mullainathan_2001_Elites.pdf

Chen, K., & Wu, A. (2016). The structure of board committees, Conference Paper, Academy of Management – Annual Meeting Proceedings. https://www.researchgate.net/profile/Andy-Wu-21/publication/320787550_The_Structure_of_Board_Committees/links/6000d44a299bf140889748c5/The-Structure-of-Board-Committees.pdf

Committee of European Banking Supervisors (CEBS). (2009). *High-level principles for Remuneration Policies.* https://www.eba.europa.eu/sites/default/documents/files/documents/10180/16094/2af16c93-a002-40e3-8c58-020e0f32065f/High-level%20principles%20for%20remuneration%20policies.pdf?retry=1

Committee of European Banking Supervisors (CEBS). (2010a). *Report on national implementation of CEBS High-level principles for Remuneration Policies.* https://www.eba.europa.eu/sites/default/documents/files/documents/10180/16151/77748a96-4f6d-4343-a6a7-ced98c241023/ImplementationReportHLPR.pdf

Committee of European Banking Supervisors (CEBS). (2010b). *Guidelines on remuneration policies and practices.* https://www.eba.europa.eu/sites/default/documents/files/documents/10180/106961/a3ab77c9-980f-4994-b2cd-397413b77084/Guidelines.pdf

Conyon, M. J., & Peck, S. I. (1998). Board control, remuneration committees, and top management compensation. *Academy of Management Journal, 41*(2), 146–157. https://www.jstor.org/stable/257099

Daily, G. M., Johnson, J. L., Ellstrand, A. E., & Dalton, D. R. (1998). Compensation committee composition as a determinant of GEO compensation. *Academy of Management Journal, 41*, 209–220. https://eds.p.ebscohost.com/eds/pdfviewer/pdfviewer?vid=3&sid=e6d362c1-6e3e-4ee5-950f-c3e68a69c507%40redis

Eisenhardt, K. (1989). Agency theory: An assessment and review. *Academy of Management Review, 14*(1), 57–74. https://www.jstor.org/stable/258191

European Banking Authority (EBA). (2016). *Guidelines on sound remuneration policies under Articles 74(3) and 75(2) of Directive 2013/36/EU and disclosure under Article 450 of Regulation (EU) No 575/2013.* https://www.eba.europa.eu/sites/default/documents/files/documents/10180/1314839/5057ed7d-8bf1-41b4-ad74-70474d6c3158/EBA-GL-2015-22%20Guidelines%20on%20Sound%20Remuneration%20Policies_EN.pdf?retry=1

European Banking Authority (EBA). (2021). *Guidelines on sound remuneration policies under Directive 2013/36/EU*, EBA/GL/2021/04. https://www.eba.europa.eu/sites/default/documents/files/document_library/Publications/Guidelines/2021/1016720/Draft%20Final%20report%20on%20GL%20on%20remuneration%20policies%20under%20CRD.pdf

European Commission (EC). (2009). *Recommendation on remuneration policies in the financial services sector, 2009/384/EC.* https://eur-lex.europa.eu/LexUriServ/LexUriServ.do?uri=OJ:L:2009:120:0022:0027:EN:PDF

European Commission (EC). (2010a). *Report on the application by Member States of the EU of the Commission 2009/384/EC.* https://eur-lex.europa.eu/legal-content/EN/TXT/PDF/?uri=CELEX:52010SC0671&from=nl

European Commission (EC). (2010b). *DIRECTIVE 2010/76/EU OF THE EUROPEAN PARLIAMENT AND OF THE COUNCIL* of 24 November 2010 amending Directives 2006/48/EC and 2006/49/EC as regards capital requirements for the trading book and for re-securitizations, and the supervisory review of remuneration policies. https://eur-lex.europa.eu/legal-content/EN/TXT/HTML/?uri=CELEX:32010L0076

European Commission (EC). (2013a). *DIRECTIVE 2013/36/EU OF THE EUROPEAN PARLIAMENT AND OF THE COUNCIL* of 26 June 2013 on access to the activity of credit institutions and the prudential supervision of credit institutions and investment firms, amending Directive 2002/87/EC and repealing Directives 2006/48/EC and 2006/49/EC. https://eur-lex.europa.eu/legal-content/EN/TXT/HTML/?uri=CELEX:32013L0036

European Commission (EC). (2013b). *REGULATION (EU) No 575/2013 OF THE EUROPEAN PARLIAMENT AND OF THE COUNCIL* of 26 June 2013 on prudential requirements for credit institutions and investment firms and amending Regulation (EU) No 648/2012. https://eur-lex.europa.eu/legal-content/EN/TXT/HTML/?uri=CELEX:32013R0575

European Commission (EC). (2019a). *DIRECTIVE (EU) 2019/878 OF THE EUROPEAN PARLIAMENT AND OF THE COUNCIL* of 20 May 2019 amending Directive 2013/36/EU as regards exempted entities, financial holding companies, mixed financial holding companies, remuneration, supervisory measures and powers and capital conservation measures. https://eur-lex.europa.eu/legal-content/EN/TXT/HTML/?uri=CELEX:32019L0878

European Commission (EC). (2019b). *REGULATION (EU) 2019/876 OF THE EUROPEAN PARLIAMENT AND OF THE COUNCIL* of 20 May 2019 amending Regulation (EU) No 575/2013 as regards the leverage ratio, the net stable funding ratio, requirements for own funds and eligible liabilities, counterparty credit risk, market risk, exposures to central counterparties, exposures to collective investment undertakings, large exposures, reporting and disclosure requirements, and Regulation (EU) No 648/2012. https://eur-lex.europa.eu/legal-content/EN/TXT/HTML/?uri=CELEX:32019R0876

Faleye, O., Hoitash, R., & Hoitash, U. (2011). The costs of intense board monitoring. *Journal of Financial Economics, 101*(1), 160–181. https://www.sciencedirect.com/science/article/pii/S0304405X11000432

Financial Stability Board (FSB). (2009). *Principles for sound compensation practices. Implementation standards*. https://www.fsb.org/wp-content/uploads/r_090925c.pdf

Financial Stability Board (FSB). (2022). *List of Global Systemically Important Banks (G-SIBs)*. https://www.fsb.org/2022/11/2022-list-of-global-systemically-important-banks-g-sibs/

Financial Stability Forum (FSF). (2009). *Principles for sound compensation practices*. https://www.fsb.org/wp-content/uploads/r_0904b.pdf

Fratini, F., & Tettamanzi, P. (2015). Corporate governance and performance: Evidence from Italian companies. *Open Journal of Business and Management, 3*(2), 199–218. https://scirp.org/journal/paperinformation.aspx?paperid=55853

Gilson, R. J., & Gordon, J. N. (2019). Board 3.0 -- An introduction. The Business Lawyer, Columbia Law and Economics, Working Paper No. 602, 74. https://ssrn.com/abstract=3332735

Gregory-Smith, I. (2012). Chief Executive Pay and Remuneration Committee Independence. *Oxford Bulletin of Economics and Statistics, 74*(4), 510–531. https://eprints.whiterose.ac.uk/86812/1/IGS1.pdf

Harymawan, I., Agustia, D., Nasih, M., Inayati, A., & Nowland, J. (2020). Remuneration committees, executive remuneration, and firm performance in Indonesia. *Heliyon, 6*(2), e03452. https://www.sciencedirect.com/science/article/pii/S2405844020302978

Holmstrom, B. (1979). Moral hazard and observability. *Bell Journal of Economics, 10*(1), 74–91. https://www.jstor.org/stable/3003320

Kanapathippillai, S., Mihret, D., & Johl, S. (2019). Remuneration committees and attribution disclosures on remuneration decisions: Australian evidence. *Journal of Business Ethics, 158*, 1063–1082. https://doi.org/10.1007/s10551-017-3736-7

Klein, A. (1998). Firm performance and board committee structure. *The Journal of Law and Economics, 41*, 275–304. https://doi.org/10.1086/467391

Kolev, K., Wangrow, D. B., Barker III, V. L., & Schepker, D. J. (2019). Board committees in corporate governance: A cross-disciplinary review and agenda for the future. *Journal of Management Studies,*

56(6), 1138–1193. https://epublications.marquette.edu/cgi/viewcontent.cgi?article=1367&context=mgmt_fac

Kovačević, S. (2009). *Understanding board remuneration committees.* A submission to the Productivity Commission. https://www.pc.gov.au/inquiries/completed/executive-remuneration/submissions/sub043.pdf

Lee, W. (2020). The determinants and effects of board committees. *Journal of Corporate Finance, 65*. https://doi.org/10.1016/j.jcorpfin.2020.101747

Main, B. G. M., & Johnson, J. (1993). Remuneration committees and corporate governance. *Accounting and Business Research, 23*, 351–362.

Newman, H. A., & Mozes, H. A. (1999). Does the composition of the compensation committee influence CEO compensation practices? *Financial Management, 28*(3), 41–53. https://www.jstor.org/stable/3666182

OECD Principles of Corporate Governance. (2015). https://www.oecd-ilibrary.org/g20-oecd-principles-of-corporate-governance_5js09wmjzz45.pdf?itemId=%2Fcontent%2Fpublication%2F9789264236882-en&mimeType=pdf

OECD Corporate Governance FactBook. (2021). https://www.oecd.org/corporate/corporate-governance-factbook.htm

Reed, D., & Upadhyay, A. (2010). Subordinate board structures. *Journal of Corporate Finance, 16*(4), 469–486. https://doi.org/10.1016/j.jcorpfin.2010.04.005

Rey, M. E. (2022). *The role of board-level committees in corporate governance.* OECD Corporate Governance Working papers, n.24. https://www.oecd-ilibrary.org/deliver/8a97a3f6-en.pdf?itemId=/content/paper/8a97a3f6-en&mimeType=pdf

Ruigrok, W., Peck, S., Tacheva, S., Greve, P., & Hu, Y. (2006). The determinants and effects of board nomination committees. *Journal of Managerial Governance, 10*, 119–148. https://doi.org/10.1007/s10997-006-0001-3

Soana, M. G., & Crisci, G. (2017). Duties and responsibilities of the nomination committee. *Corporate Ownership & Control, 15*(1), 246–252. https://www.researchgate.net/publication/320446569_Duties_and_responsibilities_of_the_nominating_committee#:~:text=Its%20main%20responsibilities%20towards%20the,monitoring%20education%20programs%20for%20directors

Suttipun, M. (2021). The influence of board composition on environmental, social and governance (ESG) disclosure of Thai listed companies. *International Journal of Disclosure and Governance, 18*, 391–402. https://www.researchgate.net/profile/Muttanachai-Suttipun/publication/350372687_The_influence_of_board_composition_on_environmental_social_and_governance_ESG_disclosure_of_Thai_listed_companies/links/62e7bfd33c0ea878877390e7/The-influence-of-board-composition-on-environmental-social-and-governance-ESG-disclosure-of-Thai-listed-companies.pdf?_sg%5B0%5D=started_experiment_milestone&_sg%5B1%5D=started_experiment_milestone&origin=journalDetail&_rtd=e30%3D

Vafeas, N., & Theodorou, E. (1998). The relationship between board structure and firm performance in the UK. *British Accounting Review, 30*, 383–407. https://doi.org/10.1006/bare.1998.0075

Vafeas, N. (1999). Board meeting frequency and firm performance. *Journal of Financial Economics, 53*, 113–142. https://www.sciencedirect.com/science/article/pii/S0304405X99000185

CHAPTER 7

Bank Deposits and Deposit Rates: The Impact of COVID-19 and the Effect of ESG Scores

Alessio Bongiovanni and Jonathan Williams

7.1 Introduction

As rational investors in bank liabilities, depositors typically discipline banks through their reactions to changes in fundamental indicators of bank performance. Depositor discipline is reported to be highly responsive to exogeneous shocks, such as financial crisis episodes. In such cases, depositors punish riskier banks by withdrawing funds and/or requiring a risk premium in the form of higher deposit interest rates to maintain balances.

A. Bongiovanni
Department of Accounting and Finance, Leeds University Business School, University of Leeds, Leeds, UK
e-mail: a.bongiovanni@leeds.ac.uk

J. Williams (✉)
Discipline of Finance and Accounting, Surrey Business School, University of Surrey, Guildford, UK
e-mail: jon.williams@surrey.ac.uk

T. King and J. Williams (eds.), *Corporate Governance in the Banking and Financial Sector*, Palgrave Macmillan Studies in Banking and Financial Institutions, https://doi.org/10.1007/978-3-031-83353-3_7

Put another way, depositors reward better performing banks by depositing funds and/or accepting lower deposit rates. In either event, the potential for exogeneous shocks to cause liquidity problems and ultimately adversely affect financial stability is unambiguous. With this in mind, our interest in depositor discipline is piqued by another more recent exogeneous shock, namely, the shock caused by the spread of COVID-19 that created both a health crisis and an economic crisis.

This chapter will provide a synthesis of contemporary analysis to distill the response of deposit markets to the pandemic. We extend our discussion and propose that during the pandemic and in the context of depositor discipline, depositors considered another indicator of bank performance, namely, ESG scores (environmental, social, governance). Our hypothesis posits that depositors perceive that ESG scores signal banks' commitment to corporate social responsibility (CSR) and, therefore, proxy for trust. Since trust is known to dissipate following an exogeneous shock, we contend that it is rationale for banks to strategically prioritise CSR (quantified by ESG scores) to enhance trust and increase customer loyalty, which is expected to produce superior bank performance outcomes. Using bank-level data for pre-shock and post-shock intervals, we examine relations between bank ESG scores and deposit market outcomes.

For our task, we construct a panel dataset of US bank holding companies (BHC) with over $3 billion in assets and collect quarterly consolidated financial statements from regulatory filings (FR-Y9C) at the Federal Reserve Bank of Chicago. To determine the impact of the shock emanating from the spread of COVID-19, our pre-shock interval covers Q2 2018 to Q4 2019 and the post-shock interval from Q1 2020 to Q2 2021. The unbalanced panel dataset includes 177 BHCs and 1755 bank-quarter observations. We augment the bank-level data with two variables that capture the health crisis and associated economic crisis. First, we construct a state-level measure of exposure to COVID-19 that we measure as the average of new COVID-19-related deaths per 100,000 inhabitants in a quarter in states where a BHC is physically present. We obtain the information necessary to construct this indicator from the New York Times and US Census, respectively. Second, our gauge of the economic crisis is captured by the State-Coincident Index sourced from the Federal Reserve Bank of Philadelphia.[1] Lastly, we source ESG scores from Refinitiv Asset4. The score is an aggregate of bank performance across constituents, namely, environment, social and governance. It is adjusted by negative news on firm-specific ESG controversies.

The chapter proceeds as follows. Section 7.2 reviews the spread of COVID-19 across states and the associated economic crisis. Section 7.3 discusses deposit market dynamics following the shock caused by the pandemic and reviews related literature. In Sect. 7.4 we review relevant literature on CSR and studies of the effects of ESG scores in banking. Section 7.5 reiterates our research hypothesis. It presents the natural experiment and fixed effects regressions approach that we use to determine the effect of ESG scores on deposit market outcomes following the shock caused by the spread of COVID-19 and discusses the results. Section 7.6 provides a short conclusion.

7.2 The COVID-19 Pandemic

As at 26 October 2023, the number of reported coronavirus cases in the US stood at 109,047,729 with 1,180,288 deaths.[2] The first reported case of COVID-19 in the US was confirmed on 21 January 2020 with the Department of Health and Human Services declaring coronavirus a public health emergency on 31 January. With the first COVID-related death on 29 February, the president declared a public health emergency on 13 March 2020 that remained in place until its expiration on 11 May 2023.

Excess deaths measured as the difference between expected deaths and recorded deaths began the week ending 28 March 2020. The spread of COVID-19 across the US reflected factors, such as the differences in the severity of lockdown measures between states that segmented along political lines. In terms of 25 deaths per 100,000 people, the northeast was hardest hit in March 2020 with peaks occurring in the midwest in

[1] In our econometric analysis we weight the two variables by a BHC's share of deposits in each state using deposit data obtained from the Summary of Deposits provided by the Federal Reserve Bank of Philadelphia. In Sect. 7.2 we analyse the unweighted data to provide a complete picture of the spread of COVID-19 across states.

[2] United States COVID - Coronavirus Statistics - Worldometer (worldometers.info).

December 2020; the south in winter 2020–21 and the west in January 2021.[3]

To illustrate the spread of the pandemic, we map the data that shows the number of cases of COVID-19 per 100,000 inhabitants by state. The analysis segments the number of cases into quartiles. The deepest blue colour indicates the largest number of cases and the lightest blue the least. The maps omit Alaska and Hawaii for presentational purposes.

Figure 7.1 shows the distribution of COVID-19 cases per 100,000 by state in Q2 2020. The legend shows that the quartile of least affected states had between 89.03 and 443.37 cases per 100,000 whereas the most affected states had between 917.88 and 1975.41 cases per 100,000. In Q2 2020, New York was the state with the highest number of cases (1975.41) followed by in rank order New Jersey (1869.89), Massachusetts (1550.54), Rhode Island (1533.71) and Connecticut (1291.96). The least affected states were Montana (89.03), West Virginia (162.25), Vermont (188.02), Oregon (205.00) and Maine (238.79).

A year later, the states with the highest number of cases were North Dakota (14,289.73), Rhode Island (13,929.50), South Dakota (13,908.79), Utah (12,438.98) and Arizona (12,298.46). Vermont, Oregon and Maine remained as the least affected alongside Washington (5861.84) and New Hampshire (7163.76). The legend indicates the severity of the pandemic. The cut-off point for the bottom quartile in Q2 2020 was 443.37 cases per 100,000 and for the upper quartile 917.88 cases. In Q2 2021, the corresponding numbers were 9670.12 and 11,286.05, respectively. To gauge the spread of COVID-19, we rank the states by cases per 100,000 in the second quarters of 2020 and 2021 and calculate the Spearman rank order correlation coefficient. The coefficient is 0.437 and significant from zero at the 1 per cent level (Fig. 7.2).

We use the State-Coincident Index from the Federal Reserve Bank of Philadelphia to proxy macroeconomic conditions across states. Table 7.1 shows the average of the index for the US as a whole from Q4 2019, the immediate pre-COVID-19 quarter, through Q2 2021. The index falls by more than 16% between Q4 2019 and Q2 2020. Although conditions subsequently improve quarter-by-quarter, the value of the index in Q2 2021 is just under two percentage points below its value in Q4 2019 (130.62 compared to 132.36). Berger and Demirgüç-Kunt (2021)

[3] How Covid shook the US: eight charts that capture the last two years | US news | The Guardian.

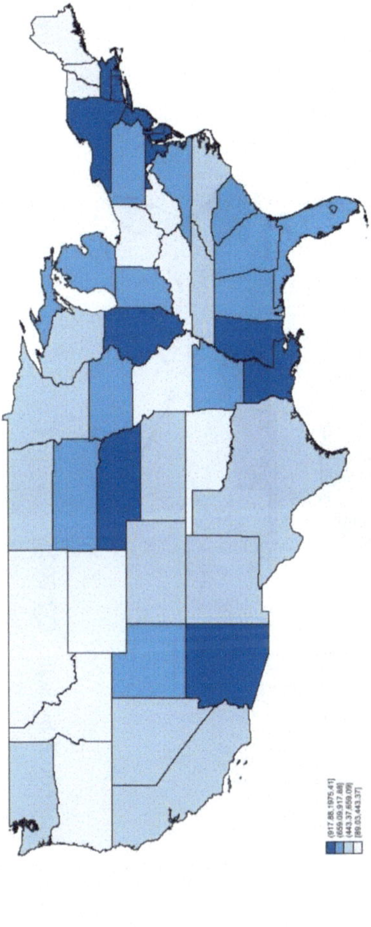

Fig. 7.1 Cases per 100,000; by State, Q2 2020

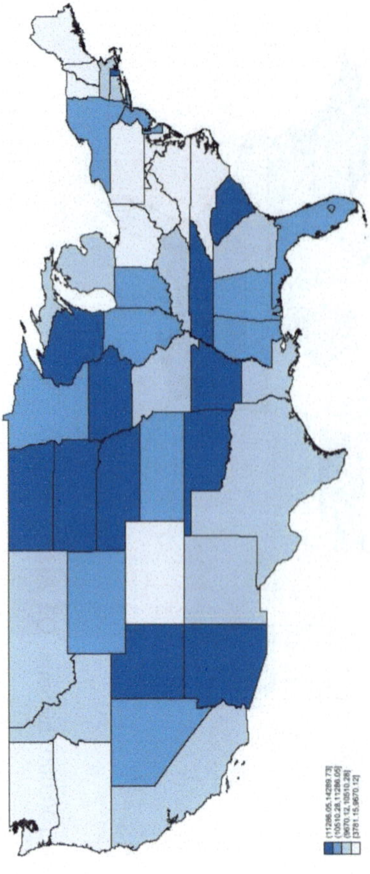

Fig. 7.2 Cases per 100,000; by State, Q2 2021

Table 7.1 Average macroeconomic conditions: by quarter

Quarters	*FRB Philadelphia State-Coincident Index*
2019 Q4	132.36
2020 Q1	132.60
2020 Q2	110.96
2020 Q3	120.11
2020 Q4	125.85
2021 Q1	128.59
2021 Q2	130.62

report that the National Bureau of Economic Research announced that the recession that began in February 2020 ended in April 2020, which made the two-month COVID-19 recession the shortest recession in the history of the US.

Table 7.2 reports results from a pairwise comparison of means. It shows a more detailed picture of the impact of the pandemic on macroeconomic conditions. The upper half of the table shows the contrasts (differences) between Q4 2019 and subsequent quarters to Q2 2021. The deterioration in macroeconomic conditions is economically largest between Q4 2019 and Q2 2020; the contrast is significant at the 1 per cent level.

The lower half of the table shows the difference-in-means on a quarter-by-quarter basis. Macroeconomic conditions bounced back between in the second half of 2020. The improvements are significant at the 1 per cent and 5 per cent levels, respectively. Although conditions did improve in 2021, the magnitude and significance of the quarterly changes diminished economically and statistically.

Lastly, we calculate the Spearman rank order correlation coefficient to show the relationship between macroeconomic conditions and cases per 100,000 by state for the second quarters of 2020 and 2021. The coefficients are -0.0646 and 0.1304 and neither are significant. In Q2 2021, California ranked ninth by the State-Coincident Index yet 34th by cases per 100,000. By contrast, Arizona ranked second and fifth, respectively. In explanation, we reiterate that the response of states to the pandemic was not uniform and varied in the severity of the measures implemented.

Table 7.2 Pairwise comparison of average macroeconomic conditions: by quarters

Quarters	*Contrast*	*Std error*	*t*	*P > |t|*	*[95% confidence interval]*	
2020 Q1 vs 2019 Q4	0.2375	2.2860	0.10	1.000	−7.46	7.93
2020 Q2 vs 2019 Q4	− 21.4022	2.2860	− 9.36	0.000	− 29.10	− 13.71
2020 Q3 vs 2019 Q4	− 12.2489	2.2860	− 5.36	0.000	− 19.94	− 4.55
2020 Q4 vs 2019 Q4	− 6.5159	2.2860	− 2.85	0.202	− 14.21	1.18
2021 Q1 vs 2019 Q4	− 3.7702	2.2860	− 1.65	0.932	− 11.46	3.92
2021 Q2 vs 2019 Q4	− 1.7456	2.2860	− 0.76	1.000	− 9.44	5.95
2020 Q2 vs 2020 Q1	− 21.6396	2.2860	− 9.47	0.000	− 29.33	− 13.95
2020 Q3 vs 2020 Q2	9.1533	2.2860	4.00	0.005	1.46	16.85
2020 Q4 vs 2020 Q3	5.7329	2.2860	2.51	0.404	− 1.96	13.43
2021 Q1 vs 2020 Q4	2.7458	2.2860	1.20	0.996	− 4.95	10.44
2021 Q2 vs 2021 Q1	2.0245	2.2860	0.89	1.000	− 5.67	9.72

7.3 Deposit Market Dynamics After the COVID-19 Shock

The nascent literature on the impact of the pandemic upon financial markets reports that a surge in bank deposits occurred during the first half of 2020 that was accompanied by a fall in deposit interest rates (Dossche & Zlatanos, 2020; Levine et al., 2021; Dursun-de Neef & Schandlbauer, 2022). Using data from our sample of BHCs, Fig. 7.3 shows the annualised growth in deposits (blue bars) and deposit interest rate (orange line) between Q2 2018 and Q2 2021. We calculate the growth rate as Q1 2020 over Q1 2019 and so forth. The vertical black line signals the beginning of the pandemic around the time when the first case of COVID-19 was reported in the US. Figure 7.3 shows that deposit growth oscillated mildly between Q2 2018 and Q4 2019 averaging 6.28

per cent. For this period, the average rate on interest-bearing deposits is 1.05 per cent.

Following the onset of the pandemic, deposit growth increases to 10.2 per cent in Q1 2020 before jumping sharply to roughly 44% in Q2 2020. Despite a temporary respite in Q3 2020, deposit growth surges in Q4 2020 (10.28 per cent) and Q1 2021 (20.10 per cent) before falling back in Q2 2021 (4.89 per cent). For the period Q1 2020 to Q1 2021, average deposit growth stood at 15.85 per cent. For the same period, the average interest rate is 0.52 per cent. Furthermore, and unlike deposit growth, interest rates continually fell from 0.98 per cent in Q1 2021 to 0.28 per cent in Q2 2021.

The extant albeit sparse literature has attempted to explain the observed behaviour in deposit markets following the onset of the pandemic, namely, the surge in deposits and fall in deposit rates. In explaining how an exogeneous shock affects deposits and deposit rates, Levine et al. (2021) consider five scenarios. First, the precautionary savings motive posits that the pandemic raised concerns over the security of jobs and incomes that caused households to save more with the surge in deposits driving down interest rates. Second, the flight to safety motive suggests that individuals reallocate their savings into safer investments like deposits. In this scenario, a larger increase in insured deposits and larger reductions in deposit rates at safer banks is expected. Third, the drawdown-and-deposit motives predict that corporations draw down pre-existing lines of credit for liquidity purposes and deposit the funds in banks; deposit growth works to drive down deposit rates. Fourth, the demand-for-deposits motive supposes that corporations draw down lines of credit, and that banks increase deposit rates to attract funds in order to provide liquidity. Fifth, the policy response motive proposes that expansionary macroeconomic policies implemented to mitigate the impact of the shock might boost deposits.

The detailed analysis presented by Levine et al. (2021) supports the precautionary savings motive because the evidence demonstrates that local COVID-19 infection rates are associated with heightened concerns over job security and expectations of losses of future income that caused current spending levels to decrease, and decreases in local deposit interest rates. Relatedly, Dursun-de Neef and Schandlbauer (2022) propose their "forced savings" hypothesis that contends that the pandemic prevented households from expending on items, such as leisure and travel. In

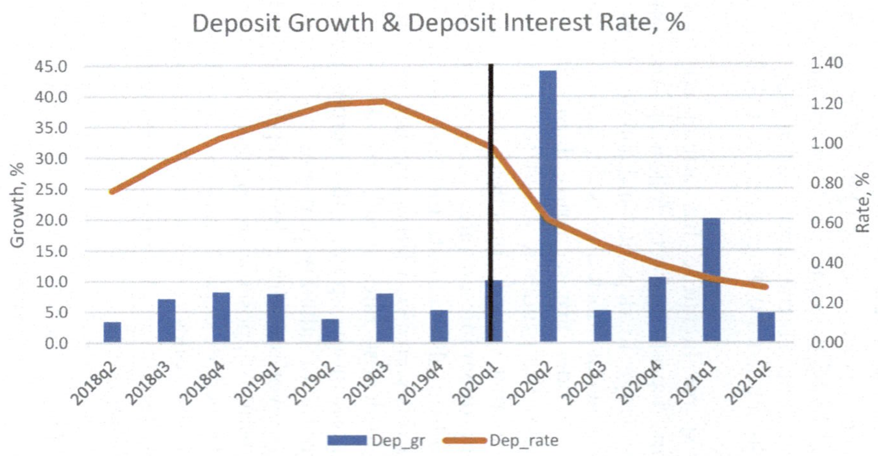

Fig. 7.3 The impact of COVID-19 on deposit markets (*Source* Author's calculations from (FR-Y9C fillings at the Federal Reserve Bank of Chicago)

support, they show that deposit growth was higher in regions that experienced larger reductions in saving. Dursun-de Neef and Schandlbauer (2022) note that the spread of COVID-19 across state lines varied in intensity and timing, and state governments responded by implementing nonpharmaceutical interventions, such as stay-at-home orders. We wish to emphasise two points. First, state-level interventions were heterogeneous in terms of type, location and timing (Abouk & Heydari, 2021). Second, the heterogeneity in interventions impacted banks differently, and while feeding precautionary saving (Levine et al., 2021) also attenuated spending on items like leisure activities that in turn caused significant economic losses (Dursun-de Neef & Schandlbauer, 2022).

We bring this section to a close by considering how the observed dynamics in deposit markets impacted the asset side of the balance sheet. Levine et al. (2021) emphasise the important role that banks play as providers of liquidity while Li et al. (2020) note that banks faced an unprecedented demand for liquidity during the pandemic as corporations drew down lines of credit. Li et al. report that the massive drawdown caused an explosion in commercial and industrial loans on bank balance sheets especially at the largest banks.[4] Analysing the last three weeks of March 2020, Li et al. (2020) find that all the increase in bank lending was attributable to drawdowns on existing credit commitments. Unsurprisingly, loan growth was greatest in areas with higher numbers of COVID-19 cases. The largest increases in lending were provided by large banks that had high levels of unused loan commitments. Furthermore, these banks could fund the demand for liquidity on the back of the massive inflows of deposits and cash, which are reported to have been twice the size of the aggregate increase in lending. In addition, Li et al. (2020) note that government interventions, such as quantitative easing and the Primary Dealer Credit Facility (introduced in March 2020) positively influenced the situation by opening up new supplies of liquidity to banks.

Beck and Keil (2022) corroborate the increase in overall bank lending during 2020. They find strong growth in small business lending on the

[4] On a weekly basis, the growth rate of commercial and industrial loans over the past 45 years averaged 0.12%. During the pandemic, in the last three weeks of March 2020 lending grew by over 6% per week. In comparison, around the time of Lehman Brothers collapse (last three weeks of October and first two weeks of November 2008), lending growth equalled 1.2% per week (Li et al., 2020).

back of government support through the Paycheck Protection Program (PPP introduced by the CARES Act of April 2020).[5] However, this development came at the expense of so-called regular lending that fell away in favour of government-supported lending. Beck and Keil find that syndicated lending exhibited the same trait as non-PPP small business lending with banks that were more exposed to the pandemic granting fewer and smaller syndicated loans and at wider spreads. The evidence in Beck and Keil (2022) shows that loan loss provisions (LLP) and nonperforming loans (NPL) increased in 2020 and were related to banks' exposure to lockdown policies, which we referenced above as varying varied across states.

Dursun-de Neef and Schandlbauer (2022) show that more exposed banks increased real estate lending if they were located in counties with a larger reduction in spending. The authors caution that this scenario mainly affected banks with higher capital ratios and banks located in counties with higher house prices. While our discussion is restricted to studies of the US banking system, we refer the reader to studies of European bank lending (Dursun-de Neef & Schandlbauer, 2021), bank lending on a global basis (Çolak & Öztekin, 2021) and cross-border lending (Park & Shin, 2021).

7.4 Corporate Social Responsibility, ESG Scores and Trust

Esteban-Sanchez et al. (2017) acknowledge the importance of the banking system and the increasing impact it has on society. Events, such as the Global Financial Crisis (GFC) and what seem like regular controversies are often perceived as the product of non-socially responsible behaviour. With corporate misbehaviour and unethical practices across industries frequently capturing the headlines, there is ever increasing pressure for corporations to demonstrate corporate social responsibility (CSR). Notwithstanding the fact that banking was one of the first industries to implement CSR programmes to protect its reputation, crises and scandals work to weaken the trust of customers in financial institutions like banks. Edmans (2023) acknowledges the intense interest on ESG

[5] PPP loans were made available by the Small Business Administration through banks to small businesses to encourage those businesses to retain or rehire furloughed workers. The loans would be forgiven upon certain conditions being met (Beck & Keil, 2022).

(environment, social and governance) principles notably by policymakers, investors and customers. As a result, a number of specialist firms have started to provide ESG scores. In response, studies are using ESG scores to proxy corporations' CSR performance or aspects of it; we shall review some of the empirical results in what follows.

Before so doing, we assess the business case for CSR/ESG from various theoretical perspectives to establish the possible effects on firm profitability, value and risk. The trade-off view suggests that prioritising CSR/ESG not only diverts firm resources, but requires substantial investment that can attenuate shareholder value creation (Aupperle et al., 1985). However, a risk mitigation view premises that investment in CSR/ESG constitutes an insurance for corporations by creating moral capital and goodwill among stakeholders (Chiaramonte et al., 2021). An agency perspective predicts that managers especially if they are entrenched face incentives to overinvest in CSR/ESG to extract private benefits and enhance personal reputation (Azmi et al., 2021; Chiaramonte et al., 2021; Jiraporn & Chintrakarn, 2013). Stakeholder theory posits a positive relationship between CSR/ESG and firm performance because non-ethical behaviour undermines trust that can produce unintended outcomes, such as regulatory sanctions or disrupting relationships with stakeholders including suppliers, financiers, employees and customers (Creyer & Ross, 1997; Freeman, 1984).

To assess the theoretical propositions we review some salient studies including of the banking industry. Asimakopoulos et al. (2023) review the notion that ESG can mitigate uncertainty. The evidence they review suggests that ESG scores reduce information asymmetry and improve access to capital markets for corporations. They also report that firms which have higher ESG scores are able to sustain a level of leverage without reducing borrowing in the face of increasing economic policy uncertainty, which leads to a smoother leverage pattern for corporations. A strand of evidence shows a positive relationship between commitment to CSR/ESG and firm value and firm profitability. It suggests that greater commitment improves customer loyalty, which implies willingness to pay more for higher CSR-related products leading to firm performance gains (Ailawadi et al., 2014; Du et al., 2011; Servaes & Tamayo, 2013). We consider a nascent strand of literature that discusses the role of trust in banking. A priori banks seek legitimacy by strategically prioritising commitment to CSR and achieving high ESG scores to enhance trust (Lins et al., 2017). By helping society banks can repair trust that is known to dissipate following an exogeneous shock like the GFC (Fungáčová et al., 2019).

The notion that higher ESG scores improve social capital is reported as the channel through which ESG affects bank performance outcomes. It implies that stronger CSR/ESG scores enhance the trust of customers especially after a shock. In support, several studies moslty surrounding the GFC show that higher CSR/ESG scoring banks realised superior performance (see, for instance, Cornett et al., 2016). Esteban-Sanchez et al. (2017) show that banks which adopt a strategic approach to corporate social performance (CSP) achieve better corporate financial performance following a shock. In a caveat to the main result, the authors note that some benefits to CSP manifest in the form of intangible assets with limited, if any, impact on short-term profitability. Therefore, CSP is thought of as a long-term performance variable. Chiaramonte et al. (2021) assess the joint and separate effects of E, S and G scores on the stability of a sample of European banks operating in 21 countries from 2005 to 2017. Consistent with results elsewhere, banks with higher total ESG scores or higher constituent scores are less exposed to financial fragility following a shock.

Li et al. (2022) investigate the effects of environment and social (ES) activities on bank stability. The authors draw their results from a large sample of commercial banks operating in over 50 countries between 2002 and 2020. Greater commitment to ES raises banks' social capital and enhances both trust and public confidence in bank oversight. As a result, higher ES scoring banks assume fewer risks during crisis episodes, which benefits financial stability. Using the same sample, Trinh et al. (2023) examine the relationship between CSR proxied by bank ES scores on tail risk. Their findings reaffirm other evidence that better ES performance works to mitigate the adverse effects of crises episodes in their case in the form of lower idiosyncratic risk and systematic tail risk following the 2008 GFC. Other evidence finds that higher ESG scoring banks realise higher profitability, fewer loan losses and higher equity values especially large banks (Bolton, 2013; Simpson & Kohers, 2002).

7.5 Deposit, Rates, ESG Scores and the Pandemic

The previous section has emphasised the role of trust in placating some of the adverse effects of an exogeneous shock. Our interest lies in the impact of the shock resulting from the COVID-19 pandemic on deposit markets.

Following Lins et al. (2017), we assume that banks prioritise achieving higher ESG scores to build trust. Our approach builds on the notion of depositor discipline. Since trust in banks is known to dissipate following an exogeneous shock, it is rational that during the pandemic depositors would assess banks' records on corporate responsibility and deem them a proxy for trust. Therefore, we hypothesise that following the onset of the pandemic, banks with higher ESG scores achieved faster deposit growth and paid lower rates than banks with poorer ESG scores. In other words, depositors assess ESG scores to reward and/or discipline banks following the shock. For our purposes, we utilise a natural experiment approach and panel fixed effects regressions to measure the impact of ESG scores on deposit markets. Equation (7.1) presents the baseline model:

$$Y_{i,t} = \alpha + \beta_1 Post_t + \beta_2 ESG_{i,t-4} + \beta_3 Post_t * ESG_{i,t-4} + \beta_4 X_{i,t-1} + \beta_5 Z_{i,t} + \gamma_t + \varphi_i + \varepsilon_{i,t} \quad (7.1)$$

Where i denotes bank and t quarter. Our dependent variable (Y) is the annualised quarterly growth rate of domestic deposits and the implicit annualised deposit rate paid by bank i on interest-bearing deposits. *Post* is a binary variable equal to unity for Q1 2020 and onwards, 0 otherwise. *ESG* is the ESG score sourced from Refinitiv and adjusted for firm-specific bad news. X is vector of six (lagged) bank-specific control variables to account for heterogeneity among BHCs. We select these variables from the extant literature. Z is vector of the two macroeconomic variables discussed earlier in this chapter. They control for the severity of banks' exposure to the health crisis and economic crisis. We augment the model with bank (φ) and quarter (γ) fixed effects to control for time-invariant unobserved heterogeneity at bank-level and time-varying shocks. Standard errors are clustered at bank level. Tables 7.3 and 7.4 show variable definitions and descriptive statistics.

Before presenting results from the econometric analysis, we briefly analyse the ESG scores. We segment the sample banks into quartiles and show the means of select variables for the full period from Q2 2018 to Q2 2021, and the two sub-periods before and after the shock. Table 7.5 shows that the average ESG score of banks in the upper quartile is 53.58 for the full period. In comparison, the mean ESG score for banks in the lower quartile is 23.61. The average ESG scores of banks in the second and third quartiles are 31.01 and 38.05, respectively. Table 7.5 shows

Table 7.3 Variable definitions

Interest-bearing deposit growth: annualised quarterly growth rate
Noninterest-bearing deposit growth: annualised quarterly growth rate
Deposit rate: annualised implicit interest rate
ESG: combined ESG score from Refinitiv Asset4 adjusted for firm-specific bad news
Size: total assets (logarithm)
Capitalisation: total equity capital/total assets
NPL ratio: total loans & leases past due 90 days or more & still accruing + nonaccruals/total loans & leases
Cash: noninterest-bearing balances and currency and coin + interest-bearing balances in U.S. offices + interest-bearing balances in foreign offices, Edge and Agreement subsidiaries and IBFs/total assets
Diversification: 1—∑ (interest income / total income) ^2 + (noninterest income/ total income)^2
Unused commitments: revolving, open-end loans secured by 1–4 family residential properties + commitments to fund commercial real estate, construction and land development loans secured by real estate + commitments to fund commercial real estate, construction and land development loans NOT secured by real estate + commercial and similar letters of credit + other unused commitments (commercial loans + loans to financial institutions + all other unused commitments)/unused commitments (as in numerator) + total loans and leases
COVID-19 exposure: average of new COVID-19-related deaths per 100,000 inhabitants where a bank is physically present weighted by its share of deposits in each state
Macroeconomic conditions: average of the FRB Philadelphia's state-coincident index in states where a bank is physically present weighted by its share of deposits in each state

Table 7.4 Descriptive statistics; N = 1755

	Mean	*Std dev*	*Min*	*Max*
Interest-bearing deposit growth	10.03	20.23	−36.89	123.45
Noninterest-bearing deposit growth	19.29	43.18	−99.81	203.75
Deposit rate	0.80	0.53	0.06	2.23
ESG	37.14	12.64	12.77	80.45
Size	16.43	1.50	14.24	21.58
Capitalisation	11.31	2.28	6.28	17.36
NPL	6.05	4.94	0.93	24.41
Cash	0.31	0.11	0.04	0.50
Diversification	0.34	0.11	0.04	0.50
Unused commitments	21.44	8.04	0.75	42.09
COVID-19 exposure	15.85	24.75	0.00	159.14
Macroeconomic conditions	128.89	12.35	80.42	155.92

unambiguously that the better ESG scoring banks are the largest institutions by a substantial margin while banks in the lowest and second quartiles are similarly sized.

Comparing the pre- and post-shock periods reveals that the average ESG scores differ little across intervals. However, some common features emerge. Across quartiles, interest-bearing deposit growth increases following the shock and marginally more so for banks in the lowest and second quartiles. In all quartiles the average bank experienced an increase in noninterest-bearing deposits by more than 30 per cent. Lastly, we find that banks in the third and upper quartiles reduced deposit rates of interest more than their smaller counterparts.

The results of the econometric analysis are shown in Table 7.6. We estimate the baseline model separately for the three dependent variables: noninterest-bearing deposit growth; interest-bearing deposit growth and the deposit interest rate. The coefficient β_1 on the variable *Post* shows the direct effect of the shock on deposit growth and the deposit rate. It measures the average changes in the deposit growth and rate variables from the pre-shock to post-shock periods that are common to banks. Columns (1) and (2) identify economically meaningful increases in noninterest-bearing deposits and interest-bearing deposits following the outbreak of the pandemic. The increase in interest-bearing deposit growth is significant at the 10 per cent level. Column (3) shows a decrease in deposit rates for all banks following the shock that is significant at the 1 per cent level. The coefficient β_2 on the variable *ESG* captures the direct effect of ESG scores on deposit outcomes across Q2 2018 to Q2 2021. None of the β_2 coefficients are statistically meaningful. It suggests that across the full period, depositors did not differentiate banks by ESG scores statistically speaking.

The coefficient β_3 on the interaction term *ESG * Post* is our main interest. It captures the effect of ESG scores on deposit outcomes following the shock and identifies if depositors used ESG scores to discipline banks during the pandemic-induced surge in bank deposits. Our results show that noninterest-bearing deposit growth at higher ESG scoring banks increased significantly at the 5 per cent level post-shock (column 1). However, the growth of interest-bearing deposits experienced a significant contraction at the 10 per cent level (column 2). The results show that higher ESG scoring banks had significantly lower deposit rates at the 1 per cent level following the shock (column 3). Our evidence suggests that after controlling for various bank-level

Table 7.5 ESG scores; by quartiles

	ESG	*Assets, $000*	*Interest-bearing deposit growth, %*	*Noninterest-bearing deposit growth, %*	*Deposit rate, %*
			Quartile 1		
Q2 2018–Q2 2021	23.61	8,507,873	13.19	20.90	0.87
Q2 2018–Q4 2019	23.47	6,905,625	12.92	13.15	1.08
Q1 2020–Q2 2021	23.80	10,766,749	13.56	32.10	0.57
			Quartile 2		
Q2 2018–Q2 2021	31.01	10,116,049	10.63	18.91	0.83
Q2 2018–Q4 2019	31.14	10,292,755	9.55	6.96	1.04
Q1 2020–Q2 2021	30.80	10,219,465	11.15	33.27	0.55
			Quartile 3		
Q2 2018–Q2 2021	38.05	68,008,640	10.77	20.52	0.80
Q2 2018–Q4 2019	37.92	67,620,504	10.70	9.91	1.01
Q1 2020–Q2 2021	38.27	68,535,482	10.77	34.38	0.48
			Quartile 4		
Q2 2018–Q2 2021	53.58	274,228,695	10.10	20.06	0.73
Q2 2018–Q4 2019	54.19	293,611,886	10.34	2.33	1.07

(continued)

Table 7.5 (continued)

	ESG	*Assets, $000*	*Interest-bearing deposit growth, %*	*Noninterest-bearing deposit growth, %*	*Deposit rate, %*
Q1 2020–Q2 2021	53.13	261,068,623	10.38	34.79	0.47
Q2 2018–Q2 2021	36.55	87,284,177	10.75	20.13	0.81

factors and the effects of the health crisis and economic crisis, depositors reward higher ESG scoring banks with significantly faster noninterest-bearing deposit growth and acceptance of significantly lower deposit rates of interest. Furthermore, we contend that the significant reduction in interest-bearing deposit growth at higher ESG scoring banks reflects the fact that falling deposit rates continually lessened the opportunity cost of holding relatively safer noninterest-bearing deposits.

7.6 Conclusions

This chapter has investigated deposit market dynamics following the shock emanating from the COVID-19 pandemic. We assess whether depositors use ESG scores that proxy for trust to discipline banks. Our rich analysis has documented the spread of COVID-19 across the US and the impact on the macroeconomic conditions of states. We review the nascent extant literature on the impact of COVID-19 on banking and an emerging strand of literature that considers the role of trust in banking. Accordingly, we develop a hypothesis, which posits that depositors discipline banks using the information content of ESG scores to proxy trust following the pandemic-induced shock. Our econometric results unequivocally show that depositors reward higher ESG scoring banks with faster growth of noninterest-bearing deposits and acceptance of lower deposit interest rates.

Table 7.6 Estimated relationships between deposit growth and rate and ESG scores

	(1)	*(2)*	*(3)*
	Noninterest-bearing deposit growth	Interest-bearing deposit growth	Deposit interest rate
Post	9.052	6.918*	−0.493***
	(6.969)	(3.719)	(0.066)
ESG_{t-4}	− 0.004	− 0.040	0.002
	(0.172)	(0.128)	(0.002)
Post x ESG_{t-4}	0.233**	− 0.133*	− 0.004***
	(0.099)	(0.069)	(0.001)
$Size_{t-1}$	− 16.534*	− 13.688**	− 0.092
	(8.853)	(6.840)	(0.103)
$Capitalisation_{t-1}$	− 0.391	1.366	0.003
	(1.319)	(1.031)	(0.012)
NPL_{t-1}	− 0.722	− 5.524***	− 0.092***
	(2.698)	(1.938)	(0.032)
$Cash_{t-1}$	− 0.863**	− 0.575**	0.013***
	(0.355)	(0.244)	(0.004)
$Diversification_{t-1}$	31.616	− 33.026	− 0.138
	(34.410)	(21.314)	(0.204)
Unused $commitments_{t-1}$	0.230	0.506	0.008
	(0.663)	(0.344)	(0.006)
COVID-19 exposure	0.136	− 0.024	− 0.001**
	(0.087)	(0.038)	(0.000)
Macroeconomic conditions	0.318	0.038	− 0.003
	(0.272)	(0.144)	(0.002)
Constant	224.062	218.003*	2.649
	(141.925)	(116.655)	(1.651)
Quarter fixed effects	Yes	Yes	Yes
Observations	1755	1755	1755
Adjusted R^2	0.419	0.128	0.842

Note The dependent variables are the annualised quarterly growth rate of noninterest-bearing and interest-bearing deposits (columns 1 and 2, respectively) and the annualised interest rate on deposits (column 3). Robust standard errors clustered by banks are in parentheses

∗ , ∗ ∗ and ∗ ∗ ∗ denote statistical significance at 10%, 5% and 1%, respectively

References

Abouk, R., & Heydari, B. (2021). The immediate effect of COVID-19 policies on social-distancing behavior in the United States. *Public Health Reports, 136*(2), 245–252.

Ailawadi, K. L., Neslin, S. A., Luan, Y. J., & Taylor, G. A. (2014). Does retailer CSR enhance behavioral loyalty? A case for benefit segmentation. *International Journal of Research in Marketing, 31*(2), 156–167.

Asimakopoulos, S., Wese Simen, C., & Vivian, A. (2023). Sustainable finance and governance: An overview. *European Journal of Finance*. https://doi.org/10.1080/1351847X.2023.2251532

Aupperle, K. E., Carroll, A. B., & Hatfield, J. D. (1985). An empirical examination of the relationship between corporate social responsibility and profitability. *Academy of Management Journal, 28*(2), 446–463.

Azmi, W., Hassan, M. K., Houston, R., & Karim, M. S. (2021). ESG activities and banking performance: International evidence from emerging economies. *Journal of International Financial Markets, Institutions and Money, 70*, 101277.

Berger, A. N., & Demirgüç-Kunt, A. (2021). Banking research in the time of COVID-19. *Journal of Financial Stability, 57*, 100939.

Beck, T., & Keil, J. (2022). Have banks caught corona? Effects of COVID on lending in the US. *Journal of Corporate Finance, 72*, 102160.

Bolton, B. J. (2013). *Corporate Social Responsibility and Bank Performance*. https://doi.org/10.2139/ssrn.2277912

Chiaramonte, L., Dreassi, A., Girardone, C., & Piserà, S. (2021). Do ESG strategies enhance bank stability during financial turmoil? Evidence from Europe. *European Journal of Finance, 28*(12), 1173–1211.

Çolak, G., & Öztekin, Ö. (2021). The impact of COVID-19 pandemic on bank lending around the world. *Journal of Banking & Finance, 133*, 106207.

Cornett, M. M., Erhemjamts, O., & Tehranian, H. (2016). Greed or good deeds: An examination of the relation between corporate social responsibility and the financial performance of US commercial banks around the financial crisis. *Journal of Banking & Finance, 70*, 137–159.

Creyer, E. H., & Ross, W. T., Jr. (1997). Tradeoffs between price and quality: How a value index affects. *Journal of Consumer Affairs, 31*(2), 280–302.

Dossche, M., Zlatanos, S. (2020). COVID-19 and the increase in household savings: Precautionary or forced? Economic Bulletin Boxes, 6.

Du, S., Bhattacharya, C. B., & Sen, S. (2011). Corporate social responsibility and competitive advantage: Overcoming the trust barrier. *Management Science, 57*(9), 1528–1545.

Dursun-de Neef, H. Ö., & Schandlbauer, A. (2021). COVID-19 and lending responses of European banks. *Journal of Banking & Finance, 133*, 106236. https://doi.org/10.1016/j.jbankfin.2021.106236

Dursun-de Neef, H. Ö., & Schandlbauer, A. (2022). COVID-19, bank deposits, and lending. *Journal of Empirical Finance, 68*, 20–33.

Edmans, A. (2023). The end of ESG. *Financial Management, 52*, 3–17.

Esteban-Sanchez, P., de la Cuesta-Gonzalez, M., & Paredes-Gazquez, J. D. (2017). Corporate social performance and its relation with corporate financial performance: International evidence in the banking industry. *Journal of Cleaner Production, 162*, 1102–1110.

Freeman, E. (1984). *Strategic management: A stakeholder approach*. Pitman.

Fungáčová, Z., Hasan, I., & Weill, L. (2019). Trust in banks. *Journal of Economic Behavior and Organization, 157*, 452–476.

Jiraporn, P., & Chintrakarn, P. (2013). How do powerful CEOs view corporate social responsibility (CSR)? *An Empirical Note. Economics Letters, 119*(3), 344–347.

Levine, R., Lin, C., Tai, M., & Xie, W. (2021). How did depositors respond to COVID-19? *Review of Financial Studies, 34*(11), 5438–5473.

Li, L., Strahan, P. E., & Zhang, S. (2020). Banks as lenders of first resort: Evidence from the COVID-19 crisis. *Review of Corporate Finance Studies, 9*(3), 472–500.

Li, T., Trinh, V.Q., Elnahass, M. (2022). Drivers of global banking stability in times of crisis: The role of corporate social responsibility. *British Journal of Management, 0*, 1–28. https://doi.org/10.1111/1467-8551.12631

Lins, K. V., Servaes, H., & Tamayo, A. (2017). Social capital, trust, and firm performance: The value of corporate social responsibility during the financial crisis. *Journal of Finance, 72*(4), 1785–1824.

Park, C. Y., & Shin, K. (2021). COVID-19, nonperforming loans, and cross-border bank lending. *Journal of Banking & Finance, 133*, 106233.

Servaes, H., & Tamayo, A. (2013). The impact of corporate social responsibility on firm value: The role of customer awareness. *Management Science, 59*(5), 1045–1061.

Simpson, W. G., & Kohers, T. (2002). The link between corporate social and financial performance: Evidence from the banking industry. *Journal of Business Ethics, 35*(2), 97–109.

Trinh, V. Q., Cao, N. D., Li, T., & Elnahass, M. (2023). Social capital, trust, and bank tail risk: The value of ESG rating and the effects of crisis shocks. *Journal of International Financial Markets, Institutions & Money, 83*, 101740.

CHAPTER 8

Do Individual Investors Drive Volatility? Evidence from the Robintrack Dataset

Timothy King and Ville Valkama

8.1 Introduction

Individual investors are often linked to volatility. Theoretical models suggest that individual investors, acting as noise traders, significantly affect volatility, and empirical studies have established a positive relationship between retail trading and volatility. In recent years, increased retail investor participation in the financial markets has occurred. The growth in participation has been influenced by newcomers in the financial services industry and facilitated by removing barriers to entry for retail investors and barriers to trading. An example that highlights this trend is the substantial growth of an electronic trading platform called Robinhood, which offers investors commission-free equity trading and investing. The

T. King (✉) · V. Valkama
School of Accounting and Finance, University of Vaasa, Vaasa, Finland
e-mail: timothy.king@uwasa.fi

V. Valkama
e-mail: a111037@student.uwasa.fi

T. King and J. Williams (eds.), *Corporate Governance in the Banking and Financial Sector*, Palgrave Macmillan Studies in Banking and Financial Institutions, https://doi.org/10.1007/978-3-031-83353-3_8

Robinhood trading application (app) disrupted the brokerage industry by introducing zero-commission trades, eliminating account minimums, and providing a user-friendly app that integrated gamification elements (Eaton et al., 2022). As a zero-commission brokerage, Robinhood generates revenue through premium services, securities lending, and payment for order flow, where user orders are forwarded to market makers for execution in return for a commission for the broker (Pagano et al., 2021).

Understanding the relationship between individual ownership and volatility is vital as individual investor participation in financial markets increases. Indeed, investigating the relationship between individual investors and volatility is a continuing concern within finance (Aharon et al., 2022; Baig et al., 2023; Foucault et al., 2011; Kyröläinen, 2008). However, studies on analyzing ownership have largely been limited to institutional investors. A possible reason is that the research on changes in institutional ownership for U.S. stocks has been made more accessible by the requirement for institutional investment managers to file Form 13F quarterly with the Securities and Exchange Commission. Representative of the literature on institutional investors, Sias (1996) shows that institutional investors tend to be attracted to stocks with higher volatility, even when controlling for company size. Moreover, he argues that while the increase in volatility does not attract institutional investors, their actions may contribute to increased volatility.

In contrast to the wide availability of institutional ownership data, micro-data related to individual investors' ownership of stocks has thus far been limited to proprietary sources. However, the new Robintrack dataset makes this type of data openly accessible to researchers and allows for re-examination of key findings from the institutional investor literature. The Robintrack dataset, which is publicly available, provides unique data that allows researchers to examine the behavior of individual investors in the stock market. This dataset includes information on daily changes in retail investor ownership in securities available at Robinhood.

To date, this rich dataset has been used in a growing number of studies, such as Barber et al. (2022) and Welch (2022). Using herding events, Barber et al. (2022) explore how attention-induced trading differs between Robinhood users and other retail traders. Welch (2022) examines Robinhood investors by evaluating the Robinhood consensus portfolio's performance using various models, including the Fama and French (2015) five-factor model. Researchers have also utilized the dataset to explore many aspects of retail investor behaviors and their impacts, including volatility. Aharon et al. (2022) investigate the impact of Robinhood investor trading on the volatility of American depositary receipts (ADRs) and find that Robinhood investors activity can intensify the cross-listed volatility of ADRs. Eaton et al. (2022) examine the behavior of Robinhood retail investors and conclude that, since changes in ownership are unrelated to future returns, they act like noise traders. Similarly, Pagano et al. (2021) find evidence that Robinhood investors exhibit both momentum and contrarian trading strategies, which is similar to recent findings for cryptocurrency markets (King & Koutmos, 2021). Eaton et al. (2021) find that a negative shock to the participation of Robinhood investors are associated with improvements in market liquidity and reduced market order imbalances and lower volatility of stock returns. Ozik et al. (2021) show that the trading activity of retail investors spikes in periods where investors have more free time such as during the COVID-19 pandemic, and that this increase in activity is associated with substantial increases in market illiquidity. Bryzgalova et al. (2023) offer a first attempt to study the options trading behavior of Robinhood retail investors using a novel measure they develop and show that such investors trade options for speculative purposes. Finally, Moss et al. (2024) analyze whether retail investors care about environmental, social, and governance (ESG) press releases, and find no evidence that ESG influences trading choices.

However, although these are important emergent findings that shed more light on the trading decisions of retail investors, the Robintrack dataset has yet to be utilized in prior studies to empirically study the volatility of ordinary shares, which is the focus of this chapter. Furthermore, financial literature on the relationship between investor ownership and volatility has typically focused on how institutional investor ownership affects and is affected by volatility, rather than the role of retail investors (e.g., Sias, 1996). To this goal, this chapter aims to address gaps in the existing literature by employing data from the Robinhood trading platform. Specifically, we utilize the Robintrack dataset to examine how volatility might influence or be impacted by individual investor ownership. We do so by adapting the core methodology of Sias (1996) to study institutional investors to the setting of individual retail investors to explore the relationship between individual investor ownership and intraday volatility.

In preview, we present several important findings that enhance the literature by providing early evidence of the impact of individual retail investors on Robinhood on volatility. Utilizing both non-parametric methods and linear regressions to study a sample of 3765 ordinary retail investor stocks, our main findings show that individual investor interest is associated with increased volatility, regardless of market capitalization. We conclude that, first, highly volatile securities can attract individual investors, while, second, increases in individual investor holdings can lead to higher volatility. The tendency for investors to maintain under-diversified portfolios could explain volatility as Robinhood investors, on average, own concentrated portfolios. Furthermore, a tendency towards risk aversion during uncertain periods may explain observed patterns of highest ownership percentages in both low and high-volatility stocks.

The rest of the chapter proceeds as follows. Section 8.2 reviews the relevant literature and presents the main study hypothesis. Section 8.3 discusses the study data and methodology. Section 8.4 presents the results and associated discussion. Section 8.5 concludes.

8.2 Literature Review and Hypothesis Development

The Behavior of Individual Investors

There is a large volume of published studies describing individual investor behavior. The literature can be generally organized under three general headings: the performance of individual investors, individual investors' risk preferences, and individual investors' risk management. We can gain insights into individual investor ownership by examining empirical literature on individual investor behaviors related to buying and selling. Conversely, studying individual investors' risk preferences can help us understand whether individual investors are attracted to volatility. Finally, exploring literature on how individual investors manage risks will give us insights into how individuals act on and react to risk.

The performance of individual investors has been a subject of interest in financial research for a considerable amount of time. Early studies include Schlarbaum et al. (1978a) who study the stock performance of investors at a full-service brokerage firm, and Schlarbaum et al. (1978b) who examine the profitability of common stock trades by individual investors. Additionally, early evidence supports the notion that individual investors tend to have more influence on stocks with smaller market capitalizations (Kumar & Lee, 2006; Nofsinger & Sias, 1999), which suggests controlling for the size of stocks is important.

The first comprehensive study of the overall performance of self-managed individual investors was done by Barber and Odean (2000), who present evidence consistent with active trading being harmful for investors. Grinblatt and Keloharju (2001), and later Barber and Odean (2013), argue that transaction costs partially explain poor investing performance. In addition, it has been documented that individual investors have poor stock selection abilities (Barber & Odean, 2013). Furthermore, Brandt et al. (2010) find higher idiosyncratic volatility levels in stocks held primarily by retail investors. The authors also demonstrate that events likely to attract the attention of retail investors lead to changes in volatility, which is also consistent with Barber et al. (2008).

The literature also highlights notable patterns in investor behavior across time. Barber et al. (2008) demonstrate that individual investors' buying and selling behaviors, observed through small trades, are highly correlated over time. These retail trade patterns forecast future returns in the short term, where trades impact stock prices, and in the long term, where small stocks are most affected. Similarly, Kumar and Lee (2006) show that individual investors' buying and selling behavior has a common directional component and that correlations exist in return comovements. Furthermore, Kelley and Tetlock (2013) find that daily buy-sell imbalances from retail orders usually indicate monthly stock returns, with trends persisting for up to a year.

The disposition effect (i.e., the tendency for investors to sell assets that have experiences increases in value) and tax-loss selling have also been found to significantly influence the decisions of retail investors to sell a stock, as shown by Grinblatt and Keloharju (2001), among others. As explained by Odean (1998), investors may choose to keep some losing investments and sell winning ones because they expect that current losers will perform better than winners in the future. However, these beliefs could be considered rational if the expected future returns for losing investments are higher than those for winners. Conversely, the beliefs are irrational if individual investors persist in holding losing investments despite evidence showing that winners have higher expected returns.

Many investors maintain concentrated portfolios despite portfolio theory advocating for diversified holdings. As Dorn and Huberman (2005) describe, investors often hold no more than three stocks even when affordable mutual funds offer an easy diversification option. Barber et al. (2022) calculate, based on 2020 statistics, that Robinhood users typically hold about three stock positions. Thus, in this case, Robinhood users represent the underdiversified investors described by Dorn and Huberman (2005).

Diversification, although beneficial, limits the potential for high returns. Investors with a strong desire for upside potential may forego diversification in pursuit of a chance for substantial gains. Mitton and Vorkink (2007) suggest that skewness-diversification trade-offs affect portfolio formation and asset prices. Theoretical modeling shows that a preference for skewness can lead to a lack of diversification. Empirical evidence indicates that underdiversified investors experience higher skewness in returns. Thus, investors intentionally select stocks to enhance skewness and prefer higher return skewness over traditional mean–variance portfolio construction. Balasubramaniam et al. (2023) attempt to explain a lack of relative diversification by investors with their individual preferences for characteristics such as market capitalization, turnover, beta, book-to-market, volatility, and skewness, which can all significantly influence investors' choices. These characteristics create similar investor clusters. In addition, individual investors are susceptible to influence from geographical location, traditional media, and social media, as Barber and Odean (2013) and Eaton et al. (2022) suggest.

Dorn and Huberman (2005) argue that many investors adopt a sequential stock-picking approach rather than optimizing their portfolio in totality, as suggested by modern portfolio theory (Markowitz, 1952). According to Dorn and Huberman (2005), this behavior is attributable to difficulties in fully optimizing portfolios and a tendency to focus narrowly on individual choices rather than on their combined impact. They assert that while investors might neglect optimal diversification strategies, their choices are not random; risk-averse investors systematically select lower-volatility stocks, and portfolio adjustments often lead to improved diversification when new funds are contributed. Thus, individual investors rely on heuristics that reflect their risk preferences and may only sometimes follow optimal portfolio construction principles.

One possible explanation as to why individual investors may be attracted to more volatile stocks could be the propensity to gamble. Kumar (2009) indicates that on an aggregate level, individual investors tend to favor stocks with characteristics resembling lotteries, with low-priced stocks exhibiting high skewness and volatility likely to be perceived as lottery-type investments.

The prevalence of high-risk, high-volatility investment options on trading platforms may give gamblers an alternative means to experience similar sensations to gambling by engaging in excessive trading (Kumar, 2009). However, as Kostopoulos et al. (2022) show, during periods of increased ambiguity investors tend to exhibit less risk-taking behavior, which persists over time. Furthermore, their result supports the idea that sentiment effects are amplified when ambiguity is high. Kostopoulos et al. (2022) also show that more ambiguity-averse investors react strongly to increases in ambiguity by reducing their exposures to the stock market.

Summarizing the main findings of the studies reviewed in this section suggests that several behavioral factors can affect the relationship between individual investors and volatility. First, the combination of a tendency of individual investors to hold under-diversified portfolios and to engage in active trading may contribute to significant daily changes in individual investor holdings which are statistically observable using a daily time frame. Second, the preference to sell winning investments and a reluctance to sell losing investments suggests that a stock's past performance and perceived risk may influence levels of individual investor ownership. Third, individual investors have poor stock selection abilities and are susceptible to behavioral biases, including local bias and media influence. These factors in combination could cause volatility or ownership of stocks to be influenced by volatility. Finally, individual investors are attracted to more volatile stocks and may seek sensations comparable to gambling in the stock market.

Measures of Volatility

Volatility represents fluctuations in stock prices commonly driven by unforeseen news related to a company's performance (Venkatachalam, 2000). Volatility metrics derived from historical price data fall into three primary groups: absolute residuals, realized volatility, and historical volatility (Blasco et al., 2012). As one of the components of mean–variance analysis, volatility is a focal point in financial analyses.

Realized volatility is vital in understanding market behaviors and how accurately volatility is estimated. The work by Merton (1980) set a precedent for accurately estimating volatility using fixed interval data, emphasizing that shorter intervals reduce estimation errors, given that price movements follow a geometric Brownian motion. French et al. (1987) highlight the accuracy of monthly standard deviation estimators for stock market returns. Instead of rolling 12-month standard deviation estimators used in previous research, their methodology accounted for the non-constant nature of stock return volatility and autocorrelation in daily returns due to non-synchronous trading, offering a more precise estimation by focusing on within-month returns. Schwert (1989) extended this approach, using daily and weekly data to estimate monthly standard deviations in stock returns, reinforcing that non-overlapping samples minimize estimation errors through time. Andersen et al. (2001) build on these earlier studies, emphasizing the importance of high-frequency data in the construction of daily, rather than monthly, realized stock volatilities and underscoring the significance of advancing towards finer, high-frequency observations to estimate volatility more accurately. This method implies that as the time between observations shortens, the accuracy of estimation increases as continuous-time diffusion processes facilitate more precise measurements of volatility.

Various studies have delved into the concept of absolute volatility in stock returns. Schwert (1990) outlines the persistent nature of stock return volatility, its tendency to rise following market downturns, and its relationship with macroeconomic factors. Using a similar methodology to French et al. (1987), Schwert (1990) employs past returns and day-of-the-week factors to estimate short-term changes in expected returns, and absolute residuals to estimate stock return variability, assuming a normal distribution of returns. Following Schwert (1990), Jones et al. (1994), Chan and Fong (2000), and Avramov et al. (2006) each employ similar models which incorporate absolute residuals from regressions, including lagged returns and day-of-the-week dummies to capture stock return volatility. These studies control for serial dependence in daily returns while exploring the effects of trade size, order imbalance, and sell-initiated transactions on daily stock volatility. Avramov et al. (2006) also include normalized sell-initiated transactions in their regression analysis as a control variable, with the goal of better understanding the influence of trading dynamics on volatility.

Historical volatility measures, mainly through range-based measures, evolved substantially with contributions from Parkinson (1980) and Garman and Klass (1980). Parkinson (1980) introduced an approach for estimating historical volatility by considering the maximum and minimum daily prices of assets. They assert that extreme price data could offer valuable insights that can help better understand volatility, particularly in predicting future volatility due to its mean-reverting nature. Garman and Klass (1980) suggest a method to estimate historical volatility using opening and closing prices and extreme prices. Their method reflects an understanding that detailed market movement data, like range-based and extreme data points, can estimate volatility more accurately than models using just open and close prices. Thus, capturing all intraday price movements is important for reliable volatility estimation. Subsequent studies and methodologies, such as those by Beckers (1983), Andersen and Bollerslev (1998), Yang and Zhang (2000), and Alizadeh et al. (2002), further validate and expand upon the initial concepts of Parkinson (1980) and Garman and Klass (1980).

Kyröläinen (2008) argues that range-based volatility is a better proxy than absolute or squared returns because range-based volatility measures have lower variance in measurement errors and accurately reflect intraday price variation and are more robust against bid-ask bounce. Thus, they may be a more efficient volatility proxy than realized volatility, which can be biased due to the sum of squared high-frequency returns. Baig et al. (2023) show that the Alizadeh et al. (2002) range-based measure has a correlation of about 48% with the GARCH(1,1) volatility measure. They propose that a range-based measure is a more dynamic measure of daily stochastic volatility. Hence, the range-based method is well suited for examining Robinhood users' behavior due to its ability to account for intraday price variations, which matches with the pattern of active and daily monitoring of stocks commonly seen among Robinhood users.

Investor Types and Volatility

Previous research connects individual investors to volatility, primarily through noise trading, herding and deviations from the decision-making processes expected by the rational choice theory. Much of the contemporary volatility literature examines either institutional or individual investors. The prevalent approach in many studies revolves around a classification scheme derived from noise trader models, which delineates between sophisticated investors—typically institutional investors—and noise traders, predominantly represented by individual investors.

Sias (1996), who examines the relationship between institutional investors and volatility directly, closely concerns the hypothesis made in this chapter; albeit the focus of Sias (1996) is on institutional investors rather than retail investors—the focus of this chapter. Sias (1996) proposes two hypotheses to explain the direct relationship between institutional investors and volatility. The first hypothesis posits that securities with greater volatility attract institutional investors. The second hypothesis posits that increased institutional holdings lead to increased volatility. Sias (1996) finds that institutional investor interest may induce volatility and that institutional investors are associated with higher levels of volatility when firm capitalization is held constant. The results support the second but not the first hypothesis, since they imply that institutional investors are more likely to sell stocks that experience increases in volatility. Similarly, research by Bushee and Noe (2000) shows that institutional investors are more likely to invest in stocks with higher volatility, and an increase in their holdings often leads to an increase in volatility. Dennis and Strickland (2002) find that on days of large market returns, mutual funds evaluated on short performance can significantly impact stock prices more than individual investors. Factors such as growth investing, as well as the rise of NASDAQ trading, contribute to increased idiosyncratic volatility (Dennis & Strickland, 2002). Greenwood and Thesmar (2011) argue that liquidity shocks associated with institutional ownership concentration or dispersion can lead to increased volatility. Bushee (1998, 2001) and Bushee and Noe (2000) utilize a classification for institutional investor types. They find that differences in investment strategies and preferences in dedicated institutions, quasi-indexers, and transient institutions impact firm management and future value distribution.

The literature on individual investor influence on volatility is extensive and focuses mainly on trading. Empirical studies by Kyröläinen (2008), Foucault et al. (2011), Aharon et al. (2022), and Baig et al. (2023) suggest that retail trading is associated with volatility, which is consistent with theoretical noise trading models. Kyröläinen (2008) demonstrates a positive relationship between individual investor trading and volatility and finds that this effect remains consistent across different periods and individual stocks. Findings further infer that less informed individual trades might impact volatility more than informed institutional trades. Foucault et al. (2011) investigate the impact of specific regulatory changes in France on stock market. Their results indicate that reforms raise trading expenses, resulting in a decrease in retail investor activity. In turn, volatility declined, thereby suggesting that retail trading contributes positively to volatility. These results also imply that the destabilizing impact of retail momentum trades could outweigh the potentially stabilizing effects of contrarian retail trades. Additionally, evidence shows contrarian trades contribute to volatility. Along the same lines, Aharon et al. (2022) find that Robinhood's trading activity negatively affects the stability of cross-listed securities. Their findings are aligned with previous studies which demonstrate how uninformed investors can negatively impact the stability and efficiency of financial and capital markets. Finally, a more recent study by Baig et al. (2023) shows that individual investor marketable buy and sell retail trades lead to increased volatility during crises.

In contrast to these studies, Kostopoulos et al. (2022), Dorn and Huberman (2010), and Baig et al. (2023) argue that ambiguity aversion, risk-aversion, and periods of crisis influence individual investor participation in financial markets. For example, Kostopoulos et al. (2022) find that there is more active trading and risk aversion during heightened ambiguity, which is consistent with the idea that investor sentiment becomes more important under ambiguous conditions (Hirshleifer & Teoh, 2003). Lastly, Dorn and Huberman (2010) propose the 'Preferred Risk Habitat Hypothesis', which posits that risk-averse investors might opt for lower-volatility stocks and lean towards mutual funds, while heavily disregarding the return correlations in their portfolios. Their results, based on analyses of data from thousands of clients of a German brokerage, support their hypothesis.

In summary, the discussions in this section support the notion that both institutional and individual investors can impact volatility. However, there are differences in the ways they influence volatility. Institutional investors have a more dominant impact on days with large market returns, and factors such as growth investing contribute to increased idiosyncratic volatility. Conversely, individual investors contribute to volatility through their trading behaviors. More importantly, less informed individual trades impact volatility more than informed institutional trades. Based on this discussion we formulate one main study hypothesis that questions whether changes in individual retail investor's interests are indicative of volatility:

Hypothesis $H1_a$: Changes in individual retail investor ownership do not predict volatility.

Hypothesis $H1_b$: Changes in individual retail investor ownership predict volatility.

8.3 Data and Methods

Motivated by the extant literature, the methodological approach we employ involves two main steps. First, we employ non-parametric analysis techniques to study the relationship between market capitalization, volatility, and popularity weight. Second, we utilize two parametric methods as the primary analytical techniques used in our study. For the sake of brevity, we discuss these methods within the context of a results section.

Sample Selection

To study the relationship between individual investor interest and volatility, we collect daily historical price data, Robinhood popularity data, and market capitalizations for a large sample of stocks following Barber et al. (2022), and Welch (2022). Our data is sourced from three sources: Robintrack, Yahoo Finance, and Financial Modelling Prep. The primary dataset for our analysis comes from the Robintrack website,[1] while we obtain historical daily price data for equities from Yahoo Finance and Financial Modeling Prep, including adjusted close, high, and low prices and market capitalizations.

As discussed by Barber et al. (2022), the Robintrack dataset contains 5,777,002 ticker day observations for 802 unique days and 8560 tickers. The mean stock has about 2000 users, and the median user count for a stock is 160. The average day has 7211 stock holdings and just under 15 million user positions; user changes are generally small. Based on the number of users reported, Robinhood users have about three stock positions on average. The sample analyzed in this sample represents a subset of the Robintrack dataset, explicitly focusing on ordinary equity stocks traded on Robinhood. Thus, this sample does not include exchange-traded funds, options, or cryptocurrencies available for clients to trade at Robinhood. After accounting for missing data, the sample used in the thesis contains 3765 tickers that can be classified as ordinary equity. Of

[1] Robintrack data available for download at https://robintrack.net/data-download. Robintrack began collecting popularity metric data made publicly available on Robinhood's API on May 2, 2018. Robinhood shut down its public API on August 13, 2020. The popularity metric in the dataset signifies the count of unique accounts holding at least one share of a particular asset. However, it is worth noting that this data set only considers long shares and does not account for options.

the 802 unique days, 546 were trading days, and the final sample results were 1,721,810 ticker day observations.

In Fig. 8.1 we plot the growth in total user stock holdings of Robinhood investors using the underlying data from Robintrack. The red dotted line represents March 11, 2020, a day the World Health Organization assessed that the coronavirus outbreak had become a global pandemic (World Health Organization, 2020). Significant growth in popularity and usage of the platform can be observed to begin at Robinhood during this time, as has been documented in Barber et al. (2022).

Variables

The main variables used in this chapter include the market capitalization of each stock (*Cap*), which is sourced directly from the underlying data; volatility (σ); returns (r); and a popularity weight (w). Except for market capitalization, variables are derived from the collected data. We describe each of the measures in this section.

Volatility: Based on the advantages outlined by Kyröläinen (2008) and Baig et al. (2023), a log-range volatility measure is chosen as it is more robust against measurement errors and accurately reflects intraday price variations. Baig et al. (2023) employ the range-based method as a volatility proxy to study the impact of retail trading on market stability. Similarly, Aharon et al. (2022) use a range-based volatility estimation to represent volatility in order to investigate Robinhood holdings' impact on American depositary receipts' volatility. Following Alizadeh et al. (2002) and Gallant et al. (1999), the log-range volatility measure we use in this study is created using daily historical price data, where volatility ($\sigma S,t$) is the first logarithmic difference between the high and low price and Ht and Lt denote the high and low price at day t.

$$\sigma S, t = \ln(Ht) - \ln(Lt) \tag{8.1}$$

Returns: Returns calculated from adjusted close prices represent the percentage change in price from one trading day to the next, considering adjustments for stock splits and dividend distributions:

$$r_t = \frac{AdjC_t}{AdjC_{t-1}} - 1 \tag{8.2}$$

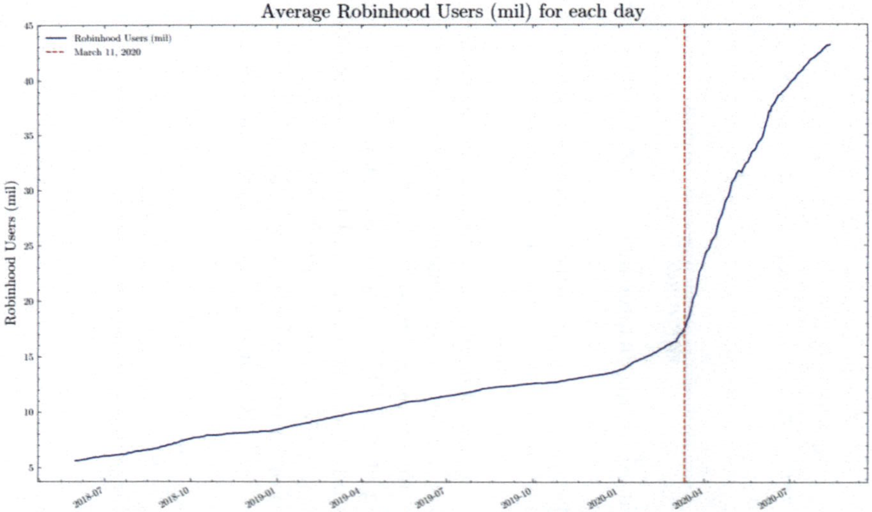

3.1.3 VARIABLES

Fig. 8.1 Robinhood total user stock holdings

Thus, the formula calculates the daily simple return (*rt*) by dividing the current day's adjusted closing price (*AdjCt*) by the previous day's adjusted closing price (*AdjCt* − *1*) and subtracting one from the result to determine the return percentage. While log-range volatility focuses on the price fluctuations seen during intraday trading sessions, returns calculated from adjusted close prices also reflect overnight returns. As a result, volatility and returns can exhibit different magnitudes, revealing different aspects of price-related market dynamics.

Popularity weight is a measure of individual investor ownership. This measure is comparable to Welch (2022), where individual stock holds weight in the 'ARH portfolio'. Thus, the measure is comparable to the percentage holding in an aggregate individual investor portfolio and results in an adequate proxy for a fraction of shares, which is the method utilized by Sias (1996) in the case of institutional ownership. Thus, the portfolio is not a market capitalization weighted portfolio but instead reflects the active choices of individual investors. Welch (2022) states that this representation is a 'very good proxy' for a household equal-weighted portfolio.

Descriptive Statistics

Table 8.1 shows the descriptive statistics for the full sample. Displayed statistics include the mean, median, standard deviation, and the 25th and 75th percentiles. The table indicates that the average and middle values for popularity weight, volatility, and changes in popularity weight and volatility are quite similar. The standard deviations for these measures imply a relatively consistent range of values around their means and medians. Additionally, the 25th and 75th percentiles values for popularity weight, volatility, and changes in popularity weight and volatility suggest a consistent spread around the average values. Overall, the statistics are quite similar to those reported in Aharon et al. (2022).

8.4 Results and Discussion

Preliminary Findings

We first examine whether firm-specific stock volatility can predict subsequent changes in individual retail investor ownership. This assessment serves two primary purposes. First, it facilitates checking if the evidence

Table 8.1 Descriptive statistics

	Popularity weight	*Volatility*	*Return*	*Δ Popularity weight*	*Δ Volatility*
Mean	0.00021	0.047	0.00058	–7.15E-08	2.19E-05
Median	2.42E-05	0.034	0	–4.31E-08	–0.00015
Std	0.0012	0.048	0.051	1.59E-05	0.041
25%	7.01E-06	0.020	–0.015	–3.19E-07	–0.011
75%	8.10E-05	0.058	0.014	4.90E-08	0.010

matches overall ownership patterns and how investors behave. Second, it allows for understanding of the temporality of the relationship between volatility and Robinhood holdings to determine how long the lags should be in our formal regression models.

We present two tables, Tables 8.2 and 8.3, with panels A and B. Tables 8.2 and 8.3 present the ten largest stocks that experienced 'Extreme one-day increases in Robinhood holdings' (Table 8.2) and 'Extreme one-day decreases in Robinhood holdings' (Table 8.3) based on popularity weights. Panel A shows Robinhood holders and changes in holdings for each date and ticker, while Panel B illustrates changes in Popularity Weight, Rate of Return, and Volatility for each company over three days. We expect volatility to be a more recurring characteristic than substantial one-day increases or decreases in the stock price as suggested by Welch (2022).

Examining the tables, the reported values are mainly in line with our expectations. From Table 8.2, the recurring characteristic seems to be above median volatility for the respective market capitalization decile of the company. It further suggests a contrarian pattern in trading behavior, where extreme increases in popularity weight follow significant negative returns that coincide with high volatility. From Table 8.3, we observe that large decreases often coincide with increased volatility that persists for three days. It also suggests a pattern of individual investors behavior corresponding with the disposition effect, in which Robinhood users sell or continue to sell stocks after high one-day stock price increases.

Next, we further explore relationships between investor ownership and volatility by running several non-parametric tests. We begin in Table 8.4 by conducting Kruskal–Wallis tests to test for significant differences in the median popularity weight and volatility for different market capitalization deciles, arranged from the smallest to the largest. This allows us to see

Table 8.2 Extreme one-day increases in Robinhood holdings

Panel A: Robinhood holdings in thousands

Date	*Ticker*	*−2*	*−1*	*±0*	*+1*	*+2*	*Δ − 1,0*
1July 26, 2018	FB	108	114	156	166	170	42,083
2April 4, 2020	UBER	144	144	196	196	196	52,329
3July 29, 2020	KODK	9	34	119	122	105	84,394
4January 6, 2020	INPX	0	0	26	26	26	26,032
5October 2, 2018	OGEN	17	27	41	39	37	14,336
6July 17, 2018	NFLX	101	107	118	118	117	11,000
7September 19, 2019	TLRY	18	18	31	31	31	12,368
8June 29, 2020	VXRT	22	22	81	86	55	58,475
9July 15, 2020	MRNA	214	223	284	305	315	60,914
10 July 27, 2018	FB	114	155	166	170	173	9832

Panel B: Robinhood change, rate of return and volatility

	Popularity weight		*Rate of return*			*Volatility*		
Company name	w*0*	Δ − *1,0*w	r − *1*	r*0*	r + *1*	σ − *1*	σ*0*	σ + *1*
1Facebook	2.49	0.65	-0.7	−18.9	1.3	3.9	3.60	2.0
2Uber	0.82	0.21	-6.8	8.1	0.3	9.1	7.59	4.8
3Kodak	0.28	0.20	−10.1	123.2	203.0	47.9	123.3	43.7
4Inpixon	0.18	0.18	8.88	-5.6	38.29	16.5	122.0	49.5
5Oragenics	0.55	0.18	−50.9	14.6	39.1	54.9	64.1	41.3
6Netflix	0.19	0.17	−1.1	45.5	1.1	28.5	11.2	2.9
7Tilray	0.42	0.16	−17.9	95.9	28.9	43.4	68.3	16.1
8Vertex Pharmaceuticals	0.20	0.14	−18.1	-0.1	28.4	43.2	30.0	59.4
9Moderna	0.69	0.14	1.9	9.6	4.5	5.7	12.4	8.5
10 Facebook	2.63	0.14	−2.1	−0.7	−18.9	5.11	3.9	3.6

Panel A shows Robinhood holders in thousands for each date and ticker and the change in holdings (Δ−1, 0). Panel B shows a change in Popularity Weight, Rate of Return, and Volatility for each company, including the initial popularity weight (w_0), change in popularity weight (Δ−1, 0w), rate of return for three days (r_{-1}, r_0, r_{+1}), and volatility for the same period (σ−1, σ_0, σ_{+1}).

whether there are significant variations in individual investor ownership and the volatility of stocks across capitalization deciles. The chi-square test statistic indicates statistically significant differences among the median popularity weight and volatility across capitalization deciles. Overall, we see an inverse relationship between market capitalization and volatility.

Table 8.3 Extreme one-day decreases in Robinhood holdings

Panel A: Robinhood Holdings in thousands

Date	*Ticker*	*−2*	*−1*	*± 0*	*+1*	*+2*	*Δ − 1,0*
1February 27, 2019	IGC	78	78	42	42	42	−36,098
2November 2, 2018	INPX	39	40	1	1	1	−35,583
3February 5, 2020	TSLA	154	163	148	152	152	−15,439
4October 1, 2018	TSLA	95	101	94	94	94	−6876
5October 4, 2018	IGC	89	84	76	72	80	−7259
6June 10, 2020	TSLA	85	85	80	73	76	−4857
7January 16, 2020	FIT	257	256	256	257	259	−924
8October 24, 2018	TSLA	113	109	103	98	95	−5885
9October 03, 2018	IGC	81	89	83	76	72	−5551
10 April 8, 2019	STZ	7	7	0	7	7	−7584

Panel B: Robinhood change, rate of return and volatility

	Popularity weight		*Rate of return*			*Volatility*		
Company name	w*0*	Δ − 1,0w	r − *1*	r*0*	r + *1*	σ − *1*	σ*0*	σ + *1*
1India Globalization	0.44	−0.54	-3.8	1.8	13.4	11.4	20.7	23.2
2Inpixon	0.02	−0.48	-2.4	−32.1	2.3	31.5	69.4	14.8
3Tesla	0.97	−0.10	13.7	−17.1	1.9	15.0	18.3	14.7
4Tesla	1.25	−0.10	−13.9	−17.3	−3.1	6.4	3.3	5.7
5India Globalization	1.00	−0.09	−30.1	27.5	−36.8	23.1	21.4	29.6
6Tesla	1.24	−0.07	0.9	16.1	−0.3	3.3	7.9	3.5
7Fitbit	1.76	−0.07	0.9	0.3	1.3	1.7	1.5	1.5
8Tesla	1.31	−0.07	12.7	−0.1	9.1	12.8	6.3	6.4
9India Globalization	1.09	−0.07	44.1	−31.9	−27.5	42.8	23.1	21.4
10 Constellation Brands	0.00	−0.07	0.2	0.5	0	2.37	1.0	1.4

Panel A shows Robinhood holders in thousands for each date and ticker and the change in holdings (Δ−1, 0). Panel B shows a change in Popularity Weight, Rate of Return, and Volatility for each company, including the initial popularity weight (w_0), change in popularity weight (Δ−1, 0w), rate of return for three days (r_{-1}, r_0, r_{+1}), and volatility for the same period (σ−1, σ_0, σ_{+1}).

Table 8.4 Median popularity weight and volatility by capitalization

Market capitalization decile	*Median popularity weight*	*Median volatility*
Smallest	0.0041%	6.76%
Decile 2	0.0019%	5.31%
Decile 3	0.0012%	4.60%
Decile 4	0.0016%	4.10%
Decile 5	0.0018%	3.73%
Decile 6	0.0016%	3.35%
Decile 7	0.0018%	3.02%
Decile 8	0.0021%	2.65%
Decile 9	0.0037%	2.36%
Largest	0.0152%	1.96%
The chi-square Statistic (all equal)	242,466.50***	319,851.19***

***indicates statistical significance at the 1 percent level

Median volatility decreases from 6.76% for the smallest decile to 1.96% for the largest decile, aligning with previous studies in finance that describe a relationship between market capitalization and volatility.

In Table 8.5 we also present the results of Wilcoxon rank-sum tests. While the Kruskal–Wallis tests examine variations in individual investor holdings and volatility across various company sizes, we cannot conclude whether increased volatility correlates with a greater individual investor presence regardless of market capitalization. The Wilcoxon rank-sum test compares whether two samples likely originate from the same population, facilitating an understanding of whether increased volatility correlates with higher individual investor presence irrespective of capitalization. To operationalize our test, we follow Sias (1996) in splitting our sample into two categories within each capitalization decile based on popularity weight. Stocks with weights greater than the overall median weight are classified as high weight, while those with weights less than the median are classified as low weight, with the median omitted from each decile. The Wilcoxon rank-sum test is then used to examine whether there are significant differences between the two groups of stocks (i.e., the one with a low-popularity weight and the other with a high popularity weight, within each decile).

The Wilcoxon rank-sum test results for popularity weight-sorted portfolios suggest significant differences between groups based on popularity

Table 8.5 Popularity weight-sorted portfolios

	Popularity weight %			*Market capitalization*			*Volatility %*		
Deciles	*High*	*Low*	*Z-stat*	*High*	*Low*	*Z-stat*	*High*	*Low*	*Z-stat*
Smallest	0.01	0.001	355.9***	20,163	24,139	–48.5***	7.65	5.81	81.8***
Decile 2	0.006	0.0006	355.9***	78,595	79,078	–7.1***	6.22	4.30	104.9***
Decile 3	0.005	0.0003	355.9***	184,642	185,036	–5.6***	5.74	3.41	148.0***
Decile 4	0.006	0.0004	355.9***	345,222	336,151	19.4***	5.04	3.15	137.2***
Decile 5	0.006	0.0005	355.9***	621,669	628,250	–12.6***	4.47	3.05	118.3***
Decile 6	0.005	0.0006	355.9***	1,141,989	1,126,469	16.7***	4.05	2.70	125.6***
Decile 7	0.006	0.0007	355.9***	1,987,486	1,969,895	6.3***	3.52	2.57	102.0***
Decile 8	0.006	0.0008	355.9***	3,694,125	3,565,540	23.6***	3.08	2.28	98.6***
Decile 9	0.011	0.001	355.9***	8,682,011	7,632,167	54.4***	2.70	2.08	87.9***
Largest	0.058	0.005	355.9***	54,294,630	24,367,425	176.4***	2.03	1.90	23.3***

***indicates statistical significance at the 1 percent level
This table presents the distribution of securities across high and low-popularity weight categories within each capitalization decile. This table sorts stocks into high-weight ('High') or low-weight ('Low') categories based on their popularity relative to the overall median weight. The median is excluded from each decile for classification.

weight for both capitalization and volatility. Noticeable variations are evident in company size and volatility between the low and high popularity weight groups within each decile. Additionally, higher volatilities were observed in the high popularity weight groups, supporting the idea that individual investors are drawn to stocks with greater volatility. Thus, individual investor ownership, measured by popularity weight, is associated with increased stock volatility, regardless of market capitalization. Which is consistent with hypothesis H1b. Individual investor ownership shows similarities to institutional investor ownership. The findings align with previous volatility research by Sias (1996) regarding institutional investors, which indicates that after controlling for capitalization, higher volatility is correlated with the presence of institutional investors.

Taken together, the results from two non-parametric methods reveal patterns of individual investor behavior observed in previous studies. Generally, Robinhood investors seem to prefer both very low-volatility and high-volatility stocks. Robinhood investors prefer smaller companies' stocks in smaller market capitalization deciles and larger companies in larger market capitalization deciles. Although higher volatility is preferred across market capitalizations, the two highest market capitalization deciles with the lowest volatilities have the highest median popularity weights. The findings from the Kruskal–Wallis and Wilcoxon rank-sum tests can be attributed to two distinct behaviors observed among individual investors in the literature review. Firstly, Robinhood investors could prefer stocks that resemble lotteries based on the characteristics outlined by Kumar (2009). Secondly, the preference for low-volatility stocks among Robinhood investors may be explained by ambiguity aversion, as suggested by Kostopoulos et al. (2022), and the preference for low volatility of risk-averse investors, as highlighted by Dorn and Huberman (2010). Finally, on average, Robinhood investors hold three stocks in their portfolios, indicating a tendency towards under-diversification. Dorn and Huberman (2005) and Mitton and Vorkink (2007) highlight the prevalence of under-diversified portfolios among investors due to challenges in optimization implementation and a propensity towards 'narrow framing'. Furthermore, some investors navigate the trade-off between skewness and diversification by opting for under-diversified portfolios to pursue high volatility and potentially higher returns.

Multivariate Regression Analysis

We continue our analyses in a multivariate regression setting, which provides the main test of our study hypothesis. To test our study hypothesis and consider whether popularity weight is associated with a subsequent change in volatility, in Eq. 8.3 we regress the volatility in day t on the volatility of day $t - 1$, the daily lagged change in popularity weight and the return in day $t - 1$. That is, we examine whether lagged change popularity weight can explain variation in volatility beyond that explained by lag volatility. We included models with two- and three-day lags based on the expected results of the extreme changes in Robinhood holdings tables.

$$\sigma t = \alpha + \beta 1 \sigma t - 1 + \beta 2(\Delta w) + \beta 3(rt - 1) + \varepsilon t \tag{8.3}$$

Thus, the regression models the relationship between current volatility (σ) and past volatility $\sigma t - 1$), change in popularity weight (Δw), and past returns ($rt - 1$). The model suggests that a stock's current volatility is a function of past volatility, change in popularity weight, and past returns.

Table 8.6 presents the results in which we test whether an increase in individual investor holdings is associated with a subsequent increase in volatility. Three models are tested, which differ only in terms of the lags for changes in popularity weight, ranging from one to three days. Specifically. Model (1) has a lag of one day, model (2) two days, and model (3) three days. In all cases, the lags for volatility and returns are held at one day.

Regarding the study hypothesis, we find evidence in support of H1b. Specifically, we find that *Change in Popularity weight* is positively associated with future volatility. In other words, an increase in stock popularity is associated with an increase in future volatility. This result is found for models (2) and (3) but is not statistically significant at conventional levels in the case of a one-day lag (model 1). One possible explanation, supported by conclusions from extreme changes tables, is that increases in Robinhood holdings may lead to volatility with a delay. Overall, the results infer that increases in individual retail investor ownership are positively and strongly associated with increases in future volatility; thus, we reject the null hypothesis that changes in individual investor ownership

Table 8.6 Change in individual investor holdings and volatility

	Estimated models		
	(1)	*(2)*	*(3)*
Intercept	0.0178***	0.0178***	0.0178***
	(0.000)	(0.001)	(0.001)
Volatility	0.6257***	0.6257***	0.6259***
	(0.002)	(0.002)	(0.002)
Change in Popularity weight	0.2060	13.0058***	24.3103***
	(7.214)	(5.040)	(5.277)
Return	–0.0271***	–0.0270***	–0.0268***
	(0.003)	(0.003)	(0.003)
Observations	1,674,204	1,666,909	1,655,981
R-squared	0.389	0.389	0.389
Adj. R-squared	0.389	0.389	0.389

***$p < 0.01$, ** $p < 0.05$, * $p < 0.1$. Standard errors are in parentheses

do not predict volatility. This result supports the idea that individual investors are attracted to stocks with greater volatility (Kumar, 2009). Moreover, it is consistent with the findings of Aharon et al. (2022) who show that the growth rate of Robinhood accounts holding the stock in ADR is correlated with increased volatility.

Regarding the other variables, the coefficients for *Volatility* are positive and highly significant across all models, which infers that increases in lagged volatility are associated with increases in future volatility. This is consistent with the notion of a volatility feedback effect whereby increases in volatility increase the expected future volatility and required return on stocks (Bae et al., 2007). It is also interesting to note that the coefficient associated with the lag return is negative and statistically significant. Therefore, increases in stock returns are associated with lower levels of future volatility. This is consistent with a body of the finance literature (see Bae et al., 2007). One often-given explanation for this effect is that a fall in stock value is associated with an increase in firm leverage, which serves to increase the stock's volatility (Bae et al., 2007).

8.5 Conclusions

Previous research connects individual investors to volatility, primarily through noise trading, herding and deviations from the decision-making processes expected by the rational choice theory. In this chapter we explore how individual retail investor ownership influences future volatility, using the novel setting of Robinhood. The Robinhood platform is unique in several ways. Most notably, it has made investing in stocks widely accessible to anyone, with no minimum investment requirements to open an account and commission-free trading. This has led to a rapid rise in the importance of retail investors overall. However, as argued by Barber et al. (2022), our academic understanding of the behavior of such investors is limited; compared to normal financial markets, Robinhood users are much more likely to be inexperienced stock investors and to be impacted more by stock attention and behavioral biases, which could lead to more herding behavior and volatility.

Using data from Robintrack, and a sample of 3765 ordinary stocks and 721,810 ticker day observations, we employ a methodology informed by prior related work on institutional investors (Sias, 1996) to test the hypothesis that changes in individual retail investor ownership of Robinhood users can influence future volatility. Our main empirical findings support the conclusion that an increase in the popularity of a stock is associated with an increase in future volatility, which is consistent with hypothesis H1b and broadly with earlier findings for other investors in the finance literature (e.g., Aharon et al., 2022; Kumar, 2009).

Given the surge in popularity of retail trading and predictions of future growth, our preliminary findings present several conclusions relevant to practice, policymakers, and regulators. Notably, our results suggest that the activity of retail traders can serve to encourage herding behavior and that an increase in the popularity of a stock can increase its future volatility. These findings, combined with the growth in retail investors and Robinhood users, are especially important to regulators and policy makers since we know from extant literature that herding can drive stock values away from fundamental values, undermining market efficiency and can lead to excess volatility (see Dennis & Strickland, 2002; Gabaix et al., 2006).

Finally, our chapter is not without limitations, which present opportunities for future research. We focus on an important new class of investors and a highly popular trading platform, yet we only consider one key research hypothesis, which we acknowledge narrows both the overall contribution and generalizability of our research findings. Given that the behavior of retail investors may naturally differ from those of institutional investors a natural progression for future research would be to analyze individual investor and institutional ownership data simultaneously. Doing so could expand our understanding of how the two investor groups interact in the markets. Further research could also be conducted to determine the effectiveness of extending the methodology of Bushee (1998) to be used with individual retail investor ownership data. He classifies institutional investors as dedicated institutions, quasi-indexers, and transient institutions. Incorporating institutional investors' preferences by categorizing stocks with this classification could be used to clarify the relationship between individual and institutional investors. Stocks could be categorized by the turnover rate in the consensus Robinhood portfolio. Thus, stocks could be classified as popular among traders or passive investors, allowing us to classify types of individual investors.

References

Aharon, D. Y., Baig, A. S., & Delisle, R. J. (2022). The impact of Robinhood traders on the volatility of cross-listed securities. *Research in International*

Business and Finance, 60, 101619. https://doi.org/10.1016/j.ribaf.2022.101619

Alizadeh, S., Brandt, M. W., & Diebold, F. X. (2002). Range-based estimation of stochastic volatility models. *Journal of Finance, 57*(3), 1047–1091. https://doi.org/10.1111/1540-6261.00454

Andersen, T. G., & Bollerslev, T. (1998). Answering the skeptics: Yes, standard volatility models do provide accurate forecasts. *International Economic Review, 39*(49), 885–905. https://doi.org/10.2307/2527343

Andersen, T. G., Bollerslev, T., Diebold, F. X., & Ebens, H. (2001). The distribution of realized stock return volatility. *Journal of Financial Economics, 61*(1), 43–76. https://doi.org/10.1016/S0304-405X(01)00055-1

Avramov, D., Chordia, T., & Goyal, A. (2006). The impact of trades on daily volatility. *Review of Financial Studies, 19*(4), 1241–1277. https://doi.org/10.1093/rfs/hhj027

Bae, J., Kim, C. J., & Nelson, C. R. (2007). Why are stock returns and volatility negatively correlated? *Journal of Empirical Finance, 14*(1), 41–58. https://doi.org/10.1016/j.jempfin.2006.04.005

Baig, A. S., Blau, B. M., Butt, H. A., & Yasin, A. (2023). Reprint of: Do retail traders destabilize financial markets? An investigation surrounding the COVID-19 pandemic. *Journal of Banking & Finance, 147*, 106744. https://doi.org/10.1016/j.jbankfin.2022.106744

Balasubramaniam, V., Campbell, J. Y., Ramadorai, T., & Ranish, B. (2023). Who owns what? A factor model for direct stockholding. *Journal of Finance, 78*(3), 1545–1591. https://doi.org/10.1111/jofi.13220

Barber, B. M., & Odean, T. (2000). Trading is hazardous to your wealth: The common stock investment performance of individual investors. *Journal of Finance, 55*(2), 773–806. https://doi.org/10.1111/0022-1082.00226

Barber, B. M., & Odean, T. (2013). The behavior of individual investors. In *Handbook of the economics of finance* (Vol. 2, pp. 1533–1570). Elsevier. https://doi.org/10.1016/B978-0-44-459406-8.00022-6.

Barber, B. M., Huang, X., Odean, T., & Schwarz, C. (2022, December). Attention-Induced Trading and Returns: Evidence from Robinhood Users. *The Journal of Finance, 77*(6), 3141–3190. https://doi.org/10.1111/jofi.13183

Barber, B. M., Odean, T., & Zhu, N. (2008). Do retail trades move markets? *Review of Financial Studies, 22*(1), 151–186. https://doi.org/10.1093/rfs/hhn035

Beckers, S. (1983). Variances of security price returns based on high, low, and closing prices. *Journal of Business, 56*(1), 97–112. https://doi.org/10.1086/296188

Blasco, N., Corredor, P., & Ferreruela, S. (2012). Does herding affect volatility? Implications for the Spanish stock market. *Quantitative Finance, 12*(2), 311–327. https://doi.org/10.1080/14697688.2010.516766

Brandt, M. W., Brav, A., Graham, J. R., & Kumar, A. (2010). The idiosyncratic volatility puzzle: Time trend or speculative episodes? *Review of Financial Studies, 23*(2), 863–899. https://doi.org/10.1093/rfs/hhp087

Bryzgalova, S., Pavlova, A., & Sikorskaya, T. (2023). Retail trading in options and the rise of the big three wholesalers. *Journal of Finance, 78*(6), 3465–3514. https://doi.org/10.1111/jofi.13285

Bushee, B. J. (1998). The influence of institutional investors on myopic R&D investment behavior. *Accounting Review, 73*(3), 305–333. https://www.jstor.org/stable/248542.

Bushee, B. J. (2001). Do institutional investors prefer near-term earnings over long run value? *Contemporary Accounting Research, 18*(2), 207–246. https://doi.org/10.1506/J4GU-BHWH-8HME-LE0X

Bushee, B. J., & Noe, C. F. (2000). Corporate disclosure practices, institutional investors, and stock return volatility. *Journal of Accounting Research, 38*, 171–202. https://doi.org/10.2307/2672914

Chan, K., & Fong, W.-M. (2000). Trade size, order imbalance, and the volatility–volume relation. *Journal of Financial Economics, 57*(2), 247–273. https://doi.org/10.1016/S0304-405X(00)00057-X

Dennis, P. J., & Strickland, D. (2002). Who blinks in volatile markets, individuals or institutions? *Journal of Finance, 57*(5), 1923–1949. https://doi.org/10.1111/0022-1082.00484C

Dorn, D., & Huberman, G. (2005). Talk and action: What individual investors say and what they do. *Review of Finance, 9*(4), 437–481. https://doi.org/10.1007/s10679-005-4997-z

Dorn, D., & Huberman, G. (2010). Preferred risk habitat of individual investors. *Journal of Financial Economics, 97*(1), 155–173.

Eaton, G. W., Green, T. C., Roseman, B., & Wu, Y. (2021). Zero-commission individual investors, high frequency traders, and stock market quality. SSRN. https://doi.org/10.2139/ssrn.3776874

Eaton, G. W., Green, T. C., Roseman, B. S., & Wu, Y. (2022). Retail trader sophistication and stock market quality: Evidence from brokerage outages. *Journal of Financial Economics, 146*(2), 502–528. https://doi.org/10.1016/j.jfineco.2022.08.002

Fama, E. F., & French, K. R. (2015). A five-factor asset pricing model. *Journal of Financial Economics, 116*(1), 1–22. https://doi.org/10.1016/j.jfineco.2014.10.010

Foucault, T., Sraer, D., & Thesmar, D. J. (2011). Individual investors and volatility. *Journal of Finance, 66*(4), 1369–1406. https://doi.org/10.1111/j.1540-6261.2011.01668.x

French, K. R., Schwert, G. W., & Stambaugh, R. F. (1987). Expected stock returns and volatility. *Journal of Financial Economics, 19*(1), 3–29. https://doi.org/10.1016/0304-405X(87)90026-2

Gabaix, X., Gopikrishnan, P., Plerou, V., & Stanley, H. E. (2006). Institutional investors and stock market volatility. *Quarterly Journal of Economics, 121*(2), 461–504. https://doi.org/10.1162/qjec.2006.121.2.461

Gallant, A. R., Hsu, C.-T., & Tauchen, G. (1999). Using daily range data to calibrate volatility diffusions and extract the forward integrated variance. *Review of Economics and Statistics, 81*(4), 617–631. https://doi.org/10.1162/003465399558481

Garman, M. B., & Klass, M. J. (1980). On the estimation of security price volatilities from historical data. *Journal of Business, 53*(1), 67–78. https://www.jstor.org/stable/2352358.

Greenwood, R., & Thesmar, D. (2011). Stock price fragility. *Journal of Financial Economics, 102*(3), 471–490. https://doi.org/10.1016/j.jfineco.2011.06.003

Grinblatt, M., & Keloharju, M. (2001). What makes investors trade? *Journal of Finance, 56*(2), 589–616. https://doi.org/10.1111/0022-1082.00338

Hirshleifer, D., & Hong Teoh, S. (2003). Herd behaviour and cascading in capital markets: A review and synthesis. *European Financial Management, 9*(1), 25–66. https://doi.org/10.1111/1468-036X.00207

Jones, C. M., Kaul, G., & Lipson, M. L. (1994). Transactions, volume, and volatility. *Review of Financial Studies, 7*(4), 631–651. https://doi.org/10.1093/rfs/7.4.631

Kelley, E. K., & Tetlock, P. C. (2013). How wise are crowds? Insights from retail orders and stock returns. *Journal of Finance, 68*(3), 1229–1265. https://doi.org/10.1111/jofi.12028

King, T., & Koutmos, D. (2021). Herding and feedback trading in cryptocurrency markets. *Annals of Operations Research, 300*(1), 79–96. https://doi.org/10.1007/s10479-020-03874-4

Kostopoulos, D., Meyer, S., & Uhr, C. (2022). Ambiguity about volatility and investor behavior. *Journal of Financial Economics, 145*(1), 277–296. https://doi.org/10.1016/j.jfineco.2021.07.004

Kumar, A. (2009). Who gambles in the stock market? *Journal of Finance, 64*(4), 1889–1933. https://doi.org/10.1111/j.1540-6261.2009.01483.x

Kumar, A., & Lee, C. M. (2006). Retail investor sentiment and return comovements. *Journal of Finance, 61*(5), 2451–2486. https://doi.org/10.1111/j.1540-6261.2006.01063.x

Kyröläinen, P. (2008). Day trading and stock price volatility. *Journal of Economics and Finance, 32*(1), 75–89. https://doi.org/10.1007/s12197-007-9006-2

Markowitz, H. (1952). Portfolio selection. *Journal of Finance, 7*(1), 77. https://doi.org/10.2307/2975974

Merton, R. C. (1980). On estimating the expected return on the market: An exploratory investigation. *Journal of Financial Economics, 8*(4), 323–361. https://doi.org/10.1016/0304-405X(80)90007-0

Mitton, T., & Vorkink, K. (2007). Equilibrium underdiversification and the preference for skewness. *Review of Financial Studies, 20*(4), 1255–1288. https://doi.org/10.1093/revfin/hhm011

Moss, A., Naughton, J. P., & Wang, C. (2024). The irrelevance of environmental, social, and governance disclosure to retail investors. *Management Science, 70*(4), 2626–2644. https://doi.org/10.1287/mnsc.2023.4822

Nofsinger, J. R., & Sias, R. W. (1999). Herding and feedback trading by institutional and individual investors. *Journal of Finance, 54*(6), 2263–2295. https://doi.org/10.1111/0022-1082.00188

Odean, T. (1998). Are investors reluctant to realize their losses? *Journal of Finance, 53*(5), 1775–1798. https://doi.org/10.1111/0022-1082.00072

Ozik, G., Sadka, R., & Shen, S. (2021). Flattening the illiquidity curve: Retail trading during the COVID-19 lockdown. *Journal of Financial and Quantitative Analysis, 56*(7), 2356–2388. https://doi.org/10.1017/S0022109021000387

Pagano, M. S., Sedunov, J., & Velthuis, R. (2021). How did retail investors respond to the COVID-19 pandemic? The effect of Robinhood brokerage customers on market quality. *Finance Research Letters, 43*, 101946. https://doi.org/10.1016/j.frl.2021.101946

Parkinson, M. (1980). The extreme value method for estimating the variance of the rate of return. *Journal of Business, 53*(1), 61–65. https://www.jstor.org/stable/2352357.

Schlarbaum, G. G., Lewellen, W. G., & Lease, R. C. (1978a). The common-stock-portfolio performance record of individual investors. *Journal of Finance, 33*(2), 429–441. https://doi.org/10.2307/2326561

Schlarbaum, G. G., Lewellen, W. G., & Lease, R. C. (1978b). Realized returns on common stock investments: The experience of individual investors. *Journal of Business, 51*(2), 299–325. https://www.jstor.org/stable/2352530.

Schwert, G. W. (1989). Why does stock market volatility change over time? *Journal of Finance, 44*(5), 1115–1153. https://doi.org/10.1111/j.1540-6261.1989.tb02647.x

Schwert, G. W. (1990). Stock volatility and the crash of '87. *Review of Financial Studies, 3*(1), 77–102. https://doi.org/10.1093/rfs/3.1.77

Sias, R. W. (1996). Volatility and the institutional investor. *Financial Analysts Journal, 52*(2), 13–20. https://doi.org/10.2469/faj.v52.n2.1976

Venkatachalam, M. (2000). Discussion of corporate disclosure practices, institutional investors, and stock return volatility. *Journal of Accounting Research, 38*, 203–207.

Welch, I. (2022). The wisdom of the robinhood crowd. *Journal of Finance, 77*(3), 1489–1527.

World Health Organization. (2020, April). Archived: WHO Timeline—COVID-19. Retrieved August 8, 2024, from https://www.who.int/news/item/27-04-2020-who-timeline---covid-19

Yang, D., & Zhang, Q. (2000). Drift-independent volatility estimation based on high, low, open, and close prices. *Journal of Business, 73*(3), 477–492. https://doi.org/10.1086/209650

CHAPTER 9

Should Shareholders Just Vote No? Examining the Impact of Shareholder Proposals

Timothy King and Jonathan Williams

> When we recognize that shareholders have significant private interests, it becomes apparent that shareholders may use any incremental power conferred upon them to pursue those interests to the detriment of shareholders as a class. As a result, transferring power from boards to shareholders may create new costs. In other words, more shareholder power could reduce overall shareholder welfare. This, of course, is a result directly opposite that predicted by proponents of increasing shareholder power. (Anabtawi, 2006, p. 5)

T. King (✉)
School of Accounting and Finance, University of Vaasa, Vaasa, Finland
e-mail: timothy.king@uwasa.fi

J. Williams
Discipline of Finance and Accounting, Surrey Business School, University of Surrey, Guildford, UK
e-mail: jon.williams@surrey.ac.uk

T. King and J. Williams (eds.), *Corporate Governance in the Banking and Financial Sector*, Palgrave Macmillan Studies in Banking and Financial Institutions, https://doi.org/10.1007/978-3-031-83353-3_9

9.1 Introduction

We explore the impact of 'shareholder voice' as an important area of firm governance (Hirschman, 1970). Specifically, we consider the role of shareholder proposals in large publicly listed U.S. firms. Such proposals are a mechanism for outside owners (shareholders) to try and induce favourable firm performance outcomes and/or instigate desirable changes by conveying shareholder expectations to firm management (Levit & Malenko, 2011).

We frame shareholder proposals as a mechanism relevant to the 'shareholder-centric', principal-agent view of firm governance, which posits that the secret to good corporate governance lies in closely aligning the interests of managers and shareholders (Jensen & Meckling, 1976; Shleifer & Vishny, 1986). Close alignment helps to reduce agency costs that leads to improvements in firm value. Yet, repeated calls are made to increase both the power of shareholders and their proxy access (Bebchuk & Fried, 2005; Bebchuk & Hirst, 2010; Bebchuk et al., 2002).[1] Typically, calls debate shareholder behaviour in terms of activity or passivity. After the Global Financial Crisis (GFC) of 2007–2009, calls intensified and advocated changes which are inconsistent with traditional agency perspectives (Bebchuk & Weisbach, 2010). Whilst some academics, policymakers and commentators argue that increased proxy access is needed, others contend that shareholders are too interested in short-term performance at the expense of the long-term. Research that provides answers to some of these questions will enhance the debate and inform policymakers.

Many changes were legislated by the Dodd-Frank Act of 21 July 2010. For instance, changes to direct proxy access, allowing shareholders to nominate board members, changes in the terms of executives' contracts and improvements in shareholder voting rights. It seems there has been a considerable shift away from board-centric towards shareholder-centric view though this movement has not been smooth. A notable illustration occurred on 4 October 2010 when the Securities and Exchange Committee (SEC) announced a significant delay to the implementation

[1] Proxy access refers to enhanced rights that give shareholders greater say over firm decisions, for example, allowing shareholders to nominate their own board candidates. Traditionally, such decisions were the preserve of company boards and senior management.

of its proxy access rule.[2] Even more surprising was the repeal of SEC's Rule 14a-11 by the United States Court of Appeals on 22 July 2011, on grounds that the SEC had not adequately considered the economic impact of increased proxy access. Berger and Murry (2009, p. 1) sum up the paucity of empirical evidence for increased shareholder empowerment ... '*Interestingly, the stockholder-centric model is not being driven by either law or statute, and the public policy benefits of this movement are far from certain. Moreover, there has been no clear empirical evidence to support the notion that the national economy or investors generally benefit from giving stockholders more control over the corporate machinery*'. If Rule 14a-11 had been passed, the proxy access rule would have allowed certain groups of shareholders, including those who had held their shares for three or more years and those with shareholdings exceeding three per cent of total shares, to nominate directors. Larcker et al. (2011) identified thirteen significant regulatory changes made by the SEC in 2007 regarding proxy access; namely, the rights of shareholders to nominate and elect company board members.

Whilst shareholder-centrism implies a significant role for shareholders in firm decision-making, the 'board-centric/director-centric' view references the superior decision-making abilities of corporate boards (Roe, 1991). An 'effective' board should deliver superior firm performance, but performance outcomes depend on decisions made by board members and senior management. As the benefits to shareholders are conditional on the capabilities of management teams, shareholders might willingly pay a premium or 'rent' to secure and retain for managerial talent. Castanias and Helfat (1991, p. 3) assess the impact of managerial talent on the generation of rents. They show how in firms with dispersed outside ownership, managers face incentives to act efficiently ... '*greater managerial discretion may not necessarily be harmful to the firm as some interpretations of agency theory might indicate, and may even play an important role in rent generation*'.

Researchers identify weaknesses in shareholder voting mechanisms resulting from rational apathy (Berle & Means, 1932) and heterogeneous shareholder interests (Bruner, 2008). Hoskisson et al. (2002) report substantial variation in shareholders' preferences which they attribute to differences in investment time horizons and incentives. Berle and Means

[2] The SEC adopted Rule 14a-11 on 25 August 2010 following a 3–2 vote.

(1932, pp. 76 and 80) explain rational apathy as … '*the normal apathy of the small stockholder is such that he will either fail to return his proxy vote, or will sign on the dotted line, returning his proxy to the [management] of the corporation*'. Given that '*his personal vote will count for little or nothing at the meeting unless he has a very large block of stock, the shareholder is practically reduced to the alternative of not voting at all or else of handing over his vote to individuals over whom he has not control and in whose selection he did not participate*'. In summary, Hayden and Bodie (2010, p. 26) explain that '*divergent interests among shareholders may point in a variety of different governance directions. That is, while shareholder heterogeneity provides general support for board primacy, it is relevant to almost any feature of corporate governance that makes the system more or less responsive to the shareholders (and it generally exerts pressure in the direction of making the system less responsive*)'. Accordingly, the non-involvement of shareholders and limitations in their access rights are '*not merely an incident of the structure of corporate law, but one of its defining and efficiency enhancing features*' (Bruner, 2008, p. 14). In accordance, Bainbridge (2003) calls shareholders 'platonic guardians'. This discussion suggests that shareholders take a passive role which affords managers considerable flexibility.

Our motivations stem from the interest and importance of corporate governance mechanisms (Certo, 2003; Ertimur et al., 2010; Hillman & Dalziel, 2003; Hillman et al., 2009; Kor & Sundaramurphy, 2009; Kroll et al., 2007). Second, the deluge of governance scandals in the early 2000s. Third, by the significant changes in corporate governance rules and regulations including the 2002 Sarbanes–Oxley Act (SOX) and 2010 Dodd-Frank Act. Fourth, increases in the importance of shareholder voice and shareholder proposal mechanism. Indeed, '*the effectiveness of shareholder voting as a mechanism to effect changes in corporate policy remains an open and controversial question*' (Armstrong et al., 2012, p. 2).

After the 2002 passage of SOX, a record number of shareholder proposals were put forward to vote between 2002 and 2006. Between 1990 and 1994, the average number of proposals submitted to proxy was 307 per annum (Gillan & Starks, 2000). In comparison, between 2002 and 2006 the average annual number of shareholder proposals was 648 (Georgeson Shareholder Annual Survey, 2006). The proportion of non-binding proposals that received majority votes by shareholders and were implemented by firms more than doubled between 1997 and 2004 to over 40% (Ertimur et al., 2010). Irrespective of any positive or negative impact on target[3] firms' financial performance attributable to decisions whether to implement shareholder proposals that had received majority vote, Ertimur et al. (2010) show that outside directors experience a significant reduction in the possibility of losing their board seats and in addition other directorships following decisions to implement majority supported non-binding shareholder proposals. These trends enrich the governance debate and focus academic and policymaker attention on firm-level corporate governance, specifically the importance of non-binding shareholder proposals as a mechanism for shareholder voice (Hirschman, 1970).

Our final motivation stems from the fact that the GFC highlighted significant corporate governance failures at firms (Kirkpatrick, 2009; The Financial Crisis Enquiry Commission, 2011). Alleged governance deficiencies led academics and regulatory bodies to strongly criticise the traditional governance model and advocate changes to governance mechanisms. Changes included improving the ease with which shareholders can propose and vote for shareholder proposals and increasing the number of types of proposals that can be put to vote. This chapter sits against this backdrop.

We examine proposals that would increase the relative power and direct access of shareholders. The 2010 Dodd-Frank Act signalled the culmination of increasing shareholder access and power in U.S. firms. The Act made it easier for shareholders to nominate board members, have greater say over director contracts, whilst strengthening shareholders' voting rights. Yet, the SEC delayed implementing its new proxy access rule on July 22, 2011, which would have further strengthened shareholders' rights and power, due to insufficient cost–benefit analysis of increasing shareholder power and access. The SEC Chair, Mary Jo White, stated that '*such transparent and robust analysis, including consideration of the costs and benefits, will help ensure that effective and optimal solutions are achieved without unnecessary burdens or competitive harm*' (Lynch, 2013, p. 1).

The chapter proceeds as follows. We develop our hypotheses in Sect. 9.2. Section 9.3 presents data and methodology. Section 9.4 discusses our results whilst Sect. 9.5 concludes.

[3] We define a target firm is a firm that is subjected to a shareholder proposal that goes to a shareholder vote.

9.2 Hypothesis Development

Bebchuk (2003) and Bebchuk and Hirst (2010) argue that greater shareholder power and letting shareholders propose board candidates yield governance benefits. However, Lipton and Rosenblum (2003) claim that higher-quality executives could be less willing to serve on boards if shareholders can forward their own candidates in the competition for board seats. Although increasing shareholders' power and access did prove popular, some criticisms followed. Bainbridge (2008) thought shareholder power was already sufficient in most firms. He suggested that increases in shareholder power and access could prove counterproductive if it granted more power to certain strongly activist investors whose objectives were incompatible with most other shareholders. Greater shareholder power could undermine firm performance if shareholders are irrational or uniform and make decisions leading to sub-optimal firm performance (Matsusaka & Ozbas, 2013). Thus, restricting shareholder access may be optimal (Greenwood, 1996). Chen et al. (2008) and Iyengar and Zampelli (2009) consider whether increasing shareholder power and direct proxy access benefits most shareholders (and firm performance). It may simply be that voting against increased power and access to the firm is a rational response by shareholders.

We analyse shareholder proposals which would grant shareholders enhanced powers, namely, to limit director terms, put forward directors to the board, call special meetings, call for enhanced disclosure of executive compensation and increase committee independence including compensation committee independence. Ultimately, we ask whether shareholders may willingly support a board-centric governance model and relinquish control providing managers achieve firm performance targets.

Theory offers ambiguous conclusions, arguments and counterarguments for and against increased shareholder access and power. However, it provides us with expectations on the potential impact of proposals. Utilising an agency theory view that shareholder power is desirable, we expect shareholders to generally vote for increased access and power and anticipate a significant number of proposals pass with over 50% of the vote. We conjecture that in such cases, the market reacts positively to proposals thereby realising positive and significant cumulative abnormal returns (CARs). Alternatively, shareholders may not desire greater access if they believe that activist shareholders would become powerful. Separately, shareholders may be concerned about attracting and keeping the best quality executives and be hesitant to allow other shareholders to nominate candidates, especially if they believe nominations will be dominated by candidates sponsored by powerful activist shareholders. If, generally, shareholders do not value increased power and proxy access we expect a significant number of proposals to fail with moderate voting percentages. Finally, if shareholders make optimal decisions on a firm-by-firm basis then we may anticipate greater distribution of voting outcomes. If most firm shareholders are satisfied with extant governance arrangements and firm performance, shareholders may take an active interest in the vote but choose to vote strongly against a proposal with a targeted 'vote no' response.

The above discussion informs the framing of our research questions. First, we consider what the relationship is between shareholder proposal voting success (pass or fail) and firm performance (measured by cumulative abnormal returns, CAR) for the sample of governance-centred shareholder proposals. Unlike studies that concentrate on pass or fail results, we examine votes on either side of a passing threshold of 50%. In addition, we examine shareholder voting percentages across the whole spectrum of outcomes and specify different voting thresholds to better understand the nature of relationship between market reaction and shareholder proposal votes. Later, we explore the value shareholders give to proposals and contemplate that if a proposal is generally unpopular with shareholders, then we may expect more negative voting outcomes are associated with positive market reaction. For example, we investigate whether shareholders value increased proxy access. We specify our first research question as follows:

> RQ1: What is the nature of the relationship between proposal voting outcome and market reaction?

Next, we examine whether the proximity of the vote to the pass threshold matters. We specify increasingly narrower thresholds closer to the pass and fail margin which allows us to examine shareholder voting decisions in greater detail. For example, shareholders may vote more negatively in some firms and/or for particular types of proposals.

Whilst past studies examine the impact of shareholder proposals on firm performance, few studies consider the impact of shareholder voting percentages on firm performance. We hypothesise that if a firm is delivering value for shareholders, we may expect shareholders to vote not only against a greater number of shareholder proposals that increase their relative power and proxy access, but also anticipate that shareholders may (rationally) vote more negatively against such proposals. We consider the impact of shareholder proposal votes by examining cumulative abnormal share price returns following votes. We examine the impact of particular proposal voting percentages on firm performance (CAR) around shareholder proposal voting dates whilst controlling for firm characteristics and instrumenting for 'over-voting'.[4] We hypothesise that strong positive market reaction corresponds to lower voting outcomes provided the low vote percentage is representative of shareholder and market interest. Alternatively, if as Thomas and Cotter (2007) suggest, shareholders view proposals as unimportant and choose not to vote, causing low vote turnouts, we expect a marginal or insignificant market reaction to the vote. Hence, an important difference exists between a deliberate 'no vote' by shareholders, which signals strong disapproval of a proposal, and proposals deemed unimportant by shareholders. To tackle this difference, we examine the impact of differences in voting percentages and pass thresholds leading to RQ2.

> RQ2: Does voting percentage matter in determining market reaction to shareholder proposals?

Next, we consider proposals designed to remove conflicts of interest on boards. This category of proposal relates to the removal of CEO duality (separation of Chair and CEO roles). Such an examination is relevant given the trend for firms to convert from duality to separating these roles. Few firms have converted from having separate roles to duality (Chen et al., 2008). Furthermore, the 2010 Dodd-Frank Act requires

[4] Over-voting itself may occur for several reasons. It might occur unintentionally because the beneficial owners of lent shares are unaware their shares have been lent to a third party and, as such, they incorrectly believe they have the right to vote whilst, similarly, a holder of lent shares believes they have acquired the right to vote. As a result, if both beneficial owners and holders of lent shares vote, over-voting occurs with twice as many votes cast relative to the number of shares. Alternatively, over-voting may reflect a deliberate strategy by certain activist shareholders who create large hedging positions prior to vote, which affords considerable voting power without exposure to the market risk associated with share ownership. Thus, one can imagine situations when certain voting outcomes may not truly reflect the opinions of most firm shareholders. Finally, the extent of over-voting depends on the extent of lending market activity from the date shareholder records are dated up until the date of a proposal vote.

firms to publicly detail the rationale behind board leadership structures which compels firms to shift from duality. However, evidence is scarce on the impact of CEO duality on firm performance and whether shareholders value the separate roles. We address whether shareholders value removal of board-level conflict of interests in our next research questions:

> RQ3: What is the nature of the relationship between shareholder proposal votes to remove conflicts of board interest and market reaction?
> RQ4: Does voting percentage matter in determining market reaction to shareholder proposals designed to remove conflicts of board interest?

Whether CEO duality is associated with improved performance remains topical and largely unresolved. Organisational theory (Cyert & March, 1963) and stewardship theory (Donaldson & Davis, 1991) view CEO duality as beneficial because establishing a clear leader of the organisational structure produces more effective, timely and efficient decision-making thereby leading to superior firm performance. Conversely, the traditional agency perspective posits a negative relationship between firm performance and duality because duality reduces shareholders' ability to monitor and assess the CEO (Fama & Jensen, 1983; Jensen & Meckling, 1976), which could cause management entrenchment with CEOs wielding enhanced power to nominate preferred board members and set executive compensation. This outcome could create further agency problems leading to even poorer firm performance (Pi & Timme, 1993; Rechner & Dalton, 1991).

Fisman et al. (2005) describe a situation when management entrenchment exerts a positive effect. If a firm fires the CEO due to poor firm performance following shareholder voice, irrespective of whether the CEO was responsible, firm performance may not improve post dismissal. Fisman et al. (2005) conjecture that under conditions of board and manager entrenchment, good quality CEOs are less likely to be fired since boards are more likely (and are able) to protect good quality board members. Notwithstanding, CEO dismissals or vote no campaigns are rare events (Taylor, 2010). Ertugrul and Krishnan (2011) studied CEO dismissals between 1996 and 2008 finding that nearly half of firms dismiss CEOs even in the absence of negative stock market returns. When board members face stronger incentives implicit in executive compensation packages, they are more likely to act on private information and dismiss the CEO. Ertugrul and Krishnan present two seemingly conflicting yet relevant findings. First, early CEO dismissals reflect proactive decisions taken by boards to remove low-quality CEOs. Second, there are no significant differences in the speed in which dismissed CEOs acquire new CEO positions which suggest that CEOs dismissed early may have comparable abilities to those dismissed later.

Duality has long been associated with a greater degree of management entrenchment (Pfeffer, 1981). Faleye (2007, 2010) finds that duality is associated with increases in organisational complexity, greater managerial ownership and CEO reputation. It suggests firms deliberately decide whether to operate with a dual structure. Nevertheless, the evidence on duality is ambiguous. Chen et al. (2008) and Iyengar and Zampelli (2009) attribute this to endogeneity emphasising that firm board structure is determined both endogenously and optimally with respect to heterogeneous firm-level characteristics and the nature of firm ownership. Elsewhere, Boyd et al. (2011) and Peng et al. (2007) find no evidence of a significant relationship between duality and firm performance whereas Yang and Zhao (2012) find a positive relationship albeit only under certain conditions, such as when firms face substantial costs of acquiring information or when firms face relatively higher processing costs, and in firms that benefit most from faster decision-making.

Our discussion helps inform expectations as to how shareholders value proposals that seek to remove CEO duality. We assess whether the market agrees with shareholder proposal vote outcomes by examining CARs around the vote date. If board structure is determined endogenously and optimally with respect to heterogeneous firm-level characteristics and the nature of firm ownership, we expect that in the absence of substantial exogenous shocks affecting a particular industry, most shareholders would prefer to continue under the existing organisational structure, especially if previous firm performance was good. Accordingly, we expect shareholders to vote against such a proposal more often. Moreover, we anticipate the market reacts more positively to strong negative voting with over-voting proving significant if the issue is particularly important to certain shareholders.

We formally test this hypothesis from the perspective that if the market agrees with a particular voting outcome it is more likely to 'vote positively' leading to positive abnormal returns around event dates. We do not focus exclusively on pass or fail outcomes and consider vote percentages. Hence, if a proposal is unpopular with shareholders, we anticipate that a strongly negative vote corresponds with stronger positive abnormal market returns (CARs).

We investigate whether the degree of management entrenchment influences shareholder proposal voting behaviour and formulate our fifth research question as:

> RQ5: What is the relationship between the degree of management entrenchment and shareholder proposal voting outcomes?

Given the ambiguity in the extant literature, we provide no exact expectation as to how management entrenchment impacts shareholders' voting. Yet, some strong indications exist on shareholder voting behaviour and market reaction. Harris and Raviv (2010) model shareholder voting behaviour and show it is optimal that they seek greater control over firm decision-making and strategy when management is entrenched irrespective of any information disadvantage shareholders face relative to board members and individual objectives. Empirically, Ertimur et al. (2010) find shareholders more likely to turn out and vote for proposals that increase firm governance quality when managers are entrenched. Thus, we expect shareholders seek more control when firm entrenchment is highest and vote strongly for proposals designed to increase shareholder access and improve governance quality and board transparency. We expect a greater percentage of proposals to pass in firms where management entrenchment is high. Intuitively, shareholders are more active in their positive voting behaviour when entrenchment is highest resulting in higher vote percentages and positive market reaction to votes.

Given the publicised movement towards a more shareholder-centric view in the U.S. away from a board-centric perspective we outline a further research question. We ask whether U.S. companies are more shareholder-centric or board-centric and discuss whether preference has changed over time.

> RQ6: Are U.S. firms more board-centric or shareholder-centric?

9.3 Data and Research Design

RiskMetrics and Thomson Reuters are our main data source on shareholder proposals. We combine this information with company financial data and equity prices from Compustat and CRSP. We download the Bebchuk et al. (2009)E-entrenchment index from the author's website and match the sample to shareholder proposal and firm financial data. The E-index is a composite index based on six equally weighted corporate governance provisions collated by the Investor Responsibility Centre (IRRC). We source data on outstanding security loans from the OTC Bulletin Board (OTCBB) and from Thomson Reuters DataStream. Finally, we source U.S. state-level economic data from the Federal Reserve Bank of Philadelphia. Our final dataset comprises 1030 corporate governance proposals for 474 publicly listed U.S. firms from 1997 to 2008.

Research Approach

Initially, we consider whether shareholders value positive governance changes by observing market reaction measured by cumulative abnormal returns around proposal event dates. We also examine whether market reactions change over time. Next, we consider two types of corporate governance proposals on increasingly popular proposal voting topics. First, proposals relating to removing conflict of interest on boards. Second, proposals explicitly relating to positively increasing shareholder power and access (direct proxy access proposals). In doing so, we investigate whether shareholders value increases in power and access. For example, whether shareholders willingly sacrifice increases in proxy access if management is making efficient choices on behalf of the firm. A potential endogeneity problem could exist since shareholders develop and file proposals, say to increase proxy access, which could induce managers to alter their behaviour and make different decisions leading to changes in current and future firm performance. In turn, this may affect the likelihood of subsequent shareholder proposals and shareholders' voting response if further proposals are put forward in future proxy seasons. We note that withdrawn shareholder proposals are nearly always withdrawn by sponsors after negotiation with firms.

We consider the possibility that outcomes are affected by other firm characteristics. Hence, our econometric models specify several control variables for firm industry, firm size and state-level economic conditions using the State composite index of the Federal Reserve Bank of Philadelphia. We control for firm size using the natural logarithm of total assets since one may expect a degree of positive correlation between total firm assets, the firm's credit rating and the stability of share price returns. Unlike previous studies, we control for the impact of over-votes (Smith, 2013) generated by lent shares to affect proposal voting outcomes.

In the second stage of analysis, we assess the impact of management and board entrenchment on firm performance. We distinguish between entrenched management firms and firms without entrenched management. Following Jochem (2012), we use scores from the E-index to proxy for degree of management entrenchment with higher scores indicating greater entrenchment. However, we depart from previous studies by adopting a regression discontinuity (RD) technique to examine the relationship between shareholder proposal voting outcomes and firm performance controlling for firm characteristics and 'over-voting'.

Like Cuñat et al. (2012) and Smith (2012, 2013), we apply a fuzzy RD approach to analyse shareholder proposal votes around acceptance thresholds. Unlike a Sharp RD approach, Fuzzy RD considers that the likelihood of receiving the treatment may be staggered around a threshold point. RD and fuzzy RD are distinguishable by whether the treatment variable is estimated using a deterministic function (RD) or stochastic function (fuzzy RD). As such the '*design allows for a smaller jump in the probability of assignment to the treatment at the threshold without requiring the jump to equal 1*' (Imbens & Lemieux, 2008, p. 4). For shareholder and management proposals, this feature of fuzzy RD is desirable since in the '*case of heterogeneous impacts, the local effect may be very different from the effect at values further away from the threshold*' (Klaauw, 2008, p. 225). Our RD approach follows Imbens and Lemieux (2008) and Smith (2013), and we follow their notation closely.

Our interest lies in the impact of votes cast on shareholder proposals which would increase shareholder proxy access, board transparency and general corporate governance. We are especially interested in differences between proposals that are narrowly voted against and proposals that receive marginal passes (majority votes) (seeCuñat et al., 2012; Imbens & Lemieux, 2008; Lee & Mas, 2012; Smith, 2013). Intuitively, the average characteristics of target firms that just pass and those that just fail should be comparable. '*However, this small difference in the vote share leads to a discrete change in the probability of implementing these proposals. In other words, for close-call proposals, passing is akin to an independent random event this is correlated with the implementation of the proposal, but it is "locally" exogenous and, therefore, uncorrelated with other firm characteristics*' Cuñat et al., (2012, p. 3).

We identify proposals that pass using a dummy variable D. The outcome variable Υ is the CARs obtained from a short window event study methodology utilising the market model and calculated across 220 previous trading days and three days event window. We specify observables, W and firm unobservables, U; treatment is a determinist function of a forcing variable, and C and V represent unobservables around the pass/fail margin. Following Smith (2013), we specify treatment firms as those in which the percentage of shareholder votes for a proposal exceeds a minimum proposal acceptance threshold, and consider the percentage of votes for, X, may be an endogenous outcome of observables, W, used to calculate the outcome equation.

$$\begin{aligned} Y &= (\tau_i(W_i, U_i))*D_i + \delta_1 W_i + U_i \\ D_i &= 1\{X_i \geq \mathrm{c}\} \\ X_i &= \delta_2 W_i + V \end{aligned} \tag{9.1}$$

Smith (2013) explains that when treatment firms are determined by the observable and unobservables and there are zero assumptions with regards to the coefficients for δ_1 and δ_2 nor the degree of collinearity between U, V and W, the model becomes a generalised model of heterogeneity.

However, we cannot estimate the treatment effect directly because the acceptance of a proposal is likely correlated with omitted variables which themselves are correlated with the outcome variable Υ (Cuñat et al., 2012). Following Smith (2013), we compute the treatment effect as the difference between the outcome variable Υ and the treatment status, and what would have been the observable outcome if the treatment status had not occurred. Since the direction of causality is unclear, any estimation of the true average treatment effect (ATE) is subject to selection (SB) and omitted variables (OVB) biases. Smith (2013) denotes this estimator as T_{Diff} and shows a simple estimation of the difference between the treatment and control groups.

$$T_{Diff} = \mathrm{E}[Y|D = 1] - \mathrm{E}[Y|D = 0]$$

$$= \underbrace{\mathrm{E}|\tau(W, U)|}_{\text{ATE}} + \underbrace{\mathrm{E}|\tau_i(W, U)D = 1]}_{\text{SB}}$$

$$+ \underbrace{\mathrm{E}|\delta_i W + U|D = 1] - \mathrm{E}[\delta_i W + U|D = 0]}_{\text{OVB}} \tag{9.2}$$

Equation 9.1 provides useful clues on the direction of causality and degree of OVB with regards to firm performance outcomes. Omitted variable bias arises because the outcome variable, Υ, is a function of a priori expectations of a shareholder proposal vote by the market. Hence, the market forms an expectation about a shareholder proposal vote and subsequently adjusts the expectation in response to the actual vote. Such adjustments are priced into the market. Since proposals affect current and future management decision-making, we hypothesise that changes affect both current and future firm performance. Thus, we expect the relationship between the likelihood of a shareholder proposal and management decision-making is endogenous. Whilst existing studies consider relations between non-binding shareholder proposals and performance metrics, such as share price returns, ROA and ROE few studies examine shareholder reaction to corporate governance proposals whilst controlling for firm-level characteristics, management entrenchment, OVB and over-voting. We address these gaps and, in doing so, inform current debate.

Following Smith (2013), the RD estimator is:

$$\tau RD = \lim_{X\downarrow c} \mathrm{E}[Y|D = 1] - \lim_{X\downarrow c} \mathrm{E}[Y|D = 0]$$

$$= \underbrace{+\mathrm{E}[\tau_i(u, w)|X = c]}_{WATE}$$

$$+ \underbrace{\lim_{X\downarrow c} \mathrm{E}[\tau_i(u, w)]|X = c] - \lim_{X\uparrow c} \mathrm{E}[\tau_i(u, w)]|X = c]}_{SB} \tag{9.3}$$

Smith (2013) redefines the problem to be one in which the proposal vote *Margin* is not precisely observable:

$$\begin{aligned} Y &= (\tau(W, U))D + \delta_1 W + U_2 \\ D &= 1\{V \geq c - (\delta_2 W + \emptyset Z)\} \end{aligned} \tag{9.4}$$

He shows how identification is achievable if $\varnothing \neq 0$ and $\mathrm{E}[UV|W = w, Z = z] = 0$ since:

$$\begin{aligned} T_{IV} &= \mathrm{E}[Y|W = w, Z = z, D = 1] - \mathrm{E}[Y|W = w, Z = z, D = 0] \\ &= \mathrm{E}[\tau(W, U)|W = w, Z = z, D = 1] \\ &\quad + \mathrm{E}[U|W = w, Z = z, D = 1] - \mathrm{E}[U|W = w, Z = z, = 0] \\ &= \mathrm{E}[\tau(W, U)|W = w, Z = z, D = 1] \\ &\quad + \mathrm{E}[U|W = w, Z = z] - \mathrm{E}[U|W = w, Z = z] \\ &= \underbrace{\mathrm{E}[\tau(W, U)|W = w, Z = z]}_{LATE} \end{aligned} \tag{9.5}$$

Smith (2013) demonstrates that by combining an instrumental variables approach with RD we can relax assumptions regarding relevant covariates since Eq. (9.5) is sensitive to conditioning correctly on *W*. Accordingly, we specify the local average treatment effect (LATE):

$$\tau_{RD+IV} = \lim_{\downarrow c - w\delta_2 - \emptyset z} (\tau|Z = z) - \lim_{\uparrow c - w\delta_2 - \emptyset z} (\tau|Z = z) \tag{9.6}$$

Whilst existing studies experience difficulties in identifying suitable governance instruments (Larcker & Rusticus, 2010), we specify two main instruments. Our main instrument is 'over-voting' (Smith, 2012, 2013), which we use in the fuzzy RD setup. We follow Smith (2013) and instrument using the number of actual lent shares relative to total shares available in the OTC securities market. We also instrument using the predicted values of lent shares by estimating the number of lent shares in the OTC on proposal voting days using an event study with three-day event window and 220-days estimation period. We use our instruments in probability models using an instrumental variable technique and later test for robustness using an IV Logit model. The approach considers over-voting as an exogenous shock that is independent to the value implication of a shareholder vote. Smith (2013) rationalises the choice of instrument on the basis that over-voting often occurs accidentally since investors often are unaware of a loss in their rights to vote. By including over-voting as an instrument, we significantly reduce the likelihood that selection bias is driving results.

We contend that withdrawn proposals influence managers' subsequent behaviour and decision-making. Furthermore, in cases where a proposal is withdrawn before going to vote, the withdrawal might be because managers made concessions to shareholders. The threat of a future proposal vote may cause managers to change their behaviour and decisions to avoid future proposals. Prior literature suggests that listening to shareholder proposals benefits board members directly. Ertimur et al. (2010) report that directors who fail to implement successful shareholder proposals suffer personally and are more likely to lose their board seat and other executive positions. To address these possibilities and reduce OVB arising from the possibility that proposals made in previous time periods affect future firm risk and efficiency and, also, the probability of subsequent shareholder proposals, we code a dummy variable equal to 1 if a firm received a proposal that went to vote or received a proposal that was withdrawn prior to vote.

$$Overvotes = VotesOverOut * Turnout \tag{9.7}$$

$$Margin = VotesOverOut - RequiredVote \tag{9.8}$$

$$Pass = \left\{ \frac{0 Margin < 0}{1 Margin \geq 0} \right\} \tag{9.9}$$

We follow Smith's (2013) approaches to arrive at our estimator. First, estimate the conditional expectation for increasingly small intervals around the proposal acceptance cut-off:

$$\tau_{RD} = \lim_{Margin \downarrow 0} \mathrm{E}[OUTCOME | PASS = 1] - \lim_{Margin \uparrow 0} \mathrm{E}[Outcome | PASS = 0]$$

Second, allow for variability around the proposal acceptance threshold using a second-order polynomial. The estimated treatment effect τ_{RD} is:

$$\tau_{RD,h} = [OUTCOME|PASS = 1, |MARGIN| < h] \\ - \mathrm{E}[OUTCOME|PASS = 0, |MARGIN| < h]$$

Following Smith (2013), and in contrast to the second approach, we apply a less parametric approach to obtain the estimator. It involves computing kernel estimates of the discontinuity around the acceptance cut-off level. Estimated returns above and below the acceptance cut-off levels are then calculated as moving averages.

$$OUTCOME = \tau_{RD} PASS + \beta_0 MARGIN + \beta_1 MARGIN \\ * PASS \beta_3 MARGIN^2 + \beta_4 MARGIN^2 * PASS + \varepsilon$$

To deal with endogeneity concerns regarding proposals around the threshold of proposal acceptance, we follow Smith (2013) and use over-voting as an instrument so that any proposals around the acceptance level are driven by variation in securities lending activity. This approach is important since we are interested in identifying the percentage of votes for a proposal which is based on the number of shares outstanding. Smith explains that the variation in approach involves moving from a sharp RD model to a fuzzy RD and specifying $VotesOverCast$ as the forcing variable as opposed to $VotesOverOut$. Formally, we specify the following model based on Smith (2013):

$$OUTCOME = \delta_1(VotesOvercast - VotesRequired) + \tau_{IV} \widehat{\widehat{PASS}} + \mathrm{u} \tag{9.10}$$

$\widehat{\widehat{PASS}}$ is calculated as:

$$\widehat{\widehat{PASS}} = \begin{cases} 0 & SharesOnLoan > |MARGIN|, \text{Observed } PASS = 0 \\ \widehat{PASS} & SharesOnLoan > |MARGIN| \\ 1 & SharesOnLoan > |MARGIN|, \text{Observed } PASS = 1 \end{cases} \tag{9.11}$$

$\widehat{PASS}$ is predicted from the following linear probability estimate:

$$PASS = \delta_2(VotesOvercast - VoteRequired) + \varnothing SharesOnLoan + \mathrm{u} \tag{9.12}$$

For observations in which: $SharesOnLoan > |MARGIN|$

We specify the following factor model for our *Output* variables (see Smith, 2013):

$$\ln(OUTPUT_{t-1,t+1} = \beta_0 + \beta_1 pass + \beta_2 margin + \beta_3 pass * margin + \beta_4 margin^2 + \beta_5 pass * margin^2 \tag{9.13}$$

where time $t = 0$ is the shareholder proposal vote date and vote *MARGIN* is calculated as:

$$MARGIN = \frac{VotesFor}{OutstandingShares} - ProposalAcceptanceThreshold \tag{9.14}$$

Estimation difficulties can arise from probability models computed using 2SLS as we are using dummy variables with a non-linear conditional expectation function. This could lead to different weighted averages of marginal effects and potentially biased results. Thus, we compute a simple IV Probit model and compute first-stage instrumental values.

9.4 Empirical Results

We discuss summary statistics by proposals that pass and fail. Table 9.1 shows that the mean market reaction to proposal votes, measured by CAR, is broadly similar for proposals that pass and fail. However, there is greater variability in market responses to proposals that fail. Firm size plays a role since the average size of firms with failed proposal votes is substantially larger. Nordén and Strand (2011) suggest that some activist shareholders may seek to bring proposals to a vote, even if they are likely to fail, for reasons other than improving firm governance or performance.

Proposals have more success when firms are less profitable (see gross profit and net profit variables), which suggests that shareholders 'punish' management for relatively poor performance (Romano, 2001). Karpoff et al. (1996) find that firms targeted by proposals from shareholders are less profitable. Furthermore, the large difference in earnings per share

Table 9.1 Selected summary statistics

Proposal pass	*Variable*	*Min*	*Mean*	*Max*	*SD*	*N*
0 (No)	Vote for per cent	0	26.06	50	15.33	1381
	CAR	–0.72	0.02	2	0.13	1756
	Total Assets	1.43	51,340	2,380,000	165,344	2280
	Gross profit/loss	–4949	5842	115,242	11,677	2280
	Net income/loss	–6417	1145	49,425	3653	2280
	Total revenue	–1670	16,954	464,603	35,696	2280
	Operating expense	0.589	13,486	378,617	30,062	2280
	Earnings per share from operations	–88.60	18.56	37,627	789	2277
	Total liabilities	0.02	42,851	2,195,000	152,623	2280
	Book value per share	–3556	218	360,944	7866	2272
1 (Yes)						
	Vote for per cent	51	65.52	100	11.73	696
	CAR	–0.6	0.01	0.57	0.11	533
	Total Assets	4.6	37,154	2,340,000	152,758	689
	Gross profit/loss	–1027	4837	87,317	9137	689
	Net income/loss	–1604	943	41,153	2880	689
	Total revenue	0	14,809	349,113	25,826	689
	Operating expense	1.73	12,121	277,896	21,126	689
	Earnings per share from operations	–17.78	1.88	14.16	2.416	689
	Total liabilities	0.02	30,395	2,218,000	142,464	687
	Book value per share	–40.81	428	282,890	10,800	686
Total						
	Vote for per cent	0	39.3	100	23.44	2077
	CAR	–0.72	0.01	2	0.13	2289
	Total Assets	1.43	48,048	2,377,000	162,595	2969
	Gross profit/loss	–4949	5609	115,242	11,146	2969
	Net income/loss	–64,167	1098	49,425	3489	2969
	Total revenue	–1670	16,456	464,603	33,672	2969
	Operating expense	0.59	13,169	378,617	28,244	2969
	Earnings per share from operations	–88.6	14.69	37,627	691	2966
	Total liabilities	0.02	39,967	2,218,000	150,400	2967
	Book value per share	–3556	267	360,944	8634	2958

This table displays selected summary statistics for all corporate governance proposals before the removal of proposals not of direct interest, including those not positively directed towards a change in firm governance. All company financial variables are in US dollars millions at 2000 prices. CAR is the cumulative abnormal return on a proposal voting day estimated using an event study methodology estimated over 220 trading days and three-day event window

from operations is almost ten times lower in firms where shareholders pass a proposal vote. The evidence suggests that targeted firms generally exhibit poorer performance and lower quality of corporate governance. Yet, the presence of systematic differences suggests some degree of selection bias (Fig. 9.1).

Figures 9.2 and 9.3 show the breakdown of shareholder proposals from 1997 to 2008 by twelve detailed proposal categories. Given arguments that executive compensation should be tied to longer-term firm performance and/or broader ethical and social concerns, we note that these proposals steadily declined in relative shareholder importance from a high of 20% in 1997 to 0.3% in 2008. There was a considerable increase in the number of proposals designed to give shareholders greater say on executive pay and, especially, to proposals seeking to align executive remuneration with shareholder value-maximising objectives. Of particular importance are governance proposals designed to remove board-level conflicts of interest and to increase shareholder access and power. On average, proposals to increase proxy access accounted for 23% of total governance proposals from 2005 to 2008. Conflict of interest and CEO duality proposals also grew in relative importance after SOX was introduced in 2002.

Table 9.2 shows results from RD regressions for the sample of corporate governance proposals. Panel A shows the simplest RD specification, and Panel C shows the fully specified model. A positive coefficient for the pass dummy $\beta 1$ indicates a positive market response to the passing of a shareholder proposal. It proxies the value placed by the market on the outcome of a particular proposal vote. In the first regressions, the pass margin threshold is pass and fail (<50%). In subsequent columns, we specify increasingly narrower thresholds. In the right-hand column, we only consider proposals within a narrow bandwidth of 12.5% above and below the pass margin.

The highly significant negative coefficient $\beta 1$ (in panels A and B) for the narrowest voting pass margin (12.5% on either side of the pass margin) implies that the market reacts most negatively to governance proposals which narrowly pass. It suggests that voting percentage matters more to shareholders when shareholder proposal votes are closely run affairs. The significant albeit small coefficient for 'Observed % votes for' in panel A for the narrowest voting margin implies that the market reacts positively to increases in voting percentage. However, this may be

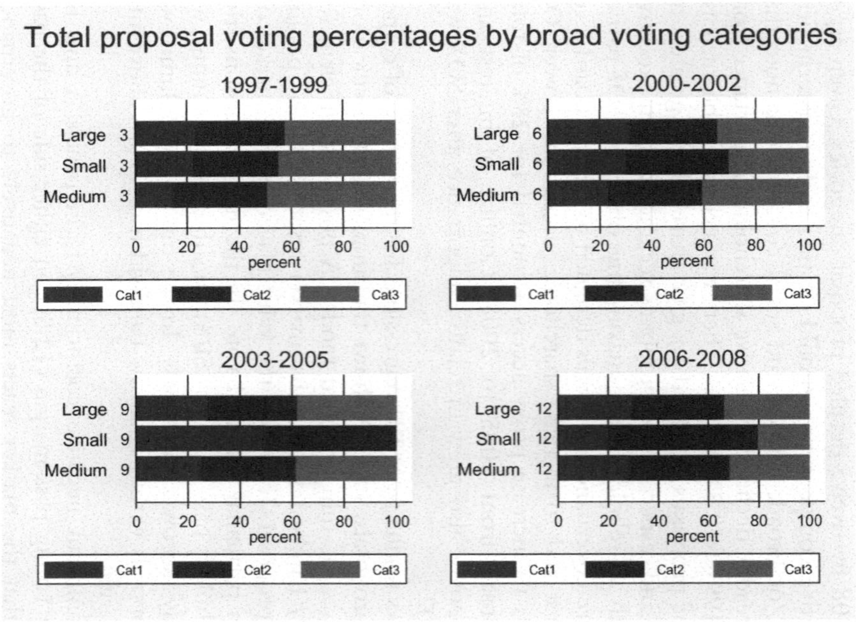

Fig. 9.1 Broad categories of corporate governance proposals (Figure shows average vote percentages for three main categories of governance proposals for small, medium and large firms measured by total assets for different years. Cat1 includes proposals to limit or give shareholders a say on executive compensation, Cat2 includes proposals to remove board conflicts of interest and Cat3 comprises proposals that directly increase shareholder access)

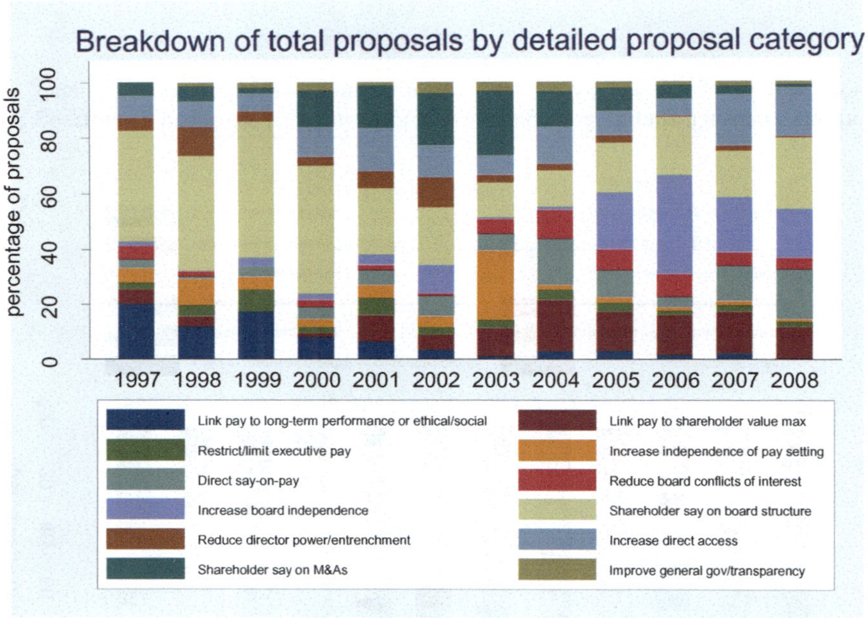

Fig. 9.2 Corporate governance proposals by detailed proposal category 1 (Figure shows the breakdown of shareholder proposals by detailed proposal category and year. From 2004 to 2008, the share of proposals designed to increase proxy access has risen as have proposals designed to decrease the level of managerial entrenchment and votes on executive remuneration)

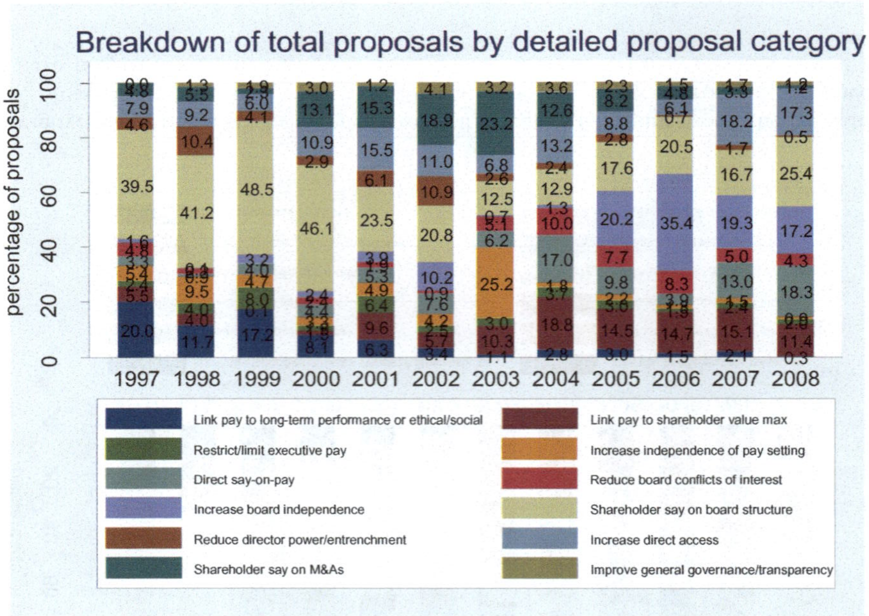

Fig. 9.3 Corporate governance proposals by detailed proposal category 2 (Figure illustrates the breakdown of shareholder proposals by detailed proposal category and year with the actual percentage of total governance proposals shown)

Table 9.2 All corporate governance proposals

Panel A				
Pass margin:	(<50%)	(<37.5%)	(<25%)	(<12.5%)
Pass (dummy)	0.0238*	0.00625	–0.0135	–0.0430***
	(1.68)	(0.42)	(–0.92)	(–2.71)
Observed % votes for	–0.000248	5.09e-05	0.000347	0.000524**
	(–0.80)	(0.16)	(1.23)	(2.40)
Constant	0.0148	0.00748	0.00834	0.0278**
	(1.40)	(0.81)	(0.93)	(2.24)
Observations	749	692	556	354
R-squared	0.006	0.003	0.004	0.013

Panel B				
Pass margin:	(<50%)	(<37.5%)	(<25%)	(<12.5%)
Pass (dummy)	–0.0249	0.0161	0.00618	–0.0364**
	(–0.55)	(1.01)	(0.33)	(–1.97)
Observed % votes for	–0.000524	–0.000823	–0.000622	0.000222
	(–1.55)	(–1.58)	(–1.02)	(0.49)
Votes for x Pass	0.000885	0.000566**	0.000554*	0.000196
	(1.20)	(2.35)	(1.90)	(0.76)
Constant	0.0225**	0.0243**	0.0211*	0.0299**
	(1.99)	(2.00)	(1.83)	(2.37)
Observations	749	692	556	354
R-squared	0.009	0.010	0.008	0.014

Panel C				
Pass requirement:	(<50%)	(<37.5%)	(<25%)	(<12.5%)
Pass (dummy)	0.353	0.0187	0.0310	–0.00996
	(1.42)	(0.83)	(1.47)	(–0.33)
Observed % votes for	–0.00351**	–0.00315*	–0.00488***	–0.00293
	(–2.33)	(–1.94)	(–2.88)	(–1.04)
Votes for x Pass	5.55e-05**	3.92e-05	6.38e-05**	4.81e-05
	(–2.44)	(1.12)	(2.35)	(1.10)

(continued)

Table 9.2 (continued)

Panel C				
Votes for squared	–0.00791	0.00127	0.00229*	0.00190
	(–1.07)	(0.74)	(1.83)	(1.06)
Votes for squared x Pass	2.73e-05	-2.24e-05	-4.20e-05	-3.70e-05
	(0.47)	(–0.60)	(–1.62)	(–1.01)
Constant	0.0501***	0.0502***	0.0630***	0.0496***
	(2.82)	(2.80)	(3.31)	(2.60)
Observations	749	692	556	354
R-squared	0.019	0.016	0.018	0.015

t statistics in parentheses. *** $p < 0.01$, ** $p < 0.05$, * $p < 0.1$
Pass is a dummy variable equal to 1 if a vote is greater than the voting pass threshold. Observed % in favour is the number of percentage votes in support of a shareholder proposal. This model is re-estimated using each individual pass dummy. The threshold is 5% on either side of the pass threshold. Pass margin is the proximity of vote percentage to the pass threshold. For example, < 12.5% includes only proposals that fall within 12.5% of the pass margin. CAR is the dependent variable. The fully specified model used in Panel C and subsequent tables is: $= (CAR_{t-1,t+1}) = \beta 0 + \beta 1 \text{pass} + \beta 2 \text{margin} + \_\beta 3 \text{pass\_margin} + \beta 4 \text{margin}^2 + \beta 5 \text{pass\_margin}^2$
In subsequent regression tables $\beta 1$ is denoted 'Pass (dummy)', $\beta 2$ 'Observed % votes for', $\beta 3$ 'Votes for x Pass', $\beta 4$ 'Votes for squared' and $\beta 5$ 'Votes for squared x Pass'

partially driven by a small number of proposals that are valuable to shareholders and narrowly pass a vote. Possibly, omitted variable bias may be driving the result since the use of more sophisticated model specifications, including those that control for the possibility of over-voting, suggest that an increase in voting percentage is associated with a negative market response (lower CAR).

Next, we control for the possibility that over-voting affects voting outcomes. Table 9.4 shows results. The significant results, especially for proposals likely to be directly affected, demonstrate the importance of accounting for over-voting in subsequent analysis and suggest that failure to include over-voting as an instrumental variable causes bias from endogenous sorting closest to the number of votes required for a proposal to be passed (Smith, 2013).

Table 9.5 presents results controlling for over-voting using the 'actual lent shares' calculated in Table 9.3. The results compare to those in Table 9.2, although differences exist in terms of the magnitude of effects. Considering all proposals on either side of the pass threshold, the larger coefficients in Table 9.5 in comparison to Table 9.2 suggest that failing to control for over-voting causes an underreporting effect.

Both Tables 9.2 and 9.5 show that for all voting outcomes an increase in vote percentage leads to lower CARs. The number of lent shares affects proposal outcomes. An increase in the number of shares on loan is similarly associated with a fall in CARs. It indicates the ability of over-votes to affect proposal voting outcomes. As before, the market reacts most negatively to proposals that narrowly pass. Increases in votes further away from the narrowest voting margins generate a positive market impact. Table 9.6 includes regressions calculated using the predicted pass margin which accounts for shares on loan in OTC markets for proposals that may be affected by over-voting. Whilst the results are consistent with Tables 9.2 and 9.5, the model fit is better and the average effect of coefficients is slightly smaller. This evidence demonstrates how over-voting affects vote outcomes.

Our findings suggest that the market rewards certain proposals that fail (or pass) by a greater margin. For instance, the difference between proposals for the whole sample and those limited to 37.5% of the pass margin. We suggest that this reaction is symptomatic of a positive (or negative) market response signalling a strong no vote (yes vote) by shareholders. Collectively, our results demonstrate that the vote percentage

Table 9.3 Estimation of predicted and actual on loan shares

	Actual % shares lent	*Predicted % shares lent*
% Shares on loan	0.0013***	
	(4.35)	
Existing % shares on loan		0.284***
		(3.60)
Votes for/votes cast	0.917***	0.485***
	(9.16)	(7.75)
Constant	−2.468***	−1.085***
	(−7.71)	(2.77)
Observations	199	114
R-squared	0.313	0.222

t statistics in parentheses. $^{***}p < 0.01$, $^{**}p < 0.05$, $^{*}p < 0.1$

This table shows robust first-stage OLS estimates for the linear pass model as a function of actual and predicted firm shares on loan in the OTC market, the number of votes for a proposal relative to the number cast, the threshold percentage required for a shareholder proposal to pass, and the percentage of shares on loan on the date of a particular proposal vote. Only proposal votes that could be affected by over-voting are included in the estimations. We use predicted residuals to generate the variables 'Actual Lent Shares' and 'Predicted Lent Shares' which are used in subsequent regressions

Table 9.4 The impact of over-voting on shareholder proposal outcomes

	Full sample	*Affected by over-vote*
% Shares on loan	0.0123**	0.243*
	(1.92)	(1.77)
Yes votes/Votes cast	−0.412***	−0.486***
	(−26.26)	(−8.68)
Constant	−1.065***	−2.855***
	(−19.05)	(−3.22)
Observations	1008	90
R-squared	0.457	0.470

t statistics in parentheses. ***$p < 0.01$, **$p < 0.05$, *$p < 0.1$
This table reports the relationship between OTC lending activity around proposal voting dates and proposal voting outcomes. It details estimations from a robust OLS model for proposal votes that have a greater pass/fail margin than the ratio of lent shares to actual shares in the OTC securities market on the day of a proposal vote. The far column shows the number of proposals likely to be affected by over-voting vis-á-vis all shareholder proposal votes

and, specifically, the proximity of the vote to the pass margin are important in determining market responses. Ours is one of a small number of studies finding that shareholder proposals induce positive market reaction (see Prevost et al., 2012; Renneboog & Szilagyi, 2011). However, our finding might reflect employment of a robust RD approach that allows us to examine proposal votes in greater scrutiny. Finally, markets reward proposals that fail but gain a substantial number of votes. The corporate social responsibility firm *As You So*, which mediates in shareholder dialogues for large publicly listed firms, argues that social proposals that attract percentages as low as 10% are difficult for management to ignore (As You So, 2013).

We turn to examine proposals designed to remove conflicts of board interest. Table 9.7 reports regressions incorporating the fitted values for actual lent shares calculated in Table 9.3 whereas regressions in Table 9.8 use the fitted values for predicted lent shares. Compared to the full sample of governance proposals analysed in Tables 9.2, 9.5 and 9.6, the average effect of coefficients is greater implying that the market reacts more strongly to these proposals. Consistent with earlier evidence, the results show that both the pass/fail outcome of a vote and the actual vote

Table 9.5 All positive corporate governance proposals using actual lent shares

Pass requirement:	*(<50%)*	*(<37.5%)*	*(<25%)*	*(<12.5%)*
Panel A				
Pass (dummy)	0.160***	0.00691	–0.0144	–0.0446**
	(2.65)	(0.45)	(–0.83)	(–2.54)
Observed % votes for	–0.00241**	7.73e-05	0.000400	0.000584**
	(–2.51)	(0.23)	(1.23)	(2.47)
Actual Lent Shares	–0.0414**	0.00257	0.000939	–0.00159
	(–2.34)	(0.60)	(0.19)	(–0.35)
Constant	0.0520***	0.00441	0.00504	0.0249**
	(2.69)	(0.47)	(0.56)	(1.97)
Observations	749	692	556	354
R-squared	0.016	0.004	0.005	0.014
Panel B				
Pass (dummy)	0.106	0.0372**	0.0232	–0.0257
	(1.61)	(2.30)	(1.20)	(–1.35)
Observed % votes for	–0.00285***	–0.00322***	–0.00274**	–0.00103
	(–2.82)	(–3.24)	(–2.54)	(–1.11)
Votes for x Pass	0.00109	0.00230***	0.00215***	0.00119
	(1.51)	(3.22)	(2.80)	(1.64)
Actual Lent Shares	–0.0432**	–0.0318***	–0.0279**	–0.0181
	(–2.47)	(–2.59)	(–2.25)	(–1.47)
Constant	0.0635***	0.0672***	0.0559***	0.0464***
	(3.04)	(3.34)	(2.88)	(2.60)
Observations	749	692	556	354
R squared	0.020	0.023	0.018	0.019
Panel C				
Pass (dummy)	0.414*	0.0180	0.0211	–0.00286
	(1.66)	(0.80)	(0.99)	(–0.09)
Observed % votes for	–0.00545***	–0.00485***	–0.00610***	–0.00516*
	(–3.25)	(–2.76)	(–3.33)	(–1.74)
Votes for x Pass	5.22e-05*	3.90e-05	6.10e-05**	5.51e-05
	(1.92)	(1.12)	(2.24)	(1.27)
Votes for squared	–0.00614	0.00423*	0.00506***	0.00506**
	(–0.87)	(1.95)	(2.71)	(2.18)
Votes for squared x Pass	1.83e-05	–4.18e-05	–6.04e-05**	–6.13e-05
	(0.32)	(–1.13)	(–2.26)	(–1.63)

(continued)

Table 9.5 (continued)

Pass requirement:	*(<50%)*	*(<37.5%)*	*(<25%)*	*(<12.5%)*
Actual Lent Shares	−0.0396**	−0.0325*	−0.0311*	−0.0319*
	(−2.27)	(−1.94)	(−1.85)	(−1.90)
Constant	0.0856***	0.0796***	0.0876***	0.0809***
	(3.62)	(3.38)	(3.62)	(3.24)
Observations	749	692	556	354
R-squared	0.029	0.024	0.025	0.023

t statistics in parentheses. ***$p < 0.01$, **$p < 0.05$, *$p < 0.1$
This table reports regressions for the whole sample and includes actual shares on loan in the OTC market on the date of a vote for proposals that may be affected by over-voting. Estimates are calculated using actual lent shares from Table 9.3 estimations

percentage matter. Considering proposals of this type (pass requirement <50%) and in contrast to Tables 9.2, 9.5 and 9.6, we find that an increase in the probability of a vote passing is associated with significant negative CARs. It suggests that most shareholders do not feel strongly about CEO duality. This result is inconsistent with agency theoretic arguments (Fama & Jensen, 1983; Jensen & Meckling, 1976) that duality negatively impacts firm performance because it is associated with increases in management entrenchment (Pfeffer, 1981), reductions in board independence (Finkelstein & D'Aveni, 1994; Rhoades et al., 2001) and, in theory, duality makes it harder for (outside) shareholders to effectively monitor management. However, the result is supportive of stewardship theory (Donaldson & Davis, 1991). It is also consistent with the proposition in Chen et al. (2008) and Iyengar and Zampelli (2009) that negative responses reflect that most shareholders already view existing board structure to be 'optimal'.

We re-examine the whole sample of corporate governance proposals and specify the E-entrenchment index (Bebchuk et al., 2009) to assess the relationship between the degree of existing management entrenchment and governance quality and market responses to proposal voting outcomes. Tables 9.9 and 9.10 show results. Results for all panels strongly imply that the extent of existing management entrenchment and governance quality have a highly significant positive impact on market returns

Table 9.6 All positive corporate governance proposals using predicted lent shares

Panel A				
Pass requirement:	(<50%)	(<37.5%)	(<25%)	(<12.5%)
Pass (dummy)	0.137***	0.00673	–0.0148	–0.0460**
	(2.67)	(0.44)	(–0.86)	(–2.57)
Observed % votes for	–0.00201**	7.89e-05	0.000407	0.000601**
	(–2.47)	(0.23)	(1.23)	(2.49)
Predicted Lent Shares	–0.0349**	0.00227	0.000604	–0.00243
	(–2.36)	(0.55)	(0.13)	(–0.53)
Constant	0.0438***	0.00444	0.00507	0.0254**
	(2.60)	(0.47)	(0.56)	(2.00)
Observations	749	692	556	354
R-squared	0.015	0.004	0.005	0.014
Panel B				
Pass requirement:	(<50%)	(<37.5%)	(<25%)	(<12.5%)
Pass (dummy)	0.0820	0.0410**	0.0237	–0.0279
	(1.43)	(2.53)	(1.23)	(–1.51)
Observed % votes for	–0.00261***	–0.00349***	–0.00282***	–0.00114
	(–2.92)	(–3.51)	(–2.69)	(–1.33)
Votes for x Pass	0.00124*	0.00249***	0.00223***	0.00132*
	(1.68)	(3.48)	(2.97)	(1.93)
Predicted Lent Shares	–0.0389***	–0.0349***	–0.0294**	–0.0207*
	(–2.59)	(–2.89)	(–2.45)	(–1.78)
Constant	0.0586***	0.0711***	0.0569***	0.0497***
	(3.08)	(3.48)	(3.02)	(2.80)
Observations	749	692	556	354
R-squared	0.020	0.025	0.019	0.020
Panel C				
Pass requirement:	(<50%)	(<37.5%)	(<25%)	(<12.5%)
Pass (dummy)	0.415*	0.0170	0.0242	–0.000614
	(1.67)	(0.77)	(1.14)	(–0.02)
Observed % votes for	–0.00640***	–0.00577***	–0.00715***	–0.00624**
	(–3.58)	(–3.09)	(–3.65)	(–2.04)
Votes for x Pass	6.79e-05**	5.33e-05	7.43e-05***	7.07e-05
	(2.50)	(1.54)	(2.72)	(1.61)
Votes for squared	–0.00551	0.00499**	0.00587***	0.00589**
	(–0.78)	(2.31)	(3.21)	(2.53)

(continued)

Table 9.6 (continued)

Panel A				
Votes for squared x Pass	5.26e-06	−5.51e-05	−7.25e-05***	−7.54e-05*
	(0.09)	(−1.46)	(−2.63)	(−1.94)
Predicted Lent Shares	−0.0413***	−0.0357**	−0.0355**	−0.0354**
	(−2.78)	(−2.52)	(−2.50)	(−2.48)
Constant	0.0948***	0.0893***	0.0992***	0.0915***
	(3.92)	(3.70)	(3.95)	(3.55)
Observations	749	692	556	354
R-squared	0.032	0.027	0.028	0.027

t statistics in parentheses. ***$p < 0.01$, **$p < 0.05$, *$p < 0.1$
This table reports regressions for the whole sample and incorporates the predicted shares on loan in the OTC market on the date of a vote for proposals that may be affected by over-voting. Estimates are calculated using predicted values from Table 9.3 estimations

following proposal votes. A higher value of the E-index indicates weaker governance quality and greater management entrenchment. Our evidence shows that both the market and shareholders value increased shareholder access and power when in comparison to other firms the existing governance quality is low and management entrenchment high. Whilst markets consistently react negatively to proposals which narrowly pass a vote, in cases when existing governance is weak and management power is especially high, markets value increased shareholder access and power (Table 9.11).

Arguably and consistent with agency theory, this desire for increased access and power may reflect shareholder concerns that highly entrenched managers consume agency goods and make decisions inconsistent with shareholder firm value-maximising objectives. Results in other studies are supportive. Berger et al. (1997) find management entrenchment is associated with lower leverage and less firm risk-taking. Kayhan (2005) also finds evidence of lower leverage in highly entrenched firms suggesting that the result is driven by managers choosing to retain more profit and rewarding shareholders via dividends sporadically.

Table 9.7 Proposals to remove conflicts of board interest

Pass requirement:	*(<50%)*	*(<37.5%)*	*(<25%)*	*(<12.5%)*
Panel A				
Pass (dummy)	0.00343	0.0583*	–0.0632	–0.0918**
	(0.02)	(1.69)	(–1.48)	(–2.52)
Observed % votes for	0.000233	–0.00108	0.00180	0.00115
	(0.09)	(–0.64)	(1.16)	(1.12)
Actual Lent Shares	0.00765	0.0103	–0.00264	–0.000958
	(0.14)	(0.23)	(1.02)	(–0.07)
Constant	–0.00582	0.0165	–0.0221	0.0480
	(–0.10)	(0.62)	(–0.18)	(1.50)
Observations	87	75	62	38
R-squared	0.005	0.043	0.043	0.084
Panel B				
Pass (dummy)	–0.727***	0.0733**	–0.0440	–0.0794**
	(–3.46)	(2.61)	(–1.02)	(–2.17)
Observed % votes for	0.000897	–0.00619***	–0.00183	–0.00195
	(0.36)	(–3.00)	(–0.65)	(–0.90)
Votes for x Pass	0.0109***	0.00499**	0.00333	0.00314
	(8.08)	(2.21)	(1.49)	(1.44)
Actual Lent Shares	0.0323	–0.0677*	–0.0516	–0.0490
	(0.69)	(–1.76)	(–1.43)	(–1.30)
Constant	–0.0152	0.121***	0.0482	0.102**
	(–0.29)	(2.71)	(0.90)	(2.24)
Observations	87	75	62	38
R-squared	0.136	0.113	0.072	0.111
Panel C				
Pass (dummy)	–1.115***	0.0573*	–0.0253	0.00550
	(–3.46)	(1.78)	(–0.61)	(0.13)
Observed % votes for	–0.00837**	–0.00597	–0.00766*	–0.00880*
	(–2.38)	(–1.59)	(–1.92)	(–1.89)
Votes for x Pass	0.000190***	0.000113	0.000192***	0.000198**
	(2.79)	(1.40)	(2.85)	(2.49)
Votes for squared	0.0276**	–0.0100**	–0.00617	–0.00661
	(2.56)	(–2.05)	(–1.36)	(–1.31)
Votes for squared x Pass	–0.000237***	9.77e-05	4.20e-06	1.14e-05
	(–2.65)	(1.32)	(0.07)	(0.17)

(continued)

Table 9.7 (continued)

Pass requirement:	*(<50%)*	*(<37.5%)*	*(<25%)*	*(<12.5%)*
Actual Lent Shares	0.0520	0.0471	0.0494	0.0529
	(1.22)	(1.17)	(1.20)	(1.27)
Constant	0.0775	0.0638	0.0682	0.0782
	(1.58)	(1.32)	(1.29)	(1.61)
Observations	87	75	62	38
R-squared	0.225	0.240	0.226	0.221

t statistics in parentheses. ***$p < 0.01$, **$p < 0.05$, *$p < 0.1$
This table reports regressions analysing proposals designed to remove conflicts of board interest, including CEO duality. Regressions incorporate actual shares on loan in the OTC market on the date of a vote for proposals that may be affected by over-voting. Estimates are calculated using actual lent shares from Table 9.3 estimations

9.5 Conclusions

Our empirical evidence informs the debate regarding shareholder power and access. For governance proposals designed to increase shareholder power, and for proposals designed to remove board level conflicts of interest, markets and shareholders do not value increased proxy access and power if evidenced by significant negative CARs. In all cases, the proximity of a vote to the pass threshold matters. It implies that markets react differently to proposal votes at varying vote levels. The degree of management entrenchment and quality of existing governance is important. Shareholders react favourably to proposals that pass in firms in which governance quality is low and the level of management entrenchment is high.

Despite strong vocal support for increased shareholder access from the SEC, we find little evidence to support the notion that shareholders desire increased access and power except in firms where the existing governance quality is particularly low and managers highly entrenched. We find little evidence to support arguments in Bebchuk (2003) and Bebchuk and Hirst (2010) that shareholders having a greater say in firm decisions benefits shareholders. Like Bainbridge (2008), we find that in most firms, shareholders consider existing shareholder access and power sufficient and vote against proposals that would increase their power. This is broadly

Table 9.8 Proposals to remove conflicts of board interest using predicted lent shares

Pass requirement:	*(<50%)*	*(<37.5%)*	*(<25%)*	*(<12.5%)*
Panel A				
Pass (dummy)	−0.220	0.0572*	−0.0583	−0.0894**
	(−1.15)	(1.68)	(−1.36)	(−2.42)
Observed % votes for	0.00379	−0.000976	0.00178	0.00120
	(1.42)	(−0.57)	(1.16)	(1.16)
Predicted Lent Shares	0.0742	0.0135	0.00237	0.00255
	(1.48)	(0.76)	(0.15)	(0.17)
Constant	−0.0728	0.0156	−0.0223	0.0454
	(−1.30)	(0.40)	(−0.73)	(1.37)
Observations	87	75	62	38
R-squared	0.026	0.047	0.043	0.085
Panel B				
Pass (dummy)	−0.948***	0.0817***	−0.0464	−0.0831**
	(−5.35)	(2.74)	(−1.06)	(−2.31)
Observed % votes for	0.00419*	−0.00638**	−0.000612	−0.00107
	(1.74)	(−2.06)	(−0.18)	(−0.41)
Votes for x Pass	0.0111***	0.00495*	0.00217	0.00228
	(9.54)	(1.68)	(0.77)	(0.86)
Predicted Lent Shares	0.0943**	−0.0673	−0.0309	−0.0341
	(2.18)	(−1.34)	(−0.67)	(−0.73)
Constant	−0.0755	0.120*	0.0220	0.0852
	(−1.46)	(1.91)	(0.35)	(1.50)
Observations	87	75	62	38
R-squared	0.165	0.101	0.053	0.097
Panel C				
Pass (dummy)	−1.067***	0.0534*	−0.0249	−0.00904
	(−3.02)	(1.67)	(−0.61)	(−0.21)
Observed % votes for	−0.00585	−0.00396	−0.00516	−0.00485
	(−1.25)	(−0.82)	(−1.03)	(−0.89)
Votes for x Pass	0.000167**	9.69e-05	0.000169***	0.000153**
	(2.55)	(1.26)	(2.64)	(2.05)
Votes for squared	0.0230*	−0.0124**	−0.00936*	−0.0106*
	(1.93)	(−2.06)	(−1.67)	(−1.71)
Votes for squared x Pass	−0.000189*	0.000124	4.15e-05	6.56e-05
	(−1.81)	(1.47)	(0.59)	(0.81)
Predicted Lent Shares	0.0750*	0.0664	0.0732*	0.0768*
	(1.70)	(1.50)	(1.74)	(1.72)
Constant	0.0433	0.0357	0.0338	0.0371
	(0.61)	(0.50)	(0.46)	(0.54)

(continued)

Table 9.8 (continued)

Pass requirement:	*(<50%)*	*(<37.5%)*	*(<25%)*	*(<12.5%)*
Observations	87	75	62	38
R-squared	0.233	0.245	0.234	0.229

t statistics in parentheses. ***$p < 0.01$, **$p < 0.05$, *$p < 0.1$
This table reports regressions for proposals designed to remove conflicts of board interest including CEO duality. Regressions incorporate predicted shares on loan in the OTC market on the date of a proposal vote for proposals that may be affected by over-voting. Estimates are calculated using predicted values from Table 9.3 estimations

Table 9.9 Governance proposals and existing governance quality 1

Pass requirement:	*(<50%)*	*(<37.5%)*	*(<25%)*	*(<12.5%)*
Panel A				
Pass (dummy)	0.242**	0.0393***	–0.00207	–0.0449***
	(2.876)	(1.835)	(–0.0827)	(–1.912)
Observed % votes for	–0.00433**	–0.000921***	–0.000188	0.000240
	(–3.156)	(–1.906)	(–0.394)	(0.720)
Actual Lent Shares	–0.0665**	–0.000202	–0.000526	–0.00452
	(–2.605)	(–0.0296)	(–0.0649)	(–0.599)
E-index	0.00902***	0.00970***	0.00936***	0.00847
	(1.694)	(1.827)	(1.742)	(1.636)
Constant	0.0970**	0.0255***	0.0193	0.0400*
	(3.646)	(1.759)	(1.341)	(2.255)
Observations	300	274	173	82
R-squared	0.053	0.032	0.023	0.035
Panel B				
Pass (dummy)	0.249**	0.0618**	0.0334	–0.0335
	(2.694)	(3.051)	(1.238)	(–1.167)
Observed % votes for	–0.00429**	–0.00399**	–0.00320*	–0.000737
	(–2.920)	(–3.098)	(–2.035)	(–0.466)
Votes for x Pass	–0.000128	0.00222*	0.00205***	0.000715
	(–0.119)	(2.234)	(1.806)	(0.585)
Actual Lent Shares	–0.0665*	–0.0338***	–0.0277	–0.0143
	(–2.592)	(–1.843)	(–1.460)	(–0.708)
E-index	0.00907***	0.00885***	0.00892***	0.00837
	(1.704)	(1.696)	(1.668)	(1.612)
Constant	0.0959**	0.0863**	0.0680*	0.0531*
	(3.241)	(3.227)	(2.540)	(2.016)
Observations	300	274	173	82
R-squared	0.053	0.052	0.036	0.036

(continued)

Table 9.9 (continued)

Pass requirement:	*(<50%)*	*(<37.5%)*	*(<25%)*	*(<12.5%)*
Panel C				
Pass (dummy)	0.398	0.0470	0.00971	–0.0297
	(1.336)	(1.455)	(0.340)	(–0.698)
Observed % votes for	–0.00647**	–0.00483*	–0.00675**	–0.00409
	(–3.253)	(–2.117)	(–3.136)	(–1.070)
Votes for x Pass	4.88e-05	1.33e-06	5.83e-05	2.52e-05
	(1.202)	(0.0237)	(1.443)	(0.415)
Votes for squared	–0.00327	0.00516***	0.00765**	0.00650*
	(–0.400)	(1.723)	(3.258)	(2.103)
Votes for squared x Pass	-8.01e-06	–2.92e-05	–8.85e-05*	–6.62e-05
	(–0.119)	(–0.506)	(–2.402)	(–1.252)
Actual Lent Shares	–0.0600*	–0.0548*	–0.0510***	–0.0511***
	(–2.186)	(–2.054)	(–1.878)	(–1.894)
E-index	0.00908***	0.00886***	0.00870	0.00841
	(1.697)	(1.687)	(1.640)	(1.630)
Constant	0.111**	0.101**	0.110**	0.0978**
	(3.815)	(3.483)	(3.822)	(3.172)
Observations	300	274	173	82
R-squared	0.059	0.058	0.053	0.055

Robust t statistics in parentheses $^{**}p < 0.01$, $^{*}p < 0.05$, $^{***}p < 0.1$

This table reports regressions for governance proposals. Regressions incorporate the Bebchuk et al. (2009) E-entrenchment index and actual shares on loan. Estimates are calculated using actual lent shares from Table 9.3

consistent with arguments in Greenwood (1996) that restricting shareholder power leads to better firm performance because management is better positioned to make firm-level decisions. Accepting this implies the response of shareholders is rational. It is plausible that shareholders desire some degree of improved power but are concerned that additional power will vest in certain powerful and influential shareholders, thereby creating conditions where greater shareholder power reduces shareholders overall welfare (Anabtawi, 2006).

Table 9.10 Governance proposals and existing governance quality 2

Pass requirement:	*(<50%)*	*(<37.5%)*	*(<25%)*	*(<12.5%)*
Panel A				
Pass (dummy)	0.304*	0.0393***	0.000262	–0.0448***
	(2.454)	(1.840)	(0.0105)	(–1.819)
Observed % votes for	–0.00542**	–0.000921***	–0.000224	0.000237
	(–2.612)	(–1.910)	(–0.473)	(0.704)
Predicted Lent Shares	–0.0843*	0.000917	0.00102	–0.00389
	(–2.298)	(0.137)	(0.128)	(–0.504)
E-index	0.00965***	0.00963***	0.00932***	0.00847
	(1.791)	(1.813)	(1.733)	(1.633)
Constant	0.112**	0.0257***	0.0193	0.0399*
	(3.033)	(1.773)	(1.342)	(2.216)
Observations	300	274	173	82
R-squared	0.052	0.032	0.023	0.034
Panel B				
Pass (dummy)	0.294*	0.0680**	0.0357	–0.0375
	(2.459)	(3.148)	(1.224)	(–1.395)
Observed % votes for	–0.00554*	–0.00457**	–0.00339	–0.000530
	(–2.416)	(–2.655)	(–1.633)	(–0.304)
Votes for x Pass	0.000237	0.00259*	0.00217	0.000573
	(0.210)	(2.024)	(1.453)	(0.417)
Predicted Lent Shares	–0.0852*	–0.0398***	–0.0290	–0.0121
	(–2.233)	(–1.730)	(–1.200)	(–0.523)
E-index	0.00957***	0.00907***	0.00913***	0.00843
	(1.779)	(1.736)	(1.698)	(1.622)
Constant	0.115**	0.0948**	0.0692*	0.0507
	(2.710)	(2.845)	(2.049)	(1.648)
Observations	300	274	173	82
R-squared	0.052	0.052	0.033	0.035
Panel C				
Pass (dummy)	0.454	0.0422	0.0193	–0.0268
	(1.471)	(1.312)	(0.685)	(–0.634)
Observed % votes for	–0.00943**	–0.00748*	–0.00961**	–0.00674
	(–3.310)	(–2.451)	(–3.190)	(–1.540)
Votes for x Pass	7.55e-05*	3.17e-05	8.28e-05*	5.15e-05
	(2.003)	(0.588)	(2.207)	(0.857)
Votes for squared	–0.00162	0.00804*	0.0104**	0.00922*
	(–0.198)	(1.990)	(2.955)	(2.249)
Votes for squared x Pass	–3.39e-05	–6.72e-05	–0.000119**	–9.93e-05***
	(–0.515)	(–1.112)	(–2.920)	(–1.754)
Predicted Lent Shares	–0.0843*	–0.0727*	–0.0710***	–0.0697***

(continued)

Table 9.10 (continued)

Pass requirement:	*(<50%)*	*(<37.5%)*	*(<25%)*	*(<12.5%)*
	(−2.209)	(−2.006)	(−1.942)	(−1.898)
E-index	0.00947***	0.00913***	0.00901***	0.00871***
	(1.758)	(1.731)	(1.694)	(1.684)
Constant	0.149**	0.133**	0.145**	0.129**
	(3.402)	(3.063)	(3.304)	(2.890)
Observations	300	274	173	82
R-squared	0.063	0.060	0.058	0.058

Robust t statistics in parentheses $^{**}p < 0.01$, $^{*}p < 0.05$, $^{***}p < 0.1$
This table reports regressions for corporate governance proposals with the Bebchuk et al. (2009)E-entrenchment index included and incorporating predicted shares on loan. Estimates are calculated using predicted values from Table 9.3 estimations

Table 9.11 Additional test for the robustness of over-voting

Variables	*OLS*	*IVPROBIT*
Pass	0.207***	
	(1.765)	
Predicted Pass		0.164***
		(1.681)
Constant	−3.326**	−3.317**
	(−24.78)	(−22.84)
Observations	400	400
R-squared	0.031	0.0160
Wald test of exogeneity		564.90
		(0.000)
First Stage F stat		264.51
		(0.000)

t statistics (OLS) and z-statistics (IVPROBIT) in parentheses. $^{**}p < 0.01$, $^{*}p < 0.05$, $^{***}p < 0.1$
This table reports a robustness test. The regressions reported show the impact of over-votes around the 50% shareholder proposal pass margin for the whole sample using the actual pass percentage computed using robust OLS and the predicted pass rate determined by estimates from Table 9.3 on loan lent shares using an IV Probit model. Our results are quantitatively similar using the alternative IV Probit approach

References

Anabtawi, I. (2006). *Some scepticism about increasing shareholder power* (UCLA, School of Law, Law & Economics Research Paper Series, No. 05-16).

Armstrong, C., Gow, I., & Larcker, D. (2012). *The efficacy of shareholder voting: Evidence from equity compensation plans* (Stanford University Working Paper). http://econpapers.repec.org/paper/eclstabus/2097.htm

As You So. (2013). *Corporate social responsibiity: Understanding shareholder votes.* http://www.asyousow.org/csr/understandingvote.shtml

Bainbridge, S. M. (2003). Board of directors as nexus of contracts. *Iowa Law Review, 88*(1), 1–34.

Bainbridge, S. M. (2008). *Remarks on say on pay: An unjustified incursion on director authority* (UCLA School of Law, Law-Econ Research Paper No. 08-06).

Bebchuk, L. A. (2003). The case for shareholder access to the ballot. *Business Lawyer, 59*(1), 43–66.

Bebchuk, L. A., Cohen, A., & Ferrell, A. (2009). What matters in corporate governance? *Review of Financial Studies, 22*(2), 783–827.

Bebchuk, L. A., & Fried, J. M. (2005). Pay without performance: The unfulfilling promise of executive compensation. *International Company and Commercial Law Review, 16*(11), 461.

Bebchuk, L. A., Fried, J. M., & Walker, D. I. (2002). Managerial power and rent extraction in the design of executive compensation. *University of Chicago Law Review, 69*(3), 751–846.

Bebchuk, L. A., & Hirst, S. (2010). Private ordering and the proxy access debate. *Business Lawyer, 65*(2), 329–360.

Bebchuk, L. A., & Weisbach, M. S. (2010). The state of corporate governance research. *Review of Financial Studies, 23*(3), 939–961.

Berger, D., & Murry, K. (2009). As the market turns: Corporate governance litigation in an age of stockholder activism. *NYU Journal of Law and Business, 5*(207), 230–231.

Berger, P. G., Ofek, E., & Yermack, D. L. (1997). Managerial entrenchment and capital structure decisions. *Journal of Finance, 52*(4), 1411–1438.

Berle, A. A., & Means, G. C. (1932). *The modern corporation and private property* (pp. 110–111). MacMillan.

Boyd, B. K., Haynes, K. T., & Zona, F. (2011). Dimensions of CEO—board relations. *Journal of Management Studies, 48*(8), 1892–1923.

Bremer, R., Buchanan, B. G., & English, P. C. (2011). The advantages of using quarterly returns for long-term event studies. *Review of Quantitative Finance and Accounting, 36*(4), 491–516.

Bruner, C. M. (2008). The enduring ambivalence of corporate law. *Alabama Law Review, 59*(5), 1385.

Castanias, R. P., & Helfat, C. E. (1991). Managerial resources and rents. *Journal of Management, 17*(1), 155–171.

Certo, S. T. (2003). Influencing initial public offerings investors with prestige: Signalling with board structures. *Academy of Management Review, 28*(3), 432–446.

Chen, C. W., Lin, J. B., & Yi, B. (2008). CEO duality and firm performance: An endogenous issue. *Corporate Ownership and Control, 6*(1), 58–65.

Cuñat, V., Gine, M., & Guadalupe, M. (2012). The vote is cast: The effect of corporate governance on shareholder value. *Journal of Finance, 67*(5), 1943–1977.

Cyert, R., & March, J. (1963). *A behavioural theory of the firm*. Prentice-Hall.

Donaldson, L., & Davis, J. (1991). Stewardship theory or agency theory: CEO governance and shareholder returns. *Australian Journal of Management, 16*, 49–64.

Ertimur, Y., Ferri, F., & Stubben, S. R. (2010). Board of Directors' responsiveness to shareholders: Evidence from shareholder proposals. *Journal of Corporate Finance, 16*(1), 53–72.

Ertugrul, M., & Krishnan, K. (2011). Can CEO dissmissals be proactive? *Journal of Corporate Finance, 17*(1), 134–151.

Faleye, O. (2007). Classified boards, firm value, and managerial entrenchment. *Journal of Financial Economics, 83*(2), 501–529.

Faleye, O. (2010). Does one hat fit all? The case of corporate leadership structure. *Journal of Management and Governance, 13*(3), 239–259.

Fama, E. F., & Jensen, M. C. (1983). Separation of ownership and control. *Journal of Law and Economics, 26*(2), 301–325.

Finkelstein, S., & D'Aveni, R. A. (1994). CEO duality as a double edged sword: How boards of directors balance entrenchment avoidance and unity of command. *Academy Management Journal, 37*(5), 1078–1108.

Fisman, R., Khurana, R., & Rhodes-Kropf, M. (2005). *Governance and CEO turnover: Do something or do the right thing?* (Working Paper, Harvard Business School).

Georgeson Shareholder. (2006). Annual corporate governance review 2005, Shareholder proposals and proxy contests. http://www.georgesonshareholder.com.

Gillan, S. L., & Starks, L. T. (2000). Corporate governance proposals and shareholder activism: The role of institutional investors. *Journal of Financial Economics, 57*(2), 275–305.

Greenwood, D. J. H. (1996). Fictional shareholders; for whom are corporate managers trustees, revisited. *Southern California Law Review, 69*, 1022–1029.

Harris, M., & Raviv, A. (2010). Control of corporate decisions: Shareholders vs. management. *Review of Financial Studies, 23*(11), 4115–4147.

Hayden, G., & Bodie, M. T. (2010). Shareholder democracy and the curious turn towards board primacy. *Williams and Mary Law Review, 51*(6), 2071–2121.

Hillman, A. J., & Dalziel, T. (2003). Boards of directors and firm performance: Integrating agency and resource dependence perspectives. *Academy of Management Review, 28*(3), 383–396.

Hillman, A. J., Withers, M. C., & Collins, B. J. (2009). Resource dependence theory: A review. *Journal of Management, 35*(6), 1404–1427.

Hirschman, A. O. (1970). *Exit, voice, and loyalty: Responses to decline in firms, organisations, and states*. Harvard University Press.

Hoskisson, R. E., Hitt, M. A., Johnson, R. A., & Grossman, W. (2002). Conflicting voices: The effect of institutional ownership heterogeneity and internal governance on corporate innovation strategies. *Academy of Management Journal, 45*(4), 697–716.

Imbens, G. W., & Lemieux, T. (2008). Regression discontinuity designs: A guide to practice. *Journal of Econometrics, 142*(2), 615–635.

Iyengar, R. J., & Zampelli, E. M. (2009). Self-selection, endogeneity, and the relationship between CEO duality and firm performance. *Strategic Management Journal, 30*(10), 1092–1112.

Jensen, M. C., & Meckling, W. H. (1976). Theory of the firm: Managerial behaviour, agency costs and ownership structure. *Journal of Financial Economics, 3*(4), 305–360.

Jochem, T. (2012). *Does proxy access increase shareholder wealth? Evidence from a natural experiment* (Working Paper, The University of Pittsburgh).

Karpoff, J. M., Malatesta, P. H., & Walkling, R. A. (1996). Corporate governance and shareholder initiatives: Empirical evidence. *Journal of Financial Economics, 42*(3), 365–395.

Kayhan, A. (2005). *Managerial entrenchment and the debt-equity choice* (Unpublished working paper, Louisiana State University).

Kirkpatrick, G. (2009). The corporate governance lessons from the financial crisis. *OEDC Journal: Financial Market Trends, 1*, 61–87.

Klaauw, W. V. D. (2008). Regression-discontinuity analysis: A survey of recent developments in economics. *Labour, 22*(2), 219–245.

Kor, Y. Y., & Sundaramurphy, C. (2009). Experience-based human capital and social capital of outside directors. *Journal of Management, 35*(4), 981–1006.

Kroll, M., Walters, B. A., & Le, S. A. (2007). The impact of board composition and top management team ownership structure on post-IPO performance in young entrepreneurial firms. *Academy of Management Journal, 50*(5), 1198–1216.

Larcker, D. F., Ormazabal, G., & Taylor, D. J. (2011). The market reaction to corporate governance regulation. *Journal of Financial Economics, 101*(2), 431–448.

Larcker, D. F., & Rusticus, T. (2010). On the use of instrumental variables in accounting research. *Journal of Accounting and Economics, 49*(3), 186–205.

Lee, D. S., & Mas, A. (2012). Long-run impacts of unions on firms: New evidence from financial markets, 1961–1999. *Quarterly Journal of Economics, 127*(1), 333–378.

Levit, D., & Malenko, N. (2011). Nonbinding voting for shareholder proposals. *Journal of Finance, 66*(5), 1579–1614.

Lipton, M., & Rosenblum, S. A. (2003). Election contests in the company's proxy: An idea whose time has not come. *Business Lawyer, 59*(1), 67–94.

Lynch, S. N. (2013). SEC makes progress on economic analysis of rules: study. *Thomson Reuters*. http://www.reuters.com/article/2013/03/12/us-usa-sec-study-idUSBRE92B14120130312

Matsusaka, J. G., & Ozbas, O. (2013). Shareholder empowerment: The right to approve and the right to propose. *American Finance Association 2013 Meetings*. http://papers.ssrn.com/sol3/papers.cfm?abstract_id=1984606

Nordén, L., & Strand, T. (2011). Shareholder activism among portfolio managers: Rational decisions of 15 minutes of fame? *Journal of Management and Governance, 15*(3), 375–391.

Pi, L., & Timme, A. (1993). Corporate control and bank efficiency. *Journal of Banking and Finance, 17*(2–3), 515–530.

Peng, M. W., Zhang, S., & Li, X. (2007). CEO duality and firm performance during China's institutional transitions. *Management and Organisation Review, 3*(2), 205–225.

Pfeffer, J. (1981). *Power in organizations*. Pitman.

Prevost, A. K., Rao, R. P., & Williams, M. A. (2012). Labor unions as shareholder activists: Champions or detractors? *Financial Review, 47*(2), 327–349.

Rechner, P. L., & Dalton, D. R. (1991). CEO duality and organizational performance: A longitudinal analysis. *Strategic Management Journal, 12*, 155–160. https://doi.org/10.1002/smj.4250120206

Renneboog, L., & Szilagyi, P. G. (2011). The role of shareholder proposals in corporate governance. *Journal of Corporate Governance, 17*(1), 167–188.

Rhoades, D., Rechner, P., & Sundaramurthy, C. (2001). A Meta-analysis of board leadership structure and financial performance: Are 'two heads better than one'? *Corporate Governance: An International Review, 9*(4), 311–319.

Roe, M. J. (1991). A political theory of American corporate finance. *Columbia Law Review, 91*(10), 10–67.

Romano, R. (2001). Less is more: Making shareholder activism a valuable mechanism of corporate governance. *Yale Journal on Regulation, 18*(2), 174–251.

Shleifer, A., & Vishny, R. (1986). Large shareholders and corporate control. *Journal of Political Economy, 94*(3), 461–488.

Smith, E. E. (2013). *Do shareholders want less governance?* (Stern University Working Paper). http://erinesmith.com/ATP_EESmith_Jan2013.pdf
Smith, E. E. (2012). *Over-voting* (Stern University Working Paper). http://www.stern.nyu.edu/cons/groups/content/documents/webasset/con_034305.pdf
Taylor, L. A. (2010). Why are CEO's rarely fired? Evidence from structural estimation. *Journal of Finance, 65*(6), 2051–2087.
The Financial Crisis Inquiry Commission. (2011). *The financial crisis inquiry report*, Official Government Edition.
Thomas, R. S., & Cotter, J. F. (2007). Shareholder proposals in the new millennium: Shareholder support, board response, and market reaction. *Journal of Corporate Finance, 13*(2–3), 368–391.
Yang, T., & Zhao, S. (2012). *CEO duality, competition, and firm performance* (Working Paper, Lehigh University).

CHAPTER 10

The Diffusion of Blockchain Technology for Financial Reporting Functions Seen Through the Lens of Norm Lifecycles

Tatiana King and Elizabeth Morton

10.1 Introduction

There is a tendency to talk about blockchain in very singular, reverential, almost religious tones… This is more than a distributed database, this is less than holy water—this is somewhere in between the two.

Tatiana King gratefully acknowledges the financial support of The Foundation for Economic Education (Liikesivistysrahasto), project number 20–11,637.

T. King (✉)
University of Vaasa, Vaasa, Finland
e-mail: tatiana.king@uwasa.fi

E. Morton
Curtin University, Perth, Western Australia, Australia
e-mail: lizzie.morton@curtin.edu.au

T. King and J. Williams (eds.), *Corporate Governance in the Banking and Financial Sector*, Palgrave Macmillan Studies in Banking and Financial Institutions,
https://doi.org/10.1007/978-3-031-83353-3_10

Hyperledger executive director Brian Behlendorf (cited in Reed, 2017).

Concern has been expressed about the process of blockchain technology adoption and the pace at which it occurs in a financial accounting and reporting context (e.g., Atzori, 2017; Dai & Vasarhelyi, 2017; Kokina et al., 2017; Tharapos & Marriott, 2020). In a 2020 report, PricewaterhouseCoopers (PwC) recognized the impact of blockchain technology in a broad context based on its five main benefits: provenance that helps organizations verify the sources of their goods and track their movements; improvements in payment systems and their effects on financial institutions; improved identity (e.g., Know Your Client 'KYC') leading to cost efficiencies and the curbing of fraud and identity theft; contract and dispute resolution resulting from the merger of ledgers, contracts, and payments; improved flow of commercial agreements; the flagging of disputes; and enhanced customer engagement through integration with customer relationship management platforms. Due to these benefits, blockchain technology has the potential to boost global domestic product (GDP) by up to US$1.76 trillion by 2030 (Panetta, 2018; PwC, 2020).

Casey and Vigna (2018, p. 64) describe a blockchain as a "distributed, append-only ledger of provably signed, sequentially linked, and cryptographically secured transactions that is replicated across a network of computer nodes, with ongoing updates determined by a software-driven consensus." Blockchain technology has been adopted across a broad range of business sectors (see, for example, Allen et al., 2020), and it is believed to offer substantial benefits for accounting and auditing functions (ACCA, 2017; Garanina et al., 2021; Kotb et al., 2020; PwC, 2020; Schmitz & Leoni, 2019; Tharapos & Marriott, 2020; Yu et al., 2018). Blockchains' inherent features of trust, transparency, and openness complement the UN's Sustainable Development Goals (SDGs)—in particular, economic growth, industry innovation, and infrastructure (United Nations, 2020)—and have the potential to offset shrinkage in global GDP stemming from the COVID-19 pandemic. Importantly, blockchains may develop differently across or within institutions at differing time points (Brunnee & Toope, 2000; Sunstein, 1996). Institutions, in turn, are shaped by their adoption (or rejection) of new technologies, such as blockchains, which may create or sustain efficiencies in current practice and/or further establish new (disruptive) practices (Brennan et al., 2019; Carlin, 2019; Kend & Nguyen, 2020).

In this chapter we offer a novel framework that complements the extant literature on blockchain technology. We merge two theories: (1) diffusion of innovation theory (Rogers, 1962, 1983, 2003) and (2) norm lifecycle theory (Bebbington et al., 2012; Brunnee & Toope, 1997; Finnemore & Sikkink, 1998; Morton, 2019; Sunstein, 1996, which help us provide a contextualized understanding of blockchain technology's potential diffusion in financial reporting functions. In doing so, we aim to clarify and contextualize blockchain technology's impact on financial reporting functions based on differing stages that underpin the norm adoption lifecycle. The framework considers social attitudes regarding what ought or ought not to ultimately drive developments in standards or practices (Krasner, 1982; Sunstein, 1996), described as norm lifecycles (Bebbington et al., 2012; Brunnee & Toope, 1997; Finnemore & Sikkink, 1998; Morton, 2019; Sunstein, 1996). We posit that blockchains can be obsolete, sustaining, or disruptive for the accounting profession, depending on when and where in the lifecycle they are adopted and for what particular aspects of accounting practices. Thus, for financial reporting functions, we present two critical limitations that hinder blockchain technology diffusion and lead to a critical tipping point for the technology to diffuse. We assert that blockchains are not yet normalized within these functions, depending on their relationships with central governance and the broader digital ecosystem.

The present study makes several contributions to literature. First, we enrich diffusion of innovation theory (Rogers, 1962, 1983, 2003) by linking it to the norm lifecycles that underpin norms in social contexts (Bebbington et al., 2012; Brunnee & Toope, 1997; Morton, 2019). Previously, innovation diffusion theory was criticized for not sufficiently considering external and social contexts (Anokhin & Schulze, 2009; Lyytinen & Damsgaard, 2001). Our study provides a more nuanced understanding and approach based on synergy between the two theories, thus providing an external context for innovation diffusion theory.

We reconciled these complementary theories to allow for multiple sources of normativity, going beyond the black-and-white positioning of blockchain technology. By exploring blockchain technology within a norm lifecycle framework, we aimed to clarify the literature on the benefits and limitations of blockchain technology and articulate blockchains' sustaining and disruptive reporting potential. The present study contributes to the diffusion of innovation theory by applying it to the development of blockchain technology in the accounting domain, viewed through a norm lifecycle lens. Our findings, on a practical level, may help practitioners reflect on the stages of blockchain diffusion in an accounting context.

We structure the rest of this chapter as follows. First, we briefly outline blockchain technology, including the initial focus on distinguishing between private and public blockchains, then toward layering, stacking and multi-chains. This then leads to consideration of their applications, as both economic elements and economic infrastructures. We then present our conceptual framework, which combines diffusion of innovation theory with norm lifecycle theory and underpinned our analysis of the diffusion of blockchain technology and innovation adoption lifecycles. We outline norm emergence through knowledge and persuasion, the related barriers to norm cascading, and decision-making for blockchain technology adoption before considering the internalization of norms and the non-redundant role of central authorities. We then contemplate the way in which blockchain technology may alter stakeholders' needs and reorientate reporting entities. We conclude with our final remarks.

10.2 Blockchain Technology

Blockchain technology broadly reflects the evolution of the digital economy and Internet capabilities. Although its early forms provided a means of payment (i.e., via Bitcoin), developments have accelerated over the last decade, particularly regarding increased functionality and, consequently, wider use cases deriving from the evolution of smart contracts, decentralized applications (DApps), non-fungible tokens (NFTs), decentralized finance (DeFi), and, most recently, decentralized autonomous organizations (DAOs) (Messari, 2021). Applications such as token systems, financial derivatives, stablecoins, identity (KYC), and reputation systems, decentralized file storage, and DAOs have been identified across blockchain communities (Ethereum, 2021).

Although Web 1.0 and Web 2.0 led to the substantial evolution of the economy by bringing economies and global activities together, blockchain technology accompanied the next evolution—Web 3.0 (Messari, 2021). By facilitating peer-to-peer networking, consensus mechanisms, and the sharing of data, blockchain technology represents a shift from an industrial to a digital economy by providing a new digital economic infrastructure. Data has become a vital economic resource, and consensus mechanisms enable trust to be industrialized (Berg et al., 2019).

The Foundations of Blockchain Technology

Blockchain technology can be broadly described as a form of decentralized ledger technology (DLT) that records transactions in chronological order on a "block," which undergo a verification process (through a consensus mechanism) before transactions are confirmed and permanently added to a "chain" (Malekan, 2018).

Information is recorded, stored, and distributed across a network of users (i.e., nodes) that compose a decentralized system without a controlling entity or external influence (Malekan, 2018). For blocks of transactions to be entered permanently into a ledger, they must be verified by blockchain miners (i.e., timestamped), which is referred to as the consensus mechanism (Brennan et al., 2019; Malekan, 2018). Each block may include business-to-business and/or business-to-consumer (or vice versa) transactions, which can be shared across a distributed network of computers anywhere in the world. The resulting interconnected "blocks" form the "blockchain," which provides a complete history of transactions (a ledger) and is considered immutable—unable to be appended without substantial collusion between participants (Malekan, 2018). Therefore, blockchain technology is known as distributed ledger technology (Cong & He, 2019; Hinchliffe, 2019).

Public Blockchains, Layering, Tech Stacks, and Multi-Chains

Blockchain technology is an institutional governance technology that may function as an infrastructure for various financial and nonfinancial commercial uses (Hinchliffe, 2019). Traditionally, systems with centralized ledgers have required the participation of a trusted third party to maintain records of transactions between organizations. A distributed ledger eliminates the need to involve a third party, which can be a significant benefit when there is no clearly trusted central organization or if the costs of intermediation are high (Chartered Accountants Australia and New Zealand, 2017). However, not all blockchains are identical.

Early considerations of blockchain technology focused on a public/private distinction. The most notable blockchains are *public* (or *permissionless*) blockchains, such as Bitcoin or Ethereum blockchains. These are open and accessible to the public: anyone can participate, view transactions, and be involved in consensus mechanisms (Lin & Liao, 2017). Overall, the core features of public blockchains can be summarized as follows: a decentralized structure with no central authority, public accessibility and participation, transparency (at least regarding transaction addresses with pseudonymous users), and security via peer participation in the consensus mechanism.

Public blockchains can be contrasted with *private* blockchains (or *permissioned* blockchains), which retain central authority. The central authority controls who can participate and in what capacity, including what can be recorded. Therefore, unlike public blockchains, private blockchains suffer from a single point of failure limitation (Lin & Liao, 2017). One example of a private blockchain is the Australian Stock Exchange's (ASX's) DLT solution, which is scheduled to replace the clearing house electronic subregister system (CHESS) (The Australian Stock Exchange, 2020). The core features of a private blockchain include a centralized structure managed by a central authority, limited accessibility and participation controlled by a central authority, transparency (but limited to those with authority), and reduced security requirements due to a limited participant pool. Generally, private blockchains reflect enterprise solutions, such as for internal management, and prompt debate regarding whether they are *truly* blockchains.[1]

As blockchain technology continues to evolve, these distinctions are becoming less pronounced. The ability of underpinning public blockchains, such as Bitcoin and Ethereum blockchains (*layer 1*), to be overlaid with *layer 2* solutions resolves scalability and transaction speed problems (Wallace, 2020). Moreover, the explosion of blockchain activity has resulted in a substantial range of applications across a multitude of blockchains.

[1] Additionally, *consortium* blockchains enable groups of entities to collaborate and form blockchains. These represent a middle ground between public and private blockchains, in that they remain permissioned but are more decentralized and offer greater security due to a broader range of participants involved in consensus protocols (Lin & Liao, 2017).

Importantly, this is creating opportunities for multi-chain, "modular" applications (Messari, 2021). Not only are trends ensuring interoperability and composability within blockchains, enabling "tech stacking," but bridging infrastructure is seen as a significant development that will come to fruition over the next five years (Messari, 2021).

Applications of Blockchain Technology

Blockchain technology underpins a broad range of digital economic infrastructures, including those for digital (private) money, assets, intellectual property rights, digital services and marketplaces, financing, and governance, to name a few (Messari, 2021). Blockchains have many uses, particularly for supply chains (i.e., provenance, protection against counterfeiting, and ensuring regulatory compliance) and credentialing and identity (e.g., KYC) (Dutta, 2020; Free & Hecimovic, 2021; Morton & Curran, 2021). Moreover, the COVID-19 pandemic has prompted a substantive shift in digital adoption, resulting in an increased willingness to adopt digital and distributed technologies (Allen et al., 2020; PwC, 2020).

Within the accounting profession, blockchain technology has the ability to simplify compliance and regulation (Deloitte, 2016), increase transparency in accounting processes (Kokina et al., 2017), improve auditing processes (CPA Canada, AISCPA, and UWCISA, 2017; Kotb et al., 2020), and facilitate tax collection (Bentley, 2019; Morton & Curran, 2021). However, the accounting, auditing, and taxation regulatory environment hinders the adoption of digitalization and automation for financial accounting and reporting (Deloitte, 2016). As Garanina et al. (2021) highlighted, there are four particularly important areas of development for the accounting field: the changing role of accountants, new challenges and opportunities for auditors, the challenges of blockchain technology applications, and the regulation of cryptoassets. The following subsections focus on core applications, first addressing different forms of digital assets, liabilities, and financial instruments, and then focusing on economic platforms, infrastructure, and entities.

Blockchains for Assets, Liabilities, and Financial Instruments

Blockchains have given birth to a vast array of private money and digital assets. Initially, blockchain technology attracted attention due to Nakamoto's white paper on Bitcoin, which examined the well-known cryptocurrency "genesis" block that was first minted at the beginning of 2009 (Nakamoto, 2008). Cryptocurrencies support peer-to-peer transactions without the need for a central bank (Nakamoto, 2008). While they are not money in a physical sense (Ramassa & Leoni, 2021), they reflect ledger entries on blockchains that are verified by miners and that are transparent to all participants. The critical difference between Bitcoin and other electronic forms of money is the way in which blockchains resolve the double-spend problem.

Besides private money, such as Bitcoin, stablecoins, central-bank digital currencies, and non-fungible tokens (NFTs) have emerged, raising questions about their accounting and taxation treatment in terms of both characterization and valuation (Hampl & Gyönyörová, 2021; Ramassa & Leoni, 2021). NFTs support a broader digitalization of property rights rather than cryptocurrencies and therefore provide access for communities and clubs, including the creative economy. Blockchain technology is also involved in initial coin offers (ICOs) for cryptoassets. Blockchain technology establishes infrastructure for decentralized finance (DeFi), thereby enabling decentralized financial products (such as liquidity pools, yield farming, or DeFi derivatives). Hence, blockchain technology has the potential to address issues such as debanking by financial institutions (AUSTRAC, 2021; Kornberger et al., 2017).

Overall, cryptoassets have an aggregate market capitalization of over $2 trillion, while cryptocurrency-based lending applications and decentralized trading venues currently command $65 billion in on boarded assets (World Economic Forum, 2021). The banking sector accounts for the highest distribution of blockchain market value and cross-border payments, and settlements comprise blockchain's largest use case (Statista, 2021).

According to Ramassa and Leoni (2021), there is a regulatory vacuum regarding accounting regulations and standard setting for cryptoassets because they have distinctive, rapidly evolving, but uncertain features. The pressures to regulate disruptive innovation inevitably result in standard setters trying to resist the pressures and defend their positions. Ramassa and Leoni's (2021) analysis of the International Accounting

Standards Board (IASB) meeting recordings showed that the IASB currently considers cryptocurrency to be too complex and uncertain to warrant time-consuming standard updating or development.

Blockchains as Economic Platforms, Infrastructure, and Entity Structures

Blockchain technology has led not only to the development of decentralized applications (DApps) that perform specific functions on blockchains, but more recently to decentralized autonomous organizations (DAOs) (Castonguay & Stein Smith, 2020; Johnston, 2020; Kornberger et al., 2017). Although numerous definitions exist, a DAO is a programmed blockchain entity that issues tokens to its stakeholders and completes its function(s) by executing smart contracts (Malekan, 2018). Rules that govern an organization and transactions undertaken therein are maintained and stored on the blockchain.

Although the introduction of DApps and smart contracts provides utility beyond money equivalents (Murray & Pirovich, 2018), DAOs attracted particular attention in 2021 due to the ability of communities of interested parties to collaborate toward a shared purpose through decentralized governance. DAOs therefore offer new forms of entity structuring that go beyond traditional companies or partnerships (Castonguay & Stein Smith, 2020; Sims, 2019).

DAOs as new forms of decentralized entities do not fit readily into existing legal structures, although some jurisdictions have established new legal structures for DAOs (e.g., Wyoming, United States; Castonguay & Stein Smith, 2020,) and the consensus is that they are most likely to fall under the definition of a partnership (Sims, 2019; Tse, 2020). For the financial reporting function, this then leads into considerations of the reporting entity itself.

While numerous benefits exist, there are also concerns about blockchain infrastructure, including the anonymity of participants, the black economy, anti-money laundering, and countering terrorist financing (AML/CTF; FATF, 2019), the energy requirements of proof of work consensus mechanisms (Dutta, 2020), and more general risks, such as the uncertain regulatory landscape and taxation ambiguity (Morton & Curran, 2022), to name a few.

10.3 Conceptual Framework

As aforementioned, through the integration of two key theories, our chapter provides the reader with a contextualized understanding of blockchain technology's potential diffusion in financial reporting functions by linking the stages of social norm emergence with the stages of innovation diffusion.

The impact of blockchains and their scope for financial reporting are not dichotomous. Like other technological advances and shifts in practice, they evolve in different ways over time as entrepreneurs experiment in various settings (i.e., some experiments fail, while others are successful). To explain the stages of blockchain development and its influence on financial reporting, we developed a conceptual theoretical framework based on two theories—diffusion of innovation theory (Rogers, 1962, 1983, 2003) and norm lifecycle theory (Bebbington et al., 2012; Brunnee & Toope, 1997; Finnemore & Sikkink, 1998; Morton, 2019; Sunstein, 1996). In particular, we posit that blockchains' effects (and benefits) will only be fully understood once they are both implemented from an infrastructure point of view and normalized from the perspective of its users.

Rogers further developed the initial 1962 diffusion of innovation theory (1983, 2003). This theory focuses on understanding how, why, and at what rate innovative technologies spread in social systems (Rogers, 1962). Instead of focusing on persuading individuals to change, diffusion of innovation theory sees change as primarily concerning the evolution of products and behaviors, so they become a better fit for the needs of individuals and groups, reflecting the infrastructural level of technology adoption (Robinson, 2009). Diffusion is the process by which an innovation is communicated through various channels over time among members of a social system (Rogers, 2003).

The innovation decision process runs from the first knowledge about an innovation to a decision's full implementation and confirmation (Rogers, 1983). For diffusion to occur, Rogers (1983) maintained that an innovation—"an idea, practice or object that is perceived as new by an individual or other unit of adoption"—must exist to be diffused. What makes diffusion different from any other type of spreading is the "newness" of the innovation. A population of potential adopters must also exist for the innovation and there must be a communication flow between the innovation's developers and potential adopters (Rogers, 2003). Diffusion is not an automatic consequence of innovation, and the ease of innovation diffusion depends on different factors (Lapsley & Wright, 2004). Rogers (2003) described the innovation-diffusion process as "an uncertainty reduction process" (Rogers, 2003, p. 232).

The literature has argued that diffusion of innovation theory, in its pure form, inadequately explains the adoption of innovation in society because it is affected by technological, social, and learning "conditions" (MacVaugh & Schiavone, 2010) in the contextual domain of a community. Lyytinen and Damsgaard (2001) found that an innovation does not necessarily need to pass through various stages of adoption, since adoptions may take place in dyadic relationships, making it difficult to identify the stages of adoption. Anokhin and Schulze (2009) provided empirical evidence indicating that external factors (such as corruption) may negatively affect innovation diffusion and reduce the chances of adopters pursuing or accepting innovative ideas. Also, diffusion of innovation theory has been combined with other theories (Davis, 1985) to better explain the development of particular technologies or to account for the influences of external environments (El-Helaly et al., 2020).

Explorations of external environments that make diffusion of innovation theory more applicable to different types of innovations are nascent (Wani & Ali, 2015). MacVaugh and Schiavone (2010) have called for further investigation of external conditions and domains that complement diffusion of innovation theory, which will help in understanding the processes by which new technology is adopted. Building on this emerging line of research, we suggest that diffusion of innovation theory (Rogers, 1962) would benefit from a more systematic acknowledgment of social norm development within society and norm lifecycles within institutions (Bebbington et al., 2012; Brunnee & Toope, 1997; Finnemore & Sikkink, 1998; Morton, 2019; Sunstein, 1996). A better understanding of such boundary conditions—norms—could extend diffusion of innovation theory, making it more context-sensitive.

Norms become defined through standards of behavior that develop over time. They are built upon social attitudes about what ought and ought not to be, resulting in collective outcomes within institutional settings (Krasner, 1982; Sunstein, 1996), reflecting interactions between participants toward an "increasingly fixed pattern of expectations about appropriate behavior" (Brunnee & Toope, 2000, p. 21) that require collective action (Sunstein, 1996).

Critically, norms relate to *individual* standards of behavior rather than institutions as a *whole* (Finnemore & Sikkink, 1998). Institutions more aptly reflect the "collection of such practices and rules," and the particular mix of practices and rules varies over time (Finnemore & Sikkink, 1998; Morton, 2019, p. 563). This is important in a contemporary (digital) society:

> Institutions are not immutable, though they are often persistent (or resistant to change). They can be reshaped through changes in the constructed identities of the actors, identities that are in turn shaped and reshaped by action within the structures. This is what Giddens refers to as the "duality of structure": structures constrain social action, but they also enable action, and in turn are affected and potentially altered by the friction of social action against the parameters of the structure. (Brunnee & Toope, 2000, p. 30)

It is therefore vital to appreciate that blockchains may develop differently across different "pockets" of or within institutions, at different time points (Brunnee & Toope, 2000; Sunstein, 1996). As a result of such shifts in behaviors, institutions will, in turn, be shaped, either by the adoption (or rejection) of new technologies such as blockchains, which may create efficiencies in current practice (be sustaining) and/or go further and establish new practices (be disruptive; Carlin, 2019; Kend & Nguyen, 2020).

Conformity in practice is generally established through increasing violations and disruptions of a preexisting norm(s) until the old norm is displaced and a new norm replaces it (Lessig, 1996). Hence, rather than perceiving developments in the financial reporting space as objective and dichotomous, through norm lifecycles we consider accepted practices to be transitory (Morton, 2019); that is, a norm progresses through a lifecycle of three stages (emergence, cascade, and internalization) before it becomes established and taken for granted (Finnemore & Sikkink, 1998; Morton, 2019; Sunstein, 1996).

The Innovation Adoption Process: Diffusion of Innovations Within a Norm Lifecycle Framework

Rogers (1983) defined an innovation adoption process of five steps that we contextualized according to the adoption of norms in society

(Bebbington et al., 2012; Brunnee & Toope, 1997; Finnemore & Sikkink, 1998; Morton, 2019; Sunstein, 1996; see Fig. 10.1).

The *knowledge stage* of innovation diffusion theory is the stage at which individuals find out about an innovation through a variety of communication channels and acquire knowledge about it. During this stage, people try to determine "what the innovation is and how and why it works" (Rogers, 2003) and come to understand the main principles of how and why it works (Rogers, 2003).

This stage is followed by the *persuasion stage*. This occurs when an individual forms a favorable or unfavorable attitude toward an innovation (Rogers, 1983). The attitude is formed after a person perceives the existence of an innovation and gains a sufficient level of knowledge about it. At this stage, the uncertainty surrounding the use of the innovation may increase (or decrease) because of information received from the public. The internal and external networks through which potential adopters learn about innovations are crucial during this stage (Lapsley & Wright, 2004).

By linking diffusion of innovation theory with norm lifecycle theory, we propose that the first two stages outlined above are characteristic of the *norm emergence* stage of the norm lifecycle. During this stage, norm entrepreneurs attempt to change preexisting norms in society by convincing norm leaders to embrace a new norm (Finnemore & Sikkink, 1998; Morton, 2019; Sunstein, 1996). Norm entrepreneurs aim to highlight a problem that needs fixing, make use of dissatisfaction, and present a solution (Sunstein, 1996).

This stage reflects what ought to be. Finnemore and Sikkink (1998) highlighted that norm entrepreneurs seek to draw attention to a problem; dramatize it; and foster values, altruism, and empathy regarding the issue. Importantly, not even common knowledge is static, and this is something that should be appreciated (Franck, 1990). The reception of new ideas at this stage is not always well received (Morton, 2019); hence, this is a complicated stage of the norm lifecycle during which increasing interactions and patterns of behavior develop in unique ways (Djelic & Quack, 2008).

The *decision stage* of diffusion of innovation theory relates to the point in time at which a choice (adoption or rejection) regarding an innovation arises. The choice to adopt means making "full use of an innovation as the best course of action available," while the choice to reject means

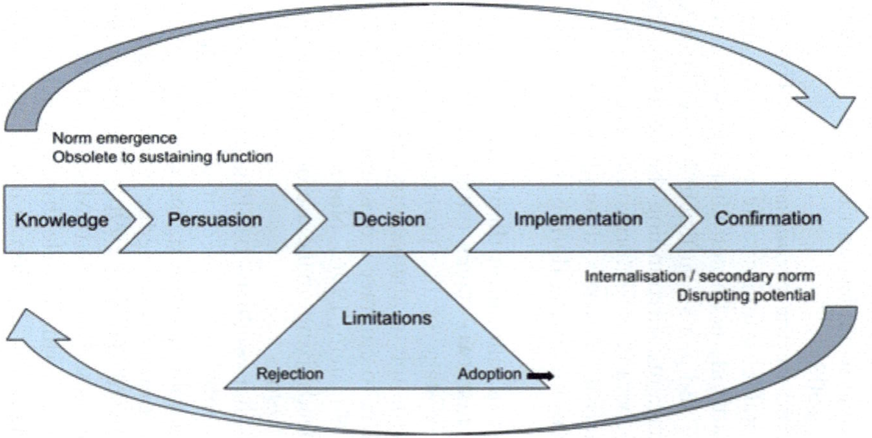

Fig. 10.1 Synergies between theories (*Source* Developed from Rogers [1983, p. 165] and Morton [2019, p. 566])

simply deciding "not to adopt an innovation" (Rogers, 2003). If adoption is chosen, the *implementation stage* follows, whereby the innovation is put into practice. The implementation of an innovation may result in behavioral changes (Rogers, 1983); for example, introducing a new technology may require adopters to learn new skills and change their behaviors (Rogers, 2003). Moreover, their attitudes toward the adoption of a new technology are shaped by mapping the benefits and costs associated with the technology (Bunduchi et al., 2011). This can be a difficult stage since the innovation may be perceived as unfamiliar and this uncertainty may hamper further adaptation. Cooperation with people who have technical skills may help to decrease such uncertainty and speed up implementation. According to Rogers (2003, p. 180), "the innovation loses its distinctive quality as the separate identity of the new idea disappears."

We propose that these two stages reflect an important process within the norm lifecycle stage of *norm cascading*: as small shifts turn into bigger shifts in meaning and understanding, a norm bandwagon develops (Sunstein, 1996). The *tipping point* toward a norm cascade occurs when a threshold number—a critical mass—of adopters is reached (Finnemore & Sikkink, 1998). This tipping point initiates a cascade of adoption, involving a shift in dynamics, including a reduction in pressure, and those previously opposed to the innovation start to follow suit (Finnemore & Sikkink, 1998). As Morton (2019, p. 567) articulated, "it is a combination of pressures—conformity, desire for legitimacy or even the enhancement of esteem—that leads norm leaders to seek out new norm followers." Finnemore and Sikkink (1998) stated that there is no true quantitative threshold at which this tipping point is reached, given the social and dynamic nature of norm entrepreneurs and norm adopters; however, they indicated a one-third proportion as the minimum level of adoption required. Norm development may, however, fail: the obsolescence of norms is equally important and relevant to institutional practices (Legro, 1997). When norms take hold, questions can arise regarding their effectiveness (Legro, 1997).

The *confirmation stage* of diffusion of innovation theory follows the implementation stage and may reverse the decision made (Rogers, 1983). When a decision about implementation is made, people may seek information about the innovation. If a person is "exposed to conflicting messages about the innovation" (Rogers, 2003, p. 189), the implementation decision may be changed; therefore, the attitude of an individual toward the innovation, formed at the persuasion stage, plays a substantial role in whether the individual continues with the adoption of the innovation.

We propose that when a decision to implement an innovation is confirmed, ***norm internalization*** takes place, since legitimization occurs when norm has cascading, compliance, and conformity become automatic (Finnemore & Sikkink, 1998) and the norm becomes entrenched (Sunstein, 1996). At this stage in the lifecycle, discussion or debate is no longer the focus (Morton, 2019):

> Within the final stage of the life cycle—internalization—conformance becomes almost automatic, norm behavior is not questioned, and conformance is no longer discussed; therefore, it is no longer the center of debate and often ignored. Norms, once internalized, can be extremely powerful due to this lack of questioning—the norm is taken for granted, accepted practice, no longer a novelty. Here, rules, norms, beliefs, values, and choices are constrained by such social conventions, or if not, at least made partially "captive" by them, where accounting actors seeking approval become "creatures" of habit and tradition and susceptible to influence. (Morton, 2019, pp. 567–568, citations omitted)

For example, for inter-period tax allocation, the debate may concern which method of deferring taxes should apply rather than whether deferred taxes should apply (Morton, 2019).

Regarding the contrast between innovations with sustaining or disruptive potential, once internalized, a norm can become binding and, critically, the lifecycle can repeat, with new norms emerging (Djelic & Quack, 2008; Finnemore & Sikkink, 1998). This can explain the apparent disconnect between normative theory and practice (Morton, 2019).

In summary, according to Rogers (1962), an innovation requires time from the date it becomes available to the point at which it is widely adopted. Similarly, although blockchain was first mentioned by Nakamoto (2008) as a means of payment, over time it has been implemented in different industries, as indicated in Sect. 10.2 of this chapter.

Blockchain technology may have a disruptive or sustaining influence on the accounting domain (Christensen et al., 2015); therefore, it was important for us to investigate the diffusion of blockchain adoption in accounting to understand which factors influenced decisions about adopting this specific type of innovation.

10.4 Diffusion of Blockchain Technology and the Innovation Adoption Landscape

Norm Emergence Through Knowledge and Persuasion Regarding Blockchain Technology

The first two stages of the innovation diffusion process (knowledge and persuasion), as outlined in Sect. 10.3, are characteristic of the process of norm emergence. Due to the lack of broad adoption of blockchains for financial reporting functions, blockchain technology is not yet legitimized as a norm within the profession and understanding of what it is and why it works is at an early stage (Rogers, 2003). We identified "norm entrepreneurs" as those seeking to offer solutions with trust and efficiency—a problem highlighted as something the profession ought to be concerned with, despite contemporary technologies such as the cloud and artificial intelligence (AI) having profound impacts on the accounting profession (Hatch, 2021). Schmitz and Leoni (2019) summarized academic and professional discussions relevant to the accounting and auditing field between 2008 and 2018. Across 16 academic and 20 professional sources, four themes emerged: (1) governance, transparency, and trust; (2) continuous auditing; (3) smart contracts; and (4) the role of auditors (Schmitz & Leoni, 2019). Based on Schmitz and Leoni's (2019) analysis, we concluded that norms—particularly knowledge dissemination—for accounting and auditing began to emerge in 2015. The first reports on blockchains by the professional community appeared only in 2015–2016 and it took several more years for the first research papers investigating the role of blockchains in accounting and auditing to be published in academic journals.

The relevant narrative for accounting reporting functions concerns the enhanced validation of entries: by keeping separate records based on transaction receipts, companies can write their transactions directly to a joint register, creating an interlocking system of enduring accounting records (Cai, 2021; Cai et al., 2019; Cong & He, 2019; Yermack, 2017). The narrative presents blockchain technology as a means of ensuring that all entries are distributed and cryptographically sealed, so falsifying or destroying them to conceal illicit activities is virtually impossible.

To explain the notion of blockchain-based accounting, some researchers have used the term *triple-entry accounting*—which refers to accounting entries of involved parties being cryptographically sealed by a blockchain (Cai, 2021; Grigg, 2005; Moll & Yigitbasioglu, 2019). The notion of triple-entry accounting was first described in 2005 by Ian Grigg, three years before blockchain was invented (Grigg, 2005). Grigg described the possibility of using cryptographically protected digital receipts to verify transactions between different parties, storing them with a third party, and showing whether any details in the records were changed or deleted. Since a blockchain is immutable to any data amendment, it is almost impossible to falsify or delete written accounting entries (at least without substantial collusion; Malekan, 2018). However, the idea that blockchain is a "triple-entry" bookkeeping system is flawed (Dutta, 2020).

The premise follows that with the advent of blockchain, processes can become cheap, automated, and more reliable as the need for a third party to hold receipts in a centralized manner is superseded by a decentralized ledger (Lazanis, 2015). Lazanis (2015) was the first to coherently describe the possibility of conventional companies using blockchain accounting. He emphasized that blockchains eliminate the need for trust in an intermediary, such as a bank or insurance company, if companies voluntarily publish their transactions on a blockchain. This would benefit companies in many ways, including standardization allowing auditors to verify large portions of the most important data underpinning financial statements, automatically reducing both the cost and time necessary to conduct an audit, which would free auditors to add value to complex transactions or to focus on internal control mechanisms (Dai & Vasarhelyi, 2017; Zhang et al., 2017).

The ability to gradually integrate blockchain technology with typical accounting procedures, starting from securing the integrity of records to implementing completely traceable and fully automated audits (Rozario & Vasarhelyi, 2018), is particularly relevant to its diffusion within the profession and therefore within reporting functions. Potekhina and Riumkin (2017) presented a real-time blockchain accounting system (RBAS)—a software solution that enables currency, financial derivative, and other digital document transactions between two or more counterparts; stores transaction data in cryptographically protected blocks whose integrity is verified through mining; and allows the composition of financial statements at any time. In some instances, early-adopting companies implement blockchains into their enterprise resource planning (ERP) systems, such as for procurement and supplier management (Wang &

Kogan, 2018). However, such uses do not reflect the open public permissionless blockchains that yield the core benefits mentioned. Instead, solutions are likely to be hybrid, permissioned versions that retain some of the shortcomings of other contemporary technologies (e.g., central authority, restricted scope of validation, and restricted transparency). For companies and their stakeholders to realize all the benefits provided by the technology, it is necessary that an RBAS comprises the following elements:

- Accessibility—the data must be easily accessible to a broad range of stakeholders.
- Immutability—there must be no programming opportunity to change data once they are entered, and to ensure this, the company using the system must not have the mining power.
- Transparency—transactions must be visible in real time, as is the case with Bitcoin.

Within this persuasion narrative, the value of trustless, intermediary-free solutions is evident, and the ongoing debate over blockchain technology's merits continues. This reflects the norm emergence stage at which the status quo is put under the spotlight. There is an increasing level of awareness, despite mixed understandings, yet nothing has changed substantially across institutions.

Blockchain technology can streamline information exchanges between organizations and foster trust between them (ACCA, 2017). However, as Schmitz and Leoni (2019) noted, perspectives across the accounting and auditing profession are diverse: "Overall, we have found that the perspectives of researchers and practitioners appear to be diverse, and neither group seems to be explicitly favourable or unfavourable towards blockchain development" (p. 338).

Researchers and practitioners are unconvinced about blockchains and critical of whether or how they will be influential and disruptive (Karajovic et al., 2019; Kend & Nguyen, 2020); for example, Fuller and Markelevich (2020) concluded that "it is hard to imagine accountants embracing blockchain in the absence of compelling arguments for the efficiencies it would bring" (p. 43). Furthermore, Kend and Nguyen (2020) concluded that we need to rethink the impact of blockchain technology, or at least engage in further debate. These concerns and suggestions are characteristic of the early diffusion stage at which blockchain technology is presently situated.

Although the benefits of blockchains are clearly articulated, their reception is complicated, and the profession has not yet been persuaded by the advocates of blockchain technology. This is particularly the case given that contemporary technologies are becoming more established (particularly big data, AI, and the cloud) in shaping the work of accountants (Moll & Yigitbasioglu, 2019). Kend and Nguyen (2020) found substantially more agreement about and legitimization of other technologies (e.g., robotics process automation, big data analytics, and AI) shaping institutions and behaviors, indicating that blockchain technology for the accounting profession remains in the earliest stages of its lifecycle.

Barriers to Norm Cascading and Decision-Making for Blockchain Technology Adoption

In theory, blockchains could fail to leave the emergence stage within a particular community. As noted in Sect. 10.3, completing the norm lifecycle is not inevitable (Finnemore & Sikkink, 1998; Morton, 2019). Norms may become obsolete (Legro, 1997), and from the perspective of innovation diffusion, adoption of an innovation may be rejected due to uncertainty about the outcome (Rogers, 2003), mirrored by the doubts surrounding blockchains. We identified two key limitations of blockchain technology that have the potential to create barriers to reaching a tipping point for cascading: (1) a *limitation of scope*, in that blockchain operates at the transactional level, and (2) a *limitation of discretion*, in that blockchain technology is fundamentally limited in its ability to cater to the discretion required by accounting standards and therefore in its ability to comply with financial reporting obligations.

Limitation of Scope: Blockchains Shift Activity at the Transactional Level

Accounting is a technical, social, and moral practice concerned with the sustainable utilization of resources and proper accountability to stakeholders to enable the flourishing of organizations, people, and nature (Carnegie et al., 2021, p. 69).

The narrative of persuasion presents compelling arguments that blockchains replace trust in intermediaries; for example, traceability of accounting policies reflected in smart contracts has increased transparency and the comparability of accounting information (Yu et al., 2018), particularly given that blockchain technology connects disclosures between companies (Watson & Mishler, 2017). However, the scope of this evolution lies in the hands of the direct participants involved in transactions. For financial reporting functions, accountants, auditors, and tax practitioners are outside this participation, and their roles involve turning transaction inputs into meaningful outputs. Hence, we distinguished between the transaction level and the reporting level. Despite Dutta (2020) dismissing the "triple entry" terminology with respect to blockchains, the technology is linked to bookkeeping functions. The influence of blockchains on accounting is currently focused on the transaction level, rather than the reporting level, for the standardization and automation of accounting services such as data collection, record checking, and bookkeeping (ACCA, 2017). Blockchains provide a verified and trusted foundation for inputs at the transaction level (Dai & Vasarhelyi, 2017).

Accounting is impactful because of what it does with basic transaction inputs, since two firms can make different financial reporting choices for similar transactions (Hodge et al., 2004) that will have enormous differences for users of financial information and not necessarily solve the problem of information asymmetry. Transparency at the transaction level is problematic (Lander & Auger, 2008) from the perspective of providing information to users of financial information because much of the information is disorganized, uninformative, and arguably meaningless. Moreover, the definition of "transaction" is somewhat problematic, as Dutta (2020) noted:

> The term "transaction" in blockchain nomenclature is over-generalized than its meaning and usage in traditional accounting and business vocabulary. In business education, we define a transaction as a business event with an unrelated third party having a monetary consequence. In accounting terminology, transaction is even more precisely and narrowly defined as having an impact on the financial statements, and thereby subject to meeting certain criteria promulgated by the accounting bodies, like the FASB or IFRS. (Dutta, 2020, p. 26)

Overall, Dutta (2020) concluded that only a fraction of blockchain transactions would "qualify" as accounting transactions.

Long-established accounting principles hold (or at least presume) that meaning is gained through the application of accounting principles and standards (Clarke et al., 2003). Accounting processes turn uninformative raw data into meaningful aggregated information that is useful for decision-making. Critically, regulatory frameworks usually take account of discretion. Moreover, more contemporary definitions of accounting go beyond basic technical practice to consider the social and moral dimensions of accounting (Adams, 2004; Carnegie et al., 2021). Carnegie et al. (2021) noted:

> Morality and accounting are interconnected. Indeed, a social practice cannot be separated from morality since a social practice affects others and is based on human interaction that creates obligations and duties. Morality is at accounting's core. Acting ethically, and in the public interest, on all occasions and in all contexts is expected of all professional accountants according to the IESBA (2018) International Code of Ethics for Professional Accountants. Accounting constructs realities which in turn dictate the conditions of human life. (p. 68)

Raw transactions, verification, and transparency have not yet reached an appropriate level to support accountability in the sense of external disclosures, whether mandatory or voluntary. Stakeholders need meaningful (timely and useful) information before conducting transactions. In theory, even if a customer or stakeholder has raw (verified and trusted) blockchain data, it may not be useful for decision-making. Meaningful information is created out of raw data via accountability—once transactions occur, organizations interpret them through accounting processes and assign meaning before making disclosures via general and specific-purpose financial statements.

O'Leary (2018, p. 149) highlighted that entities may use blockchain technology for some of their transactional activities across supply chains, enabling them to "just do peer-to-peer or consortium blockchain to provide information to a range of interested parties, whether that information is correct or not"; for example, some issues related to the reporting of property, plant, and equipment (PPE) can be embedded in smart contracts whereas others cannot. The rule-based accounting principles relating to PPE, such as classifying PPE as an asset, defining its initial cost, calculating depreciation expenses based on the length of useful life, and maintenance provisions can be accounted for in ledgers. However, when a revaluation principle of PPE is used, principle-based accounting comes into play, involving the need for an accountant's professional judgment, which is more challenging to embed in blockchains. When a judgment is executed, further technical revaluation procedures can nevertheless be followed up with the help of blockchain smart contracts. Reflecting on O'Leary (2018, p. 149), entities should retain separate internal accounting information systems "where they do their 'real' accounting and supply chain management." In this way, blockchain technology can improve the efficiency of financial reporting functions (having a sustaining impact) through collaboration, rather than completely disrupting the accounting role.

Rozario and Vasarhelyi (2018) presented a holistic audit model that encompassed blockchain and off-blockchain procedures. Simply put, blockchains support the credibility and efficiency of recorded transactions, but they do not solve the issues of categorization, valuation, correct asset disposal, and clear communication with stakeholders (ACCA, 2017; Free & Hecimovic, 2021). Concerns relate also to records uploaded to blockchains reflecting real-world activities (Kokina et al., 2017); for example, Schmitz and Leoni (2019, pp. 335–336) stated that the recognition of an asset on a blockchain "does not guarantee that the asset has been transferred or exchanged, payments have been made and transactions have been recorded in the real world." A similar concern was raised regarding the introduction of double-entry bookkeeping:

> "... For every debit there *must* be a credit, and for every credit there *must* be a debit" - Alas! How few consider, that if this *must* be the case,---this the rule to go by, nothing is more easy than to make a set of Books wear the appearance of correctness, which at the same time is *full of errors*, or of *false entries*, made on purpose to deceive! (Jones, 1796, p. 17)

Regarding the scope of blockchain technology, Dai and Vasarhelyi (2017) pointed out that blockchain technology could support a new "accounting ecosystem" (p. 6) by protecting data integrity and facilitating real-time information sharing, together with the automation of process controls. Similar descriptions were echoed by the ACCA when it stated that "the entire concept of this [blockchain] technology rests on transforming an eco-system, rather than just an individual organisation," and increasing the level of connectedness within society (ACCA, 2017). As blockchain technology continues to develop, many facets of the business ecosystem can be supported by interoperable tech stacking and multi-chain solutions. As data is distributed in new digitally enhanced ways (e.g., via blockchain layering and tech stacks), this will require a shift in professional roles:

> While some insinuate that blockchain will replace the accounting profession, it hardly seems so. Quite to the contrary, blockchain might actually make certain accounting skills and knowledge more relevant. While blockchain surely would have an effect on some accounting procedures and processes, it will also create the need for new skill-sets to be developed within the context of accounting and business. (Dutta, 2020, p. 28)

Dutta (2020) highlighted the task of "culling" blockchain transactions, which requires a sound understanding of accounting standards. Despite an appropriate focus on supply chains and internal efficiencies, external users are part of the ecosystem. Investors and broader stakeholders rely on general purpose financial statements (GPFSs), while more specific stakeholders have the power to request special-purpose financial statements (SPFSs). Reporting functions that use accounting information are a critical part of the ecosystem; however, the regulatory framework that drives reporting functions creates a further critical juncture. Blockchain technology may improve transparency by providing shareholders and stakeholders with immediate access to accounting data at the transactional level, while simultaneously providing an opportunity to create differentiated access to information for stakeholders and shareholders with different demands for information (Schmitz & Leoni, 2019). This increased transparency, combined with the verifiable nature of blockchain technology, may enhance stakeholders' trust; however, it does not necessarily meet the requirements of financial reporting in terms of understandability and meaningfulness. We now consider the limitation of discretion, which we believe is imperative for turning data into meaningful informational outputs.

Limitation of Discretion: Blockchain Lacks Capability for Discretion in Accounting Standards

The second limitation relates to the discretion allowed within accounting practice and to the limitation of scope outlined above. Discretion based on professional judgment becomes more pronounced with a shift away from traditional physical assets (such as plant and equipment) toward an increasing focus on intangible assets (such as brand or intellectual property; Lev, 2019). The profession's conceptual frameworks encompassing judgment and choice to allow fair representations are perceived as normal, legitimate practices (Hines, 1991).

As Schmitz and Leoni (2019) highlighted, firms, regulators, and standard setters are already aware of the impact blockchain technology may have on the accounting and auditing profession (e.g., Deloitte, 2016). The ICAEW (2017) reflects that blockchain technology enables cost-saving without the need to reconcile a ledger, thus streamlining the accounting process and leading to improved confidence. However, as O'Leary (2018) stated, this may not be quite as simple as recognizing the principle-based approach taken by the profession. Complexity with respect to regulation and discretion within accounting standards results in substantive limitations on the capabilities of blockchains (in particular smart contracts) and their fitness for purpose; for example, take the words of Miller and Power (2013) regarding accounting's role:

> [P]ay attention to the mutually constitutive nature of accounting, organizing, and economizing. This means viewing accounting as much more than an instrumental and purely technical activity. We identify four key roles of accounting: first, *territorializing*, the recursive construction of the calculable spaces that actors inhabit within organizations and society; second, *mediating*, that much of what accounting instruments and ideas do is to link up distinct actors, aspiration, and arenas; third, *adjudicating*, that accounting plays a decisive role in evaluating the performance of individuals and organizations, and also in determining failings and failures; and fourth, that accounting is a *subjectivizing* practice par excellence, that it both subjects individuals to control or regulation by another, while entailing the presumption of an individual free to choose. The entanglement of these four roles, we suggest, is what gives the "accounting complex" its productive force, such that it is perhaps the most powerful system of representation for social and economic life today in many national settings. (p. 557)

To achieve this, a principle-based approach to financial reporting must be adopted rather than the rule-based approach, which has a long history (Gordon, 1964). Regarding accounting standards, it is difficult to be consistent and comprehensive within a dynamic social system (Boland, 1982). Moreover, conformity with generally accepted practices is long habituated and rationalized, making it difficult to shift (Boland, 1982; Morgan, 1988; Oliver, 1997). The profession grapples with increasing complexities and shifting practices, leading to arguably redundant practices (Hopwood, 2007); for example, the idea of smart contracts enabling executable instructions based on a set of specific rules challenges the presumption of whether there is a single version of truth (or untruth) as opposed to the preferred notion of faithful representation (compare Bayou et al. [2011] with Collett [1995] on the issues of truth and fair representation). Gerboth (1972) saw it as naive to consider accounting as seeking a single truth, while Pollock (2008) regarded truth as never being simply about facts. Transactions may be recorded in an immutable form based on a set of executable conditions; however, they may evolve into a particular outcome through a process outside mathematical or logical proofs. West (2003), for example, raised concerns over the mixing of concrete and abstract facts and expectations within accounting practice (Chambers, 1968). These arguments show that, although accounting numbers appear to be objective, this is merely superficial (Hines, 1988; Moore, 2009; Morgan, 1988).

As Chambers (1991) noted, there may be many financial statement "versions" that meet the requirements for financial reporting due to the element of choice allowed within the system. Smart contracts may help digitally verify, control, and enforce transactions, and with the help of consensus protocols, lead to agreement about the sequence of actions specified in a contract (Schmitz & Leoni, 2019). Presently, smart contracts can be utilized to facilitate the terms of contracts for transactions between parties (e.g., Kim & Laskowski, 2018). However, this is still at the transaction level rather than the level at which information is aggregated with the application of necessary accounting policies.

The principles of inter-period taxation have similarly developed over a long period of time, transitioning from novelty to taken-for-granted (Morton, 2019). The normative theory of why these principles ought to apply dates to the early 1940s: incorporating principles of deferred taxation "corrects" the problems of unreal fluctuations in reported income tax (American Institute of Accountants, 1944). However, contention continued for decades and involved numerous elements, such as the classification of income tax (was it, for example, an expense, an appropriation of profit, or a redistribution of wealth?) and the appropriate interpretation of accrual mechanisms (Morton, 2019). As Chambers (1996, p. 21) explained, deferred taxes "may never happen," yet "such imaginations" are recorded. Others have described deferred taxes as "a strange twilight world" (West, 2003). Deferred taxes arguably represent expenses that are yet to occur, depending on future events (such as a tax assessment based on taxable income or dynamic tax rates; Rosenfield & Dent, 1983), and their complexity depends on tax profiles (e.g., for multinational companies, capital investments, available losses, or double tax agreements; Accounting Standards Board, 1995).

However, despite these concerns, inter-period tax allocation became an established practice within the accounting profession, and concern moved to *which* method to apply (Morton, 2019). Consequently, the accepted principles underpinning income tax reporting are highly complex and rest on income tax laws that are dynamic and subject to frequent change. The latter is a limitation for blockchains with respect to tax law (DISER, 2020; Morton & Curran, 2021). Not only are there issues for blockchains operating at the transaction level and concerns about alignment with accounting concepts, but there are also gaps in what blockchain records—such as those for income tax—require in terms of judgments within complex settings. There are substantial difficulties in contemplating the principles underpinning the conversion of inter-period tax allocations into executable smart contracts without fundamental shifts in the approach to reporting income taxes, as well as a consideration of the complexity and dynamic nature of tax laws across numerous jurisdictions (the latter considered by Morton & Curran, 2021). Hence, it is critical to appreciate the network of regulatory frameworks (both within and beyond generally accepted accounting principles (GAAP)) that apply.

Regarding deferred taxes, trust is essential in the accounting profession. Gill (2011) highlighted that it is not trust in the numbers, but trust in the accountants, that matters. Prior to the emergence of blockchain technology (and perhaps other contemporary technologies impacting the profession), trust in accountants was unavoidable, despite caution over deviant or undesirable behavior (Gill, 2011). Following rules blindly can lead to failures within the system, in what Gill (2011) described as the reduction of "the ethical to the technical." When an accountant presents information in a truthful way, Morgan (1988) claims the following:

> In actual practice, many people know that the accountant's work is based on somewhat arbitrary assumptions and conventions. They know that the accountant is really in the business of trying to persuade others that his or her concepts, or latest set of figures, "give a true and fair view" or have superior insight, when in reality this view, whatever the figures might say, is as partial as any other. The accountant's view of reality often carries more weight than other views, because of the power relations associated with the allocation and control of scarce resources. But this should in no way be seen as due to the accountant's "objectivity". (Morgan, 1988, p. 482)

Trust is what blockchains offer: the ability to reduce reliance on those parties (intermediaries) with authority and expertise and to foster trust in the (blockchain) code. Schmitz and Leoni (2019, pp. 337–338) doubted that blockchains could fully replace accounting knowledge that is capable of "prevent[ing] asset misappropriation, erroneous measurement or estimation of valid transaction[s]." In line with this argument, we argue that the incredible complexity of the accounting regulatory framework, giving substantial room for managerial judgment and discretion, constitutes a fundamental limitation on blockchain technology completely taking over the accounting function—at least without a fundamental overhaul of the regulatory and reporting framework (i.e., a shift toward a strict rule-based approach). Such an overhaul would certainly disrupt financial reporting; however, it would also raise issues regarding the rigidity and interaction of fundamental safeguards such as those found in commercial law, as well as concerns over managerial costs arising from unforeseen automated decisions (Tse, 2020).

This would be much more difficult to achieve than innovations that are more sustaining in nature (i.e., improving efficiencies across existing systems and structures); for example, increasing the quality of accounting inputs or achieving the ASX replacement of the CHESS function outlined in Sect. 10.2. Morton and Curran (2021) similarly raised the issue of discretion for the tax regulatory environment. Unless the legislation has clear black-and-white formulae (but even then), tax law is dynamic, and the authors concluded that digitalization and simplification of tax law are required for the digital economy to thrive.

As indicated in Sect. 10.4.2, it is still presumed that what is recorded on blockchains *matches* the real world (Schmitz & Leoni, 2019; Yu et al., 2018). The problems of fraudulent, illegal, unauthorized, and counterfeiting activities, or other vulnerabilities, remain (Dutta, 2020; Schmitz &

Leoni, 2019; Yu et al., 2018). Note, however, that blockchain technology's ability to facilitate tech stacking, such as by including oracles, can be adapted to resolve onboarding issues with respect to other use cases (Cho et al., 2019).

EY Global (2017) raised the question of what impact blockchain technology might have on regulatory frameworks and advocated early involvement by regulators and central banks to ensure that innovations develop in harmony with existing legal frameworks. PwC similarly highlighted the importance of considering the supporting systems and governance of disruptive technologies (PwC, 2016). The ICAEW (2017) pointed out that crafting regulations and standards to implement blockchains is not easy and can take many years. The organization noted that only with the professional guidance and expertise of leading accountancy firms and bodies can these challenges be met, by embedding innovations to revitalize the future of practice (ICAEW, 2017). Given that contemporary technologies enable innovative practices and efficiencies, the resources required to establish complex (potentially parallel or multi-level) blockchains to resolve the limitations of smart contracts for discretionary regimes may be redundant (ACCA, 2017). The ACCA (2017) highlighted the work being done on establishing interoperability and standardization for distributed ledgers, such as creating solutions in which multiple parallel and independent blockchains connect and operate together and retain their security protocols. Relevantly, Dutta (2020) highlighted that blockchains are likely to lead to particular accounting skills and knowledge becoming *more* relevant, including the ability to determine which transactions are relevant and which ought to be *culled*.

The profession may accept this innovative technology, restricted in scope as an "oracle of truth" input into accounting functions, for improving the quality and credibility of raw transaction data as a form of a verified "truth" by using blockchain oracles for on-chain inputs (Cho et al., 2019). Although the profession may find it challenging to agree on truth (or usefulness) (Moore, 2009), blockchains may enable consensus on *a* truth.

Internalization of Norms and the Non-Redundant Role of Central Authorities for Blockchain Technology

> As the physical, digital, and biological worlds continue to converge, new technologies and platforms will increasingly enable citizens to engage with governments, voice their opinions, coordinate their efforts, and even circumvent the supervision of public authorities. Simultaneously, governments will gain new technological powers to increase their control over populations, based on pervasive surveillance systems and the ability to control digital infrastructure. On the whole, however, governments will increasingly face pressure to change their current approach to public engagement and policy making, as their central role of conducting policy diminishes owing to new sources of competition and the redistribution and decentralization of power that new technologies make possible. (Schwab, 2016)

Considering the persuasive narrative for adopting blockchain technology and the move toward its implementation stage, we reflected upon balancing blockchains' facilitation of decentralized governance and a decentralized infrastructure with a continued role for central governance within the wider digital ecosystem. Given the two limitations outlined previously, we assert that for a highly regulated profession with a strong community of practice, central authority and governance will play a significant role in future developments. For blockchain technology to have an impact on the accounting profession, this duality will need to be acknowledged. With the ability of blockchains to play a decentralized infrastructure role, there is a continued need for central governance that is articulated as a new paradigm of "digital-era governance" (Andrews, 2019).

GAAP norms have become established over long periods of time through a normative process (i.e., GAAP norms are *internalized* and *binding*) (Morton, 2019). Irrespective of distributed technologies, GAAP is global and applied across jurisdictions by the International Financial Reporting Standards (IFRS). The profession has already achieved cooperation across jurisdictions, recognizing that variations are required for particular communities (e.g., Australian-equivalent IFRS [A-IFRS]). Tensions between the local and distributed are not new to the accounting profession (Ball, 2006).

Critically, we argue that statements such as "blockchain technology enables complete, conclusive verification without a trusted party" (Deloitte, 2016, p. 3), for the purposes of improving financial reporting functions, will continue to rely on centralized governance. This is fundamental, since we need to be able to trust the underlying technology and recognize that not all transactions will occur *on-chain* (Kokina et al., 2017; Yermack, 2017). Also, new technologies raise new governance issues, such as cybersecurity, privacy, and regulatory protection. Concern has already been raised over miners' arbitrage activities, referred to as miner extractable value (MEV). Within community discussion circles, the Ethereum blockchain has been described as "highly adversarial":

> If a smart contract can be exploited for profit, it eventually will be. The frequency of new hacks indicates that some very smart people spend a lot of time examining contracts for vulnerabilities. But this unforgiving environment pales in comparison to the mempool (the set of pending, unconfirmed transactions). If the chain itself is a battleground, the mempool is something worse: a dark forest. (Robinson & Konstantopoulos, 2020)

There is a need to recognize technology as supporting the human element. As Morton and Curran (2021) noted, shifting trust may shift where incentives for undesirable activities lie. They concluded that irrespective of technology evolution, "holistic checks and balances" are needed as part of a "greater, holistic, digital ecosystem" that balances rights, equity, and fairness. Also, AML/CTF (and "know your client" (KYC]) issues will continue to cause concern among regulators (FATF, 2019).

If central governance is facilitated and the fundamental limitations of scope and discretion are overcome, blockchain technology may reach the tipping point and be diffused across a critical mass of adopters. If this occurs, we will be able to observe how it moves from the norm cascade to internalization. At this point, the technology will take hold and become a "taken-for-granted" aspect of financial reporting functions. However, we argue that blockchains may yet be disruptive. They do not impact the existing patterns and paradigms of the accounting and auditing professions (Kend & Nguyen, 2020); rather, they play a sustaining role, complementing the already developing digital ecosystem alongside big data, AI, and cloud technology (Brennan et al., 2019).

10.5 Obsolete, Sustaining, or Disrupting?

This chapter clarifies the stages of blockchain technology development within the context of financial reporting by merging two theories—diffusion of innovation theory and norm lifecycle theory. We argue that it is still unclear for the accounting profession and financial reporting functions whether blockchain technology will become established and normalized within the industry, or obsolete among a suite of other contemporary technologies.

We argue that blockchain acceptance within financial reporting functions is in its infancy; it is in the *norm emergence* stage of the norm lifecycle and just at the beginning of its diffusion process. Blockchains have the potential to diffuse (Rogers, 1962, 1983, 2003) through all stages of the lifecycle only *if* and *when* their presence is normalized. For blockchains to be fully implemented and become normalized, they need legitimacy *within accounting practice* (Morton, 2019), which, according to norm theory, arises through a bundle of broad-ranging social factors, beyond enforcement, that direct people toward voluntary acceptance (Franck, 1990).

We highlight that the difficulty of blockchains moving to a norm cascade and supporting the "decision" stage lies in two key limitations: (1) a *limitation of scope* and (2) a *limitation of discretion*. What is observable in this early stage is that blockchains are perceived as offering more sustaining opportunities (e.g., Cai, 2021; Carlin, 2019) or are considered a "foundational technology" with a slow but steady uptake (e.g., Iansiti & Lakhani, 2017, p. 4). The accounting profession may see the acceptance of blockchain technology as an "oracle of truth" input to accounting functions that may improve the quality and credibility of raw transaction data. Therefore, even though the profession may find it challenging to agree on truth (or usefulness) (Moore, 2009), blockchains may help in facilitating *consensus* on *a* truth.

Critically, however, if persuasion can be achieved and the tipping point reached, what we interpret as important factors in constituting a critical mass of adopters is a bundle of factors that go beyond blockchain technology's benefits. Even if blockchains offer the benefits of transparency, trust, and traceability of financial information, it may not be sufficient for them to be accepted and adopted. We have reflected on the social lens employed here and the role of social factors (Finnemore & Sikkink, 2001) and norm communities (e.g., Karlsson-Vinkhuyzen & Vihma, 2009) and institutions (e.g., Brunnee & Toope, 2000) within which the status quo is being questioned.

Blockchains can offer improvements in transparency, security, permanence, and immutability at the infrastructural level (O'Leary, 2018; Yu et al., 2018). However, the governance and oversight of centralized, cooperating organizations will remain necessary, whether in respect of decreasing financial information asymmetry (Yermack, 2017; Yu et al., 2018), enhancing company competitiveness (Deloitte, 2019), or building trust between market participants (Yu et al., 2018). In this way, blockchain as a decentralized technology playing an important role at the infrastructure level will be underpinned by coordinated central governance comparable to IASB monitoring and management of accounting standards across a multitude of jurisdictions. Therefore, it is not the decentralized infrastructure itself but its combination with cooperative governance *central* to its operation that is likely to create opportunities for blockchain technology to diffuse across the accounting profession. As Morton and Curran (2021) noted, blockchain technology may contribute to a "technology toolkit."

We posit that blockchain technology will not yet be disruptive, since such technology adoption does not yet adequately impact the existing patterns and paradigms of the accounting and auditing professions (Kend & Nguyen, 2020); instead, such developments have a sustaining function (Carlin, 2019). Despite this, through a norm lifecycle lens, we argue that blockchains *could* have the potential to be *disruptive*. This requires an examination beyond the transactional level. This disruptive potential may arise in two ways.

First, we imagine that blockchain technology may disrupt reporting functions by shifting stakeholder needs, creating the potential for independent stakeholder-driven reporting. In doing so, in combination with the Internet of Things (IoT) and Industry 4.0, financial reporting could see a blurring (or radical overhauling) of general purpose and special-purpose financial statements (GPFSs and SPFSs) and, moreover, the redundancy of users (in particular, suppliers being less reliant on GPFSs due to interlocking/shared ledgers) within this space. In such a digital ecosystem, blockchain technology offers a verified truth and, therefore, information provenance across business networks. The notion of general users reliant on GFRS could shift since parties would build confidence in the entity with which they do business. Smart contracts automate contract terms; therefore, enacting measures to resolve misalignments between agreements and outcomes will be necessary. However, this would be a new *secondary norm* emerging from blockchain adoption once (and if) it diffuses throughout the accounting profession.

This leads us to the second disruptive impact, which is indirect but interrelated. We considered the activity-based nature of blockchain technology and the digital ecosystem in which it operates. What is core to economic activity is the economic entity that reports on economic activity according to financial reporting principles. As outlined, blockchain technology offers a new form of digital economic structuring: the DAO. DAOs enable an unlimited number of participants to collectively govern economic activity: power, control, and decision-making revert from a central authority to a decentralized, non-hierarchical, protocol-based structure (Tse, 2020). The DAO structure therefore challenges the assumptions presented in Sect. 4.3 through a reorientation of the locus of disruption of financial reporting functions from an economic activity (which is generally the focus of accounting scholarship with respect to blockchain technology) to an economic entity.

This raises questions not only about the jurisdictional relevance but also about the fundamental shift in key stakeholders that GPFS represents. For reporting entities, it is likely that there will be a separation of ownership and management, creating agency and a need for monitoring and information dissemination, with reduced agency costs for DAOs (Tse, 2020). However, simultaneously, DAOs may raise new issues over algorithm-based managerial costs arising from unforeseen automated decisions (Tse, 2020). With accounting standards largely harmonized internationally (i.e., via the IFRS), the financial reporting framework may be ideally placed for DAO-based GAAP as jurisdictions introduce new legal structures to formally recognize DAOs.

10.6 Concluding Remarks

It is fitting to appreciate that blockchains may develop differently, across and within institutions, at different points in time (Brunnee & Toope, 2000; Sunstein, 1996). As a result of these shifts in behavior, institutions will, in turn, be shaped by the adoption (or rejection) of new technologies such as blockchains, which may create efficiencies in current practice (be sustaining) and/or go further to establish new practices (be disruptive; Carlin, 2019; Kend & Nguyen, 2020).

Reflecting on the words of Carnegie et al. (2021), the profession's contemplation of blockchain technology must encompass the interconnectedness of morality and accounting. After all, as they noted and we reiterate, the realities that accounting constructs "dictate the conditions of human life" (pp. 68). Although emerging and contemporary technologies are facilitating greater efficiencies, there is an increasing need to protect—or nurture—social and moral elements.

References

ACCA. (2017). *Divided we fall, distributed we stand: The professional accountant's guide to distributed ledgers and blockchain*. Retrieved July 13, 2020, from https://www.accaglobal.com/my/en/technical-activities/technical-resources-search/2017/april/divided-we-fall-distributed-we-stand.html

Accounting Standards Board. (1995). *Discussion paper: Accounting for tax*. ASB Publications.

AUSTRAC. (2021). AUSTRAC statement 2021: De-banking. *Media release*. Retrieved December 19, 2021, from https://www.austrac.gov.au/news-and-media/media-release/austrac-statement-2021-de-banking

Adams, C. A. (2004). The ethical, social and environmental reporting performance portrayal gap. *Accounting, Auditing & Accountability Journal, 17*(5), 731–757.

Allen, D. W., Berg, C., Davidson, S., Lane, A. M., & Potts, J. (2020). *Unfreeze: How to create a high growth economy after the pandemic*. American Institute for Economic Research.

American Institute of Accountants. (1944). *Accounting research bulletin no. 23: Accounting for income taxes*. AIA.

Andrews, L. (2019). Public administration, public leadership and the construction of public value in the age of the algorithm and 'big data.' *Public Administration, 97*(2), 296–310.

Anokhin, S., & Schulze, W. S. (2009). Entrepreneurship, innovation, and corruption. *Journal of Business Venturing, 24*(5), 465–476.

Atzori, M. (2017). Blockchain technology and decentralized governance: Is the state still necessary? *Journal of Governance and Regulation, 6*(1), 45–62.

Ball, R. (2006). International financial reporting standards (IFRS): Pros and cons for investors. *Accounting and Business Research, 36*(Supl), 5–27.

Bayou, M. E., Reinstein, A., & Williams, P. F. (2011). To tell the truth: A discussion of issues concerning truth and ethics in accounting. *Accounting, Organizations and Society, 36*(1), 109–124.

Bebbington, J., Kirk, E. A., & Larrinaga, C. (2012). The production of normativity: A comparison of reporting regimes in Spain and the UK. *Accounting, Organizations and Society, 37*(2), 78–94.

Bentley, D. (2019) Timeliness principles of taxation protection. *eJournal of Tax Research, 16*(3), 679.

Berg, C., Davidson, S., & Potts, J. (2019). Blockchain technology as economic infrastructure: Revisiting the electronic markets hypothesis. *Frontiers in Blockchain*. Retrieved December 19, 2021, from, https://www.frontiersin.org/articles/10.3389/fbloc.2019.00022/full

Boland, R. J. (1982). Myth and technology in the American accounting profession. *Journal of Management Studies, 19*(1), 107–127.

Brennan, N. M., Subramaniam, N., & van Staden, C. J. (2019). Corporate governance implications of disruptive technology: An overview. *The British Accounting Review, 51*(6), 100860.

Brunnee, J., & Toope, S. J. (1997). Environmental security and freshwater resources: Ecosystem regime building. *American Journal of International Law, 91*(1), 26–59.

Brunnee, J., & Toope, S. J. (2000). International law and constructivism: Elements of an interactional international theory of international law. *Columbia Journal of Transnational Law, 39*(19), 19–74.

Bunduchi, R., Weisshaar, C., & Smart, A. U. (2011). Mapping the benefits and costs associated with process innovation: The case of RFID adoption. *Technovation, 31*(9), 505–521.

Cai, C. W. (2021). Triple-entry accounting with blockchain: How far have we come? *Accounting and Finance, 61*(1), 71–93.

Cai, C. W., Linnenluecke, M. K., Marrone, M., & Singh, A. K. (2019). Machine learning and expert judgement: Analyzing emerging topics in accounting and finance research in the Asia-Pacific. *Abacus, 55*(4), 709–733.

Carlin, T. (2019). Blockchain and the journey beyond double entry. *Australian Accounting Review, 29*(2), 305–311.

Carnegie, G., Parker, L., & Tsahuridu, E. (2021). It's 2020: What is accounting today? *Australian Accounting Review, 31*(1), 65–73.

Casey, M. J., & Vigna, P. (2018). *The truth machine*. St Martin's Press.

Castonguay, J. J., & Stein Smith, S. (2020). Digital assets and blockchain: Hackable, fraudulent, or just misunderstood? *Accounting Perspectives, 19*(4), 363–387.

Chambers, R. J. (1968). Tax allocation and financial reporting. *Abacus, 4*(2), 99–123.

Chambers, R. J. (1991). *Foundations of accounting*. VIC, Australia, Deakin University Press.

Chambers, R. J. (1996). Floccinaucinihilipilification in accounting—Does it matter? *Australian Accounting Review, 6*(1), 16–22.

Chartered ACCOUNTANTS Australia and New Zealand (CA ANZ) (2017). *The future of blockchain*. Retrieved June 23, 2021, from, https://www.charteredaccountantsanz.com/news-and-analysis/insights/research-and-insights/the-future-of-blockchain

Cho, S., Vasarhelyi, M. A., & Zhang, C. (2019). The forthcoming data ecosystem for business measurement and assurance. *Journal of Emerging Technologies in Accounting, 16*(2), 1–21.

Christensen, C. M., Raynor, M. E., & McDonald, R. (2015). *What is disruptive innovation?* Retrieved July 31, 2021, from, https://www.innosight.com/wp-content/uploads/2018/01/Innosight_HBR_What-is-Disruptive-Innovation.pdf

Clarke, F., Dean, G., & Oliver, K. (2003). *Corporate collapse: Accounting, regulatory and ethical failure*. Cambridge University Press.

Collett, P. (1995). Standard setting and economic consequences: An ethical issue. *Abacus, 31*(1), 18–30.

Cong, L. W., & He, Z. (2019). Blockchain disruption and smart contracts. *The Review of Financial Studies, 32*(5), 1754–1797.

CPA Canada, AICPA, & UWCISA. (2017). *Blockchain technology and its potential impact on the audit and assurance profession*. Retrieved July 24, 2021, from https://www.aicpa.org/content/dam/aicpa/interestareas/frc/assuranceadvisoryservices/downloadabledocuments/blockchain-technology-and-its-potential-impact-on-the-audit-and-assurance-profession.pdf

Dai, J., & Vasarhelyi, M. (2017). Toward blockchain-based accounting and assurance. *Journal of Information Systems, 31*(3), 5–21.

Davis, F. (1985). *A technology acceptance model for empirically testing new end-user information systems: Theory and results*. Retrieved June 30, 2021, from http://dspace.mit.edu/handle/1721.1/15192

Deloitte. (2016). *Blockchain technology: A game-changer in accounting?* Retrieved July 30, 2020, from https://www2.deloitte.com/content/dam/Deloitte/de/Documents/Innovation/Blockchain_A%20game-changer%20in%20accounting.pdf

Deloitte. (2019). *Deloitte global blockchain survey*. Retrieved July 30, 2020, from https://www2.deloitte.com/content/dam/Deloitte/se/Documents/risk/DI_2019-global-blockchain-survey.pdf

Department of Industry Science Energy and Resources (DISER). (2020). *The national blockchain roadmap: Progressing towards a blockchain-empowered future*. Retrieved July 24, 2021, from https://www.industry.gov.au/sites/default/files/2020-02/national-blockchain-roadmap.pdf

Djelic, M. L., & Quack, S. (2008). Institutions and transnationalization. In R. Greenwood, C. Oliver, K. Sahlin-Andersson, & R. Suddaby (Eds.), *The SAGE handbook of organizational institutionalism* (pp. 299–323). Sage Publications.

Dutta, S. K. (2020). *The definitive guide to blockchain for accounting and business*, (e1, online edition). Emerald Publishing Limited.

El-Helaly, M., Ntim, C. G., & Al-Gazzar, M. (2020). Diffusion theory, national corruption and IFRS adoption around the world. *Journal of International Accounting, Auditing and Taxation, 38*(March2020), 100305.

Ethereum. (2021). *Ethereum whitepaper*. Retrieved December 13, 2021, from, https://ethereum.org/en/whitepaper/

EY Global. (2017). *How blockchain will revolutionize finance and auditing*. Retrieved July 30, 2020, from https://betterworkingworld.ey.com/digital/blockchain-why-finance-and-auditing-willnever-be-the-same

FATF (2019). *Money laundering risks from "stablecoins" and other emerging assets*. Retrieved December 13, 2021, from, https://www.fatf-gafi.org/publications/fatfgeneral/documents/statement-virtual-assets-global-stablecoins.html

Finnemore, M., & Sikkink, K. (1998). International norm dynamics and political change. *International Organization, 52*(4), 887–917.

Finnemore, M., & Sikkink, K. (2001). Taking stock: The constructivist research program in international relations and comparative politics. *Annual Review of Political Science, 4*(1), 391–416.

Franck, T. M. (1990). Why a quest for legitimacy? In T. M. Franck (Ed.), *The power of legitimacy among nations* (pp. 3–26). Oxford University Press.

Free, C., & Hecimovic, A. (2021). Global supply chains after COVID-19: The end of the road for neoliberal globalisation? *Accounting, Auditing & Accountability Journal, 34*(1), 58–84.

Fuller, S. H., & Markelevich, A. (2020). Should accountants care about blockchain? *Journal of Corporate Accounting & Finance, 31*(2), 34–46. https://doi.org/10.1108/AAAJ-06-2020-4634

Garanina, T., Ranto, M., & Dumay, J. (2021). Blockchain in accounting research: Current trends and emerging topics, *Accounting, Auditing & Accountability Journal*, ahead-of-print. Retrieved December 13, 2021, from, https://www.emerald.com/insight/content/doi/10.1108/AAAJ-10-2020-4991/full/pdf, https://doi.org/10.1108/AAAJ-10-2020-4991

Gerboth, D. L. (1972). Muddling through with the APB. *Journal of Accountancy, 133*(5), 42–49.

Gill, M. (2011). Introduction. In *Accountant's truth, knowledge and ethics in the financial world*. Oxford University Press.

Gordon, M. (1964). Postulates, principles and research in accounting. *Accounting Review, 39*(2), 251–263.

Grigg, I. (2005). *Triple entry accounting*. Retrieved June 30, 2021, from https://www.researchgate.net/profile/Ian-Grigg/publication/308640258_Triple_Entry_Accounting/links/57e99c4408aed0a291304588/Triple-Entry-Accounting.pdf

Hampl, F., & Gyönyörová, L. (2021). Can fiat-backed Stablecoins be considered cash or cash equivalents under international financial reporting standards rules? *Australian Accounting Review, 31*(3), 233–255.

Hatch, J. (2021). *Council post: Harnessing the power of artificial intelligence in accounting*. Retrieved July 31, 2021, from, https://www.forbes.com/sites/forbestechcouncil/2021/03/05/harnessing-thepower-of-artificial-intelligence-in-accounting/?sh=4c3a9241daef

Hinchliffe, S. (2019). International dispute resolution: Circumventing the block. *Law Institute Journal, 93*(10), 40–45.

Hines, R. (1988). Financial accounting: In communicating reality, we construct reality. *Accounting, Organizations and Society, 13*(3), 251–261.

Hines, R. (1991). The FASB's conceptual framework: Financial accounting and the maintenance of the social world. *Accounting, Organizations and Society, 16*(4), 313–331.

Hodge, F. D., Kennedy, J. J., & Maines, L. A. (2004). Does search-facilitating technology improve the transparency of financial reporting? *The Accounting Review, 79*(3), 687–703.

Hopwood, A. G. (2007). Whither accounting research? *The Accounting Review, 82*(5), 1365–1374.

Iansiti, M., & Lakhani, K. R. (2017). The truth about blockchain. *Harvard Business Review, 95*(1), 3–11.

ICAEW. (2017). *Blockchain and the future of accountancy*. Retrieved July 30, 2020, from, https://www.icaew.com/-/media/corporate/files/technical/information-technology/technology/blockchainand-the-future-of-accountancy.ashx

Johnston, D. (2020). *Decentralized applications white paper*. Retrieved December 13, 2021, from, https://github.com/DavidJohnstonCEO/DecentralizedApplications

Jones, E. T. (1796). *Jones's English system of book-keeping, by single or double entry, in which it is impossible for an error of the most trifling amount to be passed unnoticed; calculated effectually to prevent the evils attendant on the methods so long established; and adapted to every species of trade*. R. Edwards.

Karajovic, M., Kim, H., & Laskowski, M. (2019). Thinking outside the block: Projected phases of blockchain integration in the accounting industry. *Australian Accounting Review, 29*(2), 319–330.

Karlsson-Vinkhuyzen, S. I., & Vihma, A. (2009). Comparing the legitimacy and effectiveness of global hard and soft law: An analytical framework. *Regulation & Governance, 3*(4), 400–420.

Kend, M., & Nguyen, L. A. (2020). Big data analytics and other emerging technologies: The impact on the Australian audit and assurance profession. *Australian Accounting Review, 30*(4), 269–282.

Kim, H. M., & Laskowski, M. (2018). Toward an ontology-driven blockchain design for supply-chain provenance. *Intelligent Systems in Accounting, Finance and Management, 25*(1), 18–27.

Kokina, J., Mancha, R., & Pachamanova, D. (2017). Blockchain: Emergent industry adoption and implications for accounting. *Journal of Emerging Technologies in Accounting, 14*(2), 91–100.

Kornberger, M., Pflueger, D., & Mouritsen, J. (2017). Evaluative infrastructures: Accounting for platform organization. *Accounting, Organizations and Society, 60*(July2017), 79–95.

Kotb, A., Elbardan, H., & Halabi, H. (2020). Mapping of internal audit research: A post-Enron structured literature review. *Accounting, Auditing & Accountability Journal, 33*(8), 1969–1996.

Krasner, S. D. (1982). Structural causes and regime consequences: Regimes as intervening variables. *International Organization, 36*(2), 185–205.

Lander, G. H., & Auger, K. A. (2008). The need for transparency in financial reporting. *Journal of Accounting & Organizational Change, 4*(1), 27–46.

Lapsley, I., & Wright, E. (2004). The diffusion of management accounting innovations in the public sector: A research agenda. *Management Accounting Research, 15*(3), 355–374.

Lazanis, R. (2015). *How technology behind bitcoin could transform accounting as we know it.* Retrieved July 16, 2021, from, https://techvibes.com/2015/01/22/how-technology-behind-bitcoin-could-transform-accounting-as-we-know-it-2015-01-22

Legro, J. W. (1997). Which norms matter? Revisiting the 'failure' of internationalism. *International Organization, 51*(1), 31–63.

Lessig, L. (1996). Social meaning and social norms. *University of Pennsylvania Law Review, 144*(5), 2181–2190.

Lev, B. (2019). Ending the accounting-for-intangibles status quo. *European Accounting Review, 28*(4), 713–736.

Lin, I., & Liao, T. (2017). A survey of blockchain security issues and challenges. *International Journal of Network Security, 19*(5), 653–659.

Lyytinen, K., & Damsgaard, J. (2001). What's wrong with the diffusion of innovation theory? In M. A. Ardis (Eds.), *Working conference on diffusing software product and process innovations* (p. 173–190). Springer.

MacVaugh, J., & Schiavone, F. (2010). Limits to the diffusion of innovation: A literature review and integrative model. *European Journal of Innovation Management, 13*(2), 197–221.

Malekan, O. (2018). *The story of the blockchain.* Triple Smoke Stack.

Messari. (2021). *Crypto theses for 2022.* Retrieved December 13, 2021, from, https://messari.io/pdf/messari-report-crypto-theses-for-2022.pdf

Miller, P., & Power, M. (2013). Economizing: Connecting accounting research and organization theory. *The Academy of Management Annals, 7*(1), 557–605.

Moll, J., & Yigitbasioglu, O. (2019). The role of internet-related technologies in shaping the work of accountants: New directions for accounting research. *The British Accounting Review, 51*(6), 100833. https://doi.org/10.1016/j.bar.2019.04.002

Moore, L. (2009). Economic reality and the myth of the bottom line. *Accounting Horizons, 23*(3), 327–340.

Morgan, G. (1988). Accounting as reality construction: Towards a new epistemology for accounting practice. *Accounting, Organizations and Society, 13*(5), 477–485.

Morton, E. F. (2019). A historical review of the rise of tax effect accounting as a financial reporting norm. *Accounting History, 24*(4), 56–590.

Morton, E., & Curran, M. (2021). Exemplifying the opportunities and limitations of blockchain technology through corporate tax losses. In T. Rana, A. Lowe & J. Svanberg (Eds.), *Handbook of big data and analytics in accounting and auditing*. Springer.

Morton, E. F., & Curran, M. F. (2022). Technical and legal aspects of tax debt collection and cryptocurrencies. *Australian Tax Forum, 37*(1), 563–598.

Murray, P., & Pirovich, J. (2018). *The taxation of cryptocurrencies*. NSW 11th Annual Tax Forum, May 25, 2018, Sofitel Sydney Wentworth, Sydney. The Tax Institute.

Nakamoto, S. (2008). *Bitcoin: A peer-to-peer electronic cash system*. Retrieved July 15, 2020, from, https://bitcoin.org/bitcoin.pdf

O'Leary, D. (2018). Open information enterprise transactions: Business intelligence and wash and spoof transactions in blockchain and social commerce. *Intelligent Systems in Accounting, Finance and Management, 25*(1), 148–158.

Oliver, C. (1997). Sustainable competitive advantage: Combining institutional and resource-based views. *Strategic Management Journal, 18*(9), 697–713.

Panetta, K. (2018). Why blockchain matters to supply chain executives. *Gartner*. Retrieved July 9, 2020, from, https://www.gartner.com/smarterwithgartner/why-blockchain-matters-to-supply-chain-executives/

Pollock, A. (2008). Fair-value accounting's "truth" is dubious. *American Banker, 173*(80), 10.

Potekhina, A., & Riumkin, I. (2017). *Blockchain—A new accounting paradigm: Implications for credit risk management*. Retrieved July 1, 2021, from http://www.diva-portal.org/smash/get/diva2:1114333/FULLTEXT01.pdf

PwC. (2016). *What's next for blockchain in 2016?* Retrieved July 30, 2020, from, https://www.pwc.com/us/en/financial-services/publications/viewpoints/assets/pwc-qa-whats-next-for-blockchain.pdf

PwC. (2020). *Time for trust: How blockchain will transform business and the economy.* Retrieved October 19, 2020, from, https://www.pwc.com/gx/en/industries/technology/publications/blockchain-report-transform-business-economy.html

Ramassa, P., & Leoni, G. (2021). Standard setting in times of technological change: Accounting for cryptocurrency holdings. *Accounting, Auditing & Accountability Journal*, ahead-of-print, https://doi.org/10.1108/AAAJ-10-2020-4968

Reed, J. (2017). *Is blockchain enterprise-ready? A hyperledger gut check with executive director Brian Behlendorf.* Retrieved June 10, 2020, from https://diginomica.com/is-blockchain-enterprise-ready-a-hyperledger-gut-check-with-executive-director-brian-behlendorf

Robinson, D., & Konstantopoulos, G. (2020). *Ethereum is a dark forest.* Retrieved August 10, 2021, from, https://www.paradigm.xyz/2020/08/ethereum-is-a-dark-forest/

Robinson, L. (2009). *A summary of diffusion of innovations.* ChangeoLogy, the Book.

Rogers, E. M. (1962). *Diffusion of innovations* (1st ed.). Free Press.

Rogers, E. M. (1983). *Diffusion of innovations* (3rd ed.). Free Press.

Rogers, E.M. (2003). *Diffusion of innovations* (5th ed.). Free Press.

Rosenfield, P., & Dent, W. C. (1983). No more deferred taxes. *Journal of Accountancy, 155*(2), 44–55.

Rozario, A. M., & Vasarhelyi, M. A. (2018). Auditing with smart contracts. *International Journal of Digital Accounting Research, 18*(1), 1–27.

Schmitz, J., & Leoni, G. (2019). Accounting and auditing at the time of blockchain technology: A research agenda. *Australian Accounting Review, 89*(29), 331–342.

Schwab, K. (2016). *The fourth industrial revolution: What it means, how to respond.* World Economic Forum. Retrieved July 31, 2020, from https://www.weforum.org/agenda/2016/01/the-fourth-industrial-revolution-what-it-means-and-how-to-respond/

Sims, A. (2019). Blockchain and decentralised autonomous organisations (DAOs): The evolution of companies? *New Zealand Universities Law Review, 28*, 423–4458. Retrieved August 23, 2020, from https://researchspace.auckland.ac.nz/bitstream/handle/2292/50346/NZULR%20DAOs%20Accepted%20Version.pdf?sequence=4

Statista. (2021). *Statistics and facts on blockchain.* Retrieved July 31, 2021, from, https://www.statista.com/topics/5122/blockchain/

Sunstein, C. R. (1996). Social norms and social roles. *Columbia Law Review, 96*(4), 903–968.

Tharapos, M., & Marriott, N. (2020). Beauty is in the eye of the beholder: Research quality in accounting education. *The British Accounting Review, 52*(5), 100934.

The Australian Stock Exchange. (2020). *CHESS replacement*. Retrieved July 24, 2021, from https://www2.asx.com.au/markets/clearing-and-settlement-services/chess-replacement

Tse, N. (2020). Decentralised autonomous organisations and the corporate form. *Victoria University of Wellington Law Review, 51*(2), 313–356.

United Nations. (2020). Innovations for infrastructure development and sustainable industrialization. Retrieved July 31, 2021, from https://www.un.org

Wallace, P. (2020). Layer 1 vs Layer 2: What you need to know about different blockchain layer solutions. Medium. Retrieved July 13, 2021, from, https://medium.com/the-capital/layer-1-vs-layer-2-what-you-need-to-know-about-different-blockchain-layer-solutions-69f91904ce40

Wang, Y., & Kogan, A. (2018). Designing confidentiality-preserving blockchain-based transaction processing systems. *International Journal of Accounting Information Systems, 30*(Sep2018), 1–18.

Wani, T. A., & Ali, S. W. (2015). Innovation diffusion theory. *Journal of General Management Research, 3*(2), 101–118.

Watson, L. A., & Mishler, C. (2017). Get ready for blockchain: Should management accountants add blockchain technology to their professional vocabulary? *Strategic Finance, 98*(7), 62–64.

West, B. P. (2003). *Professionalism and accounting rules*. Routledge.

World Economic Forum. (2021). Cryptocurrencies: A guide to getting started. Retrieved August 7, 2021, from, http://www3.weforum.org/docs/WEF_Getting_Started_Cryptocurrency_2021.pdf

Yermack, D. (2017). Corporate governance and blockchains. *Review of Finance, 21*(1), 7–31.

Yu, T., Lin, Z., & Tang, Q. (2018). Blockchain: The introduction and its application in financial accounting. *Journal of Corporate Accounting & Finance, 29*(4), 37–47.

Zhang, L., Pei, D., & Vasarhelyi, M. A. (2017). Toward a new business reporting model. *Journal of Emerging Technologies in Accounting, 14*(2), 1–15.

CHAPTER 11

ESG, Asset Quality and Financial Performance in Banking: State of the Art and Future Research Directions

María Cantero-Saiz, Salvatore Polizzi, and Enzo Scannella

11.1 Introduction

The concept of Environmental, Social and Governance (ESG) is increasingly important in the banking industry due to banks' willingness to go beyond profit maximization objectives and stakeholders' pressure to embrace a wider sustainability perspective (Azmi et al., 2021). Furthermore, ESG risks are also attracting bank managers' and supervisors'

This study was co-funded by (i) the Santander Financial Institute (SANFI), research project PRJ-1853 entitled "Risk Management and Disclosure of Traditional and Emerging Risks in Banking: New Insights from Quantitative and Qualitative Computer-Assisted Content Analysis Methodologies" (XV Convocatoria "Ayuda SANFI a la Investigación para Jóvenes Investigadores"), and (ii) the European Union—*NextGenerationEU*, Mission 4, Component 2, in the framework of the *GRINS—Growing Resilient, INclusive and Sustainable* project (GRINS PE00000018—CUP B73C22001260006). The views and opinions expressed are solely those of the authors and do not necessarily reflect those of the European Union, nor can the European Union be held responsible for them.

T. King and J. Williams (eds.), *Corporate Governance in the Banking and Financial Sector*, Palgrave Macmillan Studies in Banking and Financial Institutions,
https://doi.org/10.1007/978-3-031-83353-3_11

attention due to their impact on financial performance and financial stability (Chiaramonte et al., 2022). In this perspective, ESG practices could play a key role in making the banking system more stable, resilient to shocks and less risky, thereby making financial intermediation processes more effective.

Amongst the most relevant tangible financial consequences of bank ESG practices, it is noteworthy to mention the impact on asset quality. Theoretically speaking, according to the stakeholder theory (Freeman, 1984), stakeholders can exercise pressure on ESG-oriented banks to avoid excessive risk-taking, thereby leading to a beneficial ESG—asset quality relationship. However, certain specific factors might play a role in shaping this basic relationship. Specifically, bank financial performance can weaken the ESG-asset quality relationship. According to the so-called "skimping theory" (Berger & DeYoung, 1997), highly profitable banks particularly focused on profit maximization objectives might decide to dedicate fewer resources to loan monitoring. In doing so, they would benefit from higher levels of profitability because of these risky investments, while at the same time potentially deteriorating their asset quality. In this context, the beneficial ESG-asset quality relationship could be weaker for highly profitable banks that follow this potentially profitable but risky strategy.

In this chapter, we aim to review the extant scholarly research focusing on ESG, asset quality and the role that financial performance can play in shaping this relationship. Given that the strands of literature separately focusing on ESG and asset quality are particularly developed (Byrne & Kelly, 2019; Galletta et al., 2022), analyzing them jointly might be a suitable approach to pave the way for future research focusing on their

M. Cantero-Saiz
Santander Financial Institute (SANFI), Universidad de Cantabria - Fundación UCEIF, Santander, Spain
e-mail: maria.cantero@unican.es

S. Polizzi (✉) · E. Scannella
Department of Economics, Business & Statistics, University of Palermo, Palermo, Italy
e-mail: salvatore.polizzi@unipa.it

E. Scannella
e-mail: enzo.scannella@unipa.it

interrelationships, as well as on the potential role of financial performance as a moderating factor that could weaken the impact of bank ESG orientation on risk-taking and asset quality.

While the interrelationships between ESG, asset quality and financial performance in banking are particularly relevant from both a theoretical and practical managerial/policy perspective, the literature jointly analyzing these three factors is surprisingly scant. Thus, we contribute to literature by shedding light on their interrelationships to foster academic debate on this relevant topic.

The remainder of this chapter is organized as follows: Sect. 11.2 reviews the ESG literature focusing on the banking industry; Sect. 11.3 describes the state of the art of bank asset quality research; Sect. 11.4 analyzes the interrelationship between ESG and asset quality by focusing on the role of bank financial performance; Sect. 11.5 proposes an avenue for future research based on the potential effect of the institutional context in shaping the ESG-asset quality-financial performance interrelationships; Sect. 11.6 concludes.

11.2 ESG in Banking

The strand of literature focusing on ESG in the banking industry has recently gained momentum (Galletta et al., 2022) for two main reasons related to stakeholders' pressure to make the banking sector more sustainable from an environmental and social perspective (Azmi et al., 2021), and because of the implications of ESG risks and their management in terms of financial performance and financial stability (Buallay, 2019a; Chiaramonte et al., 2022). Amongst these studies, a specific strand has analyzed the beneficial effects of ESG practices, strategies and performance under several specific aspects. More specifically, numerous studies focus on the interrelationships with bank financial performance based on the idea that long-term economic sustainability cannot be achieved without taking into high consideration the environmental and social consequences of banking activities. For example, El Khoury et al. (2023) examine a sample of approximately 50 internationally listed banks and discover a beneficial and statistically significant association between financial performance and ESG scores by using two widely employed measures of bank profitability, namely return on equity and return on asset.[1] Along the same lines, other authors empirically confirm the existence of such positive ESG-financial performance relationship (Shakil et al., 2019). However, there is no unanimous consensus regarding the positive sign of such relationships. In fact, other studies either reject the hypothesis of the existence of such relationship (Bătae et al., 2021) or find that it could be even reversed for relatively high levels of ESG scores (El Khoury et al., 2023) or in specific geographical contexts (Menicucci & Paolucci, 2023).

Other studies analyze the relationship with bank market performance and provide empirical evidence of a positive statistically and economically significant relationship between ESG and bank market value (Azmi et al., 2021; La Torre et al., 2021). This interesting result might be explained by several different factors. For example, Al Amosh and Khatib (2022) remark on the importance of ESG activities as a way to attract more visitors in banks' institutional websites thereby improving the effectiveness of their online marketing campaigns and, consequently, enhancing financial performance. Another interesting explanation has been provided by Agnese and Giacomini (2023) who show that effective ESG strategies implemented by banks allow them to reduce the cost at issuance in bond markets thereby resulting in a reduction in funding costs. Along the same lines, Andrieş and Sprincean (2023) look at deposits and the cost of interesting-bearing liabilities and their results confirm that more ESG sustainable banks are better able to attract deposits and enjoy lower levels of funding costs compared to less sustainable banks. Lastly, another explanation might be related to lower levels of risk-taking and higher levels of stability for the best ESG performers in the banking industry (Di Tommaso & Thornton, 2020).

Broadly speaking, the benefits of effective ESG strategies go beyond the financial dimension. For instance, Houston and Shan (2022) show that banks whose ESG ratings are significantly higher than those of their borrowers positively influence the subsequent ESG performance of the borrowers themselves. This finding is particularly important because it shows that although banks' direct environmental footprint may be not particularly high, they can indirectly have a positive impact on the environment by pushing their borrowers to become more sustainable by employing better ESG strategies.

[1] More precisely, these authors find that this beneficial relationship may disappear or even be reversed for those banks whose ESG scores are particularly high.

A strictly related stream of literature has shed light on the positive consequences of ESG strategies in terms of financial stability and risk taking in the banking sector. Amongst the most relevant studies, Chiaramonte et al. (2022) show that bank better ESG practices are generally associated to higher levels of bank stability especially in financially turbulent periods such as the sovereign debt crisis in the European Union and the 2008–2009 global financial crisis. Such a type of study is particularly relevant not just from an academic and theoretical perspective, but also, most importantly, in practical terms because the finding that ESG practices play a role in improving financial stability at systemic level and guarantee that bank intermediaries avoid excessive risk taking thereby making them sounder and able to face shocks of both exogenous and endogenous nature, bring highly relevant policy and managerial implications for regulators and bank managers. Similarly, Galletta et al. (2023) provide evidence of a negative relationship between operational risk and ESG scores and consequently, banks can reduce their capital absorption when they are able to implement effective ESG strategies that are reflected in their ESG scores. With reference to bank solvency risk, Citterio and King (2023) provide empirical evidence that ESG scores represent an important determinant of bank financial distress given that they can be used as a key determinant in forecast models to identify distressed banks in an ex-ante perspective in a medium-long time horizon. In a broader perspective, other authors show that ESG scores are negatively associated with a comprehensive measure of bank risk, namely the Z-score (Di Tommaso & Thornton, 2020; Neitzert & Petras, 2022), highlighting once again the beneficial relationship between the sustainability paradigm brought by ESG practices and risk management strategies in banking.

Thus, it emerges that although this strand of literature has hitherto analyzed bank risk under several different dimensions (e.g. systemic risk, operational risk, solvency risk, overall risk), scholarly research focusing on the relationship between ESG and bank asset quality is much scarcer. This topic represents an important avenue for future research given that asset quality can substantially be interpreted as a fundamental ex-ante determinant of bank future credit risk exposure. In particular, low levels of asset quality in the banking book will likely result in high probability of insolvency for bank borrowers and, therefore, this under-researched area requires further investigations from scholars, analysts, policymakers and anyone interested in studying the positive and negative consequences of ESG scores in terms of better risk management practices, prudent risk-taking strategies and, ultimately, a sounder and more stable banking system.

11.3 The State of the Art of Bank Asset Quality Research

The literature focusing on bank asset quality is very rich and developed, although interesting avenues for future research can be identified with reference to the relationship with ESG.

This strand of literature has focused in depth on the key determinants of asset quality in the banking industry and has gained momentum in the aftermath of the 2008–2009 Global Financial Crisis and the European Sovereign Debt Crisis,[2] widely considered amongst the most important contributing causes of dramatically high levels of non-performing loans (NPLs) in the banking books of numerous financial institutions at international level (Kauko, 2012). Amongst these contributions, Arrawatia et al. (2019) show that a wide range of different factors contribute towards determining bank asset quality including industry- macroeconomic- and bank-specific characteristics, highlighting the complex nature of bank credit risk management. On a closer inspection regarding the specific determinants of asset quality, Ghosh (2015) provides evidence that amongst the bank-specific factors, profitability and capitalization have a negative and positive relationship with asset quality, respectively, while at macroeconomic level, inflation and GDP growth are found to be also crucial determinants. Similarly, Castro (2013) finds that two macroeconomic variables significantly affect bank asset quality. Specifically, these authors show that GDP growth negatively impacts asset quality while it is positively influenced by an appreciation of the exchange rate. In other words, economic cycles should be carefully monitored to detect in advance rising levels of non-performing or impaired loans in banks' balance sheets as also suggested by Beck et al. (2013). This is particularly important in the most troubled and weak economies. It is not a surprise that Castro's (2013) contribution focuses on the GIIPS countries

[2] On this regard, it is noteworthy to mention that previous studies have analyzed such important topic much earlier than 2008. See, for instance, the theoretical paper of Chan et al. (1986) which demonstrates that bank asset quality depends on their efficiency in processing borrower-specific information.

(Greece, Italy, Ireland, Portugal and Spain) widely considered amongst the most problematic economies of the European Union because of their high levels of sovereign debt (Andrés et al., 2024). Scholarly research focusing on this topic in such troubled economies is particularly developed. For instance, Louzis et al. (2012) examine the Greek banking sector and show that the levels of GDP, public debt and interest rates are relevant factors determining asset quality. Similarly, Mohaddes et al. (2017) show that persistently high levels of GDP growth in Italy are associated to a statistically significant reduction in the levels of NPLs in bank balance sheets.

In general, previous studies have demonstrated that asset quality is affected by a wide range of micro- and macroeconomic determinants. For example, Dimitrios et al. (2016) identify several bank-specific (e.g. financial performance and the loan to deposit ratio) and country-level determinants (e.g. the levels of taxation and unemployment, aside from the already mentioned effect of GDP growth) of bank asset quality.

While the probability of default of borrowers (and, therefore, also the amount of impaired/non-performing loans in bank balance sheets) is significantly affected by economic cycles as well as economic policy, regulatory and supervisory initiatives (i.e. macro-level factors), also bank-specific characteristics turn out to be highly relevant factors. In particular, financial performance is a key determinant because, on the one hand, less profitable bank intermediaries may face pressure to boost their financial performance by adopting aggressive risk-taking strategies that can soon result in lower levels of asset quality (Mare, 2015). On the other hand, banks may decide to use their retained earnings set aside when their profits are particularly high to increase lending in favour of risky borrowers that would have not been otherwise financed (Avignone et al., 2021). Another important consideration related to a bank-specific characteristic is that large banks can alternatively rely on too-big-to-fail strategies to aggressively increase lending to risky borrowers in an attempt to achieve higher levels of profitability (Afonso et al., 2014; Demirgüç-Kunt & Huizinga, 2013), or benefit from more diversified investment strategies and abilities of the top-management to achieve higher levels of asset quality (Bertay et al., 2013). Business models and asset structure also play a relevant role in that the traditional originate-to-hold business models of commercial banks expose them to loan quality deterioration compared to banks that have an originate-to-distribute or investment banking-oriented model (Altunbas et al., 2011). As for the liability side of bank balance sheet, with specific reference to the funding structure of a bank, it is noteworthy to mention that the market discipline role exercised by banks' creditors is strongly affected by the decision to rely more on wholesale rather than retail funding (Huang & Ratnovski, 2011). In this regard, as a way of example, market discipline is particularly strong in wholesale interbank markets (King, 2008). The loan to deposit ratio is another relevant bank-specific determinant as the existence of a funding gap when gross loans are much higher than the amount of deposits forces banks to look for alternative funding sources (e.g. financial markets) that are less stable and more expensive than retail funding (Van den End, 2016). Lastly, the level of capitalization is also relevant, given that highly capitalized banks have more resources to increase their credit risk-taking than less capitalized banks that are even in trouble in fulfilling the capital requirements imposed by national and international regulations (Gambacorta & Shin, 2018).

To offer a comprehensive overview of key macro- and micro-economic determinants of the levels of asset quality in the banking industry, we list them in Table 11.1 along with the names of authors who use them in their empirical analyzes. Although this list is definitely non-exhaustive, we report here some of the most important drivers that significantly influence bank asset quality (Table 11.1).

Although numerous bank-specific variables have been widely analysed in the extant bank asset quality literature, the role of ESG strategies has been hitherto overlooked by previous studies. Hence, we call for further research on the area at the intersection between asset quality and ESG in the banking and financial industry.

11.4 Financial Performance and Relationships with ESG and Asset Quality

The ESG-asset quality relationship in the banking sector deserves further research due to its important implications on financial stability and global systemic risks. ESG strategies can have positive effects on asset quality through credit risk reductions due to several reasons. First, by investing in ESG, banks state that their purpose is to integrate sustainable aspects into their business model. To achieve this purpose, banks may try to avoid excessive risk-taking and adopt more effective risk management strategies (Harjoto & Laksmana, 2016). Furthermore, ESG practices can reduce reputational risk by attracting more customers and reinforcing investors'

Table 11.1 Macro-and microeconomic determinants of asset quality in the banking industry based on the extant literature

Determinant of bank asset quality	*Authors who use them*
Macro-Economic Determinants	
GDP growth	Louzis et al. (2012), Beck et al. (2015), Ghosh (2015), Dimitrios et al. (2016), and Mohaddes et al., (2017)
Exchange rate variations	Castro (2013) and Beck et al. (2015)
Level of interest rates	Delis and Kouretas (2011) and Beck et al. (2015)
Level of inflation	Ghosh (2015)
Level of unemployment	Ghosh (2015) and Dimitrios et al. (2016)
Micro-Economic Determinants	
Level of capitalization	Ghosh (2015) and Balakrishnan and Ertan (2018)
Size	Delis and Kouretas (2011) and Balakrishnan and Ertan (2018)
Level of liquidity	Balakrishnan and Ertan (2018)
Financial performance	Delis and Kouretas (2011) and Ghosh (2015)
Amount of deposits	Dimitrios et al. (2016)
Level of efficiency	Çifter (2015) and Badunenko et al. (2022)
Asset structure	Avignone et al. (2021)
Funding structure	Avignone et al. (2021) and Bongiovanni et al. (2021)

Source Own elaboration

confidence that are convinced of the importance of sustainability, thereby reducing bank risk and increase funding stability (Agnese & Giacomini, 2023). Second, banks that are more aligned with ESG standards tend to have higher earnings quality, more transparency and are more focused on ethical principles. These key aspects can reduce adverse selection and moral hazard problems, which are amongst the main drivers of non-performing loans (Goss & Roberts, 2011; Lopatta et al., 2016). For instance, Galletta and Mazzù (2023) show that banks with fewer ESG controversies take less risk, thereby benefitting from lower risk-weighted assets and higher Z-scores. Along the same lines, Scholtens and Van't Kloster (2019) and Aevoae et al. (2023) find that banks with better ESG scores exhibit lower default risk and contribute less to financial systemic risk. Third, financial stability can be considered as a prerequisite to adopt ESG actions, so banks that normally invest in such a type of actions tend to be less risky and have better asset quality positions. In this regard,

Chollet and Sandwidi (2018) support the idea of a virtuous circle between corporate social responsibility (CSR) actions and asset quality, as good CSR scores reduce risk, thereby reinforcing also their commitment to good CSR practices.

The analysis of the ESG-asset quality binomial should also consider other aspects that can influence this relationship, especially those related to the financial side of the coin. In this regard, bank financial performance can shape the ESG-asset quality relationship through two opposing effects. On the one hand, superior financial performance may enhance the positive impact that ESG actions have on asset quality, but on the other hand, very high profits can also attenuate these positive effects. We explain now the possible reasoning behind each of these effects.

Financial performance can strengthen the benefits provided by ESG practices in terms of asset quality because more profitable banks have more resources to invest in sustainable projects as they can accumulate more capital through their retained earnings (Flannery & Rangan, 2006). Besides, banks with superior profits have less concerns about their immediate survival and can afford to implement more rigorous ESG practices (Bătae et al., 2020), which in turn can significantly reduce risks. Banks can also strengthen their legitimacy if they demonstrate that additional profitability gains are used to meet stakeholders' needs and expectations through ESG investments (Buallay, 2019b; Forcadell & Aracil, 2017). This increased legitimacy might reinforce stakeholders' confidence and reduce risk perceptions. Furthermore, financial performance can mitigate the risks associated with ESG activities. Specifically, banks with good and stable profitability levels are more capable of compensating the costs and absorbing the possible losses associated with ESG implementation (Buallay, 2019a), which leads to better asset quality positions.

However, boosting profitability beyond a reasonable level implies assuming various risky strategies (Martynova et al., 2015) that can end up attenuating the beneficial effects of ESG on asset quality. Banks that prioritize short-term profit maximization may assign fewer resources to loan monitoring, thus experiencing higher levels of non-performing loans in the future and worse asset quality positions.[3] In addition, very highly profitable banks could be more prone to use the additional resources obtained from retained earnings to finance projects that, although more

[3] This behaviour is explained by the so-called 'skimping hypothesis' proposed by Berger and DeYoung (1997).

profitable, are particularly risky, thus deteriorating their asset quality (Avignone et al., 2021). Furthermore, highly profitable banks tend to be riskier as it is more difficult to maintain such a high level of profitability in the long run (Akhtaruzzaman et al., 2021). Hence, these banks will experience more volatile profits and will be more exposed to financial stability problems. Cantero-Saiz et al. (2024) empirically support these hypotheses, as they find that very high levels of profitability attenuate, or even reverse, the beneficial effects of ESG on asset quality for a sample of banks from 33 countries between 2017 and 2022.

In summary, ESG actions may favour credit risk reductions and asset quality improvements, if banks exhibit satisfactory financial performance with realistic profitability levels that can be maintained in the long run. With stable profits and a reasonable amount of retained earnings, banks might afford more solid and rigorous ESG practices, absorbing the expensive costs and the potential losses associated with them. However, ESG efforts may be ineffective in reducing risks and improving asset quality, if banks do not really abandon their traditional short-term profit maximization perspective, which is not aligned with their stakeholders' expectations. This perspective is arduous to maintain in the long term, and excessively high profitability ambitions might lead to financial instability, uncertainty and excessive risk-taking. Hence, the mere willingness to adopt ESG initiatives might not be sufficient, and banks must be really concerned about long-term sustainability, and consider all their stakeholders' needs, aside from the pure economic motivations of their shareholders.

Although financial performance can shape the ESG-asset quality relationship in several different ways, this aspect has not been hitherto widely explored. Therefore, further research is needed to fully understand the role that financial performance plays, its two possible opposing effects and in which contexts one effect could be more important than the other.

11.5 Proposals for Future Research

The opposing effects that financial performance can exert on the ESG-asset quality relation can vary depending on the institutional context where banks operate. Institutional- and country-level factors can determine the strength of ESG regulations, countries' sustainability priorities and stakeholders' expectations, which might lead to asymmetric effects across banks in terms of profitability and asset quality. Hence, to have a more complete picture, future research endeavours could explore not only the moderating role of financial performance on the ESG-asset quality relationship, but also the possible differences across countries and institutional environments.

For instance, ESG practices have achieved enormous popularity in developed countries, which is why these nations have strong ESG regulations and non-financial disclosure requirements (Naeem et al., 2022). Besides, in these countries, stakeholders implicitly assume that banks must orient their business towards sustainable principles. Thus, domestic banks might be pushed to implement ESG practices just to maintain their legitimacy and be aligned to supervisory and stakeholders' expectations (Campbel, 2007). In these contexts, ESG actions are already institutionalized and taken as the norm (Schultz & Wehmeier, 2010), thereby leading to a certain degree of harmonization, making the differences between the 'sustainable' and the 'conventional' banks less evident (Jackson et al., 2020). In this context, it is more difficult to obtain superior competitive advantages through further ESG actions, and sustainable practices are almost taken for granted by stakeholders, as they think that it is a bank's duty to be socially and environmentally sustainable (Xiao et al., 2018). As a result, highly profitable banks may have more incentives to invest their retained earnings in profitable but risky operations. If these banks still prioritize short-term profits maximization without a real long-term sustainability perspective, their mere willingness to implement ESG strategies would not be effective in achieving asset quality improvements. In fact, it could have detrimental effects as current stakeholders' expectations would be betrayed, thus penalizing banks' balance sheets and increasing risks. Consequently, in developed countries it is more likely that excessively high financial performance attenuates the positive impact of ESG activities on asset quality.

On the other hand, ESG practices in developing countries remain at an early stage and are thus less normalized amongst stakeholders (Yin & Zhang, 2012). These countries have other more immediate priorities, such as maintaining economic growth, creating jobs or alleviating poverty, their ESG rules are less strict, there are lower concerns and education about ESG aspects, and they often lack the necessary know-how and resources to properly implement ESG strategies (Goel et al., 2022). Hence, stakeholders' expectations about banks' ESG responsibilities decrease, which is why improving ESG practices is comparatively more valuable than in developed regions. Besides, banks in developing countries generally have less profitable investment opportunities, therefore they may have fewer resources to invest in ESG actions. In these countries, there are usually more volatile economic conditions and political instability (Ogawa & Luo, 2024), which can damage bank profitability compared to more developed economies. Furthermore, in this context, financial markets are less developed, and banks have more limited access to capital markets (Abuka et al., 2019), therefore it is harder to obtain funds and invest them in growth opportunities. Consequently, if banks are capable of orienting their limited profits to ESG practices, it will be perceived as more meritorious than for banks in developed economies, given that they have fewer resources and less regulatory pressure to do it. Banks will then overcome stakeholders' expectations, thus achieving higher levels of legitimacy, competitive advantages and more investors' support (Ching & Gerab, 2017), thereby improving their financial position. Hence, the positive impact that financial performance can exert on the ESG-asset quality relationship could be more relevant in developing regions.

However, understanding whether there are actual differences in the ESG-asset quality relationship across developed and developing countries and how financial performance really shapes this relationship is an empirical question that can only be answered through empirical analyzes.

11.6 Conclusions

In this chapter, we review the literature focusing on ESG and asset quality in the banking industry as well as on their interrelationships, specifically focusing on the potential role of financial performance in shaping this relationship. In addition, we identify gaps in the literature and propose avenues for future research.

Broadly speaking, while the strands of literature on ESG and asset quality as standalone topics are very developed, the analysis of their interrelationships is still at its infancy, especially when it comes to the potential moderating role of financial performance.

Regarding the literature on ESG practices, it is a trending topic that has recently gained momentum due to stakeholders' pressure to make the banking sector more sustainable (Azmi et al., 2021), and because of the implications of ESG risks and their management in terms of performance and stability of the banking system (Buallay, 2019a). Overall, although this strand of literature has hitherto analyzed bank risk under several different dimensions (e.g. systemic risk, solvency risk, etc.), scholarly research focusing on the relationship between ESG and bank asset quality requires further investigation. This topic represents an important avenue for future research given that asset quality can substantially be interpreted as a fundamental ex-ante determinant of bank future credit risk exposure.

The topic of bank asset quality has been traditionally widely debated in banking studies (Forestieri & Mottura, 2009; Tutino, 2015). The strand of literature focusing on this topic is very rich and developed, although interesting avenues for future research can be identified with reference to the relationship with ESG. Previous studies have identified several macroeconomic and entity-specific determinants of asset quality in the banking industry, including, for instance, GDP growth (Dimitrios et al., 2016; Mohaddes et al., 2017), inflation (Ghosh, 2015), bank size (Balakrishnan & Ertan, 2018; Delis & Kouretas, 2011), efficiency (Badunenko et al., 2022; Çifter, 2015), asset and funding structure (Avignone et al., 2022; Bongiovanni et al., 2021). However, the role of ESG strategies has been hitherto overlooked. Hence, we call for further research on the area at the intersection between asset quality and ESG in the banking and financial industry.

The role of financial performance as a potential moderator of the ESG-asset quality relationship is particularly interesting. On the one hand, ESG practices may favour credit risk reductions and asset quality improvements. On the other hand, this relationship could be attenuated or even reversed for unsustainably high levels of financial performance (Cantero-Saiz et al., 2024). However, this is an empirical question that cannot be answered without a comprehensive academic debate that deserves investigation.

As an interesting avenue for future research, given that ESG practices are more spread in developed countries compared to developing economies (Naeem et al., 2022), examining the differences in the role of country-level institutional factors in shaping the ESG-asset quality-financial performance interrelationships represents an interesting gap in the literature. More specifically, banks located in developed countries might be pushed to increase their ESG orientation just to maintain their legitimacy and be aligned to supervisory and stakeholders' expectations (Campbel, 2007). Thus, ESG actions could be already institutionalized and taken as the norm in these countries (Schultz & Wehmeier, 2010), thereby leading to a certain degree of harmonization, making the differences between the 'sustainable' and the 'conventional' banks less evident (Jackson et al., 2020).

In conclusion, several financial and non-financial dimensions might play a relevant role in pushing banks to adopt more sustainable business models. In light of the recent criticism on the ESG concept (Edmans, 2023a, 2023b), we contend that the literature focusing on both non-financial (e.g. environmental sustainability) and financial (e.g. asset quality) aspects as well as on their interrelationships can play a key role to shed light on the most suitable managerial and supervisory approaches to find a balance between shareholders' and stakeholders' objectives, achieving sustainable profits as well as sound and transparent corporate governance and environmental and social sustainability.

References

Abuka, C., Alinda, R. K., Minoiu, C., Peydró, J. L., & Presbitero, A. F. (2019). Monetary policy and bank lending in developing countries: Loan applications, rates and real effects. *Journal of Development Economics, 139*, 185–202.

Aevoae, G. M., Andrieş, A. M., Ongena, S., & Sprincean, N. (2023). ESG and systemic risk. *Applied Economics, 55*(27), 3085–3109.

Afonso, G., Santos, J. A., & Traina, J. (2014). Do 'too-big-to-fail' banks take on more risk? *Economic Policy Review, 20*(2), 41–58.

Agnese, P., & Giacomini, E. (2023). Bank's funding costs: Do ESG factors really matter? *Finance Research Letters, 51*, 103437.

Akhtaruzzaman, M., Chiah, M., Docherty, P., & Zhong, A. (2021). Betting against bank profitability. *Journal of Economic Behavior & Organization, 192*, 304–323.

Altunbas, Y., Manganelli, S., & Marques-Ibanez, D. (2011). *Bank risk during the financial crisis: Do business models matter?* (European Central Bank Working Paper, No.1394/11).

Al Amosh, H., & Khatib, S. F. (2022). Websites visits and financial performance for GCC banks: The moderating role of environmental, social and governance performance. *Global Business Review*, Forthcoming.

de Andrés, P., Polizzi, S., Scannella, E., & Suárez, N. (2024). Corruption-related disclosure in the banking industry: Evidence from GIPSI countries. *The European Journal of Finance, 30*, 345–369.

Andrieş, A. M., & Sprincean, N. (2023). ESG performance and banks' funding costs. *Finance Research Letters, 54*, 103811.

Arrawatia, R., Dawar, V., Maitra, D., & Dash, S. R. (2019). Asset quality determinants of Indian banks: Empirical evidence and policy issues. *Journal of Public Affairs, 19*(4), e1937.

Avignone, G., Altunbas, Y., Polizzi, S., & Reghezza, A. (2021). Centralised or decentralised banking supervision? Evidence from European banks. *Journal of International Money and Finance, 110*, 102264.

Azmi, W., Hassan, M. K., Houston, R., & Karim, M. S. (2021). ESG activities and banking performance: International evidence from emerging economies. *Journal of International Financial Markets, Institutions and Money, 70*, 101277.

Badunenko, O., Dadoukis, A., Fusi, G., & Simper, R. (2022). The impact of efficiency on asset quality in banking. *The European Journal of Finance, 28*(6), 596–620.

Balakrishnan, K., & Ertan, A. (2018). Banks' financial reporting frequency and asset quality. *The Accounting Review, 93*(3), 1–24.

Bătae, O. M., Dragomir, V. D., & Feleagă, L. (2020). Environmental, social, governance (ESG), and financial performance of European banks. *Accounting and Management Information Systems, 19*(3), 480–501.

Bătae, O. M., Dragomir, V. D., & Feleagă, L. (2021). The relationship between environmental, social, and financial performance in the banking sector: A European study. *Journal of Cleaner Production, 290*, 125791.

Beck, R., Jakubik, P., & Piloiu, A. (2013). *Non-performing loans: What matters in addition to the economic cycle?* (European Central Bank Working Paper Series, No. 1515/2013).

Beck, R., Jakubik, P., & Piloiu, A. (2015). Key determinants of non-performing loans: New evidence from a global sample. *Open Economies Review, 26*, 525–550.

Berger, A. N., & DeYoung, R. (1997). Problem loans and cost efficiency in commercial banks. *Journal of Banking & Finance, 21*(6), 849–870.

Bertay, A. C., Demirgüç-Kunt, A., & Huizinga, H. (2013). Do we need big banks? Evidence on performance, strategy and market discipline. *Journal of Financial Intermediation, 22*(4), 532–558.

Bongiovanni, A., Reghezza, A., Santamaria, R., & Williams, J. (2021). Do negative interest rates affect bank risk-taking? *Journal of Empirical Finance, 63*, 350–364.

Byrne, D., & Kelly, R. (2019). Bank asset quality & monetary policy pass-through. *Applied Economics, 51*(23), 2501–2521.

Buallay, A. (2019a). Is sustainability reporting (ESG) associated with performance? Evidence from the European banking sector. *Management of Environmental Quality: An International Journal, 30*(1), 98–115.

Buallay, A. (2019b). Sustainability reporting and firm's performance: Comparative study between manufacturing and banking sectors. *International Journal of Productivity and Performance Management, 69*(3), 431–445.

Campbel, J. L. (2007). Why should corporations behave in socially responsible ways? An institutional theory of corporate social responsibility. *Academy of Management Review, 32*(3), 946–967.

Cantero-Saiz, M., Polizzi, S., & Scannella, E. (2024). ESG and asset quality in the banking industry: The moderating role of financial performance. *Research in International Business and Finance, 69*, 102221.

Castro, V. (2013). Macroeconomic determinants of the credit risk in the banking system: The case of the GIPSI. *Economic Modelling, 31*, 672–683.

Chan, Y. S., Greenbaum, S. I., & Thakor, A. V. (1986). Information reusability, competition and bank asset quality. *Journal of Banking & Finance, 10*(2), 243–253.

Chiaramonte, L., Dreassi, A., Girardone, C., & Piserà, S. (2022). Do ESG strategies enhance bank stability during financial turmoil? Evidence from Europe. *The European Journal of Finance, 28*(12), 1173–1211.

Ching, H., & Gerab, F. (2017). Social responsibility journal sustainability reports in Brazil through the lens of signaling, legitimacy and stakeholder theories article information. *Social Responsibility Journal, 13*, 95–110.

Chollet, P., & Sandwidi, B. W. (2018). CSR engagement and financial risk: A virtuous circle? International evidence. *Global Finance Journal, 38*, 65–81.

Çifter, A. (2015). Bank concentration and non-performing loans in Central and Eastern European countries. *Journal of Business Economics and Management, 16*(1), 117–137.

Citterio, A., & King, T. (2023). The role of Environmental, Social, and Governance (ESG) in predicting bank financial distress. *Finance Research Letters, 51*, 103411.

Delis, M. D., & Kouretas, G. P. (2011). Interest rates and bank risk-taking. *Journal of Banking & Finance, 35*(4), 840–855.

Demirgüç-Kunt, A., & Huizinga, H. (2013). Are banks too big to fail or too big to save? International evidence from equity prices and CDS spreads. *Journal of Banking & Finance, 37*(3), 875–894.

Dimitrios, A., Helen, L., & Mike, T. (2016). Determinants of non-performing loans: Evidence from Euro-area countries. *Finance Research Letters, 18*, 116–119. https://doi.org/10.1016/j.frl.2016.04.008

Di Tommaso, C., & Thornton, J. (2020). Do ESG scores effect bank risk taking and value? Evidence from European banks. *Corporate Social Responsibility and Environmental Management, 27*(5), 2286–2298.

Edmans, A. (2023a). The end of ESG. *Financial Management, 52*(1), 3–17.

Edmans, A. (2023b). Applying economics—not gut feel—to ESG. *Financial Analysts Journal, 79*(4), 16–29.

El Khoury, R., Nasrallah, N., & Alareeni, B. (2023). ESG and financial performance of banks in the MENAT region: Concavity–convexity patterns. *Journal of Sustainable Finance & Investment, 13*(1), 406–430.

Flannery, M. J., & Rangan, K. P. (2006). Partial adjustment toward target capital structures. *Journal of Financial Economics, 79*(3), 469–506.

Forcadell, F. J., & Aracil, E. (2017). European banks' reputation for corporate social responsibility. *Corporate Social Responsibility and Environmental Management, 24*(1), 1–14.

Forestieri, G., & Mottura, P. (2009). *Il Sistema Finanziario*. EGEA.

Freeman, R. E. (1984). *Strategic management: A stakeholder approach*. Cambridge University Press.

Galletta, S., & Mazzù, S. (2023). ESG controversies and bank risk taking. *Business Strategy and the Environment, 32*(1), 274–288.

Galletta, S., Mazzù, S., & Naciti, V. (2022). A bibliometric analysis of ESG performance in the banking industry: From the current status to future directions. *Research in International Business and Finance, 62*, 101684.

Galletta, S., Goodell, J. W., Mazzù, S., & Paltrinieri, A. (2023). Bank reputation and operational risk: The impact of ESG. *Finance Research Letters, 51*, 103494.

Gambacorta, L., & Shin, H. S. (2018). Why bank capital matters for monetary policy. *Journal of Financial Intermediation, 35*, 17–29.

Ghosh, A. (2015). Banking-industry specific and regional economic determinants of non-performing loans: Evidence from US states. *Journal of Financial Stability, 20*, 93–104.

Goel, R., Gautam, D., Nataluci, F., & Nataluci, M. F. M. (2022). *Sustainable finance in emerging markets: evolution, challenges, and policies priorities*. 2022-182. International Monetary Fund.

Goss, A., & Roberts, G. S. (2011). The impact of corporate social responsibility on the cost of bank loans. *Journal of Banking and Finance, 35*, 1794–1810.

Harjoto, M. A., & Laksmana, I. (2016). The impact of corporate social responsibility on risk taking and firm value. *Journal of Business Ethics, 151*, 353–373.

Houston, J. F., & Shan, H. (2022). Corporate ESG profiles and banking relationships. *The Review of Financial Studies, 35*(7), 3373–3417.

Huang, R., & Ratnovski, L. (2011). The dark side of bank wholesale funding. *Journal of Financial Intermediation, 20*(2), 248–263.

Jackson, G., Bartosch, J., Avetisyan, E., Kinderman, D., & Knudsen, J. S. (2020). Mandatory non-financial disclosure and its influence on CSR: An international comparison. *Journal of Business Ethics, 162*(2), 323–342.

Kauko, K. (2012). External deficits and non-performing loans in the recent financial crisis. *Economics Letters, 115*(2), 196–199.

King, T. B. (2008). Discipline and liquidity in the interbank market. *Journal of Money, Credit and Banking, 40*(2–3), 295–317.

La Torre, M., Leo, S., & Panetta, I. C. (2021). Banks and environmental, social and governance drivers: Follow the market or the authorities? *Corporate Social Responsibility and Environmental Management, 28*(6), 1620–1634.

Lopatta, K., Buchholz, F., & Kaspereit, T. (2016). Asymmetric information and corporate social responsibility. *Business & Society, 55*, 458–488.

Louzis, D. P., Vouldis, A. T., & Metaxas, V. L. (2012). Macroeconomic and bank-specific determinants of non-performing loans in Greece: A comparative study of mortgage, business and consumer loan portfolios. *Journal of Banking & Finance, 36*(4), 1012–1027.

Mare, D. S. (2015). Contribution of macroeconomic factors to the prediction of small bank failures. *Journal of International Financial Markets, Institutions and Money, 39*, 25–39.

Martynova, N., Ratnovski, M. L., & Vlahu, M. R. (2015). *Bank profitability and risk-taking* (International Monetary Fund Working Paper, 15/249).

Menicucci, E., & Paolucci, G. (2023). ESG dimensions and bank performance: An empirical investigation in Italy. *Corporate Governance: THe International Journal of Business in Society, 23*(3), 563–586.

Mohaddes, K., Raissi, M., & Weber, A. (2017). Can Italy grow out of its NPL overhang? A panel threshold analysis. *Economics Letters, 159*, 185–189.

Naeem, N., Cankaya, S., & Bildik, R. (2022). Does ESG performance affect the financial performance of environmentally sensitive industries? A comparison between emerging and developed markets. *Borsa Istanbul Review, 22*, S128–S140.

Neitzert, F., & Petras, M. (2022). Corporate social responsibility and bank risk. *Journal of Business Economics, 92*(3), 397–428.

Ogawa, E., & Luo, P. (2024). Macroeconomic effects of global policy and financial risks. *International Journal of Finance & Economics, 29*, 177–205.

Shakil, M. H., Mahmood, N., Tasnia, M., & Munim, Z. H. (2019). Do environmental, social and governance performance affect the financial performance of banks? A cross-country study of emerging market banks. *Management of Environmental Quality: An International Journal, 30*(6), 1331–1344.

Scholtens, B., & Van't Kloster, S. (2019). Sustainability and bank risk. *Palgrave Communications, 5*, 1–8.

Schultz, F., & Wehmeier, S. (2010). Institutionalization of corporate social responsibility within corporate communications: Combining institutional, sensemaking and communication perspectives. *Corporate Communications: An International Journal, 15*(1), 9–29.

Tutino, F. (2015). *La Banca. Economia, Finanza, Gestione*. Il Mulino.

Van den End, J. W. (2016). A macroprudential approach to address liquidity risk with the loan-to-deposit ratio. *The European Journal of Finance, 22*(3), 237–253.

Xiao, C., Wang, Q., van der Vaart, T., & van Donk, D. P. (2018). When does corporate sustainability performance pay off? The impact of country-level sustainability performance. *Ecological Economics, 146*, 325–333.

Yin, J., & Zhang, Y. (2012). Institutional dynamics and corporate social responsibility (CSR) in an emerging country context: Evidence from China. *Journal of Business Ethics, 111*(2), 301–316.

CHAPTER 12

Conclusion

Timothy King and *Jonathan Williams*

12.1 Conclusion

Building on the continued interest in corporate governance mechanisms worldwide, the chapters in this book examine issues related to the corporate governance of financial institutions and markets. As evident within these chapters, as well as the opening monologue in the introductory chapter, classical theories, including agency theory (Jensen & Meckling, 1976), stakeholder theory (Freeman, 2010), organisational theory (Cyert & March, 1963), and stewardship theory (Donaldson & Davis, 1991) are still highly relevant to the study of financial institutions and

T. King (✉)
School of Accounting and Finance, University of Vaasa, Vaasa, Finland
e-mail: timothy.king@uwasa.fi

J. Williams
Discipline of Finance and Accounting, Surrey Business School, University of Surrey, Guildford, UK
e-mail: jon.williams@surrey.ac.uk

T. King and J. Williams (eds.), *Corporate Governance in the Banking and Financial Sector*, Palgrave Macmillan Studies in Banking and Financial Institutions,
https://doi.org/10.1007/978-3-031-83353-3_12

markets. Also debates regarding the efficacy of various corporate governance structures including optimal board structures and composition as well as the degree of power given to senior managers remain unsettled and ongoing. Furthermore, they have taken new forms with the emergence of the stakeholder model of governance and the increasing importance of corporate social responsibility (CSR), ESG (environment, social and *governance*) and innovative technologies. Thus, as emphasised across the chapters in this book corporate governance remains vital and, arguably, of increasing importance to help society tackle major challenges, such as responsible behaviour and climate risks.

Although this book in no way settles such ongoing debates, and such a claim would be obtuse, it contributes to the current discourse and provides the reader with an overview of some of the most important current topics linked to the efficacy of corporate governance pursued by leading international academic authors. In recap, several chapters (Chapters 2, 5 and 6) focus on agency issues related to the separation of firm ownership and control in corporations. For example, Chapter 2 by Ahmed, King (Timothy) and Mäki look at the factors associated with the turnover of the Chief Executive Officer (CEO)s using data from the Nordic countries. They show that investors react more favourably to the appointment of externally sourced CEOs. As they argue, while internal CEO applicants have firm-specific knowledge and skills and hence should be associated with lower asymmetric information, external hires bring new skills, knowledge and networks to the firm. Similarly, Chapter 9 by King (Timothy) and Williams focuses on shareholder sponsored proposals as an important governance mechanism that allows firms stakeholders to voice their opinions regarding the decisions taken by firm management including issues related to ESG. Using data on non-binding shareholder proposals in the US, their main findings, based on examining cumulative abnormal returns and employing a regression discontinuity approach, infer, interestingly that investors only desire increased access and power in firms characterised by weak existing governance quality, including firms in which senior managers are highly entrenched.

Several further chapters (Chapters 4, 7 and 11) link corporate governance with ESG. For example, Chapter 11 by Cantero-Saiz, Polizzi and Scannella argues that, in light of recent criticisms of the ESG concept, there is a need for governance structures that can help firms strike a balance between financial and non-financial performance in light of the pressing need for sustainable business models that address key stakeholder expectations. Similarly, Chapter 7 by Bongiovanni and Williams examines how the COVID-19 pandemic influenced deposit market dynamics in the US. Using ESG as a proxy for trust they find that depositors favour higher ESG scoring banks, which is evident in faster growth of noninterest-bearing deposits and acceptance of lower deposit interest rates.

Finally, Chapters 3 and 8 examine tangential governance issues relevant to financial institutions and markets, including emergent technologies such as Blockchain (Chapter 10 by King (Tatiana) and Morton), new financial trading platforms (Chapter 8 by King (Timothy) and Valkama) as well as the impact of banks' diversification strategies on long-term bank performance and risk (Chapter 3 by Ahmed, Baselga-Pascual and King (Timothy)).

References

Cyert, R., & March, J. (1963). *A behavioural theory of the firm*, Upper Saddle River, N.J., Prentice-Hall.

Donaldson, L., & Davis, J. (1991). Stewardship theory or agency theory: CEO governance and shareholder returns. *Australian Journal of Management, 16*(1), 49–64.

Freeman, R. E. (2010). *Strategic management: A stakeholder approach*. Cambridge University Press.

Jensen, M. C., & Meckling, W. H. (1976). Theory of the firm: Managerial behaviour, agency costs and ownership structure. *Journal of Financial Economics, 3*(4), 305–360.

Index

T. King and J. Williams (eds.), *Corporate Governance in the Banking and Financial Sector*, Palgrave Macmillan Studies in Banking and Financial Institutions, https://doi.org/10.1007/978-3-031-83353-3

O

P

R

The manufacturer's authorised representative in the EU is Springer Nature Customer Service Centre GmbH, Europaplatz 3, 69115 Heidelberg, Germany. If you have any concerns regarding our products, please contact ProductSafety@springernature.com

Printed and bound by CPI Group (UK) Ltd, Croydon, CR0 4YY

30/09/2026

02225591-0006